The Law of Deliberative Democracy

Laws have colonised most of the corners of political practice, and now substantially determine the process and even the product of democracy. Yet analysis of these *laws of politics* has been hobbled by a limited set of theories about politics. Largely absent is the perspective of *deliberative democracy* – a rising theme in political studies that seeks a more rational, cooperative, informed, and truly democratic politics. Legal and political scholarship often view each other in reductive terms. This book breaks through such caricatures to provide the first full-length examination of whether and how the law of politics can match deliberative democratic ideals.

Essential reading for those interested in either law or politics, the book presents a challenging critique of laws governing electoral politics in the English-speaking world. Judges often act as spoilers, vetoing or naively reshaping schemes meant to enhance deliberation. This pattern testifies to deliberative democracy's weak penetration into legal consciousness. It is also a fault of deliberative democracy scholarship itself, which says little about how deliberation connects with the actual practice of law. Superficially, the law of politics and deliberative democracy appear starkly incompatible. Yet, after laying out this critique, *The Law of Deliberative Democracy* considers prospects for reform. The book contends that the conflict between law and public deliberation is not inevitable: it results from judicial and legislative choices. An extended, original analysis demonstrates how lawyers and deliberativists can engage with each other to bridge their two solitudes.

Ron Levy is a Senior Lecturer at the Australian National University, Australia.
Graeme Orr is a Professor of Law at the University of Queensland, Australia.

The Law of Deliberative Democracy

Ron Levy and Graeme Orr

LONDON AND NEW YORK

First published 2017
by Routledge
2 Park Square, Milton Park, Abingdon, Oxon, OX14 4RN

and by Routledge
711 Third Avenue, New York, NY 10017

First issued in paperback 2017

Routledge is an imprint of the Taylor & Francis Group, an informa business

© 2016 Ron Levy and Graeme Orr

The right of Ron Levy and Graeme Orr to be identified as author of this work has been asserted by them in accordance with sections 77 and 78 of the Copyright, Designs and Patents Act 1988.

All rights reserved. No part of this book may be reprinted or reproduced or utilised in any form or by any electronic, mechanical, or other means, now known or hereafter invented, including photocopying and recording, or in any information storage or retrieval system, without permission in writing from the publishers.

Trademark notice: Product or corporate names may be trademarks or registered trademarks, and are used only for identification and explanation without intent to infringe.

British Library Cataloguing in Publication Data
A catalogue record for this book is available from the British Library

Library of Congress Cataloging-in-Publication Data
  Names: Orr, Graeme, author. | Levy, Ron (Law teacher)
  Title: The law of deliberative democracy / Graeme Orr and Ron Levy.
  Description: New York, NY : Routledge, 2016. | Includes
  bibliographical references and index.
  Identifiers: LCCN 2016002233| ISBN 9780415705004 (hbk) |
  ISBN 9781315890159 (ebk)
  Subjects: LCSH: Constitutional law. | Deliberative democracy. |
  Representative government and representation. | Political questions
  and judicial power. | Comparative law.
  Classification: LCC K3165 .O77 2016 | DDC 342/.04--dc23LC record
  available at http://lccn.loc.gov/2016002233

ISBN 13: 978-1-138-48188-6 (pbk)
ISBN 13: 978-0-415-70500-4 (hbk)

Typeset in Baskerville by
Servis Filmsetting Ltd, Stockport, Cheshire

Table of Contents

Acknowledgements	ix

PART I
Introduction — 1

Chapter 1: Deliberation in a Juridifying World — 3

The place of law	4
Charting the law of deliberative democracy	6
a. First-order deliberation	9
b. Second-order deliberation	9
The plan of this book	11

PART II
Foundations — 19

Chapter 2: Deliberative Democracy and Elections — 21

Hallmarks	22
a. Inclusive	22
b. Cooperative	22
c. Open-minded	22
d. Reflective	22
e. Informed	23
f. Holistic	23
g. Other-regarding	23
h. Civil	23
i. Reason-giving	23
j. Uncoerced	23
Roles	24
Rationales	25
a. Democratic inclusion	26
b. Informed consent	26
c. Reflecting preferences accurately	26
d. Avoiding majority tyranny	27

vi Table of Contents

Critiques and ambiguities		27
a.	Social difference	27
b.	Self-interest as deliberative	27
c.	Unduly constrained rationality	28
d.	Empirical scepticism	29
Deliberative *electoral* democracy		29
a.	Open textured	30
b.	Sites of mass persuasion	31
c.	Personality politics	34
d.	Partisanship and inclusion	35

Chapter 3: Deliberative Democracy and the Law of Politics — 41

Law and deliberative democracy: conflict and congruence		42
a.	Collegiate judgment	42
b.	Collegiality	43
c.	Evidentiary rules	43
d.	Public reason giving	43
e.	Reasonable person	43
f.	Impartiality	44
g.	Independence	44
h.	Participation and examination	44
i.	Analogic reasoning	44
j.	Reasoning from precedent	44
Reception problems		46
Translation problems		48
Proportionality and deliberation		51
a.	Narrow framing	51
b.	Party framing	52
c.	Proportionality	53
Deliberation within a bounded legal frame		55
a.	Narrow framing	55
b.	Party framing	57
c.	Proportionality	58
Thin and thick proportionality		60
First- and second-order deliberation and law		62
Conclusion: open questions		64

PART III
Problems in the Law of Deliberative Democracy — 73

Chapter 4: Liberty v Deliberation (The Accommodation Problem) 75

Political expression and deliberation		77
Judging deliberative measures		80
a.	Individuals v collectivities	81

b. Liberty v deliberation	83
Case studies: proportionality and accommodation	85
Reporting opinion polls and election results	86
a. Other-regarding and inclusiveness	88
b. Misleading information	88
c. Representation	89
d. Feedback loops	89
e. Strategy and sincerity	90
f. Substantive discourse	91
Judicial responses to polling regulation	92
a. Redefining deliberation	95
b. Judicial deference	96
c. Elastic application	97
d. Amending the doctrines	98
Truth in political campaigning	99
a. The market analogy – consumer protection law	100
b. Self-regulation – the rise of fact-checking	103
c. Regulating truth in political advertising	104
Conclusion	108

Chapter 5: Equality v Deliberation (The Equality Problem)   **119**

The rise of equality	122
Equality of what?	124
Campaign speech	128
a. Thin equality: *Australian Capital Television (ACTV)*	128
b. Thick equality: UK examples	132
Voter equality and malapportionment	135
Conclusion	141

Chapter 6: Integrity v Deliberation (The Partisanship and Coercion Problems)   **149**

Thin integrity	153
The partisanship problem	155
The coercion problem	158
a. External perspective on coercion	160
b. Cognitive perspective on coercion	161
Thick integrity	164
Thick integrity and the partisanship problem	166
a. Veil of ignorance rules	166
b. Disembodied political representation	170
Thick integrity and the coercion problem	176
Objections from the rule of law	177
Conclusion	180

viii Table of Contents

PART IV
Conclusion   193

Chapter 7: Deliberative Democracy as an Holistic Value   **195**
    Concretising the concepts   197
        Electoral bribery as an evolving (and deliberative) regulatory issue   197
    Onwards, in conclusion   200

    Bibliography   203
    Index   233

Acknowledgements

We owe a considerable debt to each person who read parts of this work as it developed: Vito Breda, Dominique Dalla-Pozza, Chad Flanders, Larry Solum, Joo-Cheong Tham, and (especially) Kate Ogg; and to our forbearing editors, Veronica Morgan, Laura Muir and Colin Perrin. Much of this book rests on the efforts of a veritable deliberative assembly of diligent research assistants: Selena Bateman, Greg Dale, Meredith Edelman, Shay Keinan, Zsofia Korosy, Samuel Rutherford, Weng Kin San, and Cody Stephens. The book is dedicated to Kate.

Ron Levy and Graeme Orr, Canberra and Brisbane, 2015

Part I

Introduction

Chapter 1

Deliberation in a Juridifying World

Wherever there have been democracies, there have been critics of democracy concerned about the apparent tension between sound governance and mass rule.[1] On the one hand, governance should be deliberative – for instance, well-informed, cooperative, reflective, and capable of issuing sound policy and law. But it should also invite widespread democratic participation by citizens, through voting and other means.

Classically, governance was understood as either deliberative or democratic, but seldom both at once. Aristotle, among others, saw value in collective decision-making, but preferred an aristocratic 'government formed of the best men'.[2] When democracy resurfaced in the modern age, these ancient anxieties returned. JS Mill lamented the 'low calibre of the men' at the helm in government. He wished instead for elites – 'leading minds' – to assume prominent, educative roles: to demonstrate by example how to 'reason intelligently about the ends of politics'.[3]

As old as the tension between deliberation and democracy is, in recent decades it has seemed to grow more acute. Runaway policy complexity – in economics, the environment, international affairs, and much else – coexists uneasily with the global rise of procedures that require direct lay-person participation, such as referendums.[4] Timeworn models of representative democracy also frequently fall short in deliberative terms, beset as they are by polarisation and other pathologies. Many democracies have seen the potential for decisive and efficient public action decline as democratic practices have come to be characterised by more robust public distrust and scrutiny of government, and by more vigorous partisan clashes within government. The result is often either stasis or rule by technocratic and bureaucratic elites.

One promising response to the deliberative tension in contemporary governance has been the partial reorientation of political theory over more than two decades. In that time the literature on deliberative democracy has solidified a number of central questions and propositions. A particular concern in the field is whether the deliberative tension is to some extent illusory: whether in fact particular governance models can sometimes robustly encourage, at once, both democratic participation and deliberation.[5]

4 The Law of Deliberative Democracy

Deliberative models of democracy aim to reach well beyond rudimentary majoritarianism to accommodate other democratic values. Some authors in deliberative democratic theory's normative strand of research even stress that only democratic governance that is able to achieve deliberative goals qualifies as legitimate.[6] To be sure, the task of accommodating both deliberation and democracy is profoundly vexed. Yet, to many deliberativists, the status quo in governance is more problematic still, and perhaps even untenable. For instance, the deliberative tension is one likely cause of the long crisis of legitimacy afflicting developed democracies since the 1960s, reflected in largely unbroken trends of declining public trust.[7] Unable or unwilling to meet both deliberative and democratic demands, the perceived legitimacy of governments and even whole political systems may weaken – along with their capacity to respond to pressing challenges facing each polity.

Of course, deliberative democrats are aware of the many practical barriers facing their field's grand normative goals.[8] Studies in the empirical strand of deliberative democracy research often reveal a difficult environment for deliberation. For example, endemic partisan polarisation and low voter information may frustrate deliberative ideals of cooperation and informed democratic consent. Importantly, however, such empirical factors are not merely impediments to deliberative democracy; they are also the challenges to which deliberative democratic theory is geared. To many deliberative democrats, a hard empirical context only makes their work more urgent.

In its institutionalist strand, therefore, deliberative democracy scholarship offers practical solutions. These are efforts to navigate the field's freighted normative aspirations and empirical constraints.[9] Citizens' Assemblies are often-cited examples; made up of essentially randomly selected citizens, these Assemblies undertake several months of intensive learning, debate, and public consultation before issuing a recommendation for reform, such as a new voting system.[10] Early, promising experiences with these bodies in Canada inspired spin-offs, and a veritable flowering of enthusiasm among scholars and reformers. The deliberative turn in political theory – a field hardly known for unchecked optimism – has attracted many new converts intrigued by its possibilities.

The place of law

Legal scholars have been slow to join the deliberative turn. Only a handful have examined laws' roles in contributing to and constructing – or at times frustrating – more deliberative forms of democracy.[11]

Yet the use of statute and judge-made law to regulate political process has burgeoned in liberal democracies, reflecting attempts to grapple with pathologies like corruption, electoral inequality, and concentrations of official power. In most Western countries the core features of electoral law, such as campaign length and voting systems, were laid down by the early twentieth century. Beginning around the 1960s, and building on those foundations, 'modern' electoral, referen-

Deliberation in a Juridifying World 5

dum, party, and parliamentary law proliferated dramatically. By our own count, the main statutes governing elections at the national level in countries such as Australia and the United Kingdom grew nearly tenfold over the last century.[12] Sub-national (including local) statutory developments, delegated regulation, and case law have complicated this history even further. All this represents a story of striking expansion. Laws have colonised most of the corners of democratic practice and now substantially determine the process and even the product of democratic deliberation, often in dense detail.

Many countries have therefore witnessed rising juridification (subjecting politics to legal ordering) and judicialisation (court review of political controversies).[13] Especially since the 1990s, the response from the academy has been a steep rise in research into the *law of politics* – that is, law regulating the sites of political choice in a democracy. Studies in the area now divide into several subfields, the largest and best-developed of which are electoral and referendum law. There is also rising attention given to party regulation,[14] and parliamentary law.[15] Common to them all is a focus on how legal norms shape political decision-making by setting the ground rules, conditions for umpiring, and proper scope of debate among democratic participants.

But, while by now well-established, each subfield still often suffers from having developed around a limited set of substantive theories about politics. Regulatory analysis in the law of politics occurs within restricted normative confines revolving around a triad of values: political liberty, equality, and integrity. These dominant frameworks entrench assumptions that political process means intractable conflict, to the exclusion of 'the possibility of agreement'.[16] Deliberative ideals frequently are not merely absent, but are trumped by conceptualisations rooted in the marketplace or politics as a game.[17] Scholarship thus leans toward metaphors of politics as 'competitive' or 'uncompetitive'; subject to 'monopolies', 'duopolies', and 'lockup';[18] threatened by '"rent-seeking"', "agency problems" and "externalities"';[19] and fought upon level or uneven 'playing fields'.[20]

Just as studies of the law of politics have neglected deliberative theory, the converse is also true. Research on how institutions can shape deliberation to yield more trusted and effective governance is extensive, but often lacks analyses of laws as critical, and qualitatively distinct, features of the deliberative democratic institutional landscape. To the extent there is now a body of established deliberative legal theory, it is most often concerned with theorising the legitimacy of constitutional review of legislation, and with constitutional reform.[21] Work still centres on constitutional questions such as 'what ought to be in a constitution' or 'how we ought to interpret a constitution',[22] and whether deliberative innovations such as Citizens' Assemblies can enhance the legitimacy of constitutions and constitution-making.[23]

Deliberative democrats have not always recognised law's wider perfusion through democratic politics. Of the vast class of legal norms shaping political conduct, constitutional laws form an important subset; yet the far larger set is that of statutes, regulations, rules of common or judge-made law, and conventions that

6 The Law of Deliberative Democracy

variously colour and constrain politics.[24] Outside the limited constitutional arena, however, no works have previously given sustained attention to the full range of legal dimensions of deliberative democracy, nor to the deliberative dimensions of the law of politics. The deliberative and legal turns in the scholarship of politics still therefore seldom intersect.

Perhaps unsurprisingly, then, most contributions in deliberative theory demonstrate only a general understanding of the roles of law. Nearly all neglect to address law as a heterogeneous set of norms whose influences on political practice are both substantial and varied. Even Jürgen Habermas – a founder of deliberative theory, and the political theorist perhaps best apprised of law's deliberative roles – views law at a level of generality that overlooks much of what is institutionally distinctive about it. As Simone Chambers puts the point, 'Habermas is dealing with law at the highest level of abstraction', but 'questions of institutional design are best addressed within a particular legal and constitutional tradition'.[25] Omissions like his are common: the 'institutional perspective of lawyers leads to an entire apparatus of rules that are alien to' other disciplines.[26]

Yet, even if unsurprising, it is regrettable that contributions to deliberative theory continue to undervalue laws' institutional roles. Laws not only create, but are integral to (even constitutive of) the sites of political deliberation. Deliberative democrats continually hatch institutional reform schemes. However, given the deep and widespread juridification of democratic politics, such schemes might have limited impact so long as the forms and substance of the law of politics fail to align with them. The law of politics has the potential both to enable and to frustrate deliberative democrats' best-laid plans.

Charting the law of deliberative democracy

This book brings deliberative democratic perspectives squarely into the study of the law of politics, and vice versa. It extends the scholarly view of the law of politics beyond the traditional triad of normative concerns, and applies deliberation as a distinctive value. The book offers the first full-length examination of the extent to which the laws of politics match deliberative democratic ideals, and how and whether they should try to do so.

At the broadest level our goal is to describe the contours of an incipient field of legal analysis, *the law of deliberative democracy*. This encompasses a vast area of inquiry – certainly broader than we can cover in a single volume. The present volume touches on every aspect of the field, but most of all addresses *election law*: that body of laws regulating parties, candidates, voters, and other actors in the campaign and polling for representative elections. In addition to election law, the law of deliberative democracy includes other domains of the law of politics raising distinctive deliberative considerations:

- *Referendum law.* Unlike elections, referendums engage voters in deliberation on just one, or a handful, of discrete reform questions.

- *Constitutional law, adjudication, and reform.* Writing new constitutional norms, or adjudicating existing ones, raises greater-than-normal expectations for a process that is both democratic and deliberative.
- *Human rights norms.* Adjudicating fundamental rights under law can reshape and coerce political decision-making in ways occasionally contrary to democratic deliberation, though (as we see in later chapters) whether it does so depends on judicial methodology.
- *Parliamentary (or Congressional) law.* A raft of rules regarding legislative debate and lawmaking regulate the relatively elite and bounded deliberation of legislative bodies.

Each of these areas is wide and distinctive enough to deserve separate, book-length treatment. And we hope that other volumes in future will analyse them comprehensively through a deliberative lens. Some works have already ventured partway in this direction.[27] Yet election law is the branch of the law of deliberative democracy still least explored. We devote most of our attention to election law principally for this reason.

Of course there is overlap among the branches. Much election law is constitutional in nature, and many election laws assume the form of rights (an example of the former is a set legislative term; an example of the latter is a minimum voting franchise). As well, in the era of the 'permanent campaign', it can be difficult to distinguish between electoral and parliamentary law. For instance, rules about pecuniary and other corruption, or about government formation or dissolution, govern political process in the twilight spaces between electoral and parliamentary practice. However, if election law is as broadly relevant for democratic practices of deliberation as we suggest, then exploring this branch of the law of deliberative democracy is a matter of particular relevance, and even urgency. Whether implicitly or explicitly, and unintentionally or by design, election law substantially determines the deliberative quality of democratic decision-making. The main sites of legal regulation of elections arise along the path to the campaign, in the campaign itself, and at the vote and its aftermath. In the chapters of this book we look at case examples from most of these stages, exploring how law concretely affects democratic deliberation.

This is distinct from an older approach to law in deliberative theory. Deliberative democrats have long been interested in how law is made legitimate. Lawmaking often takes centre stage in their work, because deliberation is thought to be necessary for legitimate law. We can call this the *deliberation-law* relation. Yet the other side of the coin, still much neglected, is of law itself as legitimator. This is the *law-deliberation* relation. Law is an often overlooked, and yet pervasive and perhaps distinctive, element of deliberative democracy's institutional context. Thus, to understand the conditions for effective deliberative democracy, we must ask questions about the roles of law. Election lawyers are perhaps best placed to follow such questions through in detail.

A complication is that the relation between law and deliberation is a dialectical one. We might be unable to understand how deliberation helps to make law legitimate without considering how law colours and channels deliberation, and how such effects feed back to each other; by omitting either side we may fail to understand both. Nowhere is this dialectic more acute than in election law, where those who write the laws may be those who gain or lose power from them. Partisan manipulations of election law can have multiplier effects: when politicians write the ground rules of democracy – drawing up the conditions for exercising their own power – they face incentives to help themselves to more years, or more power, in government, contrary to the 'preferences of their constituents'.[28] And when factions in government regulate elections unfairly, returning themselves to power essentially uncontested, they can then rule widely and unaccountably across many other areas of public governance. Election law scholars often recognise these recursive patterns.[29] Yet we less often consider the directions for reform that deliberative democracy theory can suggest.

In this book we pursue precisely these kinds of questions. To do so we draw on our backgrounds in election law (and in the law of politics more generally) to critique, and ultimately to update, certain routine assumptions about law in deliberative democracy theory. One common position is that courts are agents or instruments of deliberation. Conceptions of deliberative democracy in relation to law often understand courts as having a distinct role. For instance, according to John Rawls, courts educate citizens by informing and disciplining public preferences that otherwise might be under-informed, aimless, unstructured.[30] In addition, in the view of Habermas and others,[31] courts (and certain other governmental elites) channel or filter raw social preferences into the more refined forms of legal rules. He writes: 'binding decisions, to be legitimate, must be steered by communication flows that start at the periphery and pass through the sluices of democratic and constitutional procedures situated at the entrance to the parliamentary complex or the courts'.[32] Governmental elites thus, in the first instance, gauge any citizen values, interests, and generalised policy choices aired in the public sphere. They then weigh and eventually set down these preferences as concrete rules. This idealised view is influential in part because it assumes that governmental elites, acting as deliberative agents, to some extent can avoid second-guessing the preferences of ordinary citizens. By instead faithfully receiving and translating preferences, elite actors can largely serve the interests of the wider citizenry, and not the other way around.[33]

These compelling visions have persisted in deliberative theory. Yet, as noted, from Rawls and Habermas onward only a few deliberative democrats have engaged with law and its practice at the level of depth that is standard in legal scholarship. Each constituent part of the deliberative ideal of law has in the past been targeted for critique. However, while we briefly rehearse such general objections in this book, our main focus is on a more distinctive set of critical perspectives, based on a fine-grained examination of the roles of law in public deliberation.

We uncover what we see as a set of legal barriers to deliberative democracy in the law of politics: that law as an institutional form imports a raft of characteristic

Deliberation in a Juridifying World 9

– if sometimes unpredictable – norms and patterns into collective decision-making. There remain key questions to answer about the quality of democratic deliberation after the encounter between democratic practice and law. In our view, at the broadest level, these questions divide into two kinds:

a. First-order deliberation

First-order democratic deliberation concerns the collective process for writing substantive policies that have direct effects on the lives of citizens (eg, a transit system, a tax, eligibility to marry). How does the law's rationalism inform the outcomes of first-order decision-making? The most optimistic view is that the judicial influence can help polities find ways to accommodate disparate citizen preferences or interests in the course of making or adjudicating law. An example is the rapid social acceptance of same-sex marriage in Canada and the United States in the period from the 1990s to the 2010s. In both countries the issue progressed for years through the courts of states/provinces before reaching the national Supreme Court. Judges along the way appeared to have had an important socially disruptive role, upending old certainties by subjecting them to the scrutiny of deliberative reconsideration and justification. Such a process can inform the public political discourse with a comparatively rigorous set of methods of reasoning (eg, analogic reasoning, public reason-giving). For example, a case that is confounding to some (eg, same-sex marriage) can be better understood by analogy to similar, settled cases (eg, interracial marriage).[34]

To be sure, the roles of courts in first-order deliberation raise a number of important questions, not all of which have been adequately answered, or even posed. For instance, how do courts deliberate in practice? Judges (and juries) have long been said to deliberate, and this assumption is reinforced by the many safeguards for deliberation embedded in legal practice (eg, rules of evidence). However, are judges on multi-member, collegiate courts sufficiently *collegial* – cooperative, communicative, mutually respectful, etc – to serve as deliberators? Moreover, legal deliberation is not the same as democratic deliberation. Courts are elite, indeed often *elitist*. Have they the institutional modesty to share their role at the apex of government with the wider public – to hear and heed representations from the 'periphery'?

b. Second-order deliberation

Whether realistic or not, deliberative accounts of law tend to keep deliberation about first-order interests foremost in mind. The judicial role in reducing social conflict treats such conflict (eg, between religious traditionalists and proponents of same-sex marriage) as first-order in nature. However, in this book we are concerned most of all with second-order questions. These are questions concerning *deliberation about the process of democratic decision-making itself*. As Dennis Thompson describes it (in the electoral context), the distinction is between deliberating *in*

10 The Law of Deliberative Democracy

elections, or deliberating *about* them.[35] The main aspects of the law of politics (eg, election law) are primarily concerned with the choices judges and legislators make about how to regulate democracy itself.

The view we noted earlier of elites filtering raw public preferences is in part an awkward fit with second-order deliberation. Instead of seeking to rationalise preferences, the task of a court in a second-order case is principally to choose among potential models of democratic practice. For example, when they review controversies over the design of party funding systems, or of electoral redistricting methods, courts at least implicitly must take account of the objectives, values, and methods of democracy – including which objectives, values, and methods are (to their minds) the most ideal. Importantly for our purposes, it often falls to judges to decide whether to sustain, strengthen, or obstruct the deliberative aspect in democracy.

Legal practice can mix poorly with deliberative democratic objectives in the second-order arena, and this mismatch can occasionally be stark. Legal practice particularly misfires, in our view, by failing to understand democracy and deliberation as elements of a coherent whole. Judges too often assume that deliberation and majoritarian democracy occupy wholly separate spheres. They are often blind to deliberative democracy as an integration of the two. A core notion of deliberative democracy theory holds that deliberation and democracy can be mutually reinforcing. This insight is mostly absent from judges' substantive reasoning about democracy. We hope to lay bare the frequent disjunction between the forms of deliberation that courts impose on democratic politics, and those that deliberative democracy entails.

It is thus in the second-order arena that law (especially the law of politics) and deliberative democracy are most dramatically at odds. Due partly to this conflict, the plans of deliberative democrats can struggle to get off the ground. The juridification of political practice has been sufficiently rapid and dense in recent decades that deliberative democrats no longer can afford to ignore law, in all its variety and nuance, if they still hope to see deliberative democratic initiatives succeed. Second-order law is the law that, more than any other, permits courts to oversee and ultimately to block schemes aiming to change the way democracy is practised. That judges (as we will see) so often step in to act as spoilers is a testament to how little deliberative democracy has penetrated into legal consciousness. It is also, however, a problem partly traceable to deliberative democracy scholarship, which as yet has done too little to engage with the finer points of legal practice. It is incumbent on both sides to bridge their solitudes.

Hence our deliberative study of the laws of politics presents a cautionary argument: that deliberative democracy theory, unapprised of the lessons and details of legal application, may have little prospect of fulfilling its own expectations. We ask whether the law of politics can play a constructive role in deliberative democracy, and at the outset we express doubt that it can. In the law of politics, deliberation is often counterpoised against more widely recognised values: liberty, equality, integrity. At best, this can distract courts and other legal decision-makers from deliberation as another value foundation of the law of politics. At worst, it can see the dominant values compete with and sideline deliberation. One of our central claims is therefore that the law of politics enforces a *thin* view of democratic politics' main normative objectives, in which deliberation as a value is mostly absent.

Yet we also consider ways around such problems. None of the difficulties we outline is wholly irredeemable. Some regulatory tools, including tools already widely available in law, can be applied creatively in order to bring the law of politics into closer alignment with democratic deliberation. Deliberation need not be in competition with, but can be read as an integral element of, other foundational political values. This conceptual move generates richer ways of expressing these values in law, yielding what we call the values' *thick* varieties (ie, thick liberty, thick equality, thick integrity).

The following chapters therefore ultimately adopt a stance of guarded optimism. We suggest that at least some of the cynicism about law's utility to deliberative democracy may be overstated. Tensions between deliberation and other values are certainly real in legal practice, yet this may only highlight a problem with how the law is presently written and practised. The problem is more illusory at a conceptual level, and in practice is far from immune to better legal design. Even within the distinctly narrow bounds of common law process, there is potential to recast the law of politics to be more consonant with democratic deliberation. By paying closer attention to law, occasionally we can better align political practice with deliberative ideals. This contention recurs throughout the book.

Notably, then, ours are chiefly questions of doctrine, not of form. We consider that the substantive practice of law matters most to the development of a more effective law of deliberative democracy. Some scholars, also concerned with whether courts help to fulfil the criteria for deliberation, have peered instead into the conduct of courts.[36] Yet only a few have carefully pored over the substance of judicial output – the patterns of legal decision-making about politics itself.[37] Our focus is on the doctrine judges and others have created to regulate democratic politics. This focus in some ways presents a less speculative take on curial deliberation. In essence we interrogate here not merely how courts are primed to function but – adopting a finer-grained view – how they function in fact. We thus look at key legal norms that judges follow (and occasionally create) when reasoning about democracy in the law of politics.

The plan of this book

The book therefore examines the deliberative dimensions of the law of politics, and the legal dimensions of deliberative democracy. While a handful of other works have gestured toward the need for such an integration of the law of politics and deliberative democracy, few have yet taken up the task. We bring our backgrounds as scholars and occasional practitioners of the law of politics to the deliberative analysis of political systems. The volume's coverage centres on the

12   The Law of Deliberative Democracy

UK, US, Canada, and Australia. Additional jurisdictions also occasionally furnish examples, to the extent that these provide illustrative contrasts or analogues. Such wide geographic breadth is in keeping with the authors' diversity of experience. It also reflects the law of deliberative democracy's potentially broad relevance across the liberal democracies of the common law world, which – despite some notable variations – have in recent decades often encountered a common suite of legal, political, and social developments and challenges.

This is not a compendium of law, but a gloss on select laws – those representing some of the key strands of legal reasoning about the function and goals of the law of politics. We want to stress that we have designed our study not as a comprehensive deliberative conspectus of every feature of the law of politics, but as a framework for better understanding some of the main questions and propositions in the new law of deliberative democracy field. In addition, informal legal norms, such as unwritten political conventions, will only occasionally form part of the survey. The focus throughout is on the key formal sources of law that help to structure political practice (eg, legislation and appellate court judgments).

Two main parts form the core of the book. The first is Part II, 'Foundations', which develops our theoretical lens. In chapter 2, the first in the part, we introduce deliberative democracy by stipulating what we understand to be its hallmarks. We do not focus on a single scholar or scholarly tradition here. Instead we aim to incorporate, as far as possible, a range of views upon the field. This mosaic approach is appropriate, we think, given our goal of stipulating the elements of the law of deliberative democracy in correspondingly general terms. Chapter 2 also introduces the practical contexts of deliberative democracy in which we focus our later analysis: campaigning, voting, and deliberating in elections.

In chapter 3 we then set out our distinctive perspective – our view of how the law of politics channels and colours democratic deliberation. We will ultimately argue that the law of politics can play a constructive role in realising deliberative democracy. However, we begin by observing how, as it is currently written and practised, the law of politics manifests its main normative fixations (ie, liberty, equality, integrity) in predominantly anti-deliberative ways. Many of the grand ideals of deliberative democracy face distinctive and formidable barriers after the superimposition of law over political practice. We describe such obstacles in this chapter at a general conceptual level, as a prelude to the case studies of Part III. The problems set out in chapter 3 raise profound complications, and in turn raise doubts about the feasibility of deliberative democracy in an era of rapid and dense juridification.

This cautionary claim rests partly on our analysis of the central role of 'proportionality' doctrines in the law of politics. The reductive inquiry of a simple proportionality test disassembles democratic deliberation into component parts – with deliberation on one side, and more dominant values (again, liberty, equality, and integrity) and their incidents on the other. Especially in the post-war period, proportionality has become entrenched throughout key areas of legal process. Its reductivity is part of its appeal: judges, faced with the wicked problem of deciding multi-faceted problems in relatively simple and final terms, rely time and again on proportionality testing to simplify the task. Beyond judges, other lawmakers and legal adjudicators (eg, bureaucratic administrators and members of official commissions) also adopt a similar, simplifying approach. But, for deliberation, simple is not always best.

This critique of legal reasoning does not in itself take us substantially beyond other contributions in the incipient law of deliberative democracy field. More novel, we think, is our approach to evaluating these critiques, and ultimately casting doubt on them. We examine the avenues for robust deliberation still open to judges, even within the narrowly bounded proportionality inquiry. Notably, we find that not all proportionality is the same. Hence it is not the law of politics' fixation on proportionality per se that presents problems for democratic deliberation. The fault lies instead in the law's habitual reliance on relatively crude proportionality methods, in which deliberative ideals are counterpoised to other values, and generally invested with lesser importance. These anti-deliberative effects are not inevitable in the law of politics. We argue they are chiefly consequences of choices about legal doctrine – choices remaining open to reform.

Next, in Part III, 'Problems in the Law of Deliberative Democracy', we survey key aspects of the law of politics, analysing them through the theoretical lens we developed in Part II. Here, therefore, we trace how the essential propositions we have just seen apply to the law of politics' doctrines of political liberty, equality, and integrity in turn. We outline both the thin (non-deliberative) and thick (deliberative) legal expressions of each of these normative political values. As we explore the doctrines, we fix upon four particular problems in the law of deliberative democracy.

In chapter 4 we examine the liberty v deliberation dichotomy in law of politics cases on, for example, political expression. (Other relevant liberties include the right to vote; but we focus less on these.) We contend that this area's focus on what we call 'conceptual balancing' raises the *accommodation problem*. Conceptual balancing, a mostly rivalrous/zero-sum form of reasoning about political values, clashes with 'accommodative' reasoning, which seeks to integrate deliberation with other aspects of democracy.

In chapter 5 we consider how the law of politics similarly constructs a clash between political equality (as traditionally understood) and deliberation. This raises the *equality problem*. In courts the focus of political equality tends to be on comparing the power enjoyed by assorted political parties; the law thus identifies these political combatants as the most relevant equality comparators. This leaves little room for a more deliberative notion of equality, understood as the robust inclusion of ideas, perspectives, and arguments into a public decision-making forum.

In chapter 6 we finish off our survey of the chief political values in the law of politics. Here we consider the particularly nebulous value of political integrity. We note how integrity – and its flipside, corruption – can resist legal ordering. And we observe how a deliberatively thick understanding of integrity allows us

14 The Law of Deliberative Democracy

to view, more clearly, extreme partisanship as a form of democratic corruption. Adopting this view allows us to visualise, and perhaps to address, not one but two key problems relating to integrity:

- The *partisanship problem*. The law of politics' approach to securing integrity is hobbled by an inflexible adherence to a limited range of traditional theories of legal regulation, relying on elaborate legal constraints on power. The long-term trend in the law of politics is towards more of the same: tightening legislative codification and judicial intervention in democratic politics. We show that such laws typically do not resolve, and indeed often aggravate, the profound partisan dysfunction endemic in this legal area, such as pathologies of 'gridlock' and 'meltdown'. And we describe an alternative regulatory method, which we term 'ambiguous positive guidance'.
- The *coercion problem*. A hallmark of deliberative theory is that nothing should compel decision-makers to reach a particular decision except rational persuasion. The aim of law, however, is often precisely to coerce: to use the force of the state to pressure a law's subjects to conform to mandates and restrictions. How, then, can law and deliberative democracy coexist, despite being so contradictory in their methods? Juridification per se might have been deliberatively unproblematic but for recurring patterns of decision-making in election law that truncate or reshape public deliberation to be more coercive. Here too, alternative regulatory models might assist, in this case by promoting integrity while avoiding the typical coercive excesses of the law of politics.

Hence in each chapter of Part III we outline worst-case scenarios first. Each chapter explores reasons why law may be unable appreciably to assist in deliberative democratic design. None of the problems is trivial; each raises profound complications. In concert, the difficulties raise doubt about the feasibility of deliberative democracy in an era of juridifying politics. This should be worrying for those of us concerned to see deliberative democratic projects succeed. Legal reasoning may comprehensively trump democratic deliberation. The dense matrix of laws and legal procedures increasingly overlying democratic practice threatens to constrain and reshape deliberation.

Yet, beyond identifying problems, any canvass of the law of deliberative democracy should also consider whether laws might actually help to establish more deliberative forms of democracy. In this book, as noted, we discuss areas in which the law of politics is indeed compatible with deliberative democracy. Perhaps because sceptical assumptions about deliberation still dominate, legal scholarship has largely neglected to mine these lines of inquiry. But blanket scepticism may be too simple a stance. The harder and more interesting question is how law might actually help effect deliberative democratic projects. An awareness of election law's deliberative deficiencies may even suggest avenues for more effective legal design. We highlight how certain tools already common in the kitbag of legal

Deliberation in a Juridifying World   15

design can mitigate the problems we have outlined. In spite of its genuine limitations, we find that law may still aid in deliberative democratic design projects.

As this work is one of the first to enter the field, we must temper these notes of optimism with caution. But we can be less cautious or equivocal in contending that deliberation still enjoys too little normative weight in studies of election law, in comparison with libertarian, egalitarian, and integrity reasoning. A central proposition in this book is that better political deliberation is already an express or unspoken goal of much legislation and jurisprudence in election law. Even if laws do not always succeed at fulfilling them, scholarship and practice should more consistently expose and evaluate the law's deliberative aims. With these objectives in mind, we set out in this book to explore whether, when, and how the pursuit of deliberative ideals is a worthwhile or plausible project of the law of politics.

Notes

1 Parts of this chapter draw from Ron Levy, 'The Law of Deliberative Democracy: Seeding the Field' (2013) 12 *Election Law Journal* 355.
2 Aristotle, 'Nicomachean Ethics' in Jonathan Barnes (ed), *Complete Works* (Princeton University Press, 1984) vol II, Book VIII, ch 10; Aristotle, 'Politics' in Jonathan Barnes (ed), *Complete Works* (Princeton University Press, 1984) vol II, Book IV, ch 7; see also at Book III, ch 11.
3 John Stuart Mill, *Considerations on Representative Government* (Parker, Son, and Bourn, 1861) Ch XV; Dennis F Thompson, *John Stuart Mill and Representative Government* (Princeton University Press, 1976) 78–80. See also Joseph Schumpeter, *Capitalism, Socialism and Democracy* (Harper Perennial Modern Classics, 3rd ed, 1950) (a choice lies between political equality for the uninformed and easily swayed masses, and the superior option of elite rule).
4 Stephen Tierney, *Constitutional Referendums: The Theory and Practice of Republican Deliberation* (Oxford University Press, 2012).
5 For example, in *Between Facts and Norms: Contributions to a Discourse Theory of Law and Democracy* (William Rehg trans, The MIT Press, 1996, first published 1992), Jürgen Habermas embraces citizen participation within a theory of deliberation. But cf his earlier contributions, eg, Jürgen Habermas, *The Theory of Communicative Action* (Thomas McCarthy trans, Beacon Press, 1984) vol 1: 'Reason and the Rationalization of Society'.
6 For example Habermas, *Between Facts and Norms*, above n 5. Many Habermasians, including Habermas himself, have softened the stringency of this requirement.
7 Russell J Dalton, *Citizen Politics: Public Opinion and Political Parties in Advanced Industrial Democracies* (Congressional Quarterly Press, 5th ed, 2008).
8 See chapter 2.
9 As an example, whereas deliberation has previously aimed at reaching consensus, theorists with an empirical bent such as Dryzek and Niemeyer have – given the reality of partisan politics – conceptualised far more realisable goals, eg, a 'normative meta-consensus': John S Dryzek and Simon J Niemeyer, 'Reconciling Pluralism and Consensus as Political Ideals' (2006) 50 *American Journal of Political Science* 634.
10 Mark Warren and Hilary Pearse (eds), *Designing Deliberative Democracy: The British Columbia Citizens' Assembly* (Cambridge University Press, 2008).
11 Forays into the field by election law scholars include Richard Pildes, 'Competitive, Deliberative and Rights-Oriented Democracy' (2004) 3 *Election Law Journal* 685; Andrew Geddis, 'Three Conceptions of the Electoral Moment' (2003) 28 *Australian Journal of Legal Philosophy* 53; James Gardner, *What Are Campaigns For? The Role of Persuasion in Electoral*

Law and Politics (Oxford University Press, 2009); and Chad Flanders, 'Deliberative Dilemmas: A Critique of Deliberation Day from the Perspective of Election Law' (2007) 23 *Journal of Law and Politics* 147.

12 For instance, Australia's original early Commonwealth Electoral Act 1902, a law of modest length at approximately 14,700 words, is now in the vicinity of 122,000 words; much of the amendment and growth in the Act took place in the post-war period. The UK's Representation of the People Act 1983 has similarly grown, from a start of approximately 16,000 to its present 128,000 words.

13 Ran Hirschl, 'The Judicialization of Politics' in Keith Whittington, R Daniel Kelemen and Gregory A Caldeira (eds), *Oxford Handbook of Law and Politics* (Oxford University Press, 2008) 120. See also, eg, Jürgen Habermas, 'Law as Medium and Law as Institution' in G Teubner (ed), *Dilemmas of Law in the Welfare State* (Walter de Gruyter, 1988); Richard Pildes, 'The Supreme Court, 2003 Term – Foreword: The Constitutionalization of Democratic Politics' (2004) 118 *Harvard Law Review* 29; John Ferejohn, 'Judicializing Politics, Politicizing Law' (2002) 61 *Law and Contemporary Problems* 41.

14 For example Anika Gauja, *Political Parties and Elections: Legislating for Representative Democracy* (Ashgate, 2010); Graeme Orr, 'Legal Conceptions of Political Parties: Through the Lens of Anti-Discrimination Law' in Joo-Cheong Tham, Brian Costar and Graeme Orr (eds), *Electoral Democracy: Australian Prospects* (Melbourne University Press, 2011); Chad Flanders, 'What Do We Want in a Presidential Primary? An Election Law Perspective' (2011) 44 *University of Michigan Journal of Law Reform* 901.

15 For example Enid Campbell, *Parliamentary Privilege* (The Federation Press, 2003).

16 Geddis, above n 11, 70–1.

17 Graeme Orr, *The Law of Politics: Elections, Parties and Money in Australia* (Federation Press, 2010) 11–15.

18 Nathaniel Persily, 'The Place of Competition in American Election Law in the Marketplace of Democracy: Electoral Competition and American Politics' in Michael P McDonald and John Samples, *The Marketplace of Democracy: Electoral Competition and American Politics* (Brookings Institution Press, 2007); JAA Lovink, 'Is Canadian Politics Too Competitive?' (1973) 6 *Canadian Journal of Political Science* 341; Bonnie M Meguid, *Party Competition between Unequals: Strategies and Electoral Fortunes in Western Europe* (Cambridge University Press, 2008).

19 Pamela Karlan, 'Politics by Other Means' (1999) 85 *Virginia Law Review* 1697, 1697.

20 Steven Levitsky and Lucan A Way, 'Why Democracy Needs a Level Playing Field' (2010) 21(1) *Journal of Democracy* 57; Jeremy N Sheff, 'The Myth of the Level Playing Field: Knowledge, Affect and Repetition in Public Debate' (2010) 75 *Missouri Law Review* 143; David Marsh, David Richards and Martin Smith, 'Unequal Plurality: Towards an Asymmetric Power Model of British Politics' (2003) 38 *Government and Opposition* 306, 310, 332.

21 For example Habermas, *Between Facts and Norms*, above n 5; Cass Sunstein, *Designing Democracy: What Constitutions Do* (Oxford University Press, 2001); Horatio Spector, 'The Right to a Constitutional Jury' (2009) 3 *Legisprudence* 111; Eric Ghosh, 'Deliberative Democracy and the Countermajoritarian Difficulty: Considering Constitutional Juries' (2010) 30 *Oxford Journal of Legal Studies* 327; Christopher F Zurn, *Deliberative Democracy and the Institutions of Judicial Review* (Cambridge University Press, 2007); Carlos Santiago Nino, *The Constitution of Deliberative Democracy* (Yale University Press, 1996).

22 Simone Chambers, 'Deliberative Democracy Theory' (2003) 6 *Annual Review of Political Science* 307, 311–12.

23 James Fishkin, *When the People Speak* (Oxford University Press, 2009); Ron Levy, 'Deliberative Voting: Realising Constitutional Referendum Democracy' (2013) *Public Law* 555; Bruce Ackerman and James Fishkin, *Deliberation Day* (Yale University Press, 2004).

24 Orr, above n 17.

25 Chambers, above n 22, 310.

26 George P Fletcher and Jens David Ohlin, *Defending Humanity: When Force Is Justified and Why* (Oxford University Press, 2008) 22.

27 John Uhr, *Deliberative Democracy in Australia: The Changing Place of Parliament* (Cambridge University Press, 1998); Tierney, above n 4; Dennis F Thompson, *Just Elections: Creating a Fair Electoral Process in the United States* (University of Chicago Press, 2002); Hoi Kong, Jeff King, Ron Levy and Graeme Orr (eds), *Deliberative Constitutionalism* (forthcoming).

28 Michael Klarman, 'Majoritarian Judicial Review: The Entrenchment Problem' (1997) 85 *Georgetown Law Journal* 491, 498.

29 Ibid.

30 John Rawls, *Political Liberalism* (Columbia University Press, Expanded Edition, 2005) 137.

31 See, eg, James Fishkin, *When the People Speak: Deliberative Democracy and Public Consultation* (Oxford University Press, 2009) 20–25.

32 Habermas, *Between Facts and Norms*, above n 5, 354–6. See also Seyla Benhabib, 'Toward a Deliberative Model of Democratic Legitimacy' in Seyla Benhabib (ed), *Democracy and Difference: Contesting the Boundaries of the Political* (Princeton University Press, 1996) 67, 74.

33 John Parkinson, 'Legitimacy Problems in Deliberative Democracy' (2003) 51 *Political Studies* 180, 183, quoting John Schaar, 'Legitimacy in the Modern State' in William Connolly (ed), *Legitimacy and the State* (Blackwell, 1984) 104–33.

34 *Kitchen v Herbert*, 755 F 3d 1193, 1210 (10th Cir 2014), citing *Loving v Virginia*, 388 US 1, 4 (1967) (Tenth Circuit Court of Appeals relying heavily on a Supreme Court case invalidating anti-miscegenation laws to find a fundamental right to same sex marriage, explaining that the Court in *Loving* had characterised the question as 'not whether there is a deeply rooted tradition of interracial marriage' but whether there is a 'freedom of choice to marry'). See also *Bostic v Schaefer*, 760 F 3d 352, 376 (4th Cir 2014) also citing *Loving* at 4 (Fourth Circuit Court of Appeals recognising that '[o]ver the decades, the Supreme Court has demonstrated that the right to marry is an expansive liberty interest that may stretch to accommodate changing societal norms'). For discussion see Hoi Kong and Ron Levy, 'Deliberative Constitutionalism' in André Bächtiger, John Dryzek, Jane Mansbridge and Mark Warren (eds), *Oxford Handbook of Deliberative Democracy* (Oxford University Press, forthcoming).

35 Dennis F Thompson, 'Deliberate About, Not In, Elections' (2013) 12 *Election Law Journal* 372.

36 Conrado Hubner Mendes, *Constitutional Courts and Deliberative Democracy* (Oxford University Press, 2013).

37 Notable contributions include Thompson, above n 27.

Part II

Foundations

Chapter 2

Deliberative Democracy and Elections

This chapter – the first of two in this part on deliberative foundations – defines deliberative democracy's core elements. The first sections of this chapter are relatively brief and compendious; readers already familiar with deliberative democracy theory may wish to skip these sections, or to skim ahead to occasional enumerated points to see which elements we select as especially relevant. The chapter concludes with initial observations about what makes deliberation distinctive in the context of *elections* – a context where others have argued that deliberation has no proper or realistic role to play. In chapter 3 ('Deliberative Democracy and the Law of Politics') we link these general background notes to the specifics of the law of politics, outlining a distinctive theoretical lens to be applied through the rest of the book. Jointly, then, these two chapters prime our later analysis, in Part III, of the relation and the fit between the law of politics and deliberative democracy.

The 'deliberative' in deliberative democracy is a term of art particular to the field. It does not refer simply to public acts of 'thinking' and 'communicating'. If it did, then all democracy would be deliberative. Instead, deliberation denotes certain forms of robust and rational collective decision-making by citizens or their representatives. In Habermas's terms, 'no force except that of the better argument is exercised'.[1] Persuasion for other reasons – majority opinion, reputation, caste, divine revelation – is devalued in comparison.[2]

Deliberativists flesh out such well-known general propositions with a range of further particulars. The synthesis to follow first covers the main hallmarks of deliberative democracy – or *what* deliberation entails – before then turning to the question of *who* plays which roles in a deliberative democracy (eg. ordinary citizens and governmental elites). To complete the description, we then discuss the rationales that give purpose, as well as further colour and detail, to these hallmarks and roles; and we raise recurring critiques that insert some ambiguity into any attempt at summary or synthesis.

Our account distils elements from numerous contributions in the field. Distilling in this way is necessary if we are to establish a workable analytic lens for judging election laws in the terms of their deliberative democratic content. However, in developing the hallmarks that follow, we remain aware of divergences of view within deliberative democracy theory. At times, in later chapters in which we read election law through a deliberative lens, such diverging views will give rise to notable (and, we think, intriguing) ambiguities.

Hallmarks

There is no single standard source describing deliberation in the context of decision-making in a democracy. However, in the literature a number of partly overlapping hallmarks frequently recur. These are *ideal* features in that they detail goals to which, according to deliberative theory, democratic discourse should aspire. In our view these distil to ten core elements:

a. Inclusive

Deliberation should be widely inclusive of citizens' interests, voices, and views; and it should air and listen to citizen representations on equal terms.[3] This may include attempting to predict and accommodate intergenerational interests.[4]

b. Cooperative

Deliberation usually involves multiple deliberators working collectively rather than individually, drawing on multiple perspectives to respond in suitably complex ways to inherently complex policy problems.[5]

c. Open-minded

Deliberation is relatively flexible and open to changes of position;[6] it 'requires that participants sincerely weigh the issues on their merits'.[7] Notably, cooperative reasoning should avoid the tendency toward 'groupthink' – a phenomenon in which group decision-making produces flawed outcomes because elements of group dynamics, such as an excessive focus on cohesion or a reluctance to question leaders' assumptions, overtake individual critical thinking.[8] Deliberativists may have given this problem too little attention thus far; as Bächtiger et al note, '[s]ocial psychologists versed in such phenomena as "groupthink" claim that deliberative democrats fail to consider, let alone actively exclude the possibility of such outcomes'.[9]

d. Reflective

Deliberative procedures aim to give deliberators sufficient opportunity to reflect – that is, to consider relevant arguments exhaustively and carefully.[10]

e. Informed

Deliberation takes account of broad sources of information (eg, about ideas, scientific facts, and affected social interests).[11]

f. Holistic

Deliberation is holistic, meaning that it accommodates or trades off diverse values, costs, and benefits, rather than viewing policy or legal options in isolation. As James Fishkin puts the point, the 'root of deliberation is "weighing"'.[12]

g. Other-regarding

Deliberative decision-makers are other-regarding – concerned both with their own interests and with those of others differently situated from themselves. This contrasts with more adversarial and reactive 'agonistic' decision-making.[13] Deliberative democrats often reject theories such as those of rational choice and social choice as explaining politics through the too-narrow lens of self-interest.[14]

h. Civil

Civility in discourse, as opposed to mutual and outward hostility, can help deliberators to realise ideals such as cooperative engagement, open-mindedness, and being other-regarding. A deep form of civility, or 'respect of others and the capacity to conceive of our social relations in terms of reciprocity', is already implicit in other deliberative hallmarks.[15] However, civility in tone is also important and may manifest, for example, in verbal cues of mutual respect in the face of substantive disagreement.[16]

i. Reason-giving

To deliberativists, a core purpose of democracy is to reflect the autonomous choices of its citizens, as opposed to viewing citizens 'as objects of legislation, as passive subjects to be ruled'.[17] This gives rise to the requirement that decision-makers justify their decisions by publicly and reciprocally providing reasons, which anyone else – assuming they share a goal of coexisting amicably in society with others – may reasonably be expected to endorse.[18] Reasons should therefore be expressed in forms that are intelligible and accessible to all. For instance, publicly stated reasons should not be based on personal divine revelation.[19]

j. Uncoerced

Finally, for a decision to be deliberative, no law or other force should unduly compel decision-makers to reach a particular decision.[20] This condition follows

24   The Law of Deliberative Democracy

from some of the hallmarks above: predetermining a decision is a procedural shortcut avoiding a more elaborate – reflective, inclusive, holistic, etc – course of deliberation.

Roles

How might these ideals of deliberation work, if indeed they do, in practice? Some deliberative democrats see a role for governmental elites as key in deliberation. These comparatively *elite-mediated* varieties of deliberative democracy expect elites to filter or translate raw social values, often initially pitched broadly and vaguely, and render them into more workable policy and law.[21] For instance, on Habermas's 'two-track' ideal, elites and ordinary citizens play complementary roles, which constitute a loose division of labour rather than a traditional hierarchy of power.[22] Ordinary citizens express and perhaps deliberate over general values, before elites then follow this general course through and concretise it in law.[23]

Similar descriptions recur throughout deliberative democracy theory. Fishkin borrows the metaphor of the 'filter' from the American constitutional founders, noting that United States '[r]epresentative institutions were supposed to refine public opinion through deliberation'.[24] Deliberativists such as Parkinson defend such arrangements because 'those who decide represent [and] express "mutuality, identification and co-performance" with those who are led', with the result that '"knowers" (philosophers, technical experts or bureaucrats) are … subordinate to "the people affected"'.[25]

Alternatively, more *populist* variants of deliberative democracy aim to encourage better deliberation by citizens themselves, relatively free from elite control. For example, in 'deliberative referendums' or 'deliberative voting',[26] and the mooted idea of a national, pre-election Deliberation Day,[27] discussion and reflection about election issues or legal reform occur through procedures designed to aid voters' sustained consideration of relevant arguments and information.

In this book, given our focus on representative elections, our analysis is situated uniquely somewhere between elite and popular deliberation. We are not concerned with direct democracy per se (ie, referendums and related models), but rather with the election of political representatives. And yet during the election period the voter has direct power. Her decisions are supreme and substantially independent: media, party-political, and other elites may influence, but never fully control, the course or quality of deliberation. Conversely, we are not here concerned with the extremes of elite-led rule in a democracy, namely parliamentary and bureaucratic leadership that loosely pay heed (if at all) to public preferences when engaging in complex, expert-driven lawmaking or regulation. The election campaign is therefore a peculiar hybrid. Though it is an election for representatives, it is uniquely the point at which Habermas's mandate for governmental insiders to listen to public voices must substantially be obeyed; no representative government will survive long electorally without so doing, and it is the very system of periodic elections that gives public opinion, throughout the term, the power to render governance relatively accountable and responsive.

These considerations will become important when we turn to law's regulation of elections, below; how we conceive of such regulation – as deliberative or otherwise – depends on how we conceive of the deliberative functions of elections.

Rationales

There are many ways to argue for deliberative democratic decision-making. Consider three principal rationales. First, a democracy featuring robust deliberation ideally rationalises decisions in an *epistemic* sense. Such a democracy better addresses problems to which we otherwise pay too little attention. These problems affect the health and success of the polity. For example, anti-deliberative, and perhaps polarised, legislators might fail to find solutions to pressing problems – environmental, geopolitical, economic, epidemic, etc – which can then persist or worsen. By contrast, deliberation may support a political system's greater sensitivity and responsiveness to relatively objective, exogenous problems.

This epistemic justification for deliberation is insufficient on its own, however, because policy choices also impact on citizen values. For example, even when a community achieves political consensus that climate change is an objective problem, it must still choose among policy responses impacting unevenly on different people and values.

Secondly, then, deliberative democracy is also concerned with decision-making in the face of disagreement. Put another way, deliberative democracy seeks to *rationalise values*. Deliberativists argue that deliberation can transform and harmonise conflicting values. Habermas draws a distinction between strategic individuals – who compete against each other to maximise their assumed self-interests – and communicatively rational people.[28] The latter are more open to reconsidering what is in their own interests. They may even find themselves better off as a result of their flexibility.

Communicatively rational decision-makers therefore seek accommodation among different values. (This notion will be particularly important in later chapters.) Accommodation is sometimes described in terms of the pursuit of 'overlapping consensus'[29] or 'normative meta-consensus'[30] – that is, areas where values are shared, despite worldview or other differences. Thus:

> different groups, countries, religious communities, and civilizations, although holding incompatible fundamental views on theology, metaphysics, human nature, and so on, would come to an agreement on certain norms that ought to govern human behavior. Each would have its own way of justifying this from out of its profound background conception.[31]

For example, environmentalists and market-oriented economists may, despite some mutually incompatible general assumptions, share common ground if they agree on the economic wisdom of, say, carbon emissions-trading as a means of opening new markets in green technology. Most of the hallmarks of deliberation noted above can contribute towards the process of deliberation over and accommodation of values. For instance, reciprocal reason-giving sees people try to explain why their views should be persuasive, using terms generally acceptable to others, whether or not the others agree with the particular reasons given.

Part of the force of the communicative description of politics stems from the fact that it is far from a new invention; it is rather embedded in a persistent strand of democratic practice. Communicative rationality is thus a modern analytic gloss on old practices – or, at the very least, on old aspirations held and advocated forcefully by a subgroup of democratic leaders. To give but one example, a contemporary observer describes (with some embellishment) US President Kennedy's international diplomacy as premised on a determination 'not to see only a distorted and desperate view of the other side, not to see conflict as inevitable, accommodation as impossible and communication as nothing more than exchange of threats'.[32]

A third key justification for deliberative democracy responds to the occasional charge that deliberation distorts or detracts from democracy.[33] Deliberativists do not yield the point that deliberative democracy departs from a purer, unfettered form of democracy. Instead, they marshal arguments for deliberative democracy's *greater democratic bona fides*. These include the following:

a. Democratic inclusion

With its stress on the force of the better argument, a deliberative democracy can place all participants on roughly the same footing, regardless of social station. On this ideal, any person's argument is influential if it is cogent and relevant.

b. Informed consent

Consent in a democracy may be a fiction to the extent that citizens do not know what they are voting on or consenting to. We should therefore understand public consent in a democracy in terms of robustly 'informed consent'.[34]

c. Reflecting preferences accurately

An ideal deliberative democracy does not channel or attempt to fit citizen values and preferences into the narrowly polarised categories of partisan debate. It therefore may provide a truer representation of often multipolar and complex communities.

d. Avoiding majority tyranny

To the extent that we persuade rather than coerce smaller or weaker groups in a democracy, we genuinely involve more people in it. This presents the best answer, normatively and practically, to the classic problem of the 'tyranny' of democratic majorities. The prevailing solution sees a judicial fiat (eg, under a bill of rights) overrule majority interests post hoc, after preferences settle in public discourses and legislation. Deliberative democracy instead seeks to accommodate majority and minority interests in the course of deciding a matter, before positions harden.

Critiques and ambiguities

Understandably, many critiques still cast doubt on whether politics might ever fulfil deliberative democratic ideals. We saw, above, the argument that deliberative democracy is less democratic than putatively purer democratic forms. Deliberative democrats frequently contend with a range of further critiques and conceptual ambiguities. These already occupy much print space in past volumes on deliberative democracy. We leave extended accounts of the basic debates to those other works, preferring to raise (in the following chapters) a fresh set of concerns arising out of the encounter between deliberative democracy and election law. Nevertheless, it is worth reviewing some of the general objections and ambiguities that frequently recur in relation to deliberative democracy, and that often defy easy or complete answers.

a. Social difference

The notion of value rationalisation attracts many of deliberative democracy's most insistent detractors, who argue that deliberation cannot adequately accommodate social difference. For instance, some feminist and other critics argue that the reason-giving of females, workers, immigrants, etc, is never held in the same esteem – it is often prejudged and written off – by others in the deliberating group. Hence the notion of citizens participating in public deliberation on an equal footing may be only a fiction, and an unconvincing one besides.[35]

Even some avowed deliberativists wonder whether politics should still preserve zones of pre-rational discourse to allow for political party, class, or other non-deliberative 'indoctrination'. Perhaps only such processes can generate citizen values in the first place, or (after formation) help to crystallise, clarify, or promote such values in the public sphere.[36]

b. Self-interest as deliberative

Relatedly, deliberative democrats also occasionally contend with how to incorporate self-interest into deliberation. Self-interest may be understood as that of an individual, or of a social group with a shared identity. In relation to both, an

28 The Law of Deliberative Democracy

important categorisation of deliberative democracy has emerged in the literature: 'Classic Deliberation' versus 'Expansion of the Classic Ideal'.[37] Both categories adhere (more or less) to the main deliberative hallmarks above. Yet a key distinction between them is the place of self-interest. In Classic Deliberation, participants ideally put their particular interests to one side, and instead seek out and clarify their common ground – that is, the set of goods or preferences shared by all. By contrast, in the Expansion of the Classic Ideal, participants are encouraged to voice their interests, including their self-interest.[38]

Even in the Expansion of the Classic Ideal participants continue to seek out some kind of common ground. Yet, because they first listen to one another's interests, the common ground they arrive at is much less abstract – it is more grounded and more tangible – than that of Classic Deliberation.[39] For example, in one version of expanded deliberative theory, self-interest acts as a check on the common ground. A participant may interject during the deliberations, saying something like, 'But that policy would hurt me [or my constituents]'.[40] The deliberating group can then revise its understanding of the common ground so that it no longer tramples upon that participant's interests.

In another version, a participant's self-interest is even a constituent part of the common ground. Indeed, here there is no common ground in the classic sense – there is no 'we' per se, or no strong sense of it in any case. Instead, there are only the constituent interests of the different group members, and each member's self-interest is in itself 'a justification, a reason in itself for adopting a particular policy'.[41] Mansbridge et al analogise this to a married couple, each with conflicting career interests: one has a job offer in one city, the other has a job offer in some other (far off) city. It would be incongruous, counter-productive, indeed somewhat dishonest, for them to discuss the dilemma solely in terms of 'what is good for "us", eg, for the "marriage" or for the children. Only by recognizing their self-interests and the conflict between them can the couple negotiate a fair, perhaps even integrative, agreement'.[42] Each of them may then 'vote' for a proposed solution entirely from the point of view of his or her self-interest.

c. Unduly constrained rationality

Also commonly, some authors sympathetic to deliberative democratic ideals seek to loosen restrictions about what counts as 'deliberative', partly so as not to exclude too many citizens from the exercise. Iris Marion Young, for one, would wish to include as deliberative certain popular narrative styles such as storytelling, which are typical of ordinary public discourse.[43] Strictly speaking, Young regards her conception of democracy as 'communicative', rather than 'deliberative'; however, regardless of what Young calls it, her democratic conception includes storytelling, rhetoric, and greeting, rather than only reason-giving.

d. Empirical scepticism

Such efforts at inclusion raise the obverse critique that citizens, once they are welcomed more robustly into political decision-making, are unlikely to be adequately informed about policy particulars. In addition, deliberative ideals of reasoned, other-regarding, and reflective decision-making may be said to naively ignore the ineradicably closed, selfish, and reactive patterns of human reasoning. A more modest version of the latter argument is that the strategic-communicative distinction is doubtful, since individuals often have a multitude of motivations for speech and actions, some strategic and others communicative.[44]

These and other critiques raise doubt about deliberative theory's empirical claims. However, note that deliberative democrats themselves do not assert that deliberation is easy. They know the flaws in their models. Certain institutional innovations, such as the Citizens' Assemblies first trialled in Canada, were by nearly all accounts successful in generating civil, cooperative, inclusive, and reflective decision-making.[45] But the best summary is that the potential for deliberation in the real world is both a matter of degree and closely dependent on context.[46] Studies have expanded the empirical record and outlined a host of specific categories in which deliberation is either relatively weak or relatively strong.[47] For instance, deliberation is often weaker in the broader public sphere than it is within the controlled conditions of a deliberative assembly.[48] Yet, in the extreme case, the sceptical view still discounts any apparent evidence of deliberative political conduct as skewed, unreliable, or misreported.[49] (Given this unfalsifiable assumption, arguments for deliberative democracy can never win.)

In our view, each of the objections and ambiguities we have just seen calls for *refining* deliberative institutions and normative goals, rather than their outright abandonment. A prevailing and sensible approach views democracies and their institutions as situated along a spectrum, from practices that are relatively deliberative to those less so. Empirical work generates a similarly complex picture of deliberation: of many gradations, arising from a variety of institutional options and their normative trade-offs. The more complex description of deliberation is usually the more accurate one. Aware of this, many deliberative democrats seek, through their institutional proposals, to edge democratic practice towards better deliberation by modest increments.

Deliberative *electoral* democracy

At one end of the deliberative spectrum, political discourse is understood as relatively agonistic, and the preferences and interests of citizens largely fixed. In an *election* characterised by wholly agonistic politics, voting would therefore matter far more than the prior campaign and its events (eg, leaders' debates, policy statements). Balloting would count up static, preformed citizen preferences to determine which sets should dominate. Pure agonism is plainly coercive because it enables the stronger faction – usually, but not always, the more populous faction

30 The Law of Deliberative Democracy

– to assert unilateral control over directions in public governance. By contrast, in an ideal deliberative electoral system the campaign period would be a key site of democratic activity. The campaign would be an extended communicative event during which candidates, parties, third-party interest groups, and media may inform and seek to sway prospective voters; and in addition where voters discursively influence each other.[50] Here the act of voting would remain important, but secondary.

Give the focus of our book on deliberation in and about elections, we spend the rest of this chapter considering elections as sites of democratic deliberation. Elections can be conducted at many levels. Representative elections may be society-wide (eg, for a president or legislature). Others may be more confined, whether regionally (eg, for a local government) or functionally (eg, for an attorney-general). Representative elections may also take many forms. For instance, representatives may be elected at-large, or from just a subset of the relevant population, and they may be elected by plurality vote or by proportional representation. Yet, despite their diversity, in key ways elections are deliberatively distinct (if not quite wholly unique), as compared with other forms of deliberation that end in voting. What are these distinctive features, and what follows from them – especially for the quality of deliberation and its amenability to legal regulation?

a. Open-textured

Deliberation within representative elections is distinct from deliberation focused on a small suite of defined issues. Juries and (in the bulk of their work) trial judges must focus on a discrete set of factual questions and, most of all, on questions of guilt or liability in a particular case. Similarly, deliberative assemblies are asked to consider a particular topic of law or policy reform. The terrain to be deliberated is relatively defined. By contrast, representative elections are not quite so programmatic. There is no easy test for relevance or salience in an electoral context. Rather there is a surfeit of election 'issues'. These include policy positions, of course, but the vision, competency, and even character or cultural identity of parties, leaders, and candidates also come into play. For this reason we call elections *open-textured*.

Electoral open-texturedness should be understood as a question of scope rather than one of scale. That is, it does not necessarily track the distinction between deliberation at a society-wide (macro) level and at a local-community (micro) level. Elections might be more focused if we had a simple job description for elected representatives or government, but we do not and perhaps cannot. The notion of political representation, as we see further below, has contradictory dimensions.

For deliberativists seeking to design institutional reform, open-texturedness poses challenges. To see why, consider how electoral open-texturedness contrasts with an act of direct as opposed to representative democracy. The point is not that referendum proposals are necessarily simple. Proposals for constitutional reform, for instance, may be modest or technical, or they may assume a high level of civics literacy or acumen.[51] This insight is captured in the anecdote of a voter, asked to vote on the constitution that would federate Australia, deliberately wasting his ballot by scrawling on it 'only lawyers understand this'.[52] But representative elections always present an extensive menu of policy issues, as well as varied options in the form of different parties and candidates.

In direct democracy, the institutional path to better popular deliberation may not be simple, but options in this regard are certainly clearer. Worldwide, conventions are commonly called to inform, promote, and shape both debate and proposals in advance of constitutional referendums. Official 'yes' and 'no' cases can be circulated in the balloting period; various US states legislated for such processes to inform ballot initiatives as early as 1909.[53] Official booklets detailing 'yes' and 'no' cases, circulated to all households, also remain a feature of Australian constitutional referendums.[54] Moreover, internet voting promises to open up space for innovations to enhance voter engagement and reflection at referendums.[55] Finally, as pioneered by Fishkin, direct democracy can be scaled-down, but deliberation ramped-up, through the mechanism of the 'deliberative poll'.[56] (In a deliberative poll, representative samples of electors are polled before and after they are exposed to, and reflect as a group upon, material relevant to a particular proposition or issue.)

Electoral open-texturedness, in contrast, renders it inconceivable that experts might calculatedly 'set' an agenda for representative elections. Rather, out of a combination of events, influential actors (notably parties and candidates, civic leaders or associations, the media), and public opinion, a variety of issues and themes emerge organically and, dare we say, democratically. Perhaps the only kind of representative election that defies this description is the US-style recall election, where an individual representative is subjected to popular dis-election, occasionally in light of specific allegations against the office-holder in question.

In our view, open-texturedness is not necessarily a bad thing. In recognising it in representative elections – and especially election campaigns – we need to embrace the fact that they are deliberatively unbounded. We should not imagine that democratic deliberation can be remade into a mechanistic calculus. In contrast to a committee working its way through a hierarchically ordered agenda, electoral democracy may appear to lack a contained or predictable agenda. Elections are not occasions for solving issues via specialist knowledge; no one can have such knowledge for every issue arising in the campaign.[57] Yet, although the open-texturedness of elections may seem to divide public attention, this feature also permits electors to vary their attention as suits their inclinations. Voters are free to engage with those agendas which are most relevant to their values, experiences, and interests.

b. Sites of mass persuasion

Some of those who doubt the potential for more deliberative electoral democracy paint elections as essentially aggregative exercises. In support of that doubt,

32 The Law of Deliberative Democracy

some point to the bald nature of voting at representative elections (one ballot per voter per office). John Dryzek sees a dichotomy between deliberative and electoral democracy, with elections understood chiefly as exercises in tallying up preferences.[58]

Others who view elections as relatively free of deliberation cite the competitive instincts of those vying for office. For instance, Dennis Thompson argues that elections function best (and are more easily regulated) as competitive contests which do not readily accommodate deliberation.[59] He offers the example of an election campaigner – a candidate for the Colorado state senate in 1996 – who bowed out because, after deliberating on the matter, she believed the other candidate was the better choice.[60] To Thompson, such capitulation made a mockery of the competitive element of campaigning for election. Indeed it did. In addition, however, a hallmark of a relatively *deliberative* election would be its inclusiveness and breadth of information, features hardly likely to be sustained if candidates withdraw and self-censor, least of all in a predominantly two-party electoral system.

Thompson advocates deliberation *about* elections (ie, about their governing rules), rather that *in* the course of election campaigns. He thinks the former more realistic.[61] Doubtless this is true, but the distinction is a porous one. Deliberative electoral rule-making is not intrinsically valuable. Its value instead depends on its capacity to promote certain democratic virtues – especially deliberation itself – in the public sphere. For instance, if a deliberative electoral redistricting body (eg, an independent commission) suppresses gerrymandering, it does so to avoid a host of more general anti-democratic and anti-deliberative vices: for example, under-representative and hence under-inclusive districts; predetermined elections and thus inflexible decision-making in election periods; or more polarised and therefore less open-minded and wide-ranging political debate.

We may also challenge the distinction between deliberation in and about elections in light of the blurred roles of political culture at these two levels. Decision-making cultures inside and outside of electoral institutions interpenetrate to some extent. For instance, as Rick Pildes notes, the perception that redistricting is a selfish partisan game can set the terms of public debate about electoral politics.[62] Thus when partisan self-interest seems to govern rule-making, we may also see a decline in wider public discourses characterised by reason and cooperation. Conversely, some studies show that deliberative bodies can set deliberative cues for citizens to follow.[63] This is an instance of the 'expressive' function of institutions and law, which several authors have explored.[64] Law and institutions perhaps may telescope the desirability, in the public arena, of certain norms. Thus carefully regulated deliberative bodies can help to structure and focus public discourses and make the latter more deliberative. For instance, by a number of accounts, public debate during and soon after British Columbia's Citizens' Assembly experiment in 2004 was relatively reflective, informed, and non-partisan.[65]

A further set of arguments marshalled against the notion of electoral deliberation points to the tendency, for many voters, to have reasonably settled allegiances and political values. James Gardner, a critic of deliberativism, goes so far as to argue, in the US at least, that there is no such thing as an election campaign capable of serving to persuade. This he believes not only to be true, but welcome: 'a deliberatively thick campaign of reasoned persuasion is not ... essential to a well-functioning democracy'.[66] To him, campaigns are 'elaborate rituals' veiling the fact that outcomes are 'settled before the campaign even gets underway'.[67] Whereas for an elitist like Joseph Schumpeter voters are a swayable mass, for Gardner they are models of relative fixity of opinion.[68]

There is force within this critique. Many voters exit the polling booth voting the way they were likely to at the start of the campaign. But the claim that election campaigns are not at all persuasive events is untenable. For counter-examples, it is enough to point to the clear and unexpected shifts that decided the outcomes of the 2015 United Kingdom and Canadian national electoral campaigns – with debate crystallising in the former around devolving power between Scotland and England, and in the latter around which opposition party offered a more acceptable progressive alternative to the long-governing Conservatives. Even in the US, voters seemed to withhold their final assessments of the candidates until the end of presidential campaigning in, for example, 1948, 1960, 1980, and 2000, as support oscillated between the Republican contender and the Democratic one.

The origins of the modern electoral campaign lie in nineteenth-century constitutional and statutory reforms. For parliamentary systems in the Westminster mould, whereas pre-modern elections were localised and often chaotic affairs, with voting spread over several days and hustings marked by rituals of largesse,[69] the latter part of the Victorian era saw reforms that rendered campaigns recognisably modern. Colourful customary practices like vote-buying and treating (eg, giving alcohol to crowds at campaign events), which configured voting as a transaction of mutual reciprocity, were reined in. A much more ordered and ascetic set of practices substituted for the overt carnival of old.[70]

The orthodox view is to see this shift in purely *democratic* terms. This is understandable given the key role played in the shift by reforms such as an expanded franchise and a less corruptible form of voting by secret ballot. But the aim was subtler. It was to replace a rowdy, physically public type of democratic politics with a more decorous and *deliberatively democratic* ideal. Coinciding with the advent of mass literacy and cheap print, electoral politics was reconceived.[71] Elections themselves were constituted not as rituals of ordination but as periods of organised, rational pitches for votes. The 'election period' now ran between a highly formalised process of candidate nomination and a single, shared polling day.[72] In the Westminster model, rules were erected to encourage respectful interactions between electors and candidates. For instance, statute law guaranteed free use of schoolrooms for election meetings, to supplant the rowdy hustings with a more discursive environment.[73] Candidates were subsidised equally to distribute their party's policy manifesto to each elector. And polling places themselves were reframed as places of quiet repose, to give voters and their consciences a final, even solemn chance to reflect on their decision (a theme we develop in chapter 4). In this way, the election 'campaign' was constructed as a regulated period of

34   The Law of Deliberative Democracy

intense focus on electoral communication and choice, whose legacy remains today.

Why have election campaigns not merely persisted, but expanded? Only some mass delusion or false consciousness could explain why so many behave as if campaigns mattered in terms of advocacy and discourse if (as Gardner argues) they do not matter in this way at all. Even if 80 per cent of electors were party loyalists, any close electoral contest depends on the campaign's effect on the deliberation of the remaining 20 per cent whose positions are more malleable. (If anything, these are overestimates. In truth, stable and strong party loyalty is in decline in many jurisdictions.[74])

More significantly, voters' positions on issues do not perfectly map onto ideological or partisan labels.[75] An election can thus be a site for political deliberation, where even staunch partisans are open to deliberation on some issues, even when the election outcome is a foregone conclusion. Adherents and critics of deliberative democracy alike often overlook these facts.

In the absence of elections, two essential and interrelated drivers of democratic political discourse would be absent. One is citizen voice, which stems from the franchise without being confined to its exercise on polling day. The other is the democratic responsiveness of politicians to the opinions of potential voters, across the electoral cycle. Public opinion is communicated to government not merely in a linear and terminal form in electoral voting but via an ongoing public sphere.[76] This occurs through a diffuse reflexive process involving a variety of consultative and deliberative mechanisms, ranging from the traditional (eg, constituency offices in parliamentary systems), through the contemporary (eg, community cabinet meetings), and on to initiatives in 'e-democracy' like www.whitehouse.gov/.[77]

Some of these mechanisms can be captured by interest groups. But this democratic deficit is salved to an extent by the ubiquity of reliable opinion polling, an inclusive and democratic methodology. Unlike other forms of public expression, such polling is a genuinely representative feedback mechanism,[78] at least (so we argue in chapter 4) if it is confined to issue-oriented polling, as opposed to merely tracking candidate or party popularity.[79]

c. Personality politics

Most deliberativists seek to prioritise policy over personality. One fear for good deliberation in representative democracy is that the necessity to elect candidates and leaders, and hence the relevance and inescapability of personality, may conflate into 'audience democracy' and even a prurient 'intimisation' of politics.[80] Yet there is nothing intrinsic about personality to preclude electors deliberating over it. As Dryzek argues, echoing Young, deliberation can embrace rhetoric, narrative, emotional appeals, and discussion about character.[81] Representative elections, after all, vest discretion in representatives to govern in circumstances of unpredictable future conditions, so questions of trust in the candidates must stand alongside policy and values in the deliberative mix.

The old Burkean dichotomy – which pits representatives as delegates voicing local interests, versus representatives as trustees serving the national interest by their own lights – offered a dualistic model of representation for a less pluralist era. Each of those representative ideals offered a deliberative focus for what was then a quite confined group of propertied, male electors, and a relatively personalised relation between representatives and constituents. In the delegate model, candidates are to be judged by their knowledge of, and sympathy for, local concerns. It is then assumed that there will be continuing deliberation and counsel between a member of parliament and her electorate. In the trustee model, electors are meant to compare candidates on their wisdom concerning broad national issues, with deliberation on particular solutions being deferred to elite, legislative debate.

But contemporary elections are, quite clearly, much more inclusive exercises than elections in eras past. Inclusiveness, it will be recalled, was the first in our list of the hallmarks of deliberative democracy. Inclusiveness embraces a breadth of perspectives and affected interests. The radical achievement of the universal suffrage instituted, most obviously, a formally inclusive basis for electoral democracy and an end to the fiction of 'virtual representation'. (Virtual representation, where some voters were taken to speak for all, meets none of the deliberative democratic rationales of inclusiveness, informed consent, accurate preference reflection, or avoiding the risk of tyranny.) It also opened up a more individualised conception of the franchise,[82] as pluralist conceptions of society came to replace organic ones. The net result has been the fragmentation of notions of representation and a multiplying of the types of concerns relevant to voters and transmitted in the media. Therefore modern elections offer a cacophonous conversation, combining a complex of policy debates, promises, and visions with often personalised questions of competence and character.

d. Partisanship and inclusion

Faced with such electoral complexity, many citizens also fall back on simplifying metrics additional to personality. One metric involves heuristics in the form of questions like 'am I and the people I care about worse off than four years ago?' and 'are we as a society heading in the right direction?' Another involves cues of loyalty to party or candidate: as John Matsusaka puts it, parties and candidates offer 'bundles'.[83] The often agonistic nature of much electoral competition is an undoubted challenge for deliberation. Partisan campaigns, it hardly needs to be said, may lead to 'inter-group polarization'.[84]

Yet, although representative elections may exacerbate this phenomenon, it is not the sole province of electoral politics. In truth, the cycle of free and fair elections temporarily opens up, then assuages, conflicting group interests. Indeed, as we explained earlier, exposure to contrasting views is essential to good deliberation, two of the hallmarks of which are open-mindedness and regard for others' interests. We need views against, as well as for, positions, and this is one upside of electoral agonism.[85] As Manin argues, 'it is the opposition of views and reasons

36 The Law of Deliberative Democracy

that is necessary for deliberation, not just their diversity'.[86] Understood in that light, the competitive debate that elections promote is a necessary precondition for deliberation.

In sum, representative elections are unique and fundamental sites for democratic deliberation. They have an open-texturedness that distinguishes them from other acts of popular deliberation, such as referendums. While elections are not programmatic in terms of the issues they throw up for deliberation, they are systematised affairs. In its modern form (which dates to the latter half of the Victorian era) the 'campaign period' arose as a more deliberatively focused and orderly successor to earlier electoral customs. In between campaigns, too, democratic opinion is channelled systematically (as we shall discuss in a later chapter) via polling on political issues. Free elections under a universal franchise have the potential to be quintessentially inclusive activities, in terms of the perspectives, interests, and concerns they embrace. These features give to elections the capacity to become more deliberative. We consider next the possible roles of law in pursuing and – at least by modest increments – realising this aspiration.

Notes

1 Jürgen Habermas, 'Reconciliation through the Public Use of Reason: Remarks on John Rawls's Political Liberalism' (1995) 92 *Journal of Philosophy* 109, 124.
2 See, eg, Amy Gutmann and Dennis Thompson, *Why Deliberative Democracy?* (Princeton University Press, 2004) 52. Habermas once thought that religious arguments should be translated to secular political claims, but changed his mind after admitting that this excludes religious people from arguing: see Jürg Steiner, *The Foundations of Deliberative Democracy: Empirical Research and Normative Implications* (Cambridge University Press, 2012) 104.
3 James Bohman, 'Deliberative Democracy and the Epistemic Benefits of Diversity' (2006) 3 *Episteme* 175; Joshua Cohen, 'Deliberative and Democratic Legitimacy' in James Bohman and William Rehg (eds), *Deliberative Democracy: Essays on Reason and Politics* (MIT Press, 1997) 67, 72; John Parkinson, *Deliberating in the Real World: Problems of Legitimacy in Deliberative Democracy* (Oxford University Press, 2006) 40.
4 Gutmann and Thompson, above n 2, 210.
5 David Estlund, *Democratic Authority: A Philosophical Framework* (Princeton University Press, 2008) 177.
6 Gutmann and Thompson, above n 2, 57–9, 110–19; Mark Warren and Hilary Pearse, 'Introduction' in Mark Warren and Hilary Pearse (eds), *Designing Deliberative Democracy: The British Columbia Citizens' Assembly* (Cambridge University Press, 2008) 6.
7 James Fishkin, *When the People Speak: Deliberative Democracy and Public Consultation* (Oxford University Press, 2009) 35.
8 See Mark Schafer, *Groupthink Versus High-Quality Decision Making in International Relations* (Columbia University Press, 2010) 6; Cass R Sunstein, 'The Law of Group Polarization' in James Fishkin and Peter Laslett (eds), *Debating Deliberative Democracy* (Blackwell, 2003) 80.
9 André Bächtiger, Simon Niemeyer, Michael Neblo, Marco R Steenbergen and Jürg Steiner, 'Disentangling Diversity in Deliberative Democracy: Competing Theories, Their Blind Spots and Complementarities' (2010) 18 *Journal of Political Philosophy* 32, 39.
10 Zsuzsanna Chappell, *Deliberative Democracy: A Critical Introduction* (Palgrave Macmillan, 2012) 8.

11 Gutmann and Thompson, above n 2, 43.
12 Fishkin, above n 7, 35.
13 Chantal Mouffe, 'Deliberative Democracy or Agonistic Pluralism?' (1999) 66 *Social Research* 745.
14 Chappell, above n 10, 4.
15 Micheline Milot, 'Conceptions of the Good: Challenging the Premises of Deliberative Democracy' in David Kahane, Daniel Weinstock, Dominique Leydet and Melissa Williams (eds), *Deliberative Democracy in Practice* (UBC Press, 2010) 30.
16 Ibid, 32; Parkinson, above n 3, 150.
17 Gutmann and Thompson, above n 2, 3.
18 John Rawls, *Political Liberalism* (Columbia University Press, Expanded Edition, 2005) 137; Gutmann and Thompson, above n 2, 3–5; Parkinson, above n 3, 99–100.
19 Gutmann and Thompson, above n 2.
20 Jürgen Habermas, *The Theory of Communicative Action* (Thomas McCarthy trans, Beacon Press, 1984, first published 1981) vol 1: 'Reason and the Rationalization of Society', 25.
21 Jürgen Habermas, *Between Facts and Norms: Contributions to a Discourse Theory of Law and Democracy* (William Rehg trans, The MIT Press, 1996, first published 1992).
22 Ibid 304.
23 Ibid 354–6. See also Seyla Benhabib, 'Toward a Deliberative Model of Democratic Legitimacy' in Seyla Benhabib (ed), *Democracy and Difference: Contesting the Boundaries of the Political* (Princeton University Press, 1996) 67, 74.
24 Fishkin, above n 7, 15.
25 John Parkinson, 'Legitimacy Problems in Deliberative Democracy' (2003) 51 *Political Studies* 180, 183, quoting John Schaar, 'Legitimacy in the Modern State' in William Connolly (ed), *Legitimacy and the State* (Blackwell, 1984), 104–33.
26 Ron Levy, 'Deliberative Voting: Realising Constitutional Referendum Democracy' (2013) *Public Law* 555.
27 Bruce Ackerman and James Fishkin, *Deliberation Day* (Yale University Press, 2004).
28 Habermas, above n 20, 285–6.
29 Rawls, above n 18, 132–72.
30 John S Dryzek and Simon J Niemeyer, 'Reconciling Pluralism and Consensus as Political Ideals' (2006) 50 *American Journal of Political Science* 634.
31 Charles Taylor, 'Conditions of An Unforced Consensus on Human Rights' in Joanne R Bauer and Daniel A Bell, *The East Asian Challenge for Human Rights* (Cambridge University Press, 1999) 124.
32 Jenny Hocking, *Gough Whitlam: The Biography* (Melbourne University Publishing/ Miegunyah Press, 2008) vol 1, 268.
33 Robert Post, 'Managing Deliberation: The Quandary of Democratic Dialogue' (1993) 103 *Ethics* 654.
34 Levy, above n 26, 563–4; Fishkin, above n 7, 34.
35 See, eg, Iris M Young, *Justice and the Politics of Difference* (Princeton University Press, 1990); Seyla Benhabib, 'Deliberative Rationality and Models of Democratic Legitimacy' (1994) 1 *Constellations* 26, 39.
36 Michael Walzer, 'Deliberation, and What Else?' in Stephen Macedo (ed), *Deliberative Politics: Essays on Democracy and Disagreement* (Oxford University Press, 1999) 58; Jane Mansbridge et al, 'The Place of Self-Interest and the Role of Power in Deliberative Democracy' (2010) 18 *Journal of Political Philosophy* 64, 84.
37 A number of scholars have highlighted these two categories, including Mansbridge et al, ibid; and Bächtiger et al, above n 9. The terms 'Classic Deliberation' and 'Expansion of the Classic Ideal' are from Mansbridge et al.
38 Another key distinction is that while Classic Deliberation relies wholly on reason-giving

38 The Law of Deliberative Democracy

by the participants, the Expansion of the Classic Ideal allows them to make verbal contributions in a variety of forms, including rhetoric, greeting, and storytelling.

39 In the Expansion of the Classic Ideal, common ground can take any of a number of forms, including (but not limited to) an aggregation of various parties' self-interests, or a recognition of interpersonal differences. This is followed first by agreement on the structure of the conflict that remains, and thereafter by either a vote or some kind of negotiation.

40 Mansbridge et al, above n 36, 73.

41 Ibid 75.

42 Ibid 76.

43 Lynn M Sanders, 'Against Deliberation' (1997) 25 *Political Theory* 347; Iris Marion Young, 'Justice, Inclusion and Deliberative Democracy' in Stephen Macedo (ed), *Deliberative Politics: Essays on Democracy and Disagreement* (Oxford University Press, 1999) 151.

44 See, eg, Jürg Steiner and Markus Spörndli, *Deliberative Politics in Action* (Cambridge University Press, 2004).

45 See, eg, contributions to Warren and Pearse, above n 6.

46 Many deliberativists echo this point: eg, Simone Chambers, 'Rhetoric and the Public Sphere: Has Deliberative Democracy Abandoned Mass Democracy?' (2009) 37 *Political Theory* 323, 325.

47 On empirical studies see, eg, Dennis Thompson, 'Deliberative Democratic Theory and Empirical Political Science' (2008) 11 *Annual Review of Political Science* 497; Kevin Mattson, 'Do Americans Really Want Deliberative Democracy?' (2002) 5 *Rhetoric & Public Affairs* 327.

48 See, eg, Robert Goodin, 'Democratic Deliberation Within' (2000) 29 *Philosophy and Public Affairs* 81.

49 See, eg, Finance and Public Administration Legislation Committee, Australian Senate, *Debate on the Citizen Initiated Referendum Bill 2013*, Melbourne, 29 April 2013, 16–17 (Sen Scott Ryan).

50 *Contra* Dennis F Thompson, 'Deliberate About, Not In, Elections' (2013) 12 *Election Law Journal* 372.

51 On 'modest' or relatively technical referendum proposals see Paul Kildea, 'Worth Talking About? Modest Constitutional Amendment and Citizen Deliberation in Australia' (2013) 12 *Election Law Journal* 524.

52 Glenn Rhodes, *Votes for Australia: How Colonials Voted at the 1899–1900 Federation Referendums* (Centre for Australian Public Sector Management, Griffith University, 2002) 12.

53 Earl R Sikes, *State and Federal Corrupt-Practices Legislation* (Duke University Press, 1928) 99–100.

54 Parliament of Australia, House of Representatives Standing Committee on Legal and Constitutional Affairs, *A Time for Change: Yes/No? Inquiry into the Machinery of Referendums* (2009).

55 Levy, above n 26.

56 James Fishkin, *Democracy and Deliberation: New Directions for Democratic Reform* (Yale University Press, 1991).

57 Compare Asimov's idea of a single, deity-like computer charged with deciding electoral contests: Isaac Asimov, 'The Franchise' in Isaac Asimov and Martin H Greenberg (eds), *Election Day 2084* (Prometheus Books, 1984).

58 John Dryzek, *Deliberative Democracy and Beyond* (Oxford University Press, 2000) 3. Posner likewise sees 'electoral law, technologies, procedures and personnel' as tabulative: Richard A Posner, *Law, Pragmatism and Democracy* (Harvard University Press, 2003) 237.

59 Thompson, above n 50, 375. See also Dennis Thompson, *Just Elections: Creating a Fair Electoral Process in the US* (University of Chicago Press, 2002).

60 Thompson, above n 50, 374.

61 Ibid.

62 Richard Pildes, 'The Supreme Court, 2003 Term – Foreword: The Constitutionalization of Democratic Politics' (2004) 118 *Harvard Law Review* 29, 219.

63 Fred Cutler et al, 'Deliberation, Information, and Trust: The British Columbia Citizens' Assembly as Agenda Setter' in Warren and Pearse, above n 6, 168–70.

64 See, eg, Cass R Sunstein, 'On the Expressive Function of Law' (1996) 144 *University of Pennsylvania Law Review* 2021; Elizabeth S Anderson and Richard H Pildes, 'Expressive Theories of Law: A General Restatement' (2000) 148 *University of Pennsylvania Law Review* 150.

65 Cutler et al, above n 63; Michael K Mackenzie and Mark E Warren, 'Two Trust-Based Uses of Minipublics in Democratic Systems' in John Parkinson and Jane Mansbridge (eds), *Deliberative Systems* (Cambridge University Press, 2012), 111–12.

66 See James A Gardner, *What are Campaigns For? The Role of Persuasion in Electoral Law and Politics* (Oxford University Press, 2009) 116.

67 Ibid 191. Rituals are important to politics as conduits for social meaning. But recognising that is quite different from arguing elections to be ritualistic in the sense of empty charades: Graeme Orr, *Ritual and Aesthetic in Electoral Systems: A Comparative Legal Account* (Ashgate, 2015) ch 2.

68 Orr, above n 67, ch 3.

69 Frank O'Gorman, 'Electoral Deference in Unreformed England, 1760–1832' (1984) *Journal of Modern History* 56; Frank O'Gorman, *Voters, Patrons and Parties: the Unreformed Electorate of Hanoverian England, 1734–1832* (Clarendon Press, 1989).

70 Orr, above n 67, chs 6, 8, and pp 190–4.

71 Compare James Vernon, *Politics and the People: A Study in English Political Culture c.1815–1867* (Cambridge University Press, 1993) ch 3.

72 The Great Reform Act 1832 decreed that polling in Britain would 'continue for Two Days only', such days to be successive. By 1853 that was reduced to a single day, and by 1918 the day had to be simultaneous across the nation.

73 Jon Lawrence, *Electing our Masters: The Hustings in British Politics from Hogarth to Blair* (Oxford University Press, 2009) 109–10 and 142 (describing local school meetings as a 'staple of electioneering' for much of the twentieth century).

74 See, eg, Paul Webb, *The Modern British Party System* (Sage, 2007) ch 2; and Ian McAllister, *The Australian Voter: 50 Years of Change* (UNSW Press, 2011) ch 2. Compare claims of increasing polarisation in the United States, eg, Alan I Abramowitz and Kyle L Saunders, 'Is Polarisation a Myth?' (2008) 70 *The Journal of Politics* 542.

75 Bernard Manin, *The Principles of Representative Government* (Cambridge University Press, 1997) 229–30.

76 Dryzek, above n 58, 50.

77 Ibid.

78 John Gastil, *By Popular Demand: Revitalizing Representative Democracy through Deliberative Elections* (University of California Press, 2000) ch 5 (comparing representations made by constituents, talkback radio, open consultations, and lobbying).

79 Compare the rather desultory fate of opinion polling under communism: Matt Henn, 'Opinion Polling in Central and Eastern Europe under Communism' (1998) 33 *Journal of Contemporary History* 229.

80 See, respectively, Manin, above n 75, 218–34; and James Stanyer, *Intimate Politics: Publicity, Privacy and the Personal Lives of Politicians in Media-Saturated Democracies* (Polity Books, 2012).

81 Dryzek, above n 58, 167–8.

82 HF Rawlings, *Law and the Electoral Process* (Sweet & Maxwell, 1988) 5–7, drawing on AH Birch, *Representation* (Macmillan, 1972).

83 John Matsusaka, 'Direct Democracy Works' (2005) 19 *Journal of Economic Perspectives* 185, 194.

84 Bernard Manin, 'Democratic Deliberation: Why We Should Promote Debate Rather than Discussion' (Paper to Program in Ethics and Public Affairs Seminar, Princeton University, 13 October, 2005) 4.

85 Nancy L Rosenblum, *On the Side of the Angels: An Appreciation of Parties and Partisanship* (Princeton University Press, 2010) 306.

86 Manin, above n 84, 15–16.

Chapter 3

Deliberative Democracy and the Law of Politics

If one were to imagine the vast collection of decision problems ... as a sea or an ocean, with the easier problems on top and more complicated ones at increasing depth, then deductive rationality would describe human behavior accurately only within a few feet of the surface.

W Brian Arthur[1]

In this chapter we begin to connect the outline of deliberative democracy theory of the previous chapter to inquiries about the roles of law in deliberative democracy. As we saw in chapter 2, a number of critiques can be raised against deliberative democracy on its own. Our aim in this chapter is not to rehearse such broad critiques, nor the responses to them; others have covered these well. We wish instead to go further by considering critiques of claims that *law* – especially *the law of politics*[2] – can play constructive roles in realising deliberative democracy.

Our focus is on law not in the abstract, but as a heterogeneous set of norms. Theorists from John Rawls and Jürgen Habermas onward have broadly characterised courts as agents or instruments of deliberation. Among later generations of deliberativists, some have even conducted detailed institutional evaluations of courts, gauging their formal features against deliberative benchmarks.[3] Few commentators, however, have looked at the substance of judicial output – that is, the instances and patterns of legal decision-making in judicial reasoning.[4] In this chapter we focus on courts, especially appellate courts, as quintessential sites for deliberation about law: its formation, interpretation, and application. Our focus is not on common law courts' institutional form or jurisdictional power, but on the doctrine at work within them. Legal scholars are presumably the most adept at such analyses, which take doctrine and substantive legal method seriously. This focus in some ways presents a less speculative take on curial deliberation. In essence we interrogate here not merely how courts are primed to function but – adopting a finer-grained view – how they function in fact. We thus look at key legal norms that judges follow (and create) when reasoning about democracy.

It is especially in the consideration of fundamental questions by appellate courts that the normative underpinnings and tensions in the law are laid bare. We raise here important concerns about anti-deliberative assumptions in the prevailing doctrines of the law of politics. These assumptions are the more concerning given the 'globally widespread' phenomenon of 'juridification' (along with 'judicialisation' and 'constitutionalisation') – in other words, given the gradual spread of law through the precincts of political power.[5] Many of the grand deliberative ideals stipulated in the previous chapter face formidable barriers after the superimposition of law on political practice. Judicial and other legal elites wield veto power over what governments, regulators, and other political actors may do. We describe such barriers in this chapter at a general level, as a prelude to Part III where we explore cases instantiating this chapter's broad claims. (Each chapter of Part III details a discrete form of clash between deliberative democracy and the law of politics.)

None of the problems to be identified is trivial; each raises profound complications. In concert, they raise doubts about the feasibility of deliberative democracy in an era of rapid juridification. Even so, in this chapter we ultimately argue that the anti-deliberative effects we identify are not inevitable, but result from currently dominant *choices* about legal doctrine and philosophies of legal practice. Importantly, none of these is immune to reform.

Law and deliberative democracy: conflict and congruence

Law is a locus of social deliberation. Its apparatus of norms and procedures enables a kind of collective decision-making that aims to resolve social disagreement only after elaborate testing of facts and normative propositions.[6] The language lawyers use to describe their own work points towards the primacy of deliberation. Judges and juries should 'deliberate', providing reasons to the wider public or just to each other. In practice they often do this after extensive collaboration, discussion, and (almost as often) disagreement. The methods and aims of law and deliberative democracy therefore overlap. That they should do so may be unsurprising: there is a clear affinity between legal iconography, especially the balance scales ubiquitous in common law courthouses, and 'deliberation', whose roots are 'de-' (entirely) and 'libra' (scales). (As we see in this chapter, the essence of deliberation is weighing of one kind or another.) Indeed, broadly deliberative objectives, many long predating modern deliberative democracy theory, evidently motivated the formation and design of common law trial and appellate procedures.[7]

Deliberative democrats and lawyers occasionally nominate the features they think prime courts to deliberate well. In many respects, higher courts have come to require these features even of lower courts and administrators. These factors include the following:

a. Collegiate judgment

The global ubiquity of multi-member high courts stems from a recognition that no individual possesses a perfectly clear view of what is morally or legally required in a social dispute. Legal scholars have long been interested in collegiate courts' implications for the quality of reasoning.[8] Deliberative democrats also note how marshalling the wisdom of a collectivity of learned judges can be the best way to test normative ideas before cementing them as law.[9] Conrado Hübner Mendes argues that, among their other benefits,[10] collegiate courts can maximise available information and 'allow for creative solutions not anticipated by any of the deliberators alone'.[11] But to remain workable, a multi-member body should remain modest in size.[12]

b. Collegiality

To the extent that judges on multi-member bodies follow curial traditions of decorous and mutually respectful interpersonal discussion, they can – like the micro-deliberative bodies discussed in chapter 2 – enhance deliberative cooperation, open-mindedness, and a sense of acceptance by those who are bound by the court's decisions.[13] (Understandably, however, some commentators doubt the collegiality of, for example, certain United States appellate courts.[14])

c. Evidentiary rules

Rules of evidence are among the common law's most recognisable deliberative safeguards. They set the conditions for a trial court to accept empirical propositions or to exclude prejudicial or otherwise unpersuasive evidence.

d. Public reason giving

Courts ultimately present their internal deliberations publicly in ways that can be understood, tested, and – if reasonable – accepted by others.[15] According to some judges, giving reasons crystallises and improves their thinking.[16] Deliberativists suggest that it can also inform and steer public debate according to salient points of logic or principle,[17] and 'educate citizens in how to reason with one another on contested issues'.[18]

e. Reasonable person

The common law's reasonable person test requires a judge to reimagine the litigants before her according to what reasonable people – people with average skills and sensitivities – would have done in their shoes.[19] The hypothetical case of the reasonable person in some ways echoes idealised assumptions in Rawls's and other deliberativists' conceptions of collective decision-making and communicative interaction.[20] This conceit allows a judge to assess litigants in light of standards that can be generalised across the whole of the community.

f. Impartiality

In one traditional view, legal judgment should avoid the distortions of judicial bias by remaining as ignorant of, or at least unmoved by, the identities of the litigating parties as it is possible to be. This principle, too, has Rawlsian overtones (and raises many of the same critiques that his work attracts).[21]

g. Independence

Only when judges can decide without fear of sanction or other interference from influential partisans can they can be impartial.[22] In addition, the *nemo judex in sua causa* rule, that no one should be a judge in her own cause, disqualifies those with an interest in the case 'through a social, economic, or political relationship with one of the parties to the dispute'.[23] These may be desirable features if they insulate judgment from the direct influence of partisan power or raw (ie, deliberatively unfiltered) popular preference.[24]

h. Participation and examination

Habermas suggests that impartial decision-making requires input through 'real discourse' among affected parties, rather than just a hypothetical assessment of relevant interests.[25] The legal rights to notice of pending litigation, and to respond to allegations, similarly ensure that decision-makers do not overlook affected interests. *Audi alteram partem* (hear the other side) is a rule of natural justice that 'requires, on notice', an open hearing 'before the decision-maker [along] with the right of cross-examination'.[26] The contributions to litigation by interested individuals and civil society groups – often appearing as amici curiae/intervenors[27] – can enhance impartiality and inclusivity by broadening the range of views available to decision-makers.[28]

i. Analogic reasoning

Courts often venture into new doctrinal territory by recasting it as familiar ground.[29] Thus a case that is confounding to some (eg, same-sex marriage) can be better understood by analogy to similar, settled cases (eg, interracial marriage).[30]

j. Reasoning from precedent

As we discuss below, legal reasoning often uses heuristics to simplify complex problems. A standard view of common law justice pictures it as engaged in a centuries-long conversation among judges, the aim of which is gradually to amass wisdom in the form of settled law. The common law method indeed collects judicial reasoning over several centuries into settled precedents, maxims, and rules (eg, evidentiary), which permit lawyers to invoke simple rubrics in place of more complex principles of justice.

Legal process is thus deliberative in some of the very same key senses in which today's deliberativists use the term. Yet, more generally, how consistent with contemporary expectations of deliberative democracy is deliberation in law and legal process? Throughout this book, we hope to lay bare the frequent disjunctions between the deliberation that deliberative democrats endorse as ideal, on the one hand, and the deliberation that the law of politics' practitioners inject into politics, on the other.

Why might law not be congruent with modern deliberative democracy theory? Begin with the most obvious criticism: that although judges may bring to lawmaking certain rigorous forms of deliberation, deliberative democracy is more than just deliberation on its own. It is deliberation in a context of robust democracy, or 'democratic deliberation, not deliberation without modifier'.[31] To repeat briefly what we said in chapter 2, members of a democratic polity must contribute to deliberation to make the latter effective. This is not merely a democratic expectation. It is also a requirement for good deliberation, because legal decisions must be responsive to the particular social needs that prompt acts of lawmaking or legal adjudication in the first place. Decisions should stem from procedures that broadly gauge the views of affected participants. In this light, deliberation practised chiefly in the isolated confines of judicial chambers may fall short not only in democratic terms, but also as a form of rigorous deliberation about public problems.

Deliberative democracy theory potentially presents a number of rejoinders. These are reasons why a role for governmental elites such as judges may in actuality be consistent with robust deliberative democracy. We saw some particularly relevant ideas in chapter 2, relating to elite-mediated varieties of deliberative democracy (as opposed to more populist versions, which stress the importance of referendums, for example). Recall that Habermas and others view elites such as elected representatives and jurists as instrumental to expressing citizens' interests coherently in law or public policy. To summarise, such deliberative elites perform two basic roles. First, they act as *receivers* of citizen preferences; that is, they gauge any citizen values, interests and generalised policy choices aired in the public sphere. Secondly, elites serve as deliberative *translators*: they undertake the complex, extended, and detailed deliberations that are necessary in order, for instance, to rewrite raw public preferences into specific legal rules. Most members of any public have neither time nor expertise to undertake such a task of deliberation about public policy arcana themselves; elite deliberators therefore aim to do it on their behalf.

On such theories, then, elites author law and policy only after weighing up disparate public preferences, and in the process drawing on their own expertise as to what is socially, scientifically, and legally practicable. The law's noted rationalising procedures may in turn assist the translation from values to law. Much deliberative democracy theory embraces elite deliberation in this way, yet still maintains a signal commitment to robust citizen involvement in democracy. In this vision of deliberative democracy, elites avoid second-guessing the preferences of ordinary citizens; by instead faithfully receiving and implementing preferences, deliberative elites do not supersede but rather serve other citizens.[32]

Each constituent part of the elite deliberative ideal can be criticised as utopian, the more so after we account for the roles of law. The main question we aim to explore in the rest of this book is whether the ideal of elites as deliberative translators sits well with the realities of legal practice. To help find answers, we rely partly on the body of legal scholarship on the law of politics. This provides deliberative democracy theory with an important and largely untapped source of insight. Deliberative democrats should become more aware of the patterns and pathologies of the law of politics, and how these challenge deliberative ideals. The law of politics imports into democratic practices a raft of characteristic modes of reasoning potentially at odds with contemporary deliberative democratic ideals.

Reception problems

Although we focus in this chapter on translation, let us first consider the reception ideal briefly. To count as deliberatively democratic, legal elites must listen to and genuinely pay attention to public preferences. On the one hand, legal process often parallels this ideal. Citizens or their values inform judicial decision-making, for instance as parties to litigation, by the interventions of amici curiae, via the influence of legislatures, and even through judges' informal and impressionistic notice of public sentiment.[33]

On the other hand, decision-making in the courtroom frequently involves not only elite reception, but elite direction. All governance is to some extent elite-centred; but legal elites, perhaps more than most, keep at least one eye fixed on norms endogenous to their own roles and process. Some of the decisional procedures, structures and values of law, maintained by a substantially autonomous legal class, risk rupturing the Habermasian two-track cooperative relation between elites and ordinary citizens. The old formalist vision of the law as a closed normative system, though often discredited, still persists: for example in self-regulation by law societies or bar associations, in the doctrines of separation of powers and judicial independence, and in the continuing construction of lawyers and judges as specially learned and apolitical actors in the formation of law. Law's practitioners might not often resemble Habermas's model elites who pay heed to citizens' diverse preferences, ideas, and values.

In law of politics disputes, legal elites (especially but not only judges) face choices such as whether to institutionalise deliberative or alternative models of governance. Empirical data suggest that assorted classes of elite citizens (eg, those with high levels of formal education, and residents of major urban areas) routinely regard deliberative democracy's keystone assumptions as unrealistic.[34] This appears to be based, first, on *institutional misrecognition*. Elites such as media commentators often confidently express sceptical views about deliberative democracy without always appearing to be apprised of its aims and methods.[35] While these opinion leaders may be relatively well-informed in general terms, they frequently overestimate themselves; many demonstrate limited basic knowledge of novel institutional varieties of democracy.

There is also a phenomenon of *empirical misrecognition* of ordinary citizens' fitness to deliberate – witnessed, for example, in one media commentator's warning about 'loopy outcome[s]' if a reform process robustly includes ordinary citizens.[36] Resistance to deliberative democracy is especially widespread among university-educated elites, who trust deliberative models of democracy least among all groups.[37] By contrast, non-elite citizens have little trouble embracing a body such as a Citizens' Assembly, and in key contexts even favour such Assemblies two-to-one over traditional lawmaking by legislatures.[38] The relative scepticism of elites appears to stem partly from doubt that fellow citizens are adequately informed on weighty policy or lawmaking matters.[39] But such elites, relying on broad presup-position or personal anecdotal experience, may not be best-placed to gauge the deliberative capacities of non-elites. Again, many classes of elites may be generally well-informed, but it does not follow that they possess a clear view of how much non-elites know or do not know on matters relevant to decisions at hand. As we saw in chapter 2, empirical work shows that ordinary citizens are often able to deliberate rigorously if provided relevant information, and more generally if given institutional support.

Relevantly, lawyers overwhelmingly fall within the elite demographic catego-ries.[40] After juridification, lawyers may constitute a problematic class of decision-makers. By litigating and adjudicating the laws that increasingly shape governance, they assume roles as elite gatekeepers of governance. (Lawyers also predominate amongst the legislative ranks and in key parts of the public service.) Deliberative democratic projects potentially clash with views based on elite (indeed, elitist) institutional and empirical preconceptions. This may be a key reason why – as we will see repeatedly in this book – many lawyers resist embracing deliberative democratic projects. They are often hostile to deliberative democratic principles, including that of inclusivity, and frequently seem guided by their own substantive choices in preference to those of ordinary citizens.[41] Hence, despite being a useful conceit, elite reception is at least occasionally problematic as a description of the realities of legal decision-making.

We do not focus further on this important and complex *elite problem* because it exists largely in the arena of rhetoric: the challenge is to convince lawyers and courts to recognise deliberative democratic models of governance as legiti-mate. To be sure, this book is intended as a contribution to an understanding of the proper roles of lawyers and courts, and as such adds to a counter-rhetoric about the benefits that might flow if legal decision-making embraces deliberative democratic ideals. Nevertheless, we are chiefly interested in more foundational conceptual questions about the fit of reasoning modes in the law of politics with deliberative democracy. These questions especially arise when we consider the ideal of translation.

Translation problems

As we know from chapter 2, Habermas suggests that 'binding decisions, to be legitimate, must be steered by communication flows that start at the periphery and pass through the sluices of democratic and constitutional procedures situated at the entrance to the parliamentary complex or the courts'.[42] As we also saw, Fishkin explains that, in the US context, '[r]epresentative institutions were supposed to refine public opinion through deliberation'.[43] Similar descriptions recur throughout theories of elite-mediated public deliberation, according to which governmental elites (eg, politicians, judges and other adjudicators, and public servants with specialised expertise) translate widely sourced public values into concrete, well-informed specific law or policy.

Our focus in this book is on four key problems raised when the law of politics places judges and other lawyers (eg, commissioners, governmental lawyers, and prosecutors; and other legal counsel, too, given that they choose how to formulate legal challenges and responses) in such a role. We call these the *accommodation* problem (explored in chapter 4), the *equality* problem (chapter 5), and the *partisanship* and *coercion* problems (chapter 6). The problems arise above all in litigation over the three political values most dominant in the law of politics: liberty, equality, and integrity. (These values, which sometimes overlap,[44] are 'dominant' in that realising them is a primary objective of the law of politics.[45])

Though the problems differ markedly, a common origin of each is legal reasoning's overreliance on certain forms of *proportionality* (also known as balancing) analysis. Proportionality is a prevailing judicial methodology in the law of politics, and a workhorse of legal decision-making more generally. As we discuss in detail in Part III, proportionality as a legal analytic method manifests in distinctive ways based on which dominant value of the law of politics is front and centre in a given case. Yet the most commonplace proportionality models in the law of politics habitually devalue, or even exclude outright, ideals of deliberative governance. This yields what we term a *deliberatively thin* legal conception of politics.

Consider this key example. In its adjudication of political liberties, the law of politics is at best awkwardly adapted to deliberative accommodation. One of deliberative democracy's greatest innovations, but also its Achilles heel, is the surprising way in which it is meant to work. Deliberative accommodation is not bargaining, meeting halfway, or aggregating and weighing the fixed preferences of opposing citizen groups. Rather it involves fitting multiple citizen preferences together simultaneously in the making of policy or law. For instance, recall from chapter 2 that the search for 'overlapping consensus' or 'normative meta-consensus' is central to some conceptions of deliberative democracy. Put simply, we expect not zero-sum, but win-win substantive outcomes from deliberative democratic decision-making.[46] Thus on Habermas's communicative ideal, as we saw, democratic citizens need not be rivals for public goods; by remaining flexible and open to preference change they might instead reach mutually agreeable decisions.

In addition, deliberative democracy is accommodative as a matter of institutional design. That is, deliberative democrats aim to preserve both deliberation and democracy, rather than placing the two in counterpoint. Theirs, confusingly, is not just a theory presenting a laundry list of requirements for better deliberation. Nor is it merely a movement for popular participation and more robust or direct democracy (eg, Citizens' Assemblies). It is often both of these, but it is neither on its own. As we saw in chapter 2, deliberative democracy is more than the sum of its parts; it is an account of what those parts are and of how the parts fit together to the benefit of both democracy and deliberation.

A sticking point for deliberative democracy is that accommodative arguments are keys to understanding deliberative democracy, yet they are often difficult to disseminate beyond the rarefied circles of academics. Media representations of deliberative democracy tend to focus on and critique either the elite (deliberative) or the populist (democratic) aspects of deliberative democracy, failing to recognise or accept that deliberative democratic accommodation integrates elements of each. Critics have thus accused deliberative democratic projects of being, paradoxically, both too elitist and too populist. Importantly for our purposes, law is another site at which accommodation is actively discouraged. Like other social and governmental elites, judges and other legal decision-makers do not usually adopt the accommodative approaches spelled out by deliberativists. The accommodation problem therefore describes a central difficulty in the law of deliberative democracy: that legal process often eschews accommodation in favour of the more rough-and-ready reasoning characteristic of law.

Judgments under bills and doctrines of rights concerning election speech illustrate how legal judgment ill-serves accommodation. In the many places where proportionality analyses dominate, including all four countries of our study, '[n]o important claim will ever be rejected' until the proportionality stage of judgment.[47] For instance, in the cases of *Bryan*[48] and *Thomson Newspapers*,[49] the Supreme Court of Canada scrutinised legislation banning the publication, respectively, of early election results and opinion polls in the lead-up to polling day. The laws' aims were unmistakably deliberative: to diminish the bandwagon or horserace character of elections.[50] However, under the doctrine of the Canadian Charter of Rights and Freedoms, courts nearly always find section 2(b), the freedom of expression, to have been infringed.[51] The bulk of legal inquiry falls to section 1 – the 'balancing clause' – under which courts determine whether a legitimate legislative purpose justifies the breach.

Similarly, within the Australian High Court the doctrine of implied constitutional rights, though somewhat vaguer, fixates on the proportionality of legal means and ends. In *Australian Capital Television (ACTV)*, the Court considered a law regulating election campaign speech.[52] The law guaranteed publicly funded television airtime, but restricted the advertising to a prescribed format and allowed regulators to apportion airtime among the parties. Before striking down the legislation, the court briefly discussed, but ultimately discounted, the deliberative ends of the law. These included encouraging a less trivial national political discourse, and curbing the role and influence of campaign money and its unequal distribution.[53]

To repeat, deliberativists hold that, with careful institutional design, deliberation reinforces democracy, and democracy in turn reinforces deliberation. Yet the reductive inquiry of a simple proportionality test disassembles democratic deliberation into component parts – with popular expression on one side, and rigour, reflection, cooperation, policy holism, etc, on the other. Indeed, this kind of analysis presupposes that such parts cannot be reconciled. Judicial enthusiasm for proportionality therefore often leads to a miscategorisation of deliberative democratic projects. Understood more thickly, as democratic deliberation, democratic speech is a coherent compound of elements.

These illustrations provide a brief first look at the difficulties deliberative democracy encounters after the superimposition of law. Law is occasionally a poor conceptual fit and may be too blunt or inflexible to embrace deliberative accommodation as a political value. Such problems potentially arise, as well, in cases under the US Constitution, much of which (eg, the First, Fourth, Fifth, Eighth and Fourteenth Amendments, and the commerce and contracts clauses) has been colonised by balancing doctrines. For example, tests of 'intermediate' or 'strict' scrutiny have assumed prominent roles in the past half-century.[54] To give just a few initial examples, in political speech cases such as *Citizens United*, *McCutcheon* and *Arizona Free Enterprise Club's Freedom Club PAC*, the possible deliberative goals of campaign expenditure and donation limits were acknowledged, but the overriding test was whether the law 'furthers a compelling interest and is narrowly tailored to achieve that interest'.[55] In each case that test was not met. Proportionality tests also extensively inform judicial practice in the law of politics under the United Kingdom Human Rights Act.[56]

The accommodation problem is, as noted, one of four key translation problems we explore in this book. Though we name them below, in this chapter we do not yet detail each problem; we leave that discussion for Part III. Our focus at present is still on conceptual groundwork. We are especially interested here in some of the common origins of key problems in the law of deliberative democracy, such as the reliance on proportionality testing. In the next section we begin by developing these basic arguments.

This alone does not take us substantially beyond past contributions. Indeed we show that others in the incipient law of deliberative democracy field have voiced related critiques. More novel is our approach to evaluating the critiques and ultimately casting doubt on them. We examine the avenues for robust deliberation still open to judges, even within a legal perspective bounded by the proportionality focus or other heuristics. And we find that, while judges gravitate toward generally anti-deliberative proportionality models, not all judicial balancing is the same. It is not the law of politics' fixation on proportionality per se that poses problems for democratic deliberation. The fault lies instead in the law's habitual reliance on relatively crude proportionality reasoning, in which deliberative ideals are either absent or of uncertain or subsidiary importance in legal doctrine.

Proportionality and deliberation

Legal process is shaped by the elusive or even quixotic aspiration to achieve objectively fair outcomes. In hard legal cases, where the reasons and consequences of judgments raise profound legal, normative, or factual complexities, such outcomes are difficult or impossible to realise. Indeed, it is not even clear among legal theorists what is meant when objectivity is invoked; for example, is it used in a 'minimal', a 'modest', or a 'strong' sense?[57]

Though objectivity is a special, vexing concern of law generally, hard cases may be even more common in the law of politics. Here political partisanship creates doubt about the very possibility of objectivity even more than is usual for law. As discussed in chapter 1, partisan manipulations of election law can have multiplier effects: political incumbents face incentives to manipulate the laws of politics to help themselves to still more years or more power in government, contrary to the 'preferences of their constituents'.[58] A court harried from all partisan sides may struggle to retain a commitment to objectivity. Mendes describes the paradigmatic constitutional court, given the role of 'co-framer of the political', as surrounded by 'power struggle' and the 'tint of *realpolitik*'.[59] Indeed, sophisticated and motivated litigating parties in disputes about the law of politics pressure judges to see things their way, and sometimes employ a range of formal and informal ways to do so effectively.[60]

Faced with the wicked problem of needing to state clear and relatively determinate legal decisions based on often markedly indeterminate criteria, and with the possibility of objectivity widely doubted,[61] common law judges tend to rely on artificially simple analytic models to aid their work. Whatever objectivity entails,[62] judges seem to strive for it using conceptual tools that fit legal reasoning within conceptually simplifying frames. In the law of politics, these come in at least three kinds.

a. Narrow framing

Litigation employs a narrowly bounded, even microscopic, field of vision. A bounded legal analysis puts into focus only a small portion of the world at once; the picture rapidly blurs as we move away from this central field of view. In part, narrowing its vision is the law's strategy to simplify and expedite judgement, in light of the inevitable frailties of imagination, reasoning, and memory with which we all contend. Bounded judgments exclude from the analytic frame as many complicating normative and empirical factors as it is possible to exclude without rendering judgment too arbitrary. By contrast, a more complex and multipolar view would include some further set of empirical factors, or more of the innumerable and often incommensurable values that bear upon a dispute before the courts.

In practice this means that courts consider the interests of the parties before them and do not often establish the global relation of a dispute to its wider context. Of course there are limited exceptions to this general principle. Yet a

52   The Law of Deliberative Democracy

strictly bounded field of vision is basic to the common law method, reflected in the convention that a judge should decide only the matters before her, and no more. She should try to avoid enunciating principles raised in hypothetical or potential future cases and, should she nevertheless moot such principles, they generally will not bind other courts.[63] Courts, required as they are to reach practicable resolutions, cannot afford to explore too many of the relevant but potentially confounding factors that bear upon a case.[64] As Justice Stephen McLeish puts it, common law practice 'defines and confines the court's task to the case at hand and thereby makes it susceptible to being managed using the resources traditionally available to judges'.[65]

To give an example, in *Bryan* the Supreme Court of Canada considered whether voters at the western end of Canada were disadvantaged vis-à-vis eastern voters whose polls closed hours earlier on the day of a national election.[66] When some media immediately publicised the eastern election results nationwide, votes in western Canada (especially those cast late in the day) seemed no longer to count; by then the countrywide outcome had been settled. The court resolved this as a two-sided dispute – mostly as a matter of 'informational equality' between classes of voters.[67] Some of what was left out or considered only obliquely included how the challenged law impacted on the quality of political debate across the country. (We consider such broader factors, and look again at this particular case, in chapter 4.) These are difficult issues for a time-poor court to take on board. Bounded judgment is, among its other uses, a cognitive tool to avoid weighing decisions down with too much information and analysis. Though it brackets many relevant factors, bounded judgment assists in the search for clear and final outcomes.

b. Party framing

Another variety of framing is particular to the law of politics. This area of law tends to conceptualise political problems of many kinds in the simple terms of a contest between *political parties*. We explore this phenomenon in chapters 5 and 6 especially. But for now note a distinct reason for this focus: political parties and parties to litigation have clear affinities. Both party types aggregate diverse citizen preferences and interests. Parties pool, concretise, and simplify what is otherwise a more profoundly complex array of decisional factors.

From the perspective of deliberation, there are potential downsides to political parties' leading roles. Parties' aggregative methods might leave little room for deliberation given that, as we saw in chapter 2, aggregative democracy is often antithetical to deliberative democracy. The former takes interests as fixed rather than fluid, and tallies and weighs them against other sets of interests to determine which should prevail. By contrast, deliberative democracy seeks to forestall majority-minority conflict. Deliberativists stress the need for citizen inclusion and uncoerced agreement above the bare levels of majority (or plurality) rule. Broader agreement is a more plausible objective if citizens engage in rational communication and argument, with the result that majority/plurality members remain open

Deliberative Democracy and the Law of Politics   53

to reconsidering their positions and finding common ground with others. Political party-focused law can frustrate such ideals. It can create or reinforce seemingly irreconcilable party oppositions in democratic politics, based on the assumption that political actors are invariably strategic competitors and must be regulated as such.

c. Proportionality

Finally, proportionality is a pre-eminent model of framing. It provides judges with 'systematizing' and 'stable procedures for arriving at decisions' in response to 'indeterminacy'.[68] And it thus finds a natural home in the common law (and other legal systems) as a powerful tool imposing another narrow frame on decision-making. In law of politics cases, proportionality often fits squarely with the focus on political parties: many proportionality judgments assess the balance between two or more such parties (see chapters 5 and 6).

Alexander Aleinikoff shows how balancing in US constitutional law arose in the 1930s–40s in the wake of the Realists' successful campaign to undermine the old presumed certainties within legal formalism.[69] Formalists insisted that correct decisions result from relatively mechanical applications of logic to abstract legal propositions and rigid categories, which were premised on 'differences of kind, not degree'.[70] Yet, particularly in the *Lochner* era,[71] when the US Supreme Court repeatedly invalidated economic legislation by asking the 'question of category: "Is [the statute] within the police power of the State?" ... [the] poor fit between doctrine and the real world led some members of the Court to question earlier constitutional truths ... with an eye more to social facts'.[72] The break with formalist notions of absolute objectivity necessitated a new and more flexible methodology, yielding the first robust balancing acts in US rights adjudication. Alec Stone Sweet and Jud Mathews show how balancing also became standard in the post-WWII global wave of rights documents.[73] Those trends resonate with Aleinikoff's observation that 'flying the flags of pragmatism, instrumentalism and science, balancing represented one attempt by the judiciary to demonstrate that it could reject mechanical jurisprudence without rejecting the notion of law'.[74]

The balancing of two counterpoised litigating parties, or of the sets of principles of law on which each side relies, is thus now a principal means by which the law channels complex disputes into a more bounded frame. This binary method is central enough to legal practice that it must be taken into account to understand how legal forms shape deliberation. *Does narrowly bounded legal judgment impede, or aid, deliberation?* Though they usually describe the problem in different terms, a handful of authors have so far suggested that legal judgment is problematic for democratic deliberation due to its bounded scope. Legal proportionality reasoning risks imposing an excessively narrow and distorted lens upon the political world – one inconsistent with deliberative notions of broadly-based holism and communicative rationality. Deliberation's aims include drawing together and accommodating diverse values, and accounting for the full set of costs and benefits of policy

54 The Law of Deliberative Democracy

and legal options, rather than viewing such options in isolation. Some of the complexity excluded from binary legal judgment may be relevant or even critical to fair and complete judgment.

Beyond these problems associated with simple and proportionate framing, there are additional reasons to doubt whether legal practitioners are deliberative. Some judges possess strong partisan or ideological pre-commitments, a characteristic sometimes inconsistent with broad-ranging, open-minded, and cooperative judicial reasoning.[75] Maya Sen shows that US 'Presidents select nominees largely on the basis of likeminded – and somewhat fixed – political ideology' and that US Supreme Court justices unsurprisingly sometimes end up arguing from positions of 'adherence to a particular worldview'.[76] Of course, this is a US-based critique, and it applies with less force in the other countries of our study.[77] But even if they are not partisan outright, judges on multi-member courts still may not always be collegial, nor open to persuasion and to reasoning cooperatively.

Whatever the cause, the risk of a deliberatively deficient court can be a critical one. The well-known symbols and structures of legal practice – the hoary curial rituals, and elaborate procedures of judicial selection and lawyer admission – raise jurists to a high status. A court might induce ordinary citizens to follow (eg, to respect and adhere to) its judgments based on appearances, claiming the mantle of a deliberative body but in actuality lacking deliberative bona fides.[78]

Most of all, however, the first contributions in the incipient law of deliberative democracy literature express reasonable doubt about law as an aid to democratic deliberation given the law's bounded view. Christopher Zurn identifies epistemic limitations of legal process as causes of anti-deliberative effects. Focusing only on the case before it 'distort[s] to some extent the Court's ability to gather relevant information, perhaps most important concerning the impact of likely decisions on the interests of all those affected'.[79] Moreover, according to Dennis Thompson, judicial focus leaves a court better suited to adjudicating claims that affect particular litigating parties than ordering broader structural changes that affect the political party system as a whole.[80] Courts' rules of standing, reliance on precedent, and emphasis on individual rights further limit their ability to adopt an institutional perspective on law of politics decisions.[81] The necessity of resolving the case before it may 'constrain the set of solutions the Court may consider'.[82]

Zurn also challenges Rawls's and others' claims that reasoning in constitutional courts embodies the ideal of public reason because they employ principled moral-political reasoning. Zurn examines several US Supreme Court cases and finds that they appeal to uniquely legal principles ('the technicalia of legal argument: jurisdiction, precedent, consistency, authorization, distinguishability, separation of doctrine from dicta, justiciability, canons of construction, and so on') and not moral and political principles.[83] To this extent, he says, legal reasoning and moral-political reasoning are dissimilar, and 'we should eschew the seductive claim that juridical discourse is a paradigmatic language for democratic deliberation'.[84] (But this equation of 'deliberation' with 'moral-political reasoning' takes a limited view of what deliberation is. Zurn does not evaluate how well legal reasoning compares

Deliberative Democracy and the Law of Politics   55

to the other deliberative ideals we have identified – accommodation, inclusivity, cooperation, holism, etc.) Similarly, Mendes extrapolates from critiques of legal theorists (eg, Mary Ann Glendon and Jeremy Waldron) regarding '"myopic" judges' with limited capacities for normative reasoning to imply that judges also may have limited facility for deliberation.[85] And Sen argues that, being beholden to precedent, judges often focus on resolving the case at hand and 'avoid addressing difficult moral questions in a comprehensive fashion'; instead they 'simply apply or distinguish prior cases on point – a significantly easier task'.[86] Sen concludes that 'deliberative democracy at an institutional level might be an untenable ideal'.[87]

There is some validity to the critique that legal forms such as proportionality lie in basic conflict with deliberative democratic ideals. Yet, as an account of anti-deliberative effects of litigation, we argue that this critique is neither complete nor unique to judicial reasoning. As we explain next, the deliberative weaknesses that some critics observe are neither straightforward nor yet fully surveyed. Conceptualising disputes within a bounded frame is not a failure of judges particularly, but a feature of human cognition generally in response to complexity. This leaves the critique of law a little less piquant. Most importantly, if judges in the law of politics make the doctrinal choices necessary to adopt *deliberatively thick* models of proportionality, democratic deliberation may even occasionally thrive within proportionality's strictly bounded frame.

Deliberation within a bounded legal frame

Each of the three key deliberative deficits of courts, mooted above, may not be unique to courts, or always even deficits.

a. Narrow framing

As noted, litigation generally focuses in on just a small subset of potentially relevant decisional factors – exposing only those points of law or fact most germane to a case, while wider concerns remain outside the picture. Yet severely restricting a decision's analytic scope to just a small number of principles, facts, and factors may make subjective decision-making less so – achieving at least passably objective solutions. This notion is familiar to economists and psychologists. The economist W Brian Arthur notes how 'human logical capacity ceases to cope' beyond a certain level of complexity; it is forced to make at best 'localized deductions'.[88] Beyond that slim zone where logical deduction is still possible, broad interactions with others are necessary, and we must guess at their behaviour – we cannot rely on the others to act rationally. In such complicated and ill-defined situations, humans employ predictable, inductive models of reasoning. Arthur notes that psychology has understood these cognitive coping methods the longest.[89] Yet economists and others have also observed the use of conceptual simplifications (described with terms such as 'satisficing' and 'optimizing') to help sustain approximately rational behaviour in complex or uncertain situations.[90]

56 The Law of Deliberative Democracy

As Kahan notes, 'it is well established that members of the public rely on heuristics and mental shortcuts'.[91] These can skew perceptions of the empirical world we live in – a problem aggravated by 'dogmatism' and 'aversion to complexity' and, unsurprisingly, by individuals' partisan and ideological commitments. But somewhat more surprising is the finding in Kahan and others' studies that it is often the most sophisticated citizens – those with the greatest knowledge resources – who use empirical data to reinforce what they already believe.[92] Whether by cherry picking or logical sophistry, these people are best equipped to bend information to match pre-existing assumptions that align with the simple, often polarised categories that dominate much political discourse.[93] This, Kahan says, is how even factual issues over which there is broad scientific consensus (eg, anthropogenic climate change) can stay forever open to political debate. Even the best-informed bodies in government and civil society, such as agencies and think tanks, can fall into patterns often similarly hostile to complexity. Many of Kahan's sophisticated but biased citizens, of course, staff such bodies.

Thus it is not clear that narrowly cast approaches to reasoning are unique to judges and law. Even election campaigns, as we described in chapter 2, are intrinsically open-textured in terms of the issues and even parties who contest them, but yield a single output in terms of who will form government. Majority-rules voting systems, at least in parliamentary systems, tend to a binary reductionism.

Ultimately, when bounded reasoning narrows the range of reasoning, it generally does so in aid of a deliberative rationale. Simplifying what is in truth complex can be a strategy for understanding complexity. A number of deliberativists explore the salutary roles of heuristics and other useful forms of simplification in the course of deliberation. Notably, Iris Marion Young thinks that metaphors, tropes, and other reductive rhetorical tools can enhance democratic deliberation, in part because they are evocative and easily understood.[94] At an extreme, Robert Goodin observes how, in some circumstances, deliberative discussion benefits when topics that are not practical, or are too impolitic to discuss, remain off the table.[95]

Hence, to reduce subjectivity, complexity, and discord, deliberation is potentially best practised within a limited sphere. Law plays a role in establishing the background consensuses that enable deliberation. Gerald Postema describes (and critiques) Samuel von Pufendorf's thesis that law aids deliberation by serving, in Postema's words, as a 'surrogate for deliberative public reason': law does not resolve, but moves a range of disputes '"off-line" out of the domain of the public and the political'. This view promotes, among other values, 'determinacy [and] finality'.[96] At the same time, bounded reasoning arguably keeps judges from engaging in hypothetical reasoning, and thus sensibly keeps common law process grounded in real-world application.

To be sure, deliberative simplification is a double-edged sword. Clearly, we should be wary about losing valuable and relevant information when we use simplification as a deliberative aid. There is ample work indicating when, for instance, certain heuristics unduly simplify and distort deliberation. We saw above that a number of academic lawyers take this view, specifically in relation to judicial reasoning. On the other hand, legal process has an important role to play in enhancing deliberation if it brings order to an otherwise formidably complex set of norms, arguments, interests, etc. Bounded judgment is not necessarily a deliberative failure. It is a common tool – in many contexts, legal and otherwise – to enable cognition where a decision-making process might otherwise fold under the weight of too much argument and information.

b. Party framing

Is giving political parties special legal status, as the law of politics tends to do, wholly inconsistent with deliberation? As noted, political parties are associated with organising electoral support for already-formed preferences, whereas deliberative democracy is generally concerned to transform preferences, interests, and citizens' understandings of the common good. Yet deliberative democratic theory does not always view political parties as deliberatively problematic.[97] In his classic theory, Joshua Cohen argues that political parties – understood as independent but publicly funded entities – can help poorer people organise and represent themselves politically.[98] He also thinks that parties can help focus the attention of deliberators on matters of general concern, rather than on narrow local issues.[99] Bernard Manin similarly argues that political parties can enrich democratic deliberation by offering participants a particular set of political solutions that they can ponder and discuss with one another.[100] And Carlos Nino believes that parties can improve the standard of democratic debate. He notes that parties usually aim to explain their views from an impartial perspective, providing a base upon which voters can build less partisan justifications for their own positions.[101]

In addition, as the last chapter noted, two categorisations of deliberative democracy ('Classic Deliberation' and 'Expansion of the Classic Ideal') are relevant to the deliberative role of entities like political parties that promote self-interested views.[102] Again, both categorisations adhere roughly to key deliberative hallmarks, but a distinction between them is the place of self-interest. In Classic Deliberation, participants ideally put their particular interests to one side, and instead seek out and clarify their common ground – that is, the set of goods or preferences shared by all. By contrast, in the Expansion of the Classic Ideal, participants are encouraged to voice their interests, including their self-interest. Even in the Expansion of the Classic Ideal, participants continue to seek out some kind of common ground. Yet, because they first listen to one another's interests, the common ground they arrive at is much less abstract – it is far more grounded and much more tangible – than that of Classic Deliberation. For example, self-interest acts as a check on the common ground. A participant may interject during the deliberations, saying something like, 'But that policy would hurt me [or my constituents]'.[103] The deliberating group can then revise its understanding of the common ground so that it no longer tramples upon that participant's interests.

Thus political parties can act as means to clarify policy options for voters. To

58 The Law of Deliberative Democracy

some extent, parties might serve as deliberative aids, much as the Expanded Ideal views some self-interested reasoning as helping to draw out both the salient differences and common ground of deliberators. Nonetheless, in chapter 5, which details the roles of political parties in deliberation, we revisit the fundamental critique that parties seed factionalism and the entrenchment of agonistic positions in politics. Yet that chapter also notes how doctrines in the law of politics can usefully respond to political parties by minimising or transforming their roles in litigation.

c. Proportionality

We come lastly to our main focus: proportionality. Writing in the UK context, Aileen Kavanagh praises the proportionality test as 'a means for disassembling the [legal] problem and breaking it down into more manageable questions and issues'.[104] Indeed, as a tool to narrow deliberation, proportionality is in one sense just an extension of the other framing tools above. Proportionality even often applies to comparisons between political parties.

Yet proportionality also aids deliberation uniquely. *Comparing* two values can be more objective than many other kinds of judgment would allow. If Paul is 5'9" and Nick 5'7", Paul is clearly the taller of the two. But absolute judgment lacks such objectivity: to call a person merely 'tall' is to raise uncounted uncertainties, since the term varies by culture, locale, cohort, age, linguistic context, etc. While there is a bona fide distinction to be drawn between people who are tall and those who are not, the line dividing the categories is a 'fuzzy' one;[105] determining tallness close to the line presents a difficult case. By contrast, proportionality is relatively objective. This helps to account for common law procedure's frequent neglect of the big picture in favour of its unending sequence of two-sided competitions.

To be relatively objective, however, a proportionality analysis ought to remain simple. Binary balancing – the insistence on counterbalancing only two parties, concepts, or values – is thus arguably the best option:

> Conflict resolution will be rendered easier the more the members of the group can limit their discursive efforts to a few problematic validity claims. ... [T]hey have a better chance of reaching agreement if they only have to resolve an empirical question about the effectiveness of two competing strategies ... .[106]

One could instead imagine a balance of threes, for example three main parties, or three key competing principles of law; picture a balance scale that works not in a one-dimensional line with just two arms, but in a two-dimensional plane, with three pans on three arms. (We might even try several kinds and levels of balancing at once – for example, weighing empirical propositions while simultaneously balancing 'fairness criteria, or what would count as a successful outcome'.[107]) But pairs are amenable to a simplified form of balancing to an extent that more complex multiples are not.[108] Proportionality is most often binary because, beyond the classic balance of twos, proportionality becomes chaotic. Larger multiples negate some, or even most, of the conceptual simplification that is balancing's principal rationale. Indeed, the chaos of threes, and higher numbers of variables, is axiomatic in the physical sciences.[109] Social choice theorists illustrate a similar problem with the example of a choice that cycles between three or more options, at least when they are put in a series of binary oppositions: where, for example, A is preferable to B, B is preferable to C, but C is preferable to A.[110]

Whatever the consequences, legal process normally resolves social complexities into bipolar competitions, shoehorning unwieldy details, factors, equities, parties, etc, into a relatively simple two-sided dispute. Most obviously, the adversarial contest between two litigating parties provides a bipolar axis for reasoning through most (but not all) cases. Procedurally this means that two main parties take the lead in court, and the case tends first to their interests and constructs those interests as mutually opposite. To be sure, rules allowing parties to be separated, or permitting complex findings of partial contribution to harm, are just some of the procedures that complicate legal procedure's binary simplicity.[111] Other exceptions include cases involving amici curiae/intervenors, who – especially in constitutional litigation – bring before the court perspectives additional or peripheral to those of the main parties.

However, in multi-member courts, majority and minority decisions nearly always emerge in relation to each legal issue directly affecting the parties. This is so even when reasons on an issue attract only a plurality of judges in favour (ie, support from the largest bloc of judges, but not an outright majority). For instance, a nine-member court might see judges produce several decisions, yet for each issue affecting the parties there can be only one outcome – the party is or is not liable, the law is or is not constitutional, etc. Even in such cases, judicial process converts complex judicial pluralities into binaries.[112]

Bounded judgment clearly can be problematic. Even if excluding detail simplifies and objectifies judgment, the detail might not be irrelevant. The simplicity of bounded judgment may enable courts to reach a practical and more objective outcome, but necessarily distorts the court's vision. Reasoning in a bounded way means trading off complexity and completeness of view, on the one hand, against objectivity and practical expedience (the need to reach some decision, however flawed), on the other. Put differently, while the 'objectivity' we achieve through a balancing frame may be genuinely objective as far as it goes, it may not go very far at all. Circumstances often call for absolute rather than relative judgments. Paul's stature may be superior to Nick's, but this provides only a weak clue as to whether Paul is suited for work in fire-fighting or professional basketball.

Nonetheless, proportionality and other forms of bounded judgment are not unique to judicial deliberation, and are in any event generally unavoidable and often indeed useful to deliberation. The law of politics' real deliberative problem, we argue next, is that in the design or practice of law, courts (or other arms of government whose members apply law) favour doctrines and methodologies that too often generate not just simpler, but markedly less deliberative reasoning. Judges

60   The Law of Deliberative Democracy

frequently choose – and it is indeed a *choice* – to follow relatively rudimentary approaches to proportionality, though it may do harm to deliberative reasoning.

Thin and thick proportionality

Deliberation, as deliberative democrats understand it, is possible even within the bounds of binary proportionality tests. What appears to matter most is not whether, but how, judges balance. We explore aspects of this contention throughout Part III, where we address the ideal by which elites serve as deliberative translators. There we specifically examine how choices between methods of proportionality determine whether the law of politics expresses each of its most dominant values – liberty, equality, and integrity – in either deliberatively thin or thick terms.

Deliberation as a value is comparatively uncommon in the law of politics, or (in a few contexts) is common but invested with relatively little urgency. The law of politics frequently devalues deliberation in part because more dominant values of liberty, equality, and integrity superficially appear to conflict with it. We argue, by contrast, that deliberatively thick doctrines can mostly seamlessly integrate deliberative concerns into these other values. This can improve democratic deliberation, especially if courts are thereby less apt to invalidate deliberative democratic legislative projects. In addition, deliberatively thicker doctrines can give fuller and more coherent effect to the dominant values themselves.

Each chapter of Part III therefore examines a choice that doctrine and practice in the law of politics make between deliberation and a more dominant value, and each chapter also details the doctrinal specifics of the choice. Focusing on one dominant value at a time, we identify discrete forms of thin proportionality reasoning, each often at odds with deliberative ideals. With some exceptions, deliberatively thicker alternatives are not more difficult to operationalise in practice than are more standard doctrines. In each chapter of Part III, then, we venture a suggestion for an approach more consonant with deliberative ideals. The main arguments to be made along these lines are summarised in Table 3.1. (A full appreciation of the table's details will only come as the reader progresses through Part III. We suggest referring back to the table from time to time.)

It should be noted that we expand the term 'proportionality' in this analysis well beyond its use by other commentators. Most read proportionality in terms similar to Stone Sweet: as 'a decision-making procedure and an "analytical structure" that judges employ to deal with tensions between two pleaded constitutional "values" or "interests"'.[113] Much proportionality reasoning in the law of politics indeed involves *rivalrous* tensions, that is, zero-sum trade-offs.

Simplifying somewhat, we label as *conceptual balancing* a first kind of proportionality reasoning in the law of politics. As we explain in chapter 4, a conceptual balancing inquiry in law presumes that values on either side of the balancing scale are conceptually distinct from each other, and also in tension with each other (eg, expressive freedoms conflict with efforts to improve electoral deliberation). By contrast, *accommodative balancing*, a deliberatively thicker alternative, is not

Deliberative Democracy and the Law of Politics   61

Table 3.1 Proportionality reasoning in the law of politics

Normative Doctrine in the Law of Politics	Thin Proportionality		Thick Proportionality	
	Type & Nature of Balance	**Objects in Balance**	**Type & Nature of Balance**	**Objects in Balance**
Liberty (chapter 4)	**'Conceptual Balance'** *Rivalrous*: zero-sum tension	Values (eg, free speech, deliberation)	**'Accommodative Balance'** *Accommodative*: win-win integration of concepts	Values (eg, free speech, deliberation)
Equality (chapter 5)	**'Strategic Balance'** *Rivalrous*: zero-sum tension	Interests of political parties/factions	**'Thick Equality'** *Inclusive*: equality enhances deliberation	Broad substantive equality criteria (eg, deliberative criteria of inclusion)
Integrity (chapter 6)			**'Thick Integrity'** (No balance) *Ambiguous positive guidance*: assorted procedural and substantive criteria for deliberation	

similarly committed to maintaining tensions and conceptual distinctions at all costs (including where they may not be justified).

As indicated in Table 3.1, the law of politics' proportionality types divide into varieties concerned either with balancing values or balancing political interests. In chapters 5 and 6 we explore what we call *strategic balancing*, a common form of proportionality in law of politics cases, and one that is relevant in relation to both political equality and integrity. This mode of proportionality is also rivalrous. But here the aim of the balancing exercise is to prevent political parties' electoral prospects from falling too far out of parity. Borrowing from notions of strategic conduct in deliberative theory, we use 'strategic balancing' to describe the assumption that political actors' principal motivations are to secure the largest share of finite political resources (eg, votes, legislative seats, money) at the expense of opponents. In chapters 5 and 6 we also seek to show how deliberatively thicker alternatives markedly differ from strategic balancing. *Thick equality* in a sense still relies on a proportionality test, but it is a test based on equalitarian comparison rather than rivalrous tension. Thick equality also transcends strategic balancing's usual focus on political parties as comparators, relying instead on a deliberative notion of equality as broad inclusion of ideas, perspectives, and participants. Finally, *thick integrity* eschews balancing exercises altogether and expressly equates integrity in law of politics decision-making with the essential hallmarks of deliberation.

First- and second-order deliberation and law

Before closing the present chapter, it bears repeating that this book also centres, uniquely, on the corpus of rules in *the law of politics*. Deliberative theory largely overlooks this area of law, but the law's influence over the design of deliberative democracy is significant and exceptional. As we saw, it is a stretch to conform the law of politics to standard descriptions of elite-mediated deliberative democracy. In the usual ideal, elected and unelected actors in government deliberate in order to make laws, while broadly gauging public sentiments and needs. Accurate or not, this vision mainly assumes that the deliberation in question is about *first-order* laws and lawmaking, the consequences of which are generally substantive and direct (eg, a transit system, a public holiday, a tax). First-order deliberation therefore includes finding ways to accommodate disparate citizen preferences or interests in the course of lawmaking. In contrast, the law of politics chiefly regulates procedures in governance and elections. As such it addresses *second-order* or meta-deliberation – *deliberation about democratic deliberation itself*. As Dennis Thompson puts it (in the electoral context), the distinction is between deliberating *in* elections, or deliberating *about* them.[114] The law of politics reflects the many choices judges and legislators make about how to regulate a democracy.

Our second-order focus adds complexity to our subject. Second-order deliberation is not just a process of translating raw preferences and interests into law. In second-order cases, deliberative elites are designers of the governmental system, and not merely participants within it. Under these circumstances, from the perspective of deliberative democracy theory, what would it mean to call elite decision-makers 'deliberative'? First, and most basically, we should still expect them to think through their task with attention to broad citizen expectations (in this case for governance). Yet atop this expectation, decision-makers should also express a commitment to deliberative forms of democracy, by helping to design or tweak governance to incorporate institutional supports for deliberation. Thus, in second-order cases, elite decision-makers should commit to deliberative democratic principles of governance. This is a recurring challenge throughout this book: encouraging legal decision-makers to recognise deliberative goals as valuable in democratic design, and to give effect to these values concretely when they write and adjudicate the law of politics. Hence, to count as 'deliberative', those who write or adjudicate the law of politics must be adept at both first- and second-order deliberation.

In theory the two might even contradict: public preferences could call for simpler, majoritarian and aggregative democracy, rather than deliberative democracy. However, at least in some contexts, this is unlikely. For instance, data in Australia indicate that popular preferences for deliberative democratic methods of constitutional reform leadership are noticeably higher than for status quo majoritarian/parliamentary approaches.[115] Yet, outside of high-profile reforms involving constitutional or fundamental institutional change, ordinary citizens may not have detailed opinions about how government should function. They may instead possess a relatively oblique and inchoate set of attitudes toward government.

Therefore if the idealised image of elite-led deliberation is convincing for first-order deliberation, it is often less so with respect to second-order deliberation. Second-order cases give to elites the onerous responsibility of calibrating and steering a political system, or even designing some of its parts de novo, often with disparate impacts on political factions. The process is always at risk of being over-shadowed by politically partisan arguments. The effect of elite involvement may be to contaminate rather than to enable deliberation, when political partisans' self-serving arguments dominate public debate.[116] Hence there are compelling reasons why second-order law is a poor fit to traditional theories of elite-led deliberative democracy. There is the possibility that many elites, invested with powers to design governmental institutions, neither deliberate well themselves when doing so nor create institutions where good deliberation is likely. These second-order difficulties complicate our subject, but also make it particularly consequential. This is fertile but mostly untilled ground.

Note that we do not deny that first-order questions are also important. Indeed, many such questions are vitally so, and still unresolved. For instance, do existing laws or conventional legal processes inform, narrow, colour, or otherwise shape discourses in the public sphere, and if so is the effect generally one that makes discourses more, or less, deliberative? The example of legal rights is illustrative. Are rights among the tropes that, in Young's framework, simplify but also improve deliberation? Laws and legal process have a potential crystallising role to play: bringing order to an otherwise formidably complex set of norms, arguments, interests, etc. Rights discourse enables the cataloguing of particular kinds of interests, reducing those interests to a simple rubric and permitting a political or legal culture to reference, at a glance, rationales and even the long narrative of the history of particular rights (eg, US equality rights invoke the experiences of slavery, anti-miscegenation, segregation, etc).[117] Rights can, in turn, impose a form of deliberative discipline upon discourses about lawmaking, both within government and in the wider arena of public debate. Postema thus notes how courts 'can take the lead in some dimensions of genuinely public deliberative reasoning'.[118] A lawmaking process must be cognisant of the review role of courts and either write law in line with rights, or risk having courts step in post hoc. Arguably, the rational rigour of legal deliberation in the courts telescopes to ordinary citizens and other governmental branches how to address public controversies fairly, logically, and dispassionately.[119] Public judicial influence is reflected, for example, in the rapid social acceptance of same-sex marriage in Canada and the US, jurisdictions where the issue first progressed through the courts. Judges, at their best, accommodate citizens' disparate values and interests and show the rest of us how it can be done.[120]

But these are not our questions. In our view questions about second-order deliberation are more interesting. For deliberative democracy the most important function of laws may be their capacity to create or limit deliberation in a democracy

64 The Law of Deliberative Democracy

by serving a gatekeeping function. Judges and other lawyers involved in the law of politics are not just governmental elites charged with translating public values into law, but also must play a role as designers of democratic systems. They review and at times second-guess the legislature's design choices. Does the law's substance create the kinds of institutions deliberative democrats dream of, and indeed can it? Do law's limits preclude such hopeful scenarios? And how does examining legal process deepen our answers to these questions? All these are questions about choices about deliberation itself. In this way second-order questions about law are prior to – that is, more foundational – than first-order questions.

Conclusion: open questions

In the law of deliberative democracy there is a set of questions external to deliberative theory that we do not address in this book, at least not in a direct way. As we see in subsequent chapters, a deep ambiguity arises whenever governments engage in apparently well-meaning interventions that can be characterised as either infringements of rights or enhancements of deliberation. How one reads such measures depends on accepting or rejecting deliberative theory's main premises. *External* arguments address such premises. They challenge our positions in this book at a foundational level by doubting the desirability of deliberation itself. Such challenges are most of all (but not exclusively) centred on questions of deliberative democracy's empirical plausibility. However, we do not set out here to answer the external problem, except incidentally at times. The question whether deliberative assumptions are empirically justified is at the core of a vast body of literature, and we aim to move beyond that literature to more particular questions about deliberative theory in relation to law.

Therefore a set of questions *internal* to deliberative theory, ignored for too long, form our main subject. Internal questions take the wisdom and desirability of deliberative theory as given, in light of reasons presented in chapter 2. Given the complexity of the subject, it is still far from clear how best to regulate democracies in law to promote deliberation. And it may never be clear, not least because, like all theories of democracy, deliberative theory has differing and often contradictory schools and strands. But despite its complexities, in the next part of this book, Part III, we assume the desirability of deliberation as a driving value in the law of politics. We then consider the fit of this value to the law – both as the law currently stands, and as it might come to look after concerted reforms.

Of course, the deliberative democrat's claim is seldom that institutional reforms can achieve ideal deliberation. As is common with other normative benchmarks, such as liberty, equality, and integrity, a deliberative analysis of law should examine just a selection of laws at one time. It should determine if those laws marginally improve or impair deliberation, without presuming to perfect it. Moreover, there is no determinate threshold above which a process counts as 'deliberative'. We saw previously that empirical work suggests a complex picture of deliberation – of many gradations, arising from a variety of institutional models and their associated

Deliberative Democracy and the Law of Politics   65

trade-offs. Shading the empirical picture of deliberation in this way brings needed nuance to debates too often coloured in primary hues. The reforms we encourage in the next chapters are therefore provisional, laying out better alternatives rather than stipulating 'best' options. Yet even this may have important consequences for the practice of politics. Given the law of politics' increasing ubiquity, deliberative democratic schemes can have limited impact so long as the law of politics remains substantially mismatched to them.

Notes

1 'Inductive Reasoning and Bounded Rationality' (1994) 84 *American Economic Review* 406, 406.
2 In chapter 1 we defined the law of politics as regulating 'the sites of political choice in a democracy'.
3 See, eg, Conrado Hübner Mendes, *Constitutional Courts and Deliberative Democracy* (Oxford University Press, 2013).
4 Among the relatively rare exceptions are, eg, Dennis F Thompson, *Just Elections: Creating a Fair Electoral Process in the United States* (University of Chicago Press, 2002); and Carlos Nino, *The Constitution of Deliberative Democracy* (Yale University Press, 1996).
5 Ran Hirschl, 'The Judicialization of Politics' in Keith Whittington, R Daniel Kelemen and Gregory A Caldeira (eds), *Oxford Handbook of Law and Politics* (Oxford University Press, 2008) 120; Richard Pildes, 'The Supreme Court, 2003 Term – Foreword: The Constitutionalization of Democratic Politics' (2004) 118 *Harvard Law Review* 29; John Ferejohn, 'Judicializing Politics, Politicizing Law' (2002) 61 *Law and Contemporary Problems* 41; Graeme Orr, 'The Law Comes to the Party: The Continuing Juridification of Australian Political Parties' (2002) 3 *Constitutional Law and Policy Review* 41.
6 Lon Fuller, 'Adjudication and the Rule of Law' (1960) 54 *American Society for International Law and Process* 1; Matthias Kumm, 'Institutionalising Socratic Contestation' (2007) 1 *European Journal of Legal Studies* 1, 31.
7 Bracton, *Bracton on the Laws and Customs of England* (1968) vol 3, ns 185b, 289, 290b.
8 Lewis A Kornhauser and Lawrence G Sager, 'Unpacking the Court' (1986) 96 *Yale Law Journal* 82, 82, 100–102; Justice Stephen Gageler, 'Why Write Judgments?' (2014) 36 *Sydney Law Review* 189; Diane P Wood, 'When to Hold, When to Fold, and When to Reshuffle: The Art of Decisionmaking on a Multi-Member Court' (2012) 100 *California Law Review* 1445 (on what motivates judges to write, or refrain from writing, separate opinions).
9 Mendes, above n 3; Maya Sen, 'Courting Deliberation: an Essay on Deliberative Democracy in the American Judicial System' (2012) 27 *Notre Dame Journal of Law, Ethics & Public Policy* 303, 311–12.
10 These include the benefits for deliberation of symbolising that decisions are products of institutions, not individual whim; and of open-ended 'argumentative' procedures: Mendes, above n 3, 63–5.
11 Ibid.
12 Sen, above n 9, 311; James Fishkin, *When the People Speak: Deliberative Democracy and Public Consultation* (Oxford University Press, 2009) 38.
13 Mendes, above n 3, 67–8, 128–34.
14 See, eg, Sen, above n 9.
15 John Rawls, 'The Idea of Public Reason' in James Bohman and William Rehg (eds), *Deliberative Democracy: Essays on Reasons and Politics* (MIT Press, 1997) 95; John Rawls, *Political Liberalism* (Columbia University Press, Expanded Edition, 2005) 137.

16 Frank Kitto, 'Why Write Judgments?' (1992) 66 *Australian Law Journal* 787; Gageler, above n 8.

17 Rawls, 'The Idea of Public Reason', above n 15, 112–14.

18 Christopher F Zurn, *Deliberative Democracy and the Institutions of Judicial Review* (Cambridge University Press, 2007) 192 (describing other authors' views), citing Ronald Dworkin, *Freedom's Law* (Harvard University Press, 1997) 345–6; Eugene V Rostow, 'The Democratic Character of Judicial Review' (1952) 66 *Harvard Law Review* 208. *Contra* Jeremy Waldron, 'Judicial Review and the Conditions of Democracy' (1998) 4 *Journal of Political Philosophy* 6.

19 Gregory C Keating, 'Reasonableness and Rationality in Negligence Theory' (1996) 48 *Stanford Law Review* 311.

20 Rawls, *Political Liberalism*, above n 15, 137; Amy Gutmann and Dennis Thompson, *Why Deliberative Democracy?* (Princeton University Press, 2004) 3–5.

21 See, eg, Laverne Jacobs, 'From Rawls to Habermas: Towards A Theory of Grounded Impartiality in Canadian Administrative Law' (2014) 51 *Osgoode Hall Law Review* 543, 547–64 (describing theories of impartiality, beginning with Rawls, as well as communitarian, contextual, feminist, and discourse theory critiques).

22 Lorne Sossin, 'Speaking Truth to Power? The Search for Bureaucratic Independence in Canada' (2005) 55 *University of Toronto Law Review* 1, 2, 6–15, 19–24; Thompson, above n 4, 161. For cases see, eg, in Canada *Canadian Pacific Limited v Matsqui Indian Band* [1995] 1 SCR 3, [76]–[84]; in Australia *Forge v ASIC* (2006) 228 CLR 45, 77; in the UK *Kruse v Johnson* [1898] 2 QB 91, 99–100 (Lord Russell); and in the US *United States v Will*, 449 US 200, 217–18 (1980).

23 Keith D Ewing, 'A Theory of Democratic Adjudication: Towards a Representative, Accountable and Independent Judiciary' (2000) 38 *Alberta Law Review* 312, 314.

24 See, eg, Robert Alexy, 'Balancing, Constitutional Review, and Representation' (2005) 3 *International Journal of Constitutional Law* 578; Mendes, above n 3, 92; Ronald Dworkin, *A Matter of Principle* (Harvard University Press, 1985) 70.

25 Jürgen Habermas, *Moral Consciousness and Communicative Action* (Christian Lenhardt and Shierry Weber Nicholsen trans, MIT Press, 1990) 68.

26 Hugh F Landerkin, 'Custody Disputes in the Provincial Court of Alberta: A New Judicial Dispute Resolution Model' (1997) 35 *Alberta Law Review* 627, 654.

27 An 'amicus curiae', or friend of the court, is a person or organisation who is not a direct party to the proceeding, but who nevertheless participates by filing a brief. Amicus curiae briefs are common in the US: D Kearney and Thomas W Merrill, 'Influence of Amicus Curiae Briefs on the Supreme Court' (1999) 148 *University of Pennsylvania Law Review* 743. Similarly, so-called 'intervenors' are appearing increasingly in Australia, and now make submissions in about half of cases before the Supreme Court of Canada: Benjamin RD Alarie and Andrew J Green, 'Interventions at the Supreme Court of Canada: Accuracy, Affiliation and Acceptance' (2010) 48 *Osgoode Hall Law Journal* 381.

28 David Mullan, *Administrative Law* (Irwin Law, 2001) 675; Frank Michelman, *Brennan and Democracy* (Princeton University Press, 1999) 59.

29 Zurn, above n 18, 278.

30 See, eg, *Kitchen v Herbert*, 755 F 3d 1193, 1210 (10th Cir 2014) (citing *Loving v Virginia*, 388 US 1, 4 (1967)) (same-sex marriage case relying heavily on *Loving* miscegenation case); *Bostic v Schaefer*, 760 F 3d 352, 4 (4th Cir 2014) (also citing *Loving*).

31 John Parkinson, *Deliberating in the Real World: Problems of Legitimacy in Deliberative Democracy* (Oxford University Press, 2006) 3.

32 John Parkinson, 'Legitimacy Problems in Deliberative Democracy' (2003) 51 *Political Studies* 180, 183, quoting John Schaar, 'Legitimacy in the Modern State' in William

Connolly (ed), *Legitimacy and the State* (Blackwell, 1984) 104–133; Jürgen Habermas, *Between Facts and Norms: Contributions to a Discourse Theory of Law and Democracy* (William Rehg trans, MIT Press, 1996, first published 1992) 304.

33 Michelman, above n 28, 59; CJ Casillas, PK Enns and PC Wohlfarth, 'How Public Opinion Constrains the US Supreme Court' (2011) 55 *American Journal of Political Science* 74.

34 Ron Levy, 'Deliberative Constitutional Change in a Polarised Federation' in Paul Kildea, Andrew Lynch and George Williams (eds), *Tomorrow's Federation* (Federation Press, 2011). See also Michael Pal, 'The Promise and Limits of Citizens' Assemblies: Deliberation, Institutions and the Law of Democracy' (2012) 38 *Queen's Law Journal* 259, 270.

35 See, eg, Paul Kelly, 'Labor Can't be Serious about Citizens' Plan', *Weekend Australian*, 24 July 2010, 1; Peter Hartcher, 'Great Procrastinator Takes Reins of Inaction on Climate Change', *Sydney Morning Herald*, 24 July 2010; Tim Blair, 'The Horror of a Year in Climate La La Land', *The Daily Telegraph*, 26 July 2010, 22; Vaughn Palmer, 'Liberals Sink into Quagmire of Electoral Reform', *Vancouver Sun*, 2 April 2003; David Brock, 'Ontario Abdicates its Duty on Electoral Reform', *The Toronto Star*, 10 May 2007.

36 Ian Urquhart, 'An Ill-Advised Leap in the Dark: Ontario Electoral Reform Panel will meet for Almost a Year and a Loopy Outcome is a Possibility', *The Hamilton Spectator*, 28 March, 2006.

37 Levy, above n 34, 368. But note that, in the poll cited, *all* groups favoured Citizens' Assemblies over the legislature-led status quo; uniquely, however, the university-educated group did so by the barest of margins.

38 Ibid.

39 Ibid 364–5.

40 Ibid.

41 David Ponet and Ethan Leib, 'Fiduciary Law's Lessons for Deliberative Democracy' (2011) 91 *Boston University Law Review* 1249, 1256.

42 Habermas, above n 32, 354–6. See also Seyla Benhabib, 'Toward a Deliberative Model of Democratic Legitimacy' in Seyla Benhabib (ed), *Democracy and Difference: Contesting the Boundaries of the Political* (Princeton University Press, 1996) 74.

43 James S Fishkin, 'Virtual Democratic Possibilities: Prospects for Internet Democracy' (Paper presented at Conference on Internet, Democracy and Public Goods, Belo Horizonte, Brazil, 6–10 November 2000) 5.

44 For instance, the 'one person, one vote' principle within the right to vote has characteristics of both a liberty and an equality guarantee.

45 What about democracy as a value? In a democratic state, democracy is indeed also a *telos* taken for granted in relation to both politics and the law of politics. However, 'democracy' is not a singular signifier, but a category encompassing a vast range of governance models based on popular rule. The nature of democracy is largely dependent upon the foundational values we have identified. For this reason, we do not isolate democracy per se as a value, but focus instead on values that instantiate democracy's basic variations: *liberties* (eg, expressive and voting rights) integral to a functioning democracy; *equality* in the scope of democracy (eg, inclusions in the franchise); *integrity*, versus corruption, the latter denoting cartelised democracy serving the needs of only a few (eg, after partisan capture of electoral rules); and *deliberation*, which concerns the essential nature of democratic communication and reasoning.

46 Dennis F Thompson, 'Deliberate About, Not In, Elections' (2013) 12 *Election Law Journal* 372; Jane Mansbridge et al, 'The Place of Self-Interest and the Role of Power in Deliberative Democracy' (2010) 18 *Journal of Political Philosophy* 64, 71.

68 The Law of Deliberative Democracy

47 Jud Mathews and Alec Stone Sweet, 'All Things in Proportion? American Rights Review and the Problem of Balancing' (2011) 60 *Emory Law Journal* 797, 802.

48 *R v Bryan* [2007] 1 SCR 527 ('*Bryan*').

49 *Thomson Newspapers Co Ltd v Canada (Attorney General)* [1998] 1 SCR 877.

50 Ibid [29]–[38]; *Bryan*, above n 48, [12]–[14], [33]–[37]. Note that, despite the poor fit of its balancing analysis, the *Bryan* court ultimately ruled in favour of the law.

51 The Constitution Act, 1982, being Sch B to the Canada Act 1982 (UK), 1982, c 11, s 2(b); *Irwin Toy Ltd v Quebec (Attorney General)* [1989] 1 SCR 927 (defining s 2(b) broadly: 'if the activity conveys or attempts to convey a meaning, it has expressive content and *prima facie* falls within the scope of the guarantee').

52 *Australian Capital Television Pty Ltd v Commonwealth* (1992) 177 CLR 106.

53 Ibid 144–5 (Mason CJ).

54 Mathews and Stone Sweet, above n 47, 800, 811–12; T Alexander Aleinikoff, 'Constitutional Law in the Age of Balancing' (1987) 96 *Yale Law Journal* 943, 963–72.

55 *Citizens United v Federal Election Commission*, 558 US 310, 312 (2010) (quoting *Federal Election Commission v Wisconsin Right to Life Inc*, 551 US 449, 464 (2007)); *McCutcheon v Federal Election Commission*, 572 US __ (2014); *Arizona Free Enterprise Club v Bennett*, 564 US __ (2011).

56 A Kavanagh, *Constitutional Review under the UK Human Rights Act* (Cambridge University Press, 2009) 233–69.

57 'Minimal' objectivity means that a majority of people agree with the truth of a statement. The 'strong' variety of objectivity is, by contrast, understood as independent of social belief; that is, whether the statement is true or not does not depend on whether a majority of people, or anyone really, thinks it is so. Somewhere in between, 'modest' objectivity denotes (like strong objectivity) that our sense of what is true may be wrong, but 'the existence and character of facts of various kinds [is] dependent on us': Jules Coleman and Brian Leiter, 'Determinacy, Objectivity, and Authority' (1993) 142 *University of Pennsylvania Law Review* 549, 616–21. Different kinds of statements (eg, aesthetic, scientific) may fit best with particular objectivity types.

58 Michael Klarman, 'Majoritarian Judicial Review: The Entrenchment Problem' (1997) 85 *Georgetown Law Journal* 491, 498.

59 Mendes, above n 3, at 80.

60 Anna Harvey and Barry Friedman, 'Pulling Punches: Congressional Constraints on the Supreme Court's Constitutional Rulings 1987–2000' (2006) 31 *Legislative Studies Quarterly* 533.

61 In the US in particular, doctrine and commentary often reflect a loss of faith in objectivity in the law of politics. Courts and commissions often shy away from issuing substantive judgments and aim instead to preserve roughly equal electoral prospects for opposing partisan factions: see chapter 5.

62 On objectivity in law see also, eg, Ronald Dworkin, *Law's Empire* (Harvard University Press, 1986); Kent Greenawalt, *Law and Objectivity* (Oxford University Press, 1992); Michael Moore, 'Moral Reality Revisited' (1992) 90 *Michigan Law Review* 2424; Nicos Stavropoulos, *Objectivity in Law* (Clarendon Press, 1996); Brian Leiter (ed), *Objectivity in Law and Morals* (Cambridge University Press, 2001); Connie S Rosati, 'Some Puzzles about the Objectivity of Law' (2004) 23 *Law and Philosophy* 273; David O Brink, 'Legal Theory, Legal Interpretation, and Judicial Review' (1988) 17 *Philosophy & Public Affairs* 105.

63 Murray Gleeson, *The Rule of Law and the Constitution* (ABC Books, 2000) 99–100; Cass R Sunstein, *A Constitution of Many Minds: Why the Founding Document Doesn't Mean What It Meant Before* (Princeton University Press, 2009) 43.

64 For kindred arguments see Gerald R Postema, 'Sweet Dissonance: Conflict, Consensus, and the Rule of Law' (2010) 17 *Harvard Review of Philosophy* 37, 48.

65 Stephen McLeish, 'Challenges to the Survival of the Common Law' (2014) 38(2) *Melbourne University Law Review* 818, 831.

66 *Bryan*, above n 48.

67 Ibid [49] (Bastarache J).

68 Mathews and Stone Sweet, above n 47, 88–9.

69 Aleinikoff, above n 54, 948–55.

70 Ibid 949.

71 *Lochner v New York*, 198 US 45 (1905).

72 Aleinikoff, above n 54, 951–4.

73 Alec Stone Sweet and Jud Mathews, 'Proportionality Balancing and Global Constitutionalism' (2008) 47 *Columbia Journal of Transnational Law* 72.

74 Aleinikoff, above n 54, 949.

75 Maya Sen, above n 9, 316–18.

76 Ibid 316–17.

77 David Weiden, 'Judicial Politicization, Ideology and Activism at the High Courts of the United States, Canada, and Australia' (2011) 64 *Political Research Quarterly* 335 (politicisation is least in Canada, followed by Australia and the US, in that order); Chris Hanretty, 'Political Preferment in English Judicial Appointments, 1880–2005' (2012) *APSA Annual Meeting Paper* (finding little evidence of partisan appointment, some evidence of partisan promotion); Mita Bhattacharya and Russell Smyth, 'The Determinants of Judicial Prestige and Influence: Some Empirical Evidence from the High Court of Australia' (2001) 30 *Journal of Legal Studies* 223, 229–31 (finding low partisanship).

78 See chapter 6 on the risk of such judicial coercion of democratic politics.

79 Zurn, above n 18, 188, 210.

80 Thompson, above n 4, 77–8.

81 Ibid 197.

82 Zurn, above n 18, 210.

83 Ibid 184, 192.

84 Ibid 164.

85 Mendes, above n 3, 84, 163, 179, citing, eg, Mary Ann Glendon, *Rights Talk: The Impoverishment of Political Discourse* (Free Press, 1993); Jeremy Waldron, 'Judges as Moral Reasoners' (2009) 7 *International Journal of Constitutional Law* 2. Note that Mendes does not clearly indicate his agreement with these sentiments.

86 Sen, above n 9, 326.

87 Ibid 331.

88 Arthur, above n 1, 406–7.

89 Ibid.

90 Herbert A Simon, 'Theories of Bounded Rationality' in CB Maguire and Roy Radner (eds), *Decision and Organization* (North-Holland Publishing Company, 1972); see also Daniel Kahneman, 'Maps of Bounded Rationality: Psychology for Behavioural Economics' (2003) 93 *The American Economic Review* 1449, 1449.

91 Dan M Kahan, 'Ideology, Motivated Reasoning, and Cognitive Reflection' (2013) 8 *Judgment and Decision Making* 407, 408.

92 Ibid 416–18. See also Jonathan Haidt, *The Righteous Mind: Why Good People are Divided by Politics and Religion* (Pantheon, 2012).

93 Kahan, above n 91, 417–18.

94 Iris Marion Young, *Inclusion and Democracy* (Oxford University Press, 2000) 64–70.

95 Robert E Goodin, 'Talking Politics: Perils and Promise' (2006) 45 *European Journal of Political Research* 235.

96 Postema, above n 64, 48.

97 See, eg, J Johnson, 'Political Parties and Deliberative Democracy?' in RS Katz and W Crotty, *Handbook of Party Politics* (Sage, 2006).

98 Joshua Cohen, 'Deliberation and Democratic Legitimacy' in A Hamlin and P Pettit (eds), *The Good Polity: Normative Analysis of the State* (Basil Blackwell, 1989).

99 A complication is that the deliberative effects of parties may vary based on whether a jurisdiction employs a two-party system (eg, in the US and, to a lesser degree, in Australia's Lower House) or a more pluralistic array of parties (eg, UK and Canada). In the latter, a greater diversity of perspectives, including some that are otherwise marginalised, may gain expression. This can in theory avoid some of the oversimplification, entrenchment, and polarisation of two-party systems. Alternatively, it might be too complex, even chaotic, to crystallise or clarify arguments.

100 Bernard Manin, 'On Legitimacy and Political Deliberation' (1987) 15 *Political Theory* 338; Bernard Manin, *The Principles of Representative Government* (Cambridge University Press, 1997) ch 6.

101 Nino, above n 4, 133.

102 A number of scholars have highlighted these two categories, including Mansbridge et al, above n 46, and Bächtiger et al, 'Disentangling Diversity in Deliberative Democracy: Competing Theories, Their Blind Spots and Complementarities' (2010) 18 *The Journal of Political Philosophy* 32. The terms 'Classic Deliberation' and 'Expansion of the Classic Ideal' are Mansbridge et al's.

103 Mansbridge et al, above n 46, 73.

104 Kavanagh, above n 56, 256. But it also 'provides an opportunity for a more precise and contextual assessment both of the substantive issues, as well as the question of the degree of deference which is appropriate with reference to them': ibid.

105 Frederick Schauer, 'Slippery Slopes' (1985) 99 *Harvard Law Review* 361, 370–1.

106 William Rehg, 'Translator's Introduction' in Jürgen Habermas, *Between Facts and Norms: Contributions to a Discourse Theory of Law and Democracy* (William Rehg trans, The MIT Press, 1996, first published 1992) xvi.

107 Ibid.

108 For a similar point, in the context of three branches of government, see M Elizabeth Magill, 'The Real Separation in Separation of Powers Law' (2000) 86 *Virginia Law Review* 1127, 1128–9.

109 See Brian L Silver, *The Ascent of Science* (Oxford University Press, 1998) 237–8.

110 John S Dryzek and Christian List, 'Social Choice Theory and Deliberative Democracy: A Reconciliation' (2003) 33 *British Journal of Political Science* 1; David Miller, 'Deliberative Democracy and Social Choice' (1992) 40 *Political Studies* 54. Deliberation may be capable of breaking such a cycle.

111 See, eg, rule 42(b) of the Federal Rules of Civil Procedure; Law Reform (Contributory Negligence) Act 1945 (US).

112 The identification of these binaries is rendered more complex by the so-called 'doctrinal paradox', raised when a court considers not just the overall outcome (eg, liability, constitutionality), but certain embedded sub-issues. Kornhauser and Sager show that a party may or may not be judged liable depending on whether the court tallies the vote on each of the sub-issues first, or whether it simply tallies the overall outcome to which each judge has independently arrived: Lewis A Kornhauser and Lawrence G Sager 'The One and the Many: Adjudication in Collegial Courts' (1993) 81 *California Law Review* 1, 11–12. Pettit has referred to this phenomenon as the 'discursive dilemma': Philip Pettit, 'Deliberative Democracy and the Discursive Dilemma' (2001) 11 *Philosophical Issues* 268, 272.

113 Stone Sweet and Matthews, above n 73, 75, citing Matthias Kumm, 'Constitutional Rights as Principles: On the Structure and Domain of Constitutional Justice' (2004) 2 *International Journal of Constitutional Law* 574, 579.

114 Thompson, above n 46.
115 Ron Levy, 'Breaking the Constitutional Deadlock: Lessons from Deliberative Experiments in Constitutional Change' (2010) 34 *Melbourne University Law Review* 805 (indicating a roughly 2:1 popular preference for a referendum led by a citizens' assembly-like model).
116 To be sure, many first-order matters also generate partisan contestation, particularly when they address matters like taxation, over which there is deep and pre-existing ideological division.
117 Louis Henkin, *The Age of Rights* (Columbia University Press, 1990) 3.
118 Postema, above n 64, 50. In this passage Postema means that judges can lead the legislative branches of government in this respect; yet later he extends the point to include using judicial deliberation to 'discipline' deliberation in the broader public sphere: at 50–52.
119 Rawls, 'The Idea of Public Reason', above n 15, 112.
120 For more on these possibilities see Hoi Kong and Ron Levy, 'Deliberative Constitutionalism' in André Bächtiger, John Dryzek, Jane Mansbridge and Mark Warren (eds), *Oxford Handbook of Deliberative Democracy* (Oxford University Press, forthcoming).

Part III

Problems in the Law of Deliberative Democracy

Chapter 4

Liberty v Deliberation (The Accommodation Problem)

We are coming to realize more completely that ... the judge has liberty of choice of the rule which he applies, and that his choice will rightly depend upon the relative weights of the social and economic advantages which will finally turn the scales of judgment in favor of one rule rather than another.

Justice Harlan Fisk Stone[1]

Liberty is a dominant value in the law of politics,[2] and the first of three we discuss in this part, each in superficial tension with deliberation. Peering through the lens of deliberative theory, in this chapter we scrutinise the proportionality methodology we call *conceptual balancing*, which dominates in litigation about expressive and other liberties. Conceptual balancing directly trades values or interests off of each other. Assuming them to be in mutual tension, it places them in counterpoint – arranges them in contest with each other on either side of a metaphoric balance scale. By contrast, deliberative *accommodation* is not a 'battleground of competing interests',[3] nor a mere aggregation and balancing of rival values. Instead, accommodative decision-making is a methodology for pursuing the kinds of common ground described in the previous chapters.

Deliberation can first involve *preference accommodation* – our term for the accommodation of those first-order matters of infinite variety that affect individual lives directly, and that so often conflict. As we noted in chapter 2, if conducted deliberatively, first-order decision-making can allow diverse citizen preferences to coexist or even to inform and modify each other.

We concentrate in this book, however, on second-order decision-making. These are decisions about the background conditions within which first-order decision-making is conducted. Second-order choices may, for example, be choices about the laws, institutions, procedures, and participants involved in first-order decision-making. In our view, only those legal decision-makers who aim to make choices instituting deliberative democratic governance may plausibly be said to deliberate well concerning second-order matters. The simple reason is that first-order democratic deliberation is usually only feasible where second-order deliberative democratic conditions are put in place.

Choices at the second-order level can seek better democratic deliberation via

76   The Law of Deliberative Democracy

a second form of accommodation, which we call *institutional accommodation*. In chapter 2 we explored at length the notion that deliberation improves democracy and democracy in turn improves deliberation. To summarise, we saw that deliberative democracy can be more inclusive, is premised on informed democratic consent, better reflects the 'real' (that is, pre-institutional and pre-legal) range of citizen preferences and interests, and lessens the coercion of dissenting democratic minorities. Conversely, we also saw that practically and politically effective law and policy must rest, at least in part, on deliberation that is sensitive to citizen values and needs. We used the example of climate change policy: even if all legislators agreed on the science, the question of how to allocate the social costs of mitigation would remain a fraught problem, and one that cannot be solved in a democratic vacuum.

It is worth recalling just how much deliberative democratic institutional accommodation marks a break with the past. Traditional assumptions in political theory and practice picture democracy at odds with deliberation. To many, democracy ought to be straightforwardly and uncompromisingly majoritarian – satisfied simply by the act of voting for representatives or in referendums.[4] Initiatives aimed at enhancing deliberation might then be seen to detract from democracy in its purest form. Other observers prefer deliberation to democracy, recalling JS Mill's idyll of governance led by 'leading minds'.[5]

Our goal in the present chapter is to explore a number of uncharted second-order questions about law. Do, or can, the doctrines of the law of politics encourage the forms of accommodation that deliberative democrats dream of? And do the law's formal processes enable or spoil such deliberative dreams? Courts seem to appreciate the deliberative implications of the law of politics at best incompletely. Thus they routinely offer resistance to deliberative democratic initiatives.[6] Indeed, even judges who implicitly recognise deliberation as an objective of law rarely use the term, much less the theory, but grasp inchoately at deliberative ideas with phrases like 'informational equality'.[7]

Particularly concerning are the effects of judicial doctrines of proportionality. Cognate terms include 'reasonably and appropriately adapted' governmental action, 'demonstrably justified limits' on liberties, 'balancing' between governmental means and ends,[8] and 'intermediate' and 'strict' scrutiny. Proportionality is commonplace in rights reasoning in Australia, Canada, the United Kingdom, and the United States. Whatever its labels and variations, much proportionality reasoning about liberties employs a rivalrous (zero-sum) conceptual balance as the main tool for reasoning about disputes concerning political liberties. In this area jurists seldom aim for the alternative of deliberative accommodation. This raises what we call the *accommodation problem*.

To repeat our claim from the previous chapter, it is not law's fixation on proportionality per se that presents the accommodation problem. Rather the difficulty lies with proportionality in relatively crude forms such as conceptual balancing. The problem is not a result of immutable forms of law, but of doctrinal choices that judges (and to a lesser extent legislatures) make to pit liberty and other dominant values in competition with deliberation. Chapter 3 showed how the common law uses proportionality as a distinctive framing device to understand multifaceted disputes more plainly. We saw that such bounded reasoning is not a failure of judges particularly, but a regular feature of human cognition in response to complexity. Indeed, it need not be a failure at all. Chapter 3 introduced the contention that, even within binary and bounded forms of legal decision-making, there is still ample scope for deliberation. Accommodative proportionality is a more nuanced and (as we called it) *deliberatively thicker* form of legal reasoning about political liberties.

In this chapter we see both how the accommodation problem manifests and how it can perhaps be mitigated. We illustrate using cases concerning a system central to the democratic enterprise: political expression. More particularly, after outlining relevant aspects of deliberative theory by way of background, we examine laws regulating, first, electoral opinion polling and, secondly, truth in political advertising.

Political expression and deliberation

In describing political expression as a 'system' we choose our words carefully.[9] From a deliberative theory perspective, expression in a democracy is ideally systemic. We contend that lawmakers and legal adjudicators should nuance law's response to expression accordingly.

Deliberative speech is systemic, first, in that deliberators do not merely speak past each other in isolated and episodic speech acts, but interact with and respond to each other over time. Not merely 'communication' but 'communicative action',[10] deliberatively thick expression involves a series of recurring and reciprocal speech acts. According to John Parkinson, deliberative 'participants agree to reciprocity in their discussions, giving each other equal speaking time'.[11] But this reciprocity is no mere trading of fixed points of view. It is rather an ongoing discussion characterised by mutual learning and persuasion (on questions of both fact and value).

Deliberative notions of communicative action at least superficially resemble a mainstay of free speech theory, the economic metaphor of the marketplace of ideas.[12] Both imagine a sustained give-and-take of ideas out of which the best propositions of fact or value emerge. But the nature of the forum and what constitute the best propositions often differ markedly between the models. Parkinson explains that deliberative 'democracy is conceived of less as a market for the exchange of private preferences, more as a forum for the creation of public agreements'.[13] With specifically accommodative goals, communicative action entails a far less mercenary and competitive collective decision-making forum than under the classic marketplace of ideas notion. To be sure, this distinction can be quite porous. Deliberative theorists often find themselves slipping into marketplace metaphors – for example, describing forum participants 'buying' ideas (see below). And, as discussed in chapter 3, the Expanded Ideal of deliberative democracy

78 The Law of Deliberative Democracy

incorporates competitive self-interest into its description of citizens' communicative interactions.

Generally, however, participants in a deliberative forum do not just make their preferences and interests known to others, but may reconsider their preferences or rethink what is in their own interests, once others make their own preferences and interests known as well. Ideally, such a process helps yield common ground in collective decisions. This goal of deep, accommodative reciprocity is reflected in deliberative criteria including inclusivity, open-mindedness, other-regarding, and reason-giving.

Consider the reason-giving, or 'publicity', criterion. A condition of deliberative democracy is 'that only those arguments which can be made public should have any force'.[14] Robert Goodin, like others,[15] suggests that having to declare publicly the reasons behind your deliberations 'works to ensure Golden Rule style outcomes' in that 'you cannot expect others to buy an argument from you that you would not buy from them'.[16] This relies on what Jon Elster calls 'the civilizing force of hypocrisy' – essentially a shaming force that encourages speakers to couch their positions in the language of general principles rather than self-interest.[17] If A is to try to persuade B based on an appeal to A's own needs, then A should be receptive when in reply B tries to do the same based on B's needs. Hence, speakers should put ideas to each other using relatively rational and widely understood forms of argumentation that others 'may reasonably be expected to endorse'.[18] This assumes (quite plausibly) that speech is not intended to be met by others passively or indifferently, but is valuable at least in part as a way to convey meanings that influence others' thoughts or behaviours.

Ideally, the system of reciprocal expression is a sustained process in which citizens both speak and listen, intending not only to sway others but to remain open to being swayed by others. (Notice the relevance of deliberative democratic criteria of open-mindedness and other-regarding.) In deliberative democracy theory, expression is not principally aimed at fulfilling the individual's desire for self-fulfilment or self-realisation, at least not in a solitary way.[19] Speakers and listeners therefore both remain front and centre. To some extent, deliberative notions of expression even muddy the coherence of the speaker-listener distinction, since in the ideal deliberative forum everyone speaks and everyone listens. In practice we might expect that some speakers dominate. But a well-designed speech system employs methods such as guaranteeing wide inclusion in a process (recalling the inclusiveness criterion), which can minimise such inequalities of expressive influence.[20]

There is also a broader sense in which deliberation is systemic. Jane Mansbridge and her co-authors outline a view of democracies as 'complex entities in which a wide variety of institutions, associations, and sites of contestation accomplish political work – including informal networks, the media, organized advocacy groups, schools, agencies, and the courts'.[21] A consequence of understanding deliberative democracy this way is that the deliberative or democratic deficiencies of one member of the system might be offset by the strengths of the others. This 'division of labour' can yield an overall system that, as a result of many parts functioning alongside each other, is more likely to approximate deliberative democratic ideals than any single part could on its own.[22]

The broader systemic theory has its share of caveats,[23] but it adds important dimensions to our discussion. It reminds us that speech acts need not occur within a narrow site or timeframe. For instance, deliberation around a single campaign event – such as a televised leaders' debate – is hardly confined to live-tweets or workplace lunchroom discussions the next day. It takes place at myriad sites and instigates longer-term campaign narratives about policies, ideologies, and personalities. Mansbridge et al's systemic view in effect concurs with some older ideas such as John Dryzek's 'discursive democracy',[24] according to which deliberation similarly transcends any narrow set of times and places, speakers and listeners, and institutions; deliberation is embodied instead in conversations 'carried on across time and space' among many participants.[25] A main thrust of such ideas is that a multiplicity of participants playing complementary roles contributes to deliberative democracy.

In either sense we have discussed, expression as a system particularly raises problems for regulation conducted by conceptual balancing. Chapter 3 briefly explained why. There we considered how, under rights regimes, almost any law more than trivially affecting political speech tends to be understood as an infringement of expressive liberty. The bulk of rights analysis then falls to the next stage, in which a court considers whether the infringement is proportionate to a legitimate public benefit and is therefore justified. Often courts have little room to manoeuvre out of this reasoning structure. They must identify and weigh distinct values or interests in tension – even if they are really neither distinct nor in tension, but parts of a systemic whole.

Let us carry forward an example from chapter 3. In *Australian Capital Television* *('ACTV')* the Australian High Court considered a law with broad effects on election campaign speech.[26] The law guaranteed publicly funded television airtime, but restricted the advertising to a prescribed format and allowed regulators to apportion airtime among the parties. As we saw, the Court briefly discussed but discounted the deliberative motivations behind the law (eg, encouraging a less trivial national political discourse, and curbing the role and influence of campaign money).[27] We offered an initial critique of this and similar cases. Conceptual balancing disassembles democratic deliberation into its component parts – placing popular expression on one side, and rigour, reflection, cooperation, policy holism, etc, on the other. The analysis thus assumes a set of irreconcilable opposites. In the cases on political expression below, a similar judicial enthusiasm for conceptually prising deliberation apart from expression leads to a miscategorisation of deliberative democratic projects. Understood more thickly, as democratic deliberation, democratic speech is a coherent compound of elements.

Why refer to such balancing as 'conceptual' if the balanced objects are in fact *values* in tension (eg, free speech versus deliberation)? The notion of conceptual balancing captures a key and problematic feature of balancing in the political

80   The Law of Deliberative Democracy

liberties context: that items on the balance scale are often presumed to be both conceptually distinct and in tension. If they were not different from each other, the tension between them would cease to make sense: on a rivalrous scale, a thing cannot be balanced against itself. However, in constitutional law in particular, the conceptual balancing test has become second nature to judges, and even indispensable. The test frequently *imposes* conceptual distinctions and tensions on controversies in the law of politics. As we see next, a common consequence is that the *deliberatively thin* judicial reading of expressive liberty is an artefact of the doctrine of conceptual balancing itself.

Judging deliberative measures

The case studies in this book illustrate what happens when judges review deliberative democratic measures – that is, initiatives to rewrite rules and conditions of political practice to bring democracy closer to deliberative democratic ideals. When such measures regulate expression, reviewing judges must make foundational normative choices between expression's thin and thick varieties. Does expression ideally involve systemic reciprocity across broad webs of interconnected speakers and listeners, or are these qualities unessential to the expressive ideal? Such choices between basic normative options matter greatly to the outcomes of legal cases, and in turn to how democracy is practised. Nevertheless, the choices and the assumptions behind them remain largely implicit, often buried in the obscure corners of written judgments or left unexpressed.

Conceptual balancing needs to be recognised as a principal (but not the only) reason for the judicial preference for deliberatively thin expression. Conceptual balancing's analytic posture is generally insensitive to systemic models of expression. It is intrinsically suspicious of government action, and especially chary of actions regulating speech. The withering scrutiny of a standard proportionality test's 'culture of justification'[28] primes courts to overrule legislative and executive actions. Courts often have little room to manoeuvre away from this posture, now so central to legal analyses of liberties.

Consider what would have happened if the *ACTV* court had tried to understand speech in deliberatively thick terms while still operating a conceptual balancing exercise. The Court in the case accepted deliberation as a legitimate (but low-value) legislative objective; had it also then read the broadcasters' speech interests as deliberative, the same concept or interest would then appear on both sides of the balance scale. This raises the logical problem noted above. Yet, even if a court must force a case to conform to the rigid pattern of binary balancing – rediscovering just *two* counterpoised items in the case before them – usually this requires little effort. At least two off-the-rack conceptual dichotomies are available to sustain a conceptual balance in many cases. Both illustrate how conceptual balancing creates thin liberties as artefacts of its own process.

a. Individuals v collectivities

Courts often pit the interests of individuals against those of broader collectivities. This distinction frequently resurfaces in free speech litigation. For instance, the *ACTV* court described the impugned law in that case as fulfilling certain public goods (described in terms of deliberation, equality, and other concepts) but viewed the broadcast companies as aggrieved smaller parties standing up for free expression. Viewing disputes about deliberative measures as contests between individual (or minority) and wider public interests adds an evocative anti-domination angle to constitutional analysis.[29]

The question raised is how strong and how inevitable is the clash between individual and collective speech interests. One set of ideas on the subject derives from free speech theory itself, which has long included deliberative arguments for protecting speech, though initially without the benefit of modern deliberative theory. Writing in the US in the 1960s, Alexander Meiklejohn comments that the 'primary purpose of the First Amendment is ... that all the citizens shall, so far as possible, understand the issues which bear upon our common life'.[30] This, he says, and not apparently competing notions such as individual self-realisation, provides the essential rationale for expressive liberty.[31] It is not the 'needs of many men to express their opinions' but rather 'the common needs of all the members of the body politic' that inform a First Amendment ultimately concerned with 'the voting of wise decisions'.[32]

Later scholars of the First Amendment also present deliberative readings of free speech. Among them are Owen Fiss, Cass Sunstein, and Lawrence Solum.[33] For his part, Solum (reading Jürgen Habermas) concludes that 'the freedom of speech should be and is best understood as the freedom to engage in communicative action, and the corollary notion that freedom of speech does not encompass the freedom to engage in strategic action'.[34] As with Meiklejohn, these authors commonly fix upon a deliberative conception of freedom of speech, which in some respects focuses more on the group than on the individual.

But this does not mean that deliberation is necessarily *incompatible* with individual expressive interests. In a systemic view of speech, individual expressive autonomy is *part of* a larger system of communicative action. As we have seen, a deliberative system ideally benefits individual expression by extending the opportunities for expression and helping to realise that expression in, for example, a more informed and persuasive mode. In Habermas's view, such collective engagement even contributes to the formation of what he calls 'that inner centre [of] personal identity'.[35] Similarly, Christian Rostbøll argues that freedom of expression, deliberation, autonomy, and respect are all interdependent. He argues that deliberation facilitates individual autonomy rather than violates it: deliberative democracy 'not only presupposes an ideal of political autonomy, it also prescribes a procedure for individuals to develop autonomous understandings of their own political preferences'.[36]

And the relation also works in reverse: robust protections for individual speech

82 The Law of Deliberative Democracy

are needed to sustain deliberative speech systems. Individual ideas help counter the tendency towards groupthink, and other deliberative pathologies that result from exclusively valuing collective interests and points of view. Indeed, we need an assortment of robust expressions – including individual and even self-interested positions[37] – to form and settle points of view in the first place. As Joshua Cohen puts the point:

> free expression is required for *determining* what advances the common good, because what is good is fixed by public deliberation, and not prior to it. It is fixed by informed and autonomous judgments ... so the ideal of deliberative democracy is not hostile to free expression, it rather presupposes such freedom.[38]

Similarly, according to Katherine Gelber, '[c]ommunicative action explains the interdependency of the individual and the community'.[39] Free speech theory is, in some views, on board with this conclusion: the 'individual interest in communicating one's ideas to others may also be stated as a societal interest in a diverse marketplace of ideas'.[40] If free speech '[i]nterests may be conceived of in both public and private terms' the distinction starts to look rather 'arbitrary'.[41]

In sum, a deliberative measure to enhance the system of expression is also likely to promote individual expression. Yet courts continue to balance individual versus collective expressive interests. One good reason is that these interests do not entirely collapse. For instance, expression can gratify individual needs like that of artistic creativity, or can promote self-expression for its own sake.[42] Part of the value of expression arguably then has little to do with communicatively rational decision-making about collective governance.

As a result, laws instituting deliberative measures may occasionally set up a clash between deliberative and non-deliberative speech goals. This is clearest for *subtractive* measures, which try to eliminate certain speakers or speech content from an expressive forum. For example, a law may seek to limit political satire that is malicious and untrue – features anathema to deliberation[43] – but whose aims are partly artistic in nature. Courts must then decide between competing principles. But this balance of principles can seem arbitrary; since deliberative and individualistic speech models are partly incommensurable, it may be unclear which should prevail over the other.[44] Cases of subtraction therefore implicate both collective-deliberative and individualistic models of free speech at once and raise unique complexities. (We cannot cover them all here.[45]) In short, it may be impossible to discount completely the need to safeguard even individually focused expression that makes no apparent contribution to deliberation.

By contrast, *additive* deliberative measures adopt a softer-touch approach and raise subtler normative choices. These initiatives only augment political discussion by encouraging new sources of information and speakers, or by adding or tweaking second-order rules (eg, laws guaranteeing broadcast time or public campaign funding). An additive scheme is thus distinguished by substantially allowing any individual (or discrete group of individuals) who previously could speak to keep doing so. Nevertheless, as we will see, many judges default to the view that, even by these relatively modest adjustments, additive interventions damage free speech interests.

Deliberative theory does not yield this point. An additive deliberative measure might censor speech trivially, or may even leave it wholly untouched. In *ACTV*, news media were exempt from any limitations; news, talkback, and other regular discussion of political affairs remained unaffected.[46] The impugned legislation merely obligated broadcasters to cede airtime on their networks for mandated political broadcasts, and provided new and more substantive opportunities for political parties to be heard.[47] As a proportion of daily airtime, the impact on the broadcasters who brought the litigation was minimal, amounting to a modest mandate for greater coverage of civic matters – hardly an unusual legislative intervention for companies licensed to use public airwaves.[48] Similarly, in the US, a law successfully challenged in *Miami Herald Publishing Co v Tornillo* required newspapers to provide a right of reply to people targeted by editorial criticisms appearing in the papers.[49] Though this cost newspapers print space, and by extension money, their rights to speak remained mostly unimpaired.

US Senate Bill 742 – the Fairness in Broadcasting Bill of 1987[50] – would even have amended the Communications Act of 1934[51] to require broadcast licensees to provide a reasonable opportunity for the discussion of conflicting views on issues of public importance. While it passed both houses of Congress, President Reagan vetoed it, saying that '[w]ell-intentioned as S 742 may be, it would be inconsistent with the First Amendment and with the American tradition of independent journalism'.[52] Of course, given that the Bill passed both houses of Congress – and that a case may be made, as Sunstein does, that the constitutional framers created a system of '"government by discussion", in which outcomes would be reached through broad public deliberation'[53] – Reagan was overstating the uniformity of American thinking on the matter.

Additive measures therefore raise a deep ambiguity, which resurfaces in a number of cases: do they limit speech at all? Does adjusting the nature – for example, the duration and substantive rigour – but not the content of political speech infringe expressive freedoms? At root this ambiguity concerns whether thick or thin conceptions of speech should prevail in the law of politics. In subtractive cases, both models of speech are raised and must be weighed against each other. By contrast, as we will see in greater depth below, when faced with substantially additive measures a court's choice between free speech models can itself conclusively decide a case.

b. Liberty v deliberation

Another way to sustain a conceptual balance is to weigh liberties against deliberation. It is common to see decisions balance speakers against censors, rightholders against governments, or simply expression (or expressive liberty) against

84 The Law of Deliberative Democracy

deliberation. Many other balancing variations are approximately synonymous with these formulations. Whatever the precise terms, such patterns of conceptual balancing draw on established, if somewhat stale, liberal-democratic suppositions. The reading of liberty in negative terms leads seamlessly to conceptual balance. This concept of liberty begins from a premise of distrust toward governmental initiatives and vigilance against official overreach. In the law of politics, a dominant assumption is that governments and their arms and agencies are primed to arrogate public power to themselves by manipulating the powers of incumbency at every turn (we explore this point in chapter 6). The role of judges should therefore principally be to second-guess, check, and (when necessary) spoil legislative schemes, not to go along with or try to improve them. From this perspective it becomes clear why even additive deliberative measures – those that censor neither speakers nor speech content – are viewed as suspect. As we see throughout the cases below, judges often view attempts to enhance the deliberative quality of speech with suspicion.

American constitutional doctrine in particular has remained vigilant against 'tyranny' since the post-revolutionary period,[54] and appears trapped in a constitutional time warp, doomed to relive an eighteenth-century struggle with an overbearing monarch. Legal design premised on distrust of government is also increasingly common in other jurisdictions.[55] Of course, we cannot entirely discount this strand of reasoning as anachronistic: governments still do overreach. But more modern, arguably richer understandings of democracy focus not only on limiting elite power, but as well on the affirmative value of democratic voice or deliberation. In any event, the assumptions behind the distrust-model of regulation too often rest on bald empirical presupposition. That government is not to be trusted is often thought axiomatic, not a proposition amenable to measurement. Nor is the assumption usually adaptable to circumstances of a given case – whether *this* government is untrustworthy at *this* time.

Another main reason why courts view liberty and deliberation as mutually opposite reflects, in our view, a different kind of error. According to Robert Post, deliberative 'procedural assumptions ... no less than substantive ones, are ultimately grounded upon a distinctive and controversial conception of collective identity'.[56] We have said that additive deliberative interventions do not limit speech if all they do is broaden inputs and participation, and tweak procedures to bring greater rationality, other-regarding, information, and so forth, to an expressive forum. But, for Post, if expression is to be truly free we cannot insist on such features.

Contrary to Post, Fiss suggests that because some actors – the media, for example – possess disproportionate power with regard to opportunities for communication, governmental inaction will simply lead to the preservation and propagation of such power imbalances.[57] Fiss thus concludes that a 'commitment to rich public debate will allow, and sometimes even require the state to act' in ways that offset inequalities in communicative power, 'however elemental and repressive they might at first seem'.[58] Similarly, Solum suggests that unless some positive action is taken to rectify existing asymmetries in communicative opportunities, the communicative ideal is undermined or compromised. For example, 'those who control newspapers and broadcast stations have inherently greater opportunities to engage in communicative action ... [and to] shape and dominate discourse on certain topics'. Therefore, '[r]ight-of-reply provisions afford those attacked by the media the opportunity to redress the imbalance' and '[t]he principle of equality of communicative opportunity would appear not only to allow, but positively require that access to the media be granted in such situations'.[59]

There is also a simpler critique of Post. His position – not uncommon, though seldom so clearly articulated – begs the question whether speech can ever be unfettered or uninfluenced by law. The lack of legal fetters he envisions can only ever be a mirage. For instance, the *ACTV* court struck down amendments to broadcasting laws, but left untouched the legal regime that had licensed – and even comprehensively shaped – television broadcasting in the first place. Indeed, we are far from the first to challenge the myth of a prior, lawless state of affairs. For instance, Sunstein argues that, as the New Deal reformers recognised, by enacting new interventions in the economy a government should not be falsely understood as disturbing an ideal of economic neutrality. He writes that '[t]he government did not "act" only when it disturbed existing distributions. What people had, in markets, was a function of the entitlements that the law conferred on them. The notion of "laissez-faire" thus stood revealed as a conspicuous fiction'.[60] Similarly, speech regulations should not be misunderstood to be necessarily contrary to the First Amendment when they function to promote deliberative aims; it is not the case that such regulation intrudes upon some neutral, pre-legal world. We are not suggesting that deliberation is equally compatible with all visions of political morality. The point is simply that critiques like Post's can apply as much to other, non-deliberative modes of regulation, which similarly leave a procedural mark on expression.

Sometimes there are independent reasons to adopt either of the conceptual dichotomies we have just outlined. But conceptual balancing itself seems to compel their adoption. Each of the noted dichotomies permits a court to maintain a conceptual balance, which in turn permits the relatively easy resolution of cases. In the rest of this chapter we explore case studies to illustrate how conceptual balancing figures prominently in proportionality doctrines, and how it shapes – and, we argue, substantially thins – legal reasoning about political liberties. On a more positive note, we also consider how proportionality doctrines can evolve to encourage deliberative accommodation.

Case studies: proportionality and accommodation

While non-standard in the law of politics, accommodation appears elsewhere in law. For instance, many anti-discrimination cases see judges finesse discriminatory norms so that legitimate goals can be met while excluding fewer people. In a leading Canadian case, fitness requirements for fire-fighters had the impact

86 The Law of Deliberative Democracy

of disproportionately disqualifying female applicants;[61] the Court accepted a newer hiring standard for fire-fighters, which gauged actual ability to carry out fire-fighting tasks rather than testing aerobic capacity or other rough markers of ability. Is the law of politics amenable to such accommodation? The interests of fire-fighters and their employers are first-order: some judicial creativity is needed to recognise as valid, or occasionally to create, norms that are mutually agreeable to parties whose interests otherwise conflict. But second-order accommodation raises more difficult problems. Here a key question is whether law can help to preserve and manifest the systemic expressive model central to deliberative democracy.

In particular, can legal proportionality tests do this? Globally, the most common approach to human rights proportionality is premised partly on Canada's venerable *Oakes* test,[62] and similar German and European models. Two steps of the test are key in the countries of our study: 'whether there were less rights-restrictive means available to achieve those same ends' (*least-restrictive means*);[63] and 'whether the effect of the measure on rights is proportionate to the ends sought to be achieved' (*proportionality*).[64] Many cases focus on the latter step, which tends to be read as a simple conceptual balance between means and ends. But more flexible models of proportionality analysis, particularly at the prior step, may create room for deliberative measures to persist or thrive. We consider four such models later in this chapter. To concretise the discussion, let us delve into a particular case study on the law of expression: whether, and if so how, to regulate political and electoral opinion polling.

Reporting opinion polls and election results

There is rising interest in and concern about political polling, especially during elections.[65] One reason is the sense that political discourse is increasingly driven by superficiality or ideological polarisation, each of which opinion polls may breed or at least magnify.[66] Many deliberative democrats insist on a 'deliberate, then vote' paradigm, according to which deliberation is not a part of the act of voting but rather precedes the act.[67] Others partly disagree, arguing that voting itself can be an opportunity for, if not deliberative communication, then at least reflection.[68] In either case, published opinion polling sometimes precludes or reduces the vibrancy of deliberation accompanying the vote.

All told, more than 90 national jurisdictions ban or delay exit polling, embargo the publication of polling during campaign periods (also known as a 'black-out'), or require the initial publication of polls to be accompanied by key information about their conduct.[69] Yet, in Anglophonic democracies, the typical assumption is that communicative liberties are trump cards and that such regulation is either unconstitutional or at least highly suspect. Exceptionally among those democracies,[70] Canada retains an election-day ban on publishing polling and election results as well as mandating disclosure obligations for surveys,[71] and New Zealand bans the publication of exit polling.[72] The Supreme Court of Canada has subjected that country's measures to scrutiny in the important cases of *Thomson Newspapers* and *R v Bryan*, discussed below.[73]

Deliberative and related concerns have inspired two main kinds of regulation of the publication of opinion polling: *embargo* and *disclosure*. Respectively, these measures are subtractive and additive, to use our earlier terminology. The embargo, the more intrusive regulatory gambit, involves prohibiting the reporting or conduct of opinion polls during an election campaign. Proponents defend such blackout periods as important times when voters can 'cool off' and the undecided can seriously consider their vote without being unduly influenced by mass media, political parties, or special interests. Some even argue that polling companies should be registered and subject to audits to ensure that polls are conducted professionally and ethically. In response, both industry bodies and libertarian groups monitor and agitate against regulation of polling. Countries that restrict electoral opinion poll reporting include half of all democracies.[74] This proportion has tended to be fairly stable,[75] despite a trend – often the result of judicial intervention – towards relatively shorter embargoes covering only the last few days of an election campaign.[76]

The second and lighter-touch regulatory approach, disclosure, mandates the publication of key information alongside reports of poll results.[77] In 1999, the Council of Europe affirmed a broad interest in the publication of opinion polls. But it qualified this finding by recognising some fundamental weaknesses in the informational value of baldly presented polling data.[78] The Council recognised that the value of any particular poll, and hence of polling as a whole, can only be assessed if polls are accompanied by essential information. This includes the identity of the body that commissioned the poll, the organisation that conducted it, the broad method and questions used, and the dates, sample size, and margin of error of the survey. Such information may be mandated by law. For example, just prior to its 2000 election, Canada enacted a provision requiring disclosure of key information about opinion polling. The bodies that commissioned and conducted the poll were to be revealed. So too were the wording of questions, the pool and sample size, and the margin of error; a methodological report also had to be made publicly available. Where a survey lacked statistical validity, that fact was to be published instead.[79]

Polling regulation is a prime example of the presumed rivalry between expression and deliberation. Regulating polling has been called a 'paternalistic' approach 'that does not coincide with the idea of democracy'.[80] Deliberative theory shows the issue to be somewhat more multifaceted. On the one hand is the claim that polling actually provides deliberatively useful information. It generates, if not dialogue, at least a kind of democratic toing-and-froing over issues between voters *en masse* and political leaders. Understood in this light, any expressive right in relation to polling belongs to the population that is sampled, more than the media outlet, interest group, or research institution conducting the polling. On the other hand, proponents of unregulated polling assert that it is 'inconsistent to demand … that voters make their decision as rationally as possible, based on factual

88 The Law of Deliberative Democracy

information, but then ... to forbid the publication of such factual information'.[81] This looks like a deliberative argument, resting as it does on a claim that all polls are informative. Yet it hides naïve assumptions about deliberation – for example, that all information is deliberatively useful, however tangential to the task at hand, and that the precondition for deliberation is the provision of raw data.

In our view, regulations that target polling and, relatedly, the live reporting of election results on election night, can benefit both deliberation and expression. To see why, consider several of political opinion polling's consequences for democratic deliberation, both pro and con.

a. Other-regarding and inclusiveness

As just noted, opinion polling may have value as a source of information about citizens' opinions. It is certainly more reliable in this sense than letters to the editor or 'vox pops'.[82] Given a mass and often segmented electorate, opinion polling can inform voters and political leaders alike about the electorate's plurality of values, and their spread among different sub-groups (poll results often being broken down by age, gender, and geography).

'Issue' polling may be particularly useful. It asks questions about particular policies or themes, as opposed to asking respondents to rate leaders or to divulge voting intentions. Citizens may adapt their positions on an issue as they become aware of the acceptance of rival positions. Opinion polling might not reveal the justifications for those alternative positions, but it brings those positions to light and measures their relative support. Issues-based opinion polling can also be a means for interest groups to raise awareness of neglected issues, and thereby broaden the deliberative and policy agenda.

b. Misleading information

Polling is part craft, part science.[83] On the one hand, margins of error have come down, either through larger sample sizes or 'polls of polls' (agglomerating data from several comparable polls). Reliability has been enhanced by more sophisticated sampling and weighting, and sub-jurisdictional polling of 'battleground' constituencies. On the other hand, polling remains problematic if understood as a predictive tool or, worse, as a factual guide for voters and a basis for deciding whom to vote for. Polls themselves may be misunderstood or even misleadingly framed. Polling predictions still occasionally miscue badly. They can suffer from insincere responses from those surveyed.[84] A lack of response from key sample populations may skew poll results.[85] There is also a lag between the design, execution, and publication of an opinion poll; and a poll can only capture present inclinations – not the moment of electoral judgment itself.[86] All of these drawbacks are magnified by a widespread and sometimes misplaced public faith in the accuracy of polls.[87]

Even with the best will in the world, pollsters find it hard to provide consistent predictions within a 2.5 to 3 per cent margin of error, both because of the phenomenon of 'rogue' polls (one in 20 samples will fall outside the margin of error, but there is no way of identifying the rogue)[88] and because huge and unaffordable sample sizes are needed to reduce the margin of error. Of course, not all pollsters and their clients have the best will. Politicians, lobbyists, and activist media companies can manipulate poll results to their advantage.[89] Polls can lend themselves to cheating by the surveys' designers, for example through loaded questions designed to tilt results, or even to spread falsehoods by so-called 'push-polling'.

c. Representation

However blunt it may be, issue-based polling in particular is a legitimate influence on policy-making. Admittedly it sometimes crystalises political issues in a binary way without offering alternative options, let alone arguments or solutions to problems.[90] But issue-polling also acts as a routine part of the democratic centrifuge, counter-balancing the elite tendency of representative governments, which are otherwise left subject only to the intermittent accountability provided by elections. If it is conducted scientifically and not tendentiously, polling may act as an inclusive counter-weight to lobby groups who have the ear of politicians and bureaucrats.[91] It can also act as an antidote to media misrepresentation of the zeitgeist. To the optimist, then, polling can act as a conduit whereby collective sentiment is publicly manifested and communicated upwards to elites.

Yet opinion polling also impinges on an old but resilient ideal of democratic deliberation by representatives. As Simone Chambers points out, '[p]oliticians use polls to find the median voter and then tailor their message to that voter. Re-election is the overarching interest when designing the message'.[92] By contrast, in Edmund Burke's classic view (his being among the first modern takes on democratic deliberation), representatives should seek election not to serve as delegates channelling constituent preferences, but principally to marshal their own expertise to deliberate carefully, with considerable latitude, about the broader public interest.[93] A focus on polling surveys can lead politicians astray from a notion that representatives should develop a considered, longer-term view of the general interest that carefully integrates diverse citizen preferences and needs.[94] Of course, Burke's view is hardly the only deliberative conception of democratic representation; however, few would reject his conception entirely.

d. Feedback loops

A particular and well-documented downside of the fixation on what others are thinking is the potential for a feedback loop to form, especially during elections. One such effect is that advocates of positions labelled, thanks to polling, as distinctly of the 'minority' may feel discouraged, thereby ensuring that those views remain in the minority. A second potential distortion can come in the form of a bandwagon effect, or simply a self-reinforcing sense of inevitability of the election result. As with the observer-effect in quantum physics, in electoral politics polls

90 The Law of Deliberative Democracy

(including exit polls released prior to the close of voting) feed back into the very dynamic that generates that politics. As Kurt Lang and Gladys Lang put it, 'polls can influence the public opinion they purport merely to measure'.[95]

The vaunted bandwagon effect involves voters being infected by enthusiasm for a frontrunner party or position. They may naïvely assume that popular positions are necessarily the most rational ones, or simply decide to back a 'winner' because it is psychologically more rewarding than backing a 'loser'.[96] A meta-analysis of research suggests that evidence for an electoral bandwagon is confined to apathetic voters, and may sometimes be balanced by an obverse 'underdog' effect.[97] Whether polls have an undue influence on voting behaviour, and hence electoral outcomes, thus remains an open and disputed question.[98]

To a deliberativist, however, the question of direct effect on voter behaviour and electoral outcomes is somewhat beside the point. The deeper question is the health of public discourse. As Susan Herbst observes:

> Conversation ... is fundamental to the construction of a democratic public sphere. ... In a way, polls may make many political discussions superfluous, since they give the illusion that the public has already spoken in a definitive manner.[99]

Claims that an underdog effect may mute any bandwagon effect are thus not particularly relevant to the cause of better deliberation. Worrying only about the ultimate effect in the ballot box reduces elections to arithmetical outcomes. Deliberation is concerned less with outcomes per se, and more with discussion and reflection involving individuals and the social whole.

It is true that the majority of surveys of voting intention are prefaced with words such as 'if an election were held today...'. In reality, injecting such a contingency into a survey muddies, rather than clarifies, the question of what is being measured. Polls purport to take a present-day pulse. Yet they invite respondents to imagine a counter-factual. This play-acting is rendered all the more complex because respondents may be aware that their responses will feed into a recursive political dynamic. Sincerity in such a situation easily gives way to partisan responses to issues or to inflating complaints in the hope that they gain traction.

e. Strategy and sincerity

Even voters immune to polling's emotional manipulations, such as bandwagon effects, may conclude that to vote rationally requires 'strategic voting'. A strategic voter holds her nose to vote not for her preferred candidate, but for some second-best candidate who seems to have a better chance at winning. Strategic voting is a concern both for opinion polls in the midst of a campaign and for exit polls or the early reporting of election results. The availability of polling information can discourage votes that reflect sincerely held views about the election's substantive issues. Strategic voters may feel they have no choice but to try to aggregate their own votes with others', based on calculations about probable electoral outcomes.

f. Substantive discourse

Gauging voting intention or candidate favourability ratings can encourage substanceless deliberation. Such polling valorises the quantifiable over the qualitative, and is at the mercy of media spin. Polling can generate superficial conclusions and skewed perspectives,[100] and an excess of polling converts election campaigns into horseraces.[101] As Chambers notes, in 'the final weeks of the 2008 American presidential election, the public was inundated with polling data, all of it based on surveys asking some version of the question "who will you vote for on November 4?"'[102] Instead of allowing campaigns to be a period of focused contemplation on party manifestos, polling may generate a win/lose sporting atmosphere.[103]

The risk, from a deliberative perspective, is that a meta-narrative based on polling swamps first order questions of policy or candidate competence. As the Inter-American Commission on Human Rights has recognised, this criticism is 'usually inscribed within a broader trend of mistrust of the relationship between the media and political processes'.[104] At root, this is a concern that the experience of elections as a shared enterprise is transformed in subtle but ontologically significant ways. Like all reductionist forms of measurement, polling tends to shift focus away from intrinsic aspects of policy and towards a focus on quantification and prediction of the outcome of the political contest. In this shift, a complex socio-cultural enterprise is reduced to a number. James Fishkin argues that what an 'ordinary poll offers [is] a representation of public opinion as it is – even if that representation reflects no more than the public's impressions of sound bites and headlines on the issue in question'.[105] Crude polls do not always 'take the public pulse' or make the will of the electorate easier to understand. For the pessimist, then, polling may act as a conduit for unconsidered and sometimes disingenuous 'opinion'.

Polling is also often reported as 'factual' with little incentive for the media, pundits, or pollsters themselves to nuance reporting with explanations about a poll's limitations. Pollsters themselves, no fans of regulation, do not deny that there is a problem to be addressed. An industry survey of some 60 countries with widespread polling found that only 31 per cent of pollsters thought that journalists had a fair or better grasp of polling; in contrast 43 per cent thought that the quality of journalistic treatment of poll data was low or fairly low.[106] As Sally Young relates, news media often fixate on drama, and hence polls are routinely spun by the media to create a sense of change and instability, even if the 'change' is well within the margin of error.[107] The plethora of polls in most western countries generates a one-dimensional meta-narrative. This narrative sublimates politics – understood as a dialogue and argument over policy, vision, and leadership – to a conception of politics as a game. The 'game' metaphor reduces political rivalry either to a relative poll ranking or to a tale about inter-party strategy, and infects political commentary with the psephological concerns of media and social

92 The Law of Deliberative Democracy

scientist insiders. The excessive focus on polling risks campaign discourse being side-tracked into a hall of mirrors, with everyone reflecting on how everyone else is leaning, without deliberating on why.

Taking all the above critiques, including both pros and cons, together, the question becomes: is it irrelevant, from a deliberative perspective, for citizens to be concerned with fluctuations in opinion polling? As we explained in chapter 2, electoral issues are open-ended, so electoral choice is potentially overdetermined. A myriad of factors motivate voters: ranging from ideology, identity, and loyalty to party, through assessments of policy proposals and overall economic and social welfare and security, and on to perceptions of trust and competence. Polling has its pathologies, but it may also assist us, in an other-regarding and hence deliberative sense, to understand the positions and priorities of our fellow citizens. As we have noted, issue-based polling particularly may have deliberative value, assisting politicians and bureaucrats in framing policy, and citizens in considering policy debates, by providing information about shifting public values and adjusting the agenda democratically.

Studies are revealing voter dissatisfaction with the ubiquity of opinion polls during elections and referendums.[108] Many voters are 'switching off' from politics due in part to the increasingly polarised, superficial, and disputatious tenor of public discourse.[109] Some of these people may pay less conscious attention to polls as a result. For yet others, information from polling may prove overwhelming if not addictive, leading to a vicious cycle where graphical and simplistic reporting of polls comes to substitute for more challenging or richer political dialogue.

Judicial responses to polling regulation

In our view, carefully targeted regulations can sometimes reap deliberative benefits without significantly suppressing individual speech interests. For the reasons just discussed, banning issues-based polls would almost certainly do more harm than good from a deliberative perspective. But polling about general voting intentions and leadership – the sort of polling that predominates in electoral seasons – is a reductive and over-used device. Publication of the latter can legitimately be prohibited or embargoed, once the campaign period commences, to help ensure a deliberative focus on substantive electoral issues. Binding requirements for methodological and statistical rigour would also help curb polling's misleading use and reporting. At a minimum, the deliberative benefit of publication of any poll should be strengthened with laws requiring disclosure of key information about the source and methods used in those polls. Yet, in the countries of our study, polling regulations frequently battle uphill when they are subjected to legal scrutiny. Around the world, judicial responses to regulation of opinion polling have been mixed,[110] reflecting the conceptual ambiguities discussed above. But the liberty position has too often been played as a trump in the countries of our study.

Official US considerations of political poll regulations are few, and hostile. The issue was treated by an appellate court in *Daily Herald Co v Munro*, which held that restrictions on media-run exit polls violated the First Amendment.[111] The Ninth Circuit found that the law, which prevented exit polling within 300 feet of a polling place (to deter exit polling altogether), restricted political speech and thus triggered strict scrutiny. The Court found that, 'just as with election-day broadcasts or newspaper editorials that may affect voters' choices', if the state's aim is to protect voters from hearing the results of polling which may influence their voting decisions, this would be an impermissible purpose under the First Amendment.[112]

The Congressional Reports Service later published a report considering the First Amendment issues raised by publication of election day projections of results. It concluded that prohibiting such publication would clearly violate the First Amendment.[113] The analysis was brief and, in the US context, unsurprising: political reporting is speech whose regulation is subject to strict scrutiny and highly likely to fail justification.[114] In the US, then, First Amendment liberties, as judicially developed into a strict form of conceptual balancing, trump even the narrowest of subtractive measures like a restriction on exit polling. However, according to the report, mandating information on polling methodology *might* pass constitutional muster despite it compelling speech in a modest way.[115]

There has been greater judicial engagement with opinion polling and reporting of election results in Canada. In *Thomson Newspapers*, the Supreme Court of Canada struck down a three-day, pre-election blackout on new polls.[116] The appellant media company relied on the protections for expression and the franchise in sections 2(b) and 3 of the Canadian Charter of Rights and Freedoms. The federal government had argued that a short ban on opinion polling insulated voters from potentially inaccurate or deliberately misleading last-minute polls. As is standard, the Court considered the case under section 1, the Charter's balancing clause. A low threshold leaves Canadian courts quick to find speech infringements: a court will ask whether an attempt to 'convey meaning' has been impeded.[117] 'The freedom of expression is clearly infringed by this ban', wrote Justice Bastarache for the majority, with no hint yet that the deliberative benefit of the blackout could have an ameliorative effect on expression.[118]

Crucially, the majority in *Thomson Newspapers* drew contrasts with past cases where laws had sought to repair social conditions that undermined the 'dignity' and 'membership in the community' of a 'specific and identifiable group'.[119] (US readers will notice echoes of 'discrete and insular minorities', which *Carolene Products* singled out.[120]) The Court cited regulations affecting pornography,[121] ads targeted at children,[122] and the unequal influence of political campaign money:[123] laws that purportedly aided discrete and disadvantaged groups such as women, children, and minority voices respectively. In those cases the Court had deferred to legislative choices. But in *Thomson Newspapers* the Court found that polling embargoes pursued a different kind of goal: 'The social science evidence did not establish that the Canadian voter is a vulnerable group relative to pollsters and the media who publish polls'.[124] This vividly reflects conceptual balancing's uneasy fit with deliberation. Systemic, polity-wide legislative efforts are hardly cognisable under the test. Geared to competitive opposites, conceptual balancing addresses

94   The Law of Deliberative Democracy

contests between, for example, dominant versus discrete and disadvantaged societal groups. The Court said that this legislation and its deliberative goals, however, left 'many unanswered questions as to the proper approach to the [section] 1 analysis'.[125] The judgment canvassed deliberative goals at length, but these were too 'vague'.[126]

In comparison with other value foundations in the law and politics, is deliberation too vague? One gets a sense that it is rather too new, in comparison with legal notions of liberty, equality, and integrity. In *Thomson Newspapers*, even the Attorney General sought to characterise the opinion polling regulations as if they had only the narrow purpose of securing political integrity (eg, because misleading polls just prior to election day cannot be scrutinised or debunked in time).[127] That deliberation as a political value still has a hard time gaining notice or respect in the law of politics is richly ironic. Law is very much focused upon deliberation in its own processes. For example, as we saw in chapter 3, common law judges reimagine litigants as reasonable persons to avoid capricious legal claims and defences. Both sides are judged according to what a reasonable person would do in their shoes. Deliberative theory's publicity requirement similarly assumes that citizens communicatively engage with each other in rational and mutually relatable terms.

But, despite parallels between the rationalism of deliberative theory and the rationalism of the common law, the latter remains under-informed by deliberative democracy scholarship. This omission is particularly acute and regrettable in the law of politics. Here the reasonable person test can import unhelpful assumptions about individual *political* behaviour into cases. In *Thomson Newspapers* Bastarache declared:

> I cannot accept, without gravely insulting the Canadian voter, that there is any likelihood that an individual would be so enthralled by a particular poll result as to allow his or her electoral judgment to be ruled by it. ... The presumption in this Court should be that the Canadian voter is a rational actor who can learn from experience and make independent judgments about the value of particular sources of electoral information.[128]

Bastarache relied on an empirically naïve image of the reasonable person, or 'rational actor', to explain his distaste for the deliberative measures. Similar to critiques surveyed in chapter 2, this one rests on hasty thought-experiments and presupposition. Yet data on deliberation (most of which, to be fair, emerged after *Thomson Newspapers*) show nothing quite so simple. Political deliberation is context-specific, turning on myriad social conditions and – relevantly – institutional supports.[129] Most deliberativists express some faith in ordinary citizens' native deliberative capacities, but seek to understand the conditions precedent for better citizen deliberation. Bastarache failed to recognise how the shape of a political forum, including its quality of background information and robust opportunities for citizen expression, affects whether citizens can avail themselves of their underlying deliberative capacities.

He also committed the fallacy of posing the legal issue as if it turned on whether an 'individual' voter would be unduly influenced by a 'particular' poll. This atomises the electorate, implying that the liberty of individual pollsters or reasoning of individual voters is all that matters. Such an approach ignores both the collective aspect of politics and the fact that the legislation was not aimed at any single poll. Rather, it was concerned with the overall influence of *many* polls on the *shared* deliberative space that is an electoral campaign.

Intriguingly, after several years the very same court, and even the same judge, found a way to a markedly different result. In the case of *Bryan*, Bastarache and Justice Fish, each writing for the majority, upheld a law delaying the reporting of election results from Eastern Canada before the polls in Western Canada had closed.[130] To be sure, each of these judgments conceded a violation of the freedom of expression and proceeded, as usual, to the balancing test. Neither judge second-guessed the assumption that expression was infringed, nor issued more than a conclusory sentence or two to explain the nature of the infringement.[131] But notice how limited the subtractive effects of the law were: after just two, two-and-a-half, or three hours (depending on the region), suppressed information could be reported in full. Yet neither majority judgment accepted that such regulation, rather than imposing a limit on expression, might constitute a modest tweak of democratic procedure to avoid certain deliberative pathologies. Interestingly, a dissent by Justice Abella came closest to acknowledging the deliberative pathologies we canvassed at length above, by considering concerns about strategic voting and voter apathy.[132] Yet, entrenched in the conceptual balancing paradigm, all the judgments pitted what they called the law's goal of 'informational equality' against expressive liberty, or focused on the clash between Western voters and the majority of voters in the east of Canada.

Significantly, however, the *Bryan* court upheld the information embargo. In one country of our study, then, a court has embraced a deliberative measure related to the publication of electoral results. *Bryan* rather vividly illustrates some of the strategies judges may use to slip past the borders of conceptual balancing to achieve such an end. We detect four of these strategies:

a. Redefining deliberation

Courts can redefine deliberation as something else, such as equality or integrity, which may better serve as a counter-weight to liberty interests. In *Bryan*, according to the majority judgments, at the balancing stage informational equality outweighed expressive liberty.[133] To Bastarache, '*the mere fact* that one voter could have general access to information about election results that another voter does not have is *in and of itself problematic*' (emphases in original).[134] Hence, he accepted that informational equality is 'a central assumption of electoral democracy'.[135] This is perhaps an overstatement, or a conflation of two genuinely essential electoral values: information and equality. Since information is essential to elections, it may indeed follow that governments should try to make information

96 The Law of Deliberative Democracy

equally accessible. Yet the term 'informational equality' is under-descriptive of the law's deliberative effects – just a single ingredient of the recipe. The term grasps at the wider notion of deliberation, but deliberation denotes far more than simply ensuring adequate or equal levels of information. Still, highlighting the equality element in deliberation provides a comfortable fit with existing Charter values, and lands a court on the legal terra firma of equality reasoning (and the established concept of 'information asymmetry' in the context of economic contracts).[136]

This work-around seems to have helped the deliberative measure to squeak by in *Bryan*'s 5-4 judgment. But a strategy of mischaracterisation is hardly a coherent model generalisable for future use. It retains the basic conceptual balancing structure of weight-versus-counterweight. And it remains implicit, and thus likely to lead to muddled judicial reasoning in future. *Bryan* does little to resolve the conceptual confusion about how to treat deliberation under the *Charter*. Simply redefining deliberation as something else may yield unpredictable and unrepeatable results.[137] And, as a work-around, it may not always work. In *Thomson Newspapers*, the Court considered the risk of rogue/manipulated polls entering the public discourse at the last minute as an integrity matter. But the gravity of the law's infringement of expression was still said to outweigh this possibility.

b. Judicial deference

Courts that defer to legislative choices about how to regulate democracy might of course invalidate fewer deliberative measures. Aileen Kavanagh, in her work on the UK Human Rights Act, concludes that 'deference has a crucial role to play in determinations of whether particular laws or Executive decisions satisfy the doctrine of proportionality, because it sets the intensity and intrusiveness of review which the court will adopt in assessing the importance of the competing values at stake'.[138] In the important context of rights, she says, '[i]t is beyond doubt that automatic or complete deference is no longer appropriate. ... The courts should not adopt an uncritical or supine approach: they have a constitutionally important reviewing role which should not be abdicated'.[139]

Talk of judicial deference is commonplace in relation to proportionality tests,[140] particularly when there are 'concerns about the limits of the courts' expertise, competence and/or legitimacy'.[141] Deference by judges is also common on questions of institutional design of democracy – and not only in the UK. Canada's test for least-restrictive means ('minimal impairment') is sometimes softened so that 'if the law falls within a range of reasonable alternatives, the courts will not find it overbroad merely because they can conceive of an alternative which might better tailor objective to infringement'.[142] In *Bryan*, at the minimal impairment step, Bastarache in particular gave deference to Parliament's electoral design choices. The dissenting opinion by Abella rested partly on her more limited reading of the proper scope of judicial deference:[143] 'harm to the Charter right is demonstrable; the benefits of the ban are not'.[144] But both judges' concepts of deference focused on what to do when conclusive social science evidence in favour of a measure is not available.

The judicial deference approach is not one we prefer for cases on expressive liberty. Conceptual balancing will sometimes help nudge a court away from deference. In *Thomson Newspapers*, as noted, the Court refused to defer to legislative choices because Bastarache saw no discernible disadvantaged social group benefited by the legislation. On the other hand, this effect is unpredictable, even more than is usual for the law of politics. The same social-group analysis could have applied in *Bryan*. And, in *Thomson Newspapers*, the Court failed to defer even though the legislature's choices were premised on the considered findings of the Canadian Government's Lortie Commission on Electoral Reform and Party Financing a few years before,[145] while in *Bryan* the majority made extensive use of the same report.[146] Why the two cases applied different deference standards is ultimately obscure.

More importantly, deference is too blunt to distinguish between deliberative measures and other, more pernicious expressive infringements. Uniform judicial deference could too often allow partisan manipulations of electoral speech to survive unchecked. An implicit rationale for judicial deference about institutional choices is that what is 'best' for political system design is never wholly clear. Courts are also concerned with their own competence here: the limited nature of their ability to render complex social science-based decisions.[147] However, rather than practice more deference on questions apparently beyond their competence, we think that it would be preferable for judges to embrace the kinds of systemic judgment necessary for competent decision-making. The next two options we discuss can be more sensitive to systemic political values in the law of politics.

c. Elastic application

Some judges apply conceptual balancing loosely, claiming to follow its strict forms but departing from them in practice. This is a relatively effective and useful option for preserving deliberative measures. If a judge wishes to take a systemic view of political expression, the *formal* scope for doing so may be limited. But, in *Bryan*, the majority judgments noted that electoral democracy is part of a tightly ordered system. Bastarache abstractly noted the need to view the 'electoral system as a whole'.[148] Fish echoed this need for whole-system vision: the measure was 'part of the elaborate statutory scheme crafted by Parliament in response to the findings and recommendations of the [Lortie] Royal Commission'.[149] En route to arguing that the law should be upheld, both judges still found the freedom of expression in section 2(b) of the Charter to have been violated. Indeed, arguably they had little choice but to so find given the established doctrine about that freedom. Nevertheless, Fish, in particular, stretched the doctrine to bring it closer in practice to a systemic reading. Though he found an infringement, he severely minimised it. The infringement involved 'no suppression of any information at all, but only a brief delay in its communication'.[150] Based partly on this approach, Fish thought that the law should not be struck down.

The best illustration of the flexible model is the dissent in *Thomson Newspapers*. Justice Gonthier would have upheld the polling regulations. Following the usual protocol, the judge found an infringement, and continued on to the balancing test. Yet, in a lengthy preamble, he canvassed deliberative rationales for the 'infringement', including some similar to those we discussed above.[151] Gonthier's understanding of the expressive interests involved in the case clearly ranged system wide. He explained that the 'freedom of expression should not be considered as an end *per se*'[152] – a nice way of expressing the view that expression, understood as deliberation, has no singular means and end. And neither does deliberative expression divide people into those who speak and those who merely listen. It is rather a system of reciprocal elements. The 'promotion of an informed vote over a misinformed vote … serves the core values of the freedom of expression in a free and democratic society'.[153] The measures in the case were not primarily limits upon speech, he wrote; their 'primary objective is positive rather than negative'.[154] Apparently responding to the majority's confusion about how to deal with an additive (ie, 'positive') measure, rather than a subtractive one aimed at countering discrete social disadvantages, Gonthier said that the law 'does not purport to suppress an evil *per se*, such as obscenity … or hate propaganda'; rather it 'aims at balancing and enhancing *Charter* rights, namely … informed participation in the electoral process'.[155]

Hence, the *Thomson Newspapers* dissent and the *Bryan* majorities show how an elastic approach can sustain a deliberative measure, despite the awkward fit between systemic values and current models of proportionality testing. One viable option, then, is to preserve the proportionality test essentially as is, but to encourage judges to apply the test flexibly, with a view to systemic interests.

d. Amending the doctrines

Arguably, however, a problem with such elastic application of doctrine is its disingenuousness. Why concede that freedom of expression has been infringed upfront, only to deny the same later on? An approach more consistent with frank judicial reasoning would question the assumption of violation at the outset, and focus more overtly on a measure's 'positive impact on freedom of expression'.[156] Doctrinal changes, imposed for instance by judges, could expand the judicial field of view to be more consistent with second-order deliberative accommodation. This would be appropriate specifically for proportionality tests in the law of politics. Such changes would make clear that proportionality can embrace systemic political values, thus for example departing from assumptions that deliberative measures uniformly infringe expression.

At least three specific doctrinal changes can assist here. First, the *threshold for infringement* can be redefined. A few of the judgments we have seen question whether the impacts of deliberative measures 'limit' any party's speech, or whether they merely modify the deliberative character of the speech. For example, Gonthier held that polling regulations infringed speech interests, but also concluded that no substantial restriction occurred. A more consistent proportionality doctrine would go a step further by bringing the systemic view to the forefront. The threshold step could permit judges to find that no infringement has occurred if a law can be characterised, especially at a systemic level, as merely additive and ameliorative for expression.

Secondly, systemic accommodation can also occur in later proportionality steps. For instance, *least-restrictive means* reasoning is already accommodative for first-order interests: after recognising a restriction of a liberty and a legitimate government objective, a court assesses whether a different substantive policy would preserve the objective without infringing the liberty quite so severely. But the test as it stands is unsuitable for second-order accommodation. The least-restrictive means standard focuses, by definition, on 'restriction' (or 'impairment'). Hence it presupposes that regulations infringe liberties. But, rather than purport to search for a less 'rights-restrictive' alternative, a court should flexibly seek out a version of the law that best fulfils all the litigating parties' – including the legislature's – requirements for the law. Again, Gonthier came closest to this approach with his focus not on *less restriction* but on finding any '*equally effective* alternative' (emphasis added).[157]

Finally, the most prominent step in a proportionality test is often called, confusingly, 'proportionality'. In practice this step amounts to conceptual balancing. That a law should be read as a 'limit' is often explicit (eg, in references to 'effects of the measures which are responsible for limiting' a right[158]). The term 'proportionality' should, however, be interpreted more expansively to allow for an *accommodative* notion of proportionality that does not presuppose infringement. We suggest that, for analyses of liberties in the law of politics, this final step should be one of 'proportionality and accommodation' to make clear the potential that the values or interests undergoing proportionality analysis may not be in tension.

Truth in political campaigning

Sincerity is an aspect of good deliberation, implied in deliberative criteria such as that communication should be informed and uncoerced. To deliberative democrats, the 'better argument' does not refer to the argument that sways interlocutors by any means, even including trickery. Rational communication is truthful, and at the very least this means that it does not involve the telling of lies.[159] However, much of politics deals with vision rather than facts. Vision involves expressing hopes and values about an uncertain future, rather than expressing content with a truth-value, such as fine-grained policies based on explicit factual assumptions. Political promises, in turn, may be concrete or they may be vague. Political promises therefore occupy a middle ground between vision and claims about facts. As one English judgment in the law of deceit puts it, 'the state of a man's mind is as much a fact as the state of his digestion'.[160] What the judge neglected to add is that the human mind is a little more subjective, and harder to penetrate forensically, than the flora of the gut.

100 The Law of Deliberative Democracy

These caveats aside, much of politics and electioneering *is* susceptible to assessment as to its truth or falsity. In political debates, many claims are made about economic and social indicators, about policy positions, or about what a rival said or did on a particular occasion. Yet with a few exceptions – discussed below – it is unusual to find laws mandating truth in political speech or campaigning. This contrasts starkly with the regulation of commercial speech. That this is so presents us with another example of the over-emphasis, in the law of politics, of a naïve form of liberty interest prevailing over subtler deliberative concerns. We begin here by examining the commercial markets analogy, before turning to truth in political and electoral campaigning and whether and how it might be regulated.

a. The market analogy – consumer protection law

Thanks to consumer protection legislation, speech in trade or commerce is unlawful if it is likely to mislead or deceive. Such statutory rules are policed through individual complaint, through competitor complaint, or via watchdog agencies.[161] While such legislation may be subject to judicial elaboration, it is not the product of judicial balancing tests and so in that sense is unlike the case law we surveyed above. The common law courts, in fact, were only ever able to develop a very limited form of protection for consumers. Courts in earlier centuries managed to erect civil torts involving deceit and negligent misrepresentation. But these only covered actual transactions where individuals relied to their detriment on some misleading pitch directed at them. Everything else in commercial speech fell beneath the radar of the common law judges. It tended to be treated, by classical (libertarian) common law, as puffery governed by the principle of *caveat emptor*, 'let the buyer beware'.[162] Worse, commercial speakers could, especially through clauses in fine print, contract out of judicial attempts to hold them to higher standards.

It took concerted legislative efforts to develop a set of statutory guidelines mandating more ethical behaviour from businesses and corporations. These laws evolved to achieve a set of interrelated aims, weaving together concerns best labelled as relating to liberty, equality, integrity *and* deliberation. The liberty consideration is obvious. Market mechanisms assume a significant level of freedom to promote and sell all lawful products. Without it, new entrants to markets and new goods and services find it difficult to gain traction.

However, free and fair competition, an equality consideration, is not achieved merely by having a level playing field between suppliers. The integrity of the marketplace overall is dependent on *informed* consumer choices. Consumers, like voters, are in a position of relative disadvantage, in this case vis-à-vis corporations.[163] Modern law recognises this power differential by imposing obligations on businesses when they market themselves or their wares (eg, through disclosure obligations). It recognises that consumers deliberate over purchases, relying on promotional statements made by businesses, and as part of that deliberation share opinions, experiences, and information in a discourse with fellow consumers.

This is not to say that deliberating over information about products and services is all consumers do. (Information is only part of a jigsaw puzzle. Brands seek to build images, just as politicians and parties project visions. Those public relations projects are relatively unsusceptible to metrics of accuracy versus deceit.) Rather, it is to ask why misleading speech is legally proscribed in trade and commerce, but not politics. Indeed this disparity raises a paradox: we normally expect higher standards from public life than commercial activity.

Legislation against misleading commercial discussion does not generally extend into the realm of political, religious, or social debate. The point is illustrated in a Federal Court of Australia case involving the former New South Wales Premier, Nick Greiner.[164] Greiner successfully defended a lawsuit which asserted that he had made false electioneering commitments about avoiding school closures. Without a clear legislative basis for doing so, the Court was understandably wary of extending the market-focused notion of falsity to cover political debate.

Such a case would likely turn out differently were a government itself to act in the role of commercial transactor. Governments are usually bound by contract law; and they might, like other contractors, fall foul of laws against misleading comments made in providing paid services, or in labour negotiations with public sector employees. By analogy, it has been held that while the truth value of creation science arguments was not caught by consumer protection law, a false claim in *marketing* a creation science speech, merchandise, or speaker's qualifications could be.[165]

What then distinguishes political speech from commercial speech? We would caution against lazy analogies between the political and commercial realms. Politics, after all, is irreducibly about the construction of a public good. Whatever role the invisible hand of market competition plays, the market is not intrinsically structured as a collective enterprise. Consumers retire to their personal spaces to enjoy their property rights over goods that they purchase. Individual citizens, however, do not 'own' or even 'employ' the politicians they elect or policy proposals they endorse; rather these decisions are made collectively, for collective purposes.

Yet to make these distinctions is to draw attention to the paradox noted earlier. Informed deliberation in politics, being a collective and shared activity, is surely no less important than informed deliberation over consumption. The epistemic concern that politics is too fluid or vague, when compared to producers' claims about the nature of their widgets, is not a good explanation for why misleading market speech should be regulated but not political speech. Corporate entities, as much as politicians and parties, engage in marketing based on woolly themes of 'brand vision and values'. It may be true that political values are shared, in the sense of democratically constructed, in ways that are more open-ended than brand values. But this does not justify a hands-off approach to political 'marketing'. On the contrary, the more that politics is practised via sophisticated marketing techniques, the more we might want to subject it to ethical standards similar to those of corporate speech.

102   The Law of Deliberative Democracy

Why then does the law baulk at extending the principle behind laws governing commercial speech into broader realms of social and political speech? The explanation usually cited is a concern with a chilling effect. The law, while trying to promote accurate and truthful speech, could deter people who engage in such debates from being open or sincere. A preference for abstaining from regulation reflects a faith that misleading speech can best be answered by more speech. The net effect of the absence of a general legal norm against misleading or deceptive political speech is to erect a principle of 'caveat elector' – let the elector beware.

In US First Amendment jurisprudence there is almost a 'constitutional right to lie in campaigns and elections' (to borrow Richard Hasen's phrase).[166] This position is reflected in judicial reasoning. It is not that appellate courts recognise an inherent value in false speech: the US Supreme Court has suggested that 'demonstrable falsehoods are not protected by the First Amendment in the *same manner* as truthful statements'.[167] Indeed, private reputations are protected against unreasonably false assault, through defamation law. But the 'same manner' qualification is crucial.

In *United States v Alvarez*, the Supreme Court struck down Stolen Valor Act provisions that penalised malicious (in the sense of knowingly false) claims to military honours.[168] While the case did not directly implicate electoral speech, Alvarez's false aggrandising of himself as a decorated military hero included claims that he made on a political stage, namely his first meeting as a member of a municipal board. In subjecting the prohibition against 'stolen valor' to exacting constitutional scrutiny, a four-judge majority ran with the claim (derived from the seminal *Sullivan*[169] defamation case) that free debate necessarily involves erroneous debate. It extended this nostrum into a full blown embrace of a 'common understanding that some false statements are inevitable if there is to be an open and vigorous expression of views'.[170]

Two additional judges, applying 'intermediate scrutiny' to the prohibition, also held that the rule against 'stolen valor' claims was unconstitutionally broad. They reasoned against the law precisely *because* it could apply in political contexts, where the judges feared that the risk of censorship, for example by prosecutorial decisions, was too great.[171] Even the three-judge minority, which found there to be no general constitutional principle against prohibiting false speech, rejected such prohibitions in 'matters of public concern' for fear of 'the state [using] its power for political ends'.[172] The closest a US court has come to accepting a power to limit false campaign speech appears to be an Ohio decision permitting candidates to be reprimanded for making knowingly or recklessly false claims. However, the decision rejected the use of penalties or legal injunctions, or any redress for negligently false claims.[173]

As we noted earlier, the origins of the US constitutional system in a rebellion against governmental power has left the system haunted by a variety of spectral apparitions. By all means, judges should criticise a disproportionality in a legal remedy involving speech. But why judge the *principle* underlying the law more harshly where the speech occurs in a political context – that is, before a wider audience where public power relations are at stake – rather than in a purely social context? It is ironic that courts, which insist on laws against perjury to ensure that their own deliberations are not tainted, so peremptorily object to similar laws designed to safeguard popular political and electoral discourse. This is doubly so given that in legislatures, another forum of elite deliberation, there have also long been prohibitions against misleading statements. Sanctions for misleading legislatures, admittedly, are largely left to self-enforcement, through the law of 'parliamentary privilege'.[174] But these sanctions are not toothless. Indeed they have extended to the power not merely to suspend or fine a deliberately misleading legislator or minister, but to expel him or her altogether.[175] Like a good deal of such 'parliamentary law', dealing with the method and manner of debate in legislative chambers, such provisions are designed to create an accommodation of values. Specifically, they accommodate the absolute privilege of freedom of speech, which attaches to the role of legislator,[176] with an obligation to speak respectfully and honestly to improve the deliberative capacity of the chamber as a whole.

b. Self-regulation – the rise of fact-checking

Journalism, for all its foibles, has a significant ability to inform and even guide political discourse. The liberty of the media and its capacity to self-regulate (eg, over alleged unfair investigative techniques or misleading reporting) are perennial topics of controversy.[177] One development has been the rise of 'fact-checking'. This movement, prominent during electoral seasons, has been driven by public-spirited media sites run by a variety of organisations. These include ostensibly dispassionate media outlets, notably the BBC in the UK and ABC in Australia, and the *Tampa Bay Times'* devised, Pulitzer prize-winning PolitiFact. com in the US. There are quasi-academic outlets, such as the cross-national website *The Conversation*. And there are also philanthropically funded institutes, such as FactCheck.org. The proliferation of professional fact-checking seems to fill a desire, among both journalists and citizens alike, for reasonably reliable, independent, and expert assessments of political claims.

Far from fact-checking being an elitist injection into the partisan process, a study commissioned by the American Press Institute showed that at least half the US population was familiar with fact-checking. The same study revealed extraordinarily high levels of trust in fact-checking, with approximately 94 per cent of those familiar with the process having favourable views of it.[178] Exposure to fact-checking, in itself, appeared to increase factual literacy. Partisanship was not, of course, irrelevant to the equation: Republicans were somewhat less enamoured with fact-checking than Democrats. Yet partisanship did not overwhelm trust in fact-checking. Further, while 'motivated reasoning' (see chapter 3) means that partisans are reflexively cynical about statements made by candidates from rival parties, the reverse does not seem to apply. Thus, even partisans appear quite open to fact-checked corrections of inaccuracies perpetrated by their favoured party.[179]

Conversely, citizens have relatively low trust in both politicians and journalists when they are perceived as parts of a closed or 'beltway' caste. These findings, therefore, are encouraging for anyone interested in improving popular deliberation. They suggest that the overlay of a meta-discourse – a discussion about political discussion – need not always descend into a hall of mirrors, with media and political commentators impeaching each other's motivations. It can be genuinely informative. This is not to gloss over fact-checking's imperfections. It can be subject to partiality, and to obsessing over the relatively trivial (of the 'did candidate X make the under-informed or embarrassing statement his opponent alleges?' variety) rather than focusing on the key claims in the key issues of the day. But we ought to recognise the worthwhile aims and only partly tapped potential of fact-checking.

Fact-checking is a product of civil society and a form of self-regulation. What, then, of actual regulatory measures relating to truth in political campaigning? As we shall see, there are in place, in regions within one of the countries in our study at least, laws penalising misleading statements in electioneering. The laws may cover only part of campaign discourse, namely paid election advertising. But they are suggestive of the potential for regulation to accommodate deliberative and expressive values in a framework that integrates liberty of speech with informed debate rather than painting those values as if they were in intractable tension.

c. Regulating truth in political advertising

Often dubbed 'truth in political advertising', the concept that misleading campaign statements should be subject to legal proscription has a history of support in Australia.[180] The national parliament, between 1983–84, briefly legislated an offence against publishing or authorising an electoral advertisement which contained statements that were untrue or likely to mislead or deceive.[181] After the 1984 national election, however, a parliamentary committee on electoral reform recommended its repeal. The committee argued that political advertising was a mix of 'intangibles, ideas, policies and images' and that the law might create defensive publishers and mischievous complaints.[182]

Since that time, minor parties have supported the reintroduction of truth in political advertising laws at national level in Australia.[183] This is unsurprising, as smaller political groups are less likely to have the ear of the media, let alone the resources to counter-advertise, to challenge misleading political statements. Interest in legislation against misleading political advertising has been reinforced because the Australian media no longer engage in robust self-regulation of misleading political advertisements as they once did via bodies like the Press Council and the Federation of Australian Commercial Television Stations.

An alternative approach might be simply to restrict political or electoral advertising altogether. The UK has long had an outright ban on paid broadcast advertising for political purposes. Such a formal prohibition is cleaner than seeking to nuance content (such as the truth value of claims). It encapsulates a fear of the power of broadcast advertising and of its pathologies, as well as a desire to keep campaigning focused on textual and face-to-face communications. The ban is not purely subtractive. There is an additive dimension in that parties are allotted air-time for 'party political broadcasts', slots designed to be positive statements of campaign proposals rather than to be used for attacking rival positions and parties. However, even aside from limiting the size of political campaigns, such restrictions still leave open misleading content in other forms of advertising, such as in print or online. Misleading statements may also be fed through other forms of outreach such as press releases and conferences, and by viral-marketing on social media, whose regulation would be particularly controversial or difficult.

Taking seriously the objections to regulation laid down in *United States v Alvarez*, a key question about 'truth in political advertising law' concerns who administers it. This question has two elements. One is who should have standing (ie, a right to litigate) to complain about misleading claims. Since rival parties or interest groups have a clear stake in the matter, they should have standing. In theory any voter should also be able to object, but procedures are needed to dispose quickly of vexatious complaints. The second, more contentious element concerns who decides when a claim is misleading. Under consumer protection law, independent regulators act as primary guardians of the wider public or consumer interest. However, electoral authorities are loath to become involved in policing political debates, lest they attract accusations of partisanship.

Contrary to libertarian fears, however, experience at the sub-national level in Australia shows that regulation of misleading political advertising *can* function in a deliberatively valuable way that supports, rather than encroaches on, freedom of speech. The experience in South Australia is instructive. That state has had a law against misleading political advertising for many electoral cycles, without chilling robust electoral commentary. At elections, it is an offence to publish or authorise an electoral advertisement containing a purported 'statement of fact' that is 'inaccurate and misleading in a material extent'.[184] Radio and television advertisements are explicitly covered. A related provision in the Northern Territory of Australia applies to 'untrue or incorrect' statements made in the distribution of electoral advertisements, flyers, or 'how-to-vote' material; the Northern Territory law even targets online dissemination.[185]

In *Cameron v Becker*, a court of appeal upheld the South Australian law under Australia's constitutionally implied freedom of political communication. The Court found that the freedom is not absolute: it 'neither involves the right to disseminate false or misleading material nor limits any power' to restrict such material. While this judgment is more sympathetic to deliberative understandings than is the US jurisprudence, it is still couched in a test that purports to 'balance the concept of freedom of speech and the [individual voter's] right to be properly informed'.[186] Such binary, conceptual balancing is, as we have argued, an example of judicial blindness to accommodative reasoning. In limiting the flow of misleading material into the systemic discourse of an election campaign, the law, far from impugning liberty of political expression, may actually reinforce it.

106 The Law of Deliberative Democracy

A more holistic approach was evident in a judgment of the High Court of Australia a century ago, prior to the rise of constitutionalised rights jurisprudence (including proportionality testing) in that country.[187] In upholding a law prohibiting anonymous electoral pamphleteering and advertising, the Court avoided proceeding from some putative liberty of speech. Rather, it cast the requirement that candidates publicly authorise and avow electoral material (an additive rule) as one that could assist electors to deliberate. In doing so, the Court compared the deliberative reasons for and against anonymous speech. On the one hand, attention should focus on 'abstract arguments'; but on the other hand, knowing the source of an argument allows a listener to weigh the speaker's authority, expertise, and motivation. This latter approach, which won the day, is consistent with the general deliberative principle that 'publicity is justified by the notion that speakers should be held accountable for their claims and representations before the audiences potentially affected by them'.[188]

The formal consequences of a breach of the South Australian truth in electoral advertising provision can be three-fold. The simplest consequence is a request by either a political opponent or the South Australian Electoral Commission to retract the advertisement. The Commission can reinforce its power to act by seeking a court order to withdraw and retract an offending advertisement.[189]

The second consequence is a possible prosecution, with a fine of up to A\$5,000 for an individual and A\$25,000 for a corporation. The option of a corporate fine acts as an incentive to publishers to guard against advertisements with obvious misstatements (few political parties are incorporated). Publishers are nonetheless protected by the availability of a legal defence of 'innocent involvement'.[190] An example of a successful prosecution is the case of *Cameron v Becker* itself. In that dispute, a Labor Party television advertisement alleged that the Liberal Party leader had made a statement about the possible closure of small schools. The magistrate found that the only possible basis of the claim was a statement by a Liberal education spokesperson that a few very small schools might face closure. The claim was quintessentially factual but unfounded, and hence at the heart of the mischief addressed by the law, namely political misinformation.

A third consequence is a formal political one. A serious enough breach in a close electoral race may be the basis of a petition to an election court, to unseat a successful candidate, if there is evidence that the misleading advertising was likely to have swayed the result. In *King v Electoral Commissioner*, an independent candidate established that the Liberal Party had engaged in misleading electoral advertising.[191] Its advertisements had claimed, pictorially and in words, that 'A vote for ... an independent candidate (thanks to preferences) ... gives you' a Labor Premier. The advertisements were materially inaccurate for misrepresenting how the state's preferential, or 'instant-runoff', voting system worked. Because it is up to electors to distribute their second preferences as they please, the act of voting for an independent candidate did not benefit either of the major parties. However, on the facts, the petitioner was unable to show that the advertising was likely to have affected the result.

Another significant case involving allegations of misleading advertising was the (failed) petition in *Featherston v Tully*.[192] In that case, an independent MP representing a conservative seat fielded a challenge in court after he decided to support a minority Labor government in a hung parliament. His conservative opponent pointed to advertisements and 'how-to-vote' cards in which the independent had denied that he would ever contemplate supporting a Labor government. The case squarely raised the problem of whether or when a statement about intentions and the future can be false or inaccurate. To hold candidates to such stated intentions might discourage cynicism in the electorate, but at a cost of binding candidates to promises made in a state of uncertainty about the political or economic future. Although the pre-election statements in this case were declamatory, they were held to be not untrue: the candidate was permitted a Damascene conversion after the election. Pre-election promises would be deceitful only if their utterer had no intention, at the time they were made, of pursuing or upholding them.

The absence of truth in political advertising laws in most other common law jurisdictions is probably a stimulus for negative or attack advertising – a particular bugbear for deliberativists. Advertising that is highly critical of opponents is more likely to fall into misstatement, whether through ignorance or malice. Uniquely, during campaigns in the Australian state of Tasmania, no electoral advertisement can mention a candidate by name without his or her written consent.[193] Although this rule was originally designed to limit false or unwanted endorsements, it also limits the scope for attack advertising. Like the truth in political advertising laws in Australia, it too has been upheld as constitutional.[194] In a similar vein, a longstanding UK law makes it an offence to utter false claims about the personal conduct or character of a candidate.[195] In contrast, a Washington State Supreme Court struck down a law prohibiting false allegations against rival candidates.[196]

In describing the legislative options for regulation, our purpose is not to endorse them unequivocally. Instead, our aim is to debunk, using comparisons and examples, the assumption that liberties of speech and deliberative measures are in irresolvable tension. On the contrary, even when it comes to subtractive regulation, the experience of South Australia has been that robust freedom of political expression can accommodate a graded set of sanctions to counter misleading electoral speech.

Free speech doctrine, particularly (but not only) in the US, often implies that 'free' means as unaffected or unconstrained by binding norms as possible. We have sought to challenge this presumption. Electoral politics is not played out in a virgin jungle, but in the shadow of the law of politics. As in the realm of opinion polling discussed earlier, there is a clear bias in the countries of our study towards treating 'free speech' as a trump-card, rather than considering the accommodative potential of tailored regulation and its potential to promote thicker forms of electoral expression. Of course, even ardent deliberativists would not pretend that implementing the injunction 'don't lie' will, on its own, bring about a deliberative nirvana. But it would be a start. And, in this regard, the law could bring benefits not merely in the particular instances of its application, but perhaps over time by

108 The Law of Deliberative Democracy

exerting a salutary effect on the culture of electoral campaigning and discourse. Already achieved in the commercial arena, there is reason to believe that that kind of cultural nudging can be achieved, too, in the electoral one.

Conclusion

This chapter has presented a detailed critique of an assumed dichotomy between political liberty and deliberation. That dichotomy is in large part a product of judicial approaches to conceptual balancing of liberties against the still-emerging language of deliberative democratic values. We argued in chapter 3 that conceptual balancing is popular among judges due to its promise of passably objective judgment in the face of extreme complexity. If we had perfect vision we could dispense with conceptual balancing. Instead of teasing apart the elements of a legislative scheme and forcing them onto a set of scales, we could view the elements as part of an integrated whole. But, having merely human vision, we are left with conceptual balancing and other imperfect instruments by which judges and others simplify reasoning tasks. We have sought here to describe and advocate a more accommodative approach and jurisprudence, which understands liberties of expression not as one-dimensional rights, but as part of a deliberative system of discourse.

Two case studies concretised the discussion. These illustrated the additive and subtractive approaches legal regulation may take. We chose them because they are topical but neglected aspects of the law of politics. If space permitted, we would have delved into a broader conspectus of the many techniques and legal provisions capable of improving the reliability and flow of political information. These range from simple additive measures, such as disclosure of political donations (classically conceived as an integrity measure, but which also brings to light networks of ideological and policy influences),[197] through to more complex additive measures. Examples of the latter include the work done by bodies like the Congressional Budget Office, or through Charters of Budget Honesty, to cost policies and campaign pledges; would legally mandated independent evaluations be deliberatively beneficial, and legally feasible? Another example concerns who should be included in leadership debates, a question that raises difficult deliberative and expressive considerations, as well as recurring litigation.

Similarly, there are a host of subtractive measures that should be considered, also ranging from the relatively simple to the more challenging. An example of a more straightforward measure is a rule limiting campaigning on election day and around polling stations. Such a restriction is susceptible to naïve liberty objections, yet it enacts a deliberative goal of allowing a window of repose before polling. An example with more nuanced regulatory aims is a media code requiring broadcasters to exercise 'balance'. None of these measures alone would ensure good deliberation. Yet, just as no single vote makes much difference but together many do, collectively a variety of incremental measures may do much to improve deliberation.

Notes

1 'The Common Law in the United States' (1936) 50 *Harvard Law Review* 4, 10.
2 Distinctions among 'liberties', 'rights', and 'freedoms' generally are not relevant to our discussions below; for simplicity we usually elide these as 'liberties'.
3 T Alexander Aleinikoff, 'Constitutional Law in the Age of Balancing' (1987) 96 *Yale Law Journal* 943, 946.
4 See, eg, Joseph Schumpeter, *Capitalism, Socialism, and Democracy* (Harper, 3rd ed, 1950) ch 22; James Gardner, *What are Campaigns For? The Role of Persuasion in Electoral Law and Politics* (Oxford University Press, 2009) 155–7.
5 John Stuart Mill, *Considerations on Representative Government* (Parker, Son, and Bourn, 1861) ch XV. See also, eg, James Madison, 'The Federalist No. 63' in Isaac Kramnick (ed), *The Federalist Papers* (Penguin, 1987) 371.
6 At least two Australian judgments on free speech have even expressly held that maintaining civility in democratic discourse is not a legitimate legislative goal compatible with the country's system of government: *Coleman v Power* (2004) 220 CLR 1, 122; *Monis v The Queen* (2013) 249 CLR 92, 134.
7 *R v Bryan* [2007] 1 SCR 527, [12]–[14], [20]–[23].
8 Proportionality: see *R (Daly) v Secretary of State for the Home Department* [2001] 2 AC 532. Reasonably appropriate and adapted: see *Roach v Electoral Commissioner* (2007) 233 CLR 162. Demonstrably justified: see *Sauvé v Canada (Chief Electoral Officer)* [2002] 3 SCR 519. Balancing: see *Wisconsin v Yoder*, 406 US 205, 214, 237 (1972). In the United States, courts will apply strict scrutiny to government measures falling into certain categories, such as those affecting a 'suspect classification'. Where strict scrutiny is applied, the measure will only be upheld if it furthers a compelling government interest, and is narrowly tailored to further that interest: see, among numerous examples, *Grutter v Bolinger*, 539 US 306 (2003). For discussion of US proportionality see, eg, Frederick Schauer, 'Proportionality and the Question of Weight' in Grant Huscroft, Bradley W Miller and Gregoire Webber (eds), *Proportionality and the Rule of Law* (Cambridge University Press, 2014) 173, 181.
9 But we are hardly the first: see, eg, Thomas Emerson, *The System of Freedom of Expression* (Harvard University Press, 1970).
10 Jürgen Habermas, *The Theory of Communicative Action* (Thomas McCarthy trans, Beacon Press, 1984, first published 1981) vol 1: 'Reason and the Rationalization of Society'.
11 John Parkinson, *Deliberating in the Real World: Problems of Legitimacy in Deliberative Democracy* (Oxford University Press, 2006) 3.
12 *Abrams v United States*, 250 US 616, 630 (1919).
13 Parkinson, above n 11, 3.
14 Ibid 99.
15 Amy Gutmann and Dennis F Thompson, *Democracy and Disagreement* (Harvard Belknap Press, 1996) 52–94.
16 Robert Goodin, *Motivating Political Morality* (Blackwell, 1992) 132–3.
17 Jon Elster, 'Deliberation and Constitution-Making' in Jon Elster (ed), *Deliberative Democracy* (Cambridge University Press, 1998) 97–122. However, this 'does not eliminate base motives, but forces and induces speakers to hide them': at 111. See also Cass Sunstein, *Democracy and the Problem of Free Speech* (The Free Press, 1993) 244.
18 John Rawls, *Political Liberalism* (Columbia University Press, Expanded Edition, 2005) 137. See also Gutmann and Thompson, above n 15, 4; Parkinson, above n 11, 99.
19 Even in variations of the theory that do not require inter-personal communication, but instead accept that individual contemplation about other people's interests can make others 'imaginatively present', others are still present in a virtual sense. See,

eg, Robert Goodin, 'Democratic Deliberation Within' (2009) 29 *Philosophy and Public Affairs* 81, 99.

20 Parkinson, above n 11, 40, 151.

21 Jane Mansbridge et al, 'A Systemic Approach to Deliberative Democracy', in John Parkinson and Jane Mansbridge (eds), *Deliberative Systems* (Cambridge University Press, 2012) 1, 2.

22 Ibid 2–4.

23 Ibid 22–24.

24 John Dryzek, *Discursive Democracy* (Cambridge University Press, 1990).

25 Parkinson, above n 11, 6. See also Amy Gutmann and Dennis F Thompson, *Why Deliberative Democracy?* (Princeton University Press, 2009) 6; Caroline Hendriks, 'Integrated Deliberation: Reconciling Civil Society's Dual Role in Deliberative Democracy' (2006) 54 *Political Studies* 486.

26 *Australian Capital Television Pty Limited v Commonwealth* (1992) 177 CLR 106.

27 Ibid [50].

28 David Dyzenhaus, 'Proportionality and Deference in a Culture of Justification' in Grant Huscroft, Bradley W Miller and Gregoire Webber (eds), *Proportionality and the Rule of Law* (Cambridge University Press, 2014).

29 TRS Allan, 'Democracy, Legality and Proportionality' in Grant Huscroft, Bradley W Miller and Gregoire Webber (eds), *Proportionality and the Rule of Law* (Cambridge University Press, 2014) 205, 220.

30 Alexander Meiklejohn, *Political Freedom: The Constitutional Powers of the People* (Oxford University Press, 1965) 75.

31 Ibid. On self-realisation as a rationale for free speech see, eg, Frederick Schauer, *Free Speech: A Philosophical Enquiry* (Cambridge University Press, 1982) 49; Martha Nussbaum, 'Capabilities as Fundamental Entitlements: Sen and Social Justice' (2003) 9 *Feminist Economics* 33, 41–2.

32 Meiklejohn, above n 30, 26, 75.

33 Owen Fiss, 'Why the State?' (1987) 100 *Harvard Law Review* 781, 785; Cass Sunstein, 'Preferences and Politics' (1991) 20 *Philosophy and Public Affairs* 3.

34 Lawrence Byard Solum, 'Freedom of Communicative Action: A Theory of the First Amendment Freedom of Speech' (1988) 83 *Northwestern University Law Review* 54, 56, 108–18.

35 Katharine Gelber, 'Freedom of Political Speech, Hate Speech and the Argument from Democracy: The Transformative Contribution of Capabilities Theory' (2010) 9 *Contemporary Political Theory* 304, 312, quoting Jürgen Habermas, *Moral Consciousness and Communicative Action* (MIT Press, 1990) 199–200.

36 Christian F Rostbøll, 'Freedom of Expression, Deliberation, Autonomy and Respect' (2011) 10 *European Journal of Political Theory* 5, 6. See also Solum, above n 34, 118.

37 Jane Mansbridge et al, 'The Place of Self-Interest and the Role of Power in Deliberative Democracy' (2010) 18 *Journal of Political Philosophy* 64.

38 Joshua Cohen, 'Deliberation and Democratic Legitimacy' in James Bohman and William Rheg (eds), *Deliberative Democracy: Essays on Reason and Politics* (MIT Press, 1997) 67, 83–4 (emphasis in original).

39 Gelber, above n 35, 312.

40 Aleinikoff, above n 3, 981.

41 Ibid.

42 Schauer and Nussbaum, above n 31.

43 Mansbridge et al, above n 21, 21.

44 Aleinikoff, above n 3, 972–6 (on problems of balancing incommensurables).

45 For instance, how much weight should a court give to the liberty of an individual who purports to seek private self-fulfilment, but chooses to do so in a public way – with

public consequences? Does the inherently social nature of expression make individualistic rationales for free speech less convincing?

46 *Contra:* John O McGinnis, 'Against the Scribes: Campaign Finance Reform Revisited' (2000–2001) 24 *Harvard Journal of Law & Public Policy* 25, 28 (arguing that such schemes are discriminatory between speakers of different classes).

47 In chapter 5 we describe the Court's further concerns about unequal distribution of airtime among political parties. We think that this is a more serious concern, but still misplaced.

48 See, eg, *FCC v League of Women Voters*, 468 US 364, 380–81 (1984); *Turner Broadcasting System Inc v FCC*, 512 US 622, 637–88 (1994).

49 418 US 241 (1974); cf *Red Lion Broadcasting Co v FCC*, 395 US 367 (1969) (accepting a right of reply on broadcast networks).

50 S 742, 100th Congress (1987).

51 47 USC §§ 151–622 (current).

52 Ronald Reagan, *Message to the Senate Returning Without Approval the Fairness in Broadcasting Bill* (19 June 1987) Ronald Reagan Presidential Library and Museum <www.reagan. utexas.edu/archives/speeches/1987/061987h.htm> accessed 23 February 2016

53 Sunstein, above n 17, xvi; see also at 130, 242. Sunstein, on the other hand, does not believe that 'the existence of an unjust status quo should be a reason to allow content or viewpoint based regulation of speech' because there is a risk that such decisions about the power of various groups and who is owed redistribution are going to be biased or unreliable: ibid, 179.

54 See, eg, James Madison, 'The Federalist No. 47' in Isaac Kramnick (ed), *The Federalist Papers* (Penguin Books, 1987) 303. On anti-tyranny's continuing influence in constitutional law see, eg, *Olmstead v United States*, 277 US 348 (1928); *INS v Chadha*, 462 US 919 (1983); *New York v United States*, 505 US 144 (1992); *Wyeth v Levine*, 555 US 555 (2009).

55 Ron Levy, 'Regulating Impartiality: Electoral Boundary Politics in the Administrative Arena' (2008) 53 *McGill Law Journal* 1, 16.

56 Robert Post, 'Managing Deliberation: The Quandary of Democratic Dialogue' (1993) 103 *Ethics* 654, 661.

57 Owen Fiss, 'Free Speech and Social Structure' (1985) 71 *Iowa Law Review* 1405, 1410–12.

58 Ibid 1415.

59 Solum, above n 34, 127–9. See also Sunstein, above n 17, 18.

60 Sunstein, above n 17, 31.

61 *British Columbia (Public Service Employee Relations Commission) v British Columbia Government and Service Employees' Union* [1999] 3 SCR 3.

62 *R v Oakes* [1986] 1 SCR 103.

63 Janina Boughey, 'The Reasonableness of Proportionality in the Australian Administrative Law Context' (2015) 43 *Federal Law Review* 59, 72; Schauer, above n 8, 181–3.

64 Boughey, above n 63; Kai Möller, 'Proportionality and Rights Inflation' in Grant Huscroft, Bradley W Miller and Gregoire Webber (eds), *Proportionality and the Rule of Law* (Cambridge University Press, 2014) 155–6.

65 We expand on ideas in this section in Graeme Orr and Ron Levy, 'Regulating Opinion Polling: A Deliberative Democratic Perspective' (2016) 39 *UNSW Law Journal* 381.

66 See SJA Ward, *Ethics and the Media* (Cambridge University Press, 2011), 108–109.

67 Jürgen Habermas, 'Constitutional Democracy: A Paradoxical Union of Contradictory Principles?' (2001) 29 *Political Theory* 766, 772; Simone Chambers, 'Deliberative Democracy Theory' (2003) 6 *Annual Review of Political Science* 307, 308–309.

68 Ron Levy, 'Deliberative Voting: Realising Constitutional Referendum Democracy' (2013) *Public Law* 555 (focusing on the referendum context).

69 ACE Electoral Knowledge Network, *Blackout Period for Release of Opinion Poll Results* (26 November 2014) <https://aceproject.org/epic-fr/CDMap?question=ME062&questions=all&set_language=en> accessed 23 February 2016.

70 See Tim Bale, 'Restricting the Broadcast and Publication of Pre-Election and Exit Polls: Some Selected Examples' (2002) 39 *Representation* 15.

71 Canada Elections Act, SC 2000, c 9, s 328.

72 Electoral Act 1993 (NZ), s 197(1). See also Andrew Geddis, *Electoral Law in New Zealand* (LexisNexis, 2007) 184.

73 *Thomson Newspapers v Canada (Attorney General)* [1998] 1 SCR 877 (*'Thomson Newspapers'*); *R v Bryan* [2007] 1 SCR 527 (*'Bryan'*).

74 Thomas Petersen, 'Regulation of Opinion Polls: A Comparative Perspective' in Christina Holtz-Bacha and Jesper Strömbäck (eds), *Opinion Polls and the Media: Reflecting and Shaping Public Opinion* (Palgrave-Macmillan, 2012) 47, 57–8, updating Frits Spangenberg, *The Freedom to Publish Opinion Poll Results: Report on a Worldwide Update* (Foundation for Information, 2003). Similarly see Robert Chung, 'The Freedom to Publish Opinion Poll Results: A Worldwide Update of 2012' (The University of Hong Kong, December 2012) <http://hkupop.hku.hk/english/report/freedom/FTP_2012.pdf> accessed 19 February 2016, reporting 46 per cent of 83 countries having some form of embargo on election period publication.

75 See Article 19 Global Campaign for Free Expression, *Comparative Study of Laws and Regulations Restricting the Publication of Election Opinion Polls* (2003) <www.article19.org/data/files/pdfs/publications/opinion-polls-paper.pdf> accessed 19 February 2016. A pair of industry group surveys identified 30 democracies with polling embargoes (out of 66 and 78 countries surveyed, respectively): Wolfgang Donsbach and Uwe Hartung, 'The Legal Status of Public Opinion Research in the World' in Wolfgang Donsbach and Michael Traugott (eds), *The SAGE Handbook of Public Opinion Research in the World* (SAGE, 2008) 431, 437–8; Wolfgang Donsbach, 'Who's Afraid of Opinion Polls?: Normative and Empirical Arguments for the Freedom of Pre-Election Surveys' (European Society for Opinion and Marketing Research, 2001) <http://wapor.org/pdf/who-is-afraid-of-opinion-polls.pdf> accessed 19 February 2016, 7.

76 The longest embargo currently in force appears to be Luxembourg, with a one-month blackout. Of major democracies, several such as France, Italy, South Korea, Taiwan, and Switzerland have had substantial embargoes extending longer than the final week of the campaign period. Many South American countries embrace embargoes: Argentina's lasts over a week, Bolivia's a week, and Mexico's four days: Donsbach and Hartung, above n 75, 438.

77 World Association for Public Opinion Research, *ESOMAR/WAPOR Guideline on Opinion Polls and Published Surveys* (ESOMAR/WAPOR, 2014) <http://wapor.org/esomarwapor-guide-to-opinion-polls/> accessed 19 February 2016.

78 Council of Europe, Committee of Ministers, 'Measures Concerning Media Coverage of Election Campaigns', Recommendation No R 99 (15) (9 September 1999).

79 Canada Elections Act, SC 2000, c 9, ss 326–7.

80 Organization of American States, *Annual Report of the Inter-American Commission on Human Rights 2005: Report of the Special Rapporteur for Freedom of Expression* (Inter-American Commission on Human Rights OEA/Ser L/V/II122, Washington DC, 27 February 2008) vol III, ch VI, 155.

81 Petersen, above n 74, 65.

82 Donsbach and Hartung, above n 75, 436. 'Vox pops' are 'person on the street interviews', or other anecdotal samples of opinion.

83 Amy J Berinsky, 'American Public Opinion in the 1930s and 1940s: The Analysis of

Quota-Controlled Sample Survey Data' (2006) 40 *Public Opinion Quarterly* 499; Amy Fried, *A Crisis in Public Opinion Polling* (Routledge, 2011).

84 Leo P Crespi, 'The Cheater Problem in Polling' (1945) 9 *Public Opinion Quarterly* 431.

85 Ibid.

86 Charles K Atkin and James Gaudino, 'The Impact of Polling and the Mass Media' (1984) 472 *Annals of the American Academy of Political and Social Science* 119.

87 Dennis F Thompson, *Just Elections* (University of Chicago Press, 2002) 100.

88 Charles E Parker, 'Polling Problems in State Primary Elections' (1948) 12 *Public Opinion Quarterly* 728.

89 Human Rights Council, 'Report of the Special Rapporteur on the promotion and protection of the right to freedom of opinion and expression, Frank La Rue' (2014) UN Doc A/HRC/26/30 (30 May 2014) [72].

90 Drew E Altman and Brodie Mollyann, 'Opinion on Public Opinion Polling' (2003) *Health Affairs* W276; Angus Campbell, 'Polling, Open Interviewing, and The Problem of Interpretation' (1946) 2(4) *Journal of Social Issues* 67.

91 Frank Teer and James D Spence, *Political Opinion Polls* (Hutchinson, 1973) 10–11.

92 Chambers, above n 67, 338.

93 Edmund Burke, 'Speech to the Electors of Bristol, November 3, 1774', in *Select Works of Edmund Burke* (A New Imprint of the Payne Edition, Liberty Fund, 1999) vol IV, 3.

94 Rick Henderson, 'Polling Error' (1993) 25(1) *Reason* 11.

95 Kurt Lang and Gladys E Lang, 'The Impact of Polls on Public Opinion' (1984) 472 *Annals of the American Academy of Political and Social Science* 129.

96 Sibylle Hardmeier, 'The Effects of Published Polls on Citizens' in W Donsbach and M Traugott (eds), *The SAGE Handbook of Public Opinion Research in the World* (SAGE, 2008) 504, 508–509.

97 Lang and Lang, above n 95, 506–507.

98 Eg, Guy Lachapelle, *Polls and the Media in Canadian Elections: Taking the Pulse* (Research Studies for the Royal Commission on Electoral Reform and Party Financing, vol 16, Dundurn Press, 1991). See also Donsbach, above n 75, 22–31.

99 Susan Herbst, *Numbered Voices: How Opinion Polling has Shaped American Politics* (University of Chicago Press, 1993) 166. See also Colin Feasby, 'Public Opinion Poll Restrictions, Elections and the *Charter*' (1997) 55 *University of Toronto Faculty of Law Review* 241.

100 Robert Weissberg, 'The Problem with Polling' (2002) 148 *Public Interest* 37; Elias Walsh, Sarah Dolfin and John DiNardo, 'Lies, Damn Lies, and Pre-Election Polling' (2009) 99 *American Economic Review* 316.

101 Thomas Fitzgerald, 'Public Opinion Sampling' (2002) 39(6) *Society* 53.

102 Simone Chambers, 'Rhetoric and the Public Sphere: Has Deliberative Democracy Abandoned Mass Democracy?' (2009) 37 *Political Theory* 323, 343.

103 Atkin and Gaudino, above n 86, 124.

104 Organization of American States, above n 80.

105 James S Fishkin, 'Consulting the Public Through Deliberative Polling' (2002) 22 *Journal of Policy Analysis and Management* 128.

106 Chung, above n 74, 20.

107 Sally Young, 'Media Reporting on the Next Federal Election: What Can We Expect?' (Papers on Parliament No 58, Australian Senate, 2012) 78.

108 Eg, Robert Anderson, 'Reporting Public Opinion Polls: The Media and the 1997 Canadian Election' (2000) 12 *International Journal of Public Opinion Research* 285; CH de Vreese and HA Semetko, 'Public Perception of Polls and Support for Restrictions on the Publication of Polls: Denmark's 2000 Euro Referendum' (2002) 14 *International Journal of Public Opinion Research* 410.

109 Andrew Russell, 'The Truth about Youth? Media Portrayals of Young People and Politics in Britain' (2004) 4 *Journal of Public Affairs* 347.

110 Striking laws down: *Social Weather Stations Inc v Commission on Elections*, Philippines Supreme Court, GR No 147571 (5 May 2001); Cour de cassation [French Court of Cassation], 00-85329, 4 September 2001 reported in (2001), Bull crim No 170, 562, involving the *Le Parisien* newspaper; Constitutional Court of Colombia, Decision C-488/1993 (28 October 1993). Upholding laws: Supreme Court of Justice of Paraguay, Constitutional Chamber, Decision 99 of 1998 (5 May 1998), involving Teledifusora Paraguay; A682.XXXVI (7 June 2005) brought by the Asociación de Teleradiodifusoras Argentina and Asociación de Radiodifusoras Privadas Argentina; Constitutional Court of Colombia, Decision C-089/1994 (3 March 1994); *Kim Jong-Cheol v Republic of Korea*, Human Rights Committee, UN Doc CCPR/C/84/D/968/2001 (23 August 2005).

111 *Daily Herald Co v Munro*, 838 F 2d 380 (9th Cir Wash 1988).

112 Ibid 387 (citing *Mills v Alabama*, 384 US 214, 218–20 (1966), which held 'that no test of reasonableness can save a state law from invalidation as a violation of the First Amendment when that law makes it a crime for a newspaper editor to do no more than urge people to vote one way or another in a publicly held election'); *Vanasco v Schwartz*, 401 F Supp 87, 100 (ED NY, 1975): 'When the State through the guise of protecting the citizen's right to a fair and honest election tampers with what it will permit the citizen to see and hear even that important state interest must give way to the irresistible force of protected expression under the First Amendment', affirmed by memorandum, *Schwartz v Vanasco*, 423 US 1041 (1976).

113 Henry Cohen, *Election Projections: First Amendment Issues* (CRS Report for Congress, 2001).

114 Ibid 2. See *Sable Communications of California Inc v Federal Communications Commission*, 492 US 115, 126 (1989).

115 Cohen, above n 113.

116 *Thomson Newspapers*, above n 73. The case and issues involved were prophesied in H Kushner, 'Election Polls, Freedom of Speech and the Constitution' (1983) 15 *Ottawa Law Review* 515.

117 *Libman v Quebec (Attorney General)* [1997] 3 SCR 569, [31].

118 *Thomson Newspapers*, above n 73, [85] (Bastarache J).

119 Ibid [92].

120 *United States v Carolene Products Co*, 304 US 144, 152, fn 4 (1938). For analysis of similarities see Vanessa A MacDonnell, 'The Constitution as Framework for Governance' (2013) 63 *University of Toronto Law Journal* 624, 636.

121 *R v Butler* [1992] 1 SCR 452.

122 *Irwin Toy Ltd v Quebec (Attorney General)* [1989] 1 SCR 927.

123 *Libman v Quebec (Attorney General)* [1997] 3 SCR 569.

124 Ibid [112], [114].

125 Ibid [100], [96].

126 Ibid.

127 *Thomson Newspapers*, above n 73, 902, 888.

128 Ibid [101], [112]. See similarly Nicholas Devlin, 'Opinion Polls and the Protection of Political Speech – A Comment on *Thomson Newspapers Co v Canada*' (1997) 28 *Ottawa Law Review* 411, 430.

129 See chapter 2.

130 Canada Elections Act, SC 2000, c 9, s 329.

131 *Bryan*, above n 73, [26] (Bastarache J), [58] (Fish J), [96]–[97] (Abella J, dissenting).

132 Ibid [92], [111]–[117] (Abella J).

133 Ibid [14] (Bastarache J), [73] (Fish J).

134 Ibid [12]–[14], [35] (Bastarache J, joining majority).

135 Ibid.

136 Ronen Avraham and Liu Zhiyong, 'Incomplete Contracts with Asymmetric Information: Exclusive Versus Optional Remedies' (2006) 8 *American Law and Economics Review* 523.

137 Note that despite some judicial shaving of the period of repose, Canada still embargoes publication of new polls on election day (just as it still bans most election advertising on election day): Canada Elections Act, SC 2000, c 9, ss 323–4. A paradox however arises in that relatively short embargoes on electoral opinion polling – of the kind most common today, covering just the last few days of the campaign period – are harder to justify on deliberative grounds than an embargo lasting the whole of that campaign. Short bans form a brief period of repose prior to polling day in which undecided voters focus on whether and how to vote. Deliberative concerns with electoral opinion polling extend beyond such limited horizons.

138 Aileen Kavanagh, *Constitutional Review under the UK Human Rights Act* (Cambridge University Press, 2009) 254.

139 Ibid.

140 On deference to legislatures in least-restrictive means testing, see Allan, above n 29, 217. See also more generally Dyzenhaus, above n 28.

141 Kavanagh, above n 138, 177, 233–69.

142 *RJR-MacDonald Inc v Canada (Attorney General)* [1995] 3 SCR 199, [160].

143 *Bryan*, above n 73, [100]–[103] (Abella J).

144 Ibid [131].

145 *Thomson Newspapers*, above n 73, [108], citing Royal Commission on Electoral Reform and Party Financing, *Reforming Electoral Democracy* (Canadian Government, June 1991) vol 1 (*'Lortie Commission Final Report'*).

146 *Bryan*, above n 73 (eg, [4], [18], [25], [36], [41], [45]–[60], [63]).

147 *Thomson Newspapers*, above n 73, [104]–[107].

148 *Bryan*, above n 73, [50].

149 Ibid [63] (Fish J), citing *Lortie Commission Final Report*, above n 145. See also at [59].

150 Ibid [80]–[81] (Fish J).

151 *Thomson Newspapers*, above n 73, [2]–[18] (Gonthier J).

152 Ibid [25].

153 Ibid.

154 Ibid [29].

155 Ibid.

156 Ibid [61] (Gonthier J, dissenting).

157 Ibid [47] (Gonthier J, dissenting).

158 *R v Oakes* [1986] 1 SCR 103, [70].

159 Habermas, above n 10, 94–5.

160 *Edgington v Fitzmaurice* (1885) 29 Ch D 459.

161 See, eg, Australian Consumer Law (aka Competition and Consumer Act 2011 (Australia)), Sch 2; Trade Descriptions Act 1968 (UK); Federal Trade Commission Act, 15 USC §§ 41–58 and Uniform Deceptive Trade Practices Act of 1966 (US); Competition Act, RSC 1985, c C-34 (Canada).

162 Geraint Howells and Stephen Weatherill, *Consumer Protection Law* (Ashgate, 2nd ed, 2005) 14–16.

163 Ross Cranston, *Consumers and the Law* (Weidenfeld and Nicholson, 1978) 21–6.

164 *Durant v Greiner* (1990) 21 NSWLR 119.

165 *Plimer v Roberts* (1997) 150 ALR 235: *Global Sportsman Pty Ltd v Mirror Newspapers Ltd* (1984) 55 ALR 25. But 'information providers' are now exempt as to non-advertising content: Australian Consumer Law, s 19.

166 Richard L Hasen, 'A Constitutional Right to Lie in Campaigns and Elections' (2013) 74 *Montana Law Review* 53.

167 *Brown v Hartlage*, 456 US 45 (1982).

168 *United States v Alvarez*, 132 SCt 2537 (2012).

169 *New York Times Co v Sullivan*, 376 US 254 (1964).

170 *United States v Alvarez*, above n 168, 2544.

171 Ibid 2556 (Breyer J).

172 Ibid 2563 (Alito J).

173 *Pestrak v Ohio Elections Commission*, 926 F 2d 573 (6th Circuit, 1991).

174 Enid Campbell, *Parliamentary Privilege* (Federation Press, 2003) ch 5. Exceptionally, there may be criminal penalties for misleading legislative committees: eg, Criminal Code (Queensland), s 57.

175 The power to expel has been neutered in some parliaments: eg, Parliamentary Privileges Act 1987 (Australia), s 8.

176 Traceable to the Bill of Rights 1688 (Eng), art 9.

177 Lord Justice Leveson, *An Inquiry into the Culture, Practices and Ethics of the Press* (4 vols, The Stationery Office, November 2012); Ray Finkelstein QC, *Report of the Independent Inquiry into the Media and Media Regulation* (Australian Government, 28 February 2012). The fate of these reports and their recommendations for regulation (eg, to enable better recourse to rein in abuse of media power) replayed the debate between libertarians and those who stress the media's public obligations: see Post versus Fiss and Solum, text above nn 52–7.

178 Brendan Nyhan and Jason Reifler, 'Estimating Fact-checking's Effects: Evidence from a Long-Term Experiment during Campaign 2014' (American Press Institute, 28 April 2015) <www.americanpressinstitute.org/wp-content/uploads/2015/04/Estimating-Fact-Checkings-Effect.pdf> accessed 23 February 2016.

179 Michelle A Amazeen et al, 'A Comparison of Correction Formats: the Effectiveness and Effects of Rating Scale versus Contextual Corrections on Misinformation' (American Press Institute, February 2015) <www.americanpressinstitute.org/wp-content/uploads/2015/04/The-Effectiveness-of-Rating-Scales.pdf> accessed 19 February 2015.

180 For an account of the debate see George Williams, *Truth in Political Advertising Legislation in Australia* (Australian Parliamentary Library, Research Paper No 13 of 1996–97); George Williams and Natalie Gray, 'A New Chapter in the Regulation of Truth in Political Advertising in Australia' (1997) 8 *Public Law Review* 110; Queensland Parliament, Legal, Constitutional and Administrative Review Committee, *Report on Truth in Political Advertising* (December 1996).

181 Commonwealth Electoral Legislation Amendment Act 1983 (Cth).

182 Senate Joint Select Committee on Electoral Reform, Parliament of Australia, *Second Report* (1984), [2.79–80] and [2.77]. For political context see Colin A Hughes, 'The Rules of the Game' in Clive Bean, Ian McAllister and John Warhurst (eds), *The Greening of Australian Politics: The 1990 Federal Election* (Longman Cheshire, 1990) 147–51.

183 Electoral Amendment (Political Honesty) Bill 2003 (Australian Democrats) and Joint Standing Committee on Electoral Matters, *Report on the Conduct of the 2007 Federal Election and Matters Relating Thereto* (Parliament of Australia, 2009).

184 Electoral Act 1985 (South Australia), s 113.

185 Electoral Act 2004 (Northern Territory), ss 268, 271(2).

186 *Cameron v Becker* (1995) 64 SASR 238, 243, 247–8, 253–8.

187 *Smith v Oldham* (1912) 15 CLR 355, 358.

188 Mark E Warren, 'Institutionalizing Deliberative Democracy' in Shawn W Rosenberg, *Deliberation, Participation and Democracy: Can the People Govern?* (Palgrave Macmillan, 2007) 272, 281, invoking Habermas, Gutman and Thompson, and Bohman.

189 Electoral Act 1985 (South Australia), s 113(4), (5).

190 Under ibid s 113(3), it is a defence to have no part in the content of the advertisement and no reason to have known of the inaccuracy. There is also the general criminal law defence of honest and reasonable mistake: *Cameron v Becker* (1995) 64 SASR 238, 246–7, 251.

191 *King v Electoral Commissioner* (1998) 78 SASR 172.

192 *Featherston v Tully* (2002) 83 SASR 302 and especially *Featherston v Tully (No 2)* (2002) 83 SASR 347.

193 Electoral Act 2004 (Tasmania), s 196. Compare Commonwealth Electoral Act 1918 (Australia), s 351; Electoral Act 1992 (Australian Capital Territory), s 301.

194 *Taylor v McLean* (Unreported, Court of Petty Sessions, Launceston, Schott CM, 9 June 2004).

195 Representation of the People Act 1983 (UK), s 106(1).

196 *Rickert v Washington Public Disclosure Commission* 168 P 3d 826 (2007).

197 See discussion in the South African Constitutional Court as to whether freedom of information demands disclosure of political donation: *My Vote Counts NPC v Speaker of the National Assembly* [2015] ZACC 31.

Chapter 5

Equality v Deliberation (The Equality Problem)

To the extent that political struggle takes place on the basis of deliberation rather than of power, it is more evenly matched. The deliberative playing field is more nearly level. Moral appeals are the weapon of the weak – not the only weapon, to be sure, but one that by its nature gives them an advantage over the powerful.

Amy Gutmann and Dennis Thompson[1]

One of the realities of the [2000 Florida presidential] recount and life is that lawyers and political folks don't really speak the same language.

US Senator Ted Cruz[2]

We next consider another apparent value conflict in the law of politics: equality versus deliberation. Equality reasoning in the law of politics has escalated as judges, and to some degree legislatures, subject more of political life to equality standards involving strict comparativism and numerism (faith in numbers). In this chapter we query whether such equalitarian reasoning is consistent with democratic deliberation and, if not, then what particular reforms of the law of politics might be desirable. Similar to the other value binaries we identify in this book (liberty versus deliberation in the previous chapter, integrity versus deliberation in the next), our claim is that conflicts between equality and deliberation are not inevitable. Rather, they result from the conceptually meagre vision of equality often implicit in the law of politics' rules and judgments.

Especially since the 1960s in the United States, and the 1980s–1990s in Canada, Australia, and the United Kingdom, equalitarian reasoning has assumed a central place in the law of politics. Within each of the jurisdictions of our study, despite variations, there is generally an equalising trajectory in, for instance, the regulation of electoral speech and voting. Some equality standards in the law of politics remain rather loose, calling only for reversals of the most egregious cases of unequal regulation. Other standards are stricter. In the cases we canvass in this chapter, there is a sporadic but overall marked pattern of tightening equalisation affecting the key participants in elections – the candidates and parties who run for election, and the voters who elect them.

Before describing what we aim to do in this chapter, it is worth repeating what this and the next chapter share in common. The two should be read together. Both explore legal reasoning based on *strategic* forms of balancing. (At this point it may be helpful to review Table 3.1 in chapter 3, detailing our typology of thick and thin legal balancing.) The thin, *conceptual* balancing test we saw in the last chapter was rivalrous; its conceptually distinct comparators lay in conflict on opposite sides of the balance scale. Conceptual balancing is thus a weighing of pros against cons: of legislative objectives against violations of liberties or other human interests. Strategic balancing is similarly thin, and also similarly rivalrous. But in this case the rivalry lies between the competing interests of assorted political parties (or factions).[3]

Balancing focused on equality is common across many areas of law, not just the law of politics. Such balancing highlights *sameness or difference*. Its core question is whether items on the balance scale differ in kind or weight. Under standard equality law, courts might disallow such differential treatment. For instance, when a group of persons is excluded from a public institution, such as marriage or employment in government, courts will often inquire into whether those excluded are – in relevant ways and to the same degree – just like others who are habitually included.

By contrast, models of equality in the law of politics frequently (but not invariably) involve strategic balancing. On the one hand, this form of equality is just an instance of equality reasoning. Courts will often seek to curb inequalities in the political opportunities afforded to political parties. There may be remediable inequalities in the effects the law of politics has on parties' electoral prospects (eg, unfairly unequal formulae for public funding). A court might therefore attempt to correct such structural inequalities.

On the other hand, as a variety of equality, strategic balancing also generates a distinctive form of equality test. Particularly unique is its *rivalrous*, or zero-sum, assessment centring on the fates of *political parties*. Greater political opportunity enjoyed by one party assumedly comes at a cost to the party's main rival or rivals. Strategic balancing can serve as a simple, legally imposed rule of thumb for electoral system fairness. Yet its assumptions are problematic. As we argue in this chapter, strategic balancing presents an impoverished view of equality, far thinner than the deliberative democratic notions of equality we will canvass. Deliberatively thick equality does not assume parties to be the primary and proper comparators of a test of political equality. Nor does it assume a rivalrous relation between political actors. Ranging well beyond political parties, deliberative notions of equality favour the inclusion into collective deliberation of a heterogeneous array of actors and information.

To be sure, more standard forms of equality testing – that is, equality premised neither on the centrality of political parties nor on any presumed relation between them – also figure in the law of politics. However, even when it considers the equality of individual voters, or of groups of voters, this area of law routinely neglects deliberative equality ideals. Partly this is a consequence of the law's frequent and simplistic focus on *numeric* equality tests. This approach imposes a strict quantitative test of equality of opportunity (eg, numbers of voters distributed among voting districts). Sometimes it even concentrates on equality of outcomes (eg, numbers of legislative seats won). We see below, by contrast, how deliberatively thick equality requires judges to make a host of more flexible judgments often at odds with the law of politics' naïve numerism.

After assuming greater centrality in the law of politics, equality standards have renovated much of what was, to some, a disconcertingly messy array of electoral practices and legal norms. Part of the explanation for this expanding use of equality to override other values is equality's intuitive normative appeal. And, being relatively simply articulable in law, equality tests are easy to understand and apply. Yet simplicity is not always a virtue. The equalising drive in the law of politics presents a problem for a value like deliberation characterised by a thoroughgoing and protean complexity. The normative appeal of applying equality more extensively within the law of politics should invite critique. Does the standard genuinely improve the law of politics? If so, in what demonstrable ways, and at what cost to the contrary values it displaces?

On the surface we appear to be in the uncomfortable position of arguing against equality. And it is true that, as we examine cases in this chapter, we are critical of the overuse of certain equalitarian habits of reasoning in the law of politics. However, our ultimate claim is, once again, that an apparent conflict between deliberation and an alternative value like equality in the law of politics is illusory. This is not a difficult conceptual move when it is recalled, from chapter 2, that equality of a certain kind is a criterion of deliberative democracy. Deliberation should be widely inclusive of citizens of varying identities,[4] and of broad sources of information,[5] and these inclusions should be on approximately equal terms for all.[6] In its treatment of political equality, we argue, the law of politics should favour this thick conception, which gives to equality a novel aspect largely distinct from other, well-worn legal equality categories (eg, formal versus substantive equality). Thick equality incorporates lessons from deliberative theory to generate a unique picture of what political equality should entail in the law of politics. We explore this picture below.

Note once again that our focus is on second-order deliberation. As we saw, lawmakers and courts engage in this when they deliberate about deliberative processes or rules themselves, for instance when they choose between electoral rules with deliberative or anti-deliberative consequences. We omit more straightforward, first-order questions here because they generally fall outside the ambit of the law of politics. But let us briefly review their importance to equality law. Courts applying certain equalitarian tools of deliberation, such as reasoning by analogy to past cases, can perhaps inform and improve public debate. For instance, in the controversy over legal recognition of same-sex marriage, proponents pointed to powerful lessons from historical examples; they often drew links to long-discredited anti-miscegenation laws and the cases that overturned them.[7] Moreover, weak or unsupported arguments (that 'tradition' provides reason enough to discriminate, that marriage entails the possibility of procreation, etc) have frequently collapsed

122 The Law of Deliberative Democracy

when exposed to the scrutiny of equalitarian reasoning in court.[8] Advocates and opinion-writers often incorporate legal arguments, backed by judicial authority, into their rhetorical arsenals. Equality rights discourse may help to account for the rapid changes in public sentiment in the US and Canada on same-sex marriage through the 2000s and 2010s.[9]

But such questions belong to another book. Our main focus is instead on how and whether equality's sweep through many second-order doctrines – through the legal rules that critically shape democratic politics – reflects deliberative democratic ideals. We ask here again how, if the law of politics took deliberation more seriously, decisions in a range of cases would come out differently. How, in turn, might politics itself change? Thin forms of equality are common and comparatively easy to conceptualise and operate in law. But they fall short from a deliberative perspective. And, though the thick doctrine of equality we propose is more consistent with deliberation, it is no less robust a model of equality. Thick equality is not merely a compromise between deliberation and equality, but is consistent with each, and may thus appeal both to deliberativists and equalitarians alike.

The rise of equality

Equality law's central dogma of treating likes alike reaffirms deeply embedded patterns of reasoning in the common law. When courts use administrative, human rights, and constitutional law to review government action, common law decision-making generally does not allow for unequal treatment of groups of citizens to go unjustified. In other words, there is a presumption against arbitrary action. A government that provides or guarantees an interest or a liberty must do so on equal terms, or else state a good reason for not doing so.[10] David Dyzenhaus describes equality as stemming from the 'idea of law as a culture of justification'.[11] Laws that either implicitly or explicitly allow space for officials to make arbitrary decisions upset the notion of dignity; and when the law disavows the entitlement of its subjects to dignity, 'something goes wrong not just morally speaking, but also legally speaking'.[12]

Such a claim should be relatively uncontroversial to those versed in the law of politics. For example, the right to vote has tended to evolve into a right to vote *on equal terms* – such as in the US guarantee of 'one man, one vote'.[13] By the 1970s, the High Court of Australia was still holding that the constitutional provision that Parliament should be 'directly chosen by the people' could be satisfied by any form of direct election, equal or not.[14] But this permissive approach is no more. In *Roach*[15] – a 2007 case on the disenfranchisement of prisoners – the Court mooted hypothetical laws excluding for example, women, Catholics, Indigenous Australians, members of a particular political party, or bankrupts from voting at general elections.[16] In the present day, the Court asked, would such a law comply with the guarantee of direct election? It would not; when the right to vote is denied to any class of people there must be a good reason for it. This conclusion is the more striking given that, when the Constitution came into force in 1901, women were yet to be included in the federal franchise. The equality principle even therefore takes precedence over original constitutional intentions (such as we understand them).[17]

In countries with comprehensive, written constitutional or quasi-constitutional equality guarantees – that is, in most liberal democracies other than Australia – equality doctrines might be expected to permeate democratic practice even more completely. Cases in Canada[18] and the UK[19] have indeed challenged prisoner disenfranchisement laws more robustly than did *Roach*. (*Roach* still permits the disenfranchisement of inmates serving sentences that are not 'short-term': in current practice more than three years in prison.) Yet the presence or absence of an express equality guarantee is not always determinative. A court in any of the four jurisdictions of our study might still place stress on the elected branches' democratic interests in designing their own political procedures, or the difficulties posed when judges seek to answer questions 'of a political nature about which opinions may vary considerably'.[20] Indeed, democratic design must always choose from a menu of multiple and often incompatible democratic goals.[21] In the 1973 case of *Richardson v Ramirez*, citing the need for deference, the US Supreme Court upheld widespread prisoner voting bans.[22]

At the *permissive* end of a spectrum of cases, then, we sometimes see full judicial deference over democratic system design. But the cases that wholly decline to adopt equality standards are often now decades old. Perhaps buttressed by more egalitarian assumptions in the political culture at large, courts now regularly invoke the concept of equality.

A little further down the spectrum, some cases offer *qualified deference*. Here courts generally defer to the elected branches, but also signal a willingness to intervene when necessary. Particularly in Australian and Canadian cases on electoral district malapportionment, judges have often neglected to strike down substantial inequalities. In *McGinty*, Western Australian state legislative districts packed urban areas with up to four times as many voters per district as rural regions, leaving urbanites with significantly less influence in elections.[23] To American eyes, malapportionment on that scale (at least in the House of Representatives) may seem extreme, even inexcusable. But a majority in *McGinty* upheld the apportionment; judges, they noted, should seldom second-guess choices about governance design, about which there can be no right answer.[24] As we will see, a similar flexibility is the norm in Canada, as well as the UK. However, judges in Australia, Canada, and the UK reserve a backstop role: a willingness to block electoral rules so unequal as to be plainly partisan or wildly under-representative. For instance, a majority of the judges in *McGinty* were prepared to accept that a 'grossly disproportionate' disparity (ie, inequality) in electorate sizes would offend the constitutionally mandated system of representative democracy.[25]

US cases and legislation tend now to present a different picture (outside the exceptional prisoner voting situation). Much of the US law of politics has moved beyond equality as a mere backstop, and towards equality *perfectionism*. Here, judges eschew deference in favour of stricter formal equality standards. (We use

124 The Law of Deliberative Democracy

the qualifier 'formal' because US courts are somewhat less zealous in striking down laws in which indirect – that is, substantively unequal – effects are asserted.[26]) The one person, one vote standard in the US is a prime example, which we discuss below in the case studies. As we shall also see, UK, Canadian, and Australian laws have come under pressure from lower courts and legislatures to adopt strict equality tests in the law of politics.

Equality law's quiet march throughout the many corners of politics has marked implications for politics in practice. Once adopted, equality perfectionism can be difficult to dislodge; the 'sphere of democracy may widen, but not so easily contract'.[27] And, importantly, by introducing stricter equality scrutiny, the law of politics transplants a greater portion of politics into the courts. A key question is how these developments reshape democracy.

We explore this next by first asking, *equality of what?* Does equality in the law of politics compare the right items? What critical standards does, or should, a 'culture of justification' bring to bear here? More particularly, should balancing out the powers or status of competing political parties exhaust the law's commitment to political equality? As noted, the laws of political equality commonly fixate on equalities of parties, including both parties to *litigation* and *political* parties, the two often being conflated in legal cases. Also common is the strict, numeric comparison brought to bear on individual voter equality, another potentially thin methodology. Are deliberatively thicker forms of equality viable in law? If so, what might these entail?

Equality of what?

Equality is often valued in democratic theory in light of the basic notion that people who are subject to collective decisions should have a hand in those decisions. No one should be excluded arbitrarily from the decision-making process, nor from influencing its outcome.[28] This rationale for equality is common to many conceptions of democracy.

Yet equality also has a more distinctive rationale in deliberative democracy theory. Understood as *broad inclusivity*, equality can be a tool of deliberation. That is, equality can enhance the quality of discussion in a deliberative forum. (We use 'deliberative forum' to denote, first, carefully structured micropublics like Citizens' Juries and Assemblies, which stand in for the broader community. Secondly, the term can refer to macro-level public discourse, such as an election campaign and its less formalised involvement of 'citizens, politicians, the government, civil society and the media'.[29]) Inclusive decision-making can be more epistemically rigorous and can yield decisions more responsive and acceptable to a broad cross-section of citizens.[30] Conversely, when 'entire social perspectives – such as those of minorities or women – are excluded from the political arena' the problematic result is 'an impoverishment of political life'.[31]

When we speak of wide inclusion of information and people, what precisely do we mean? Information can denote ideas, arguments, interests, values, preferences, social perspectives, discourses, and intellectual frameworks (eg, scientific or ideological systems of thought).[32] As for who should bring such information to the deliberative forum, an inclusive process can seek to represent or directly engage individuals, identity groups (eg, organised by ethnicity, race, gender, geography, language), or groups formed to promote certain causes (eg, policy preferences shared in common, interests, ideas, social perspectives, ideologies). Such inclusions widen the range of inputs into decision-making in the forum.

To be sure, some exclusion is inevitable. For instance, as Iris Marion Young describes, in 1996 the South African government invited public comment on its draft constitution by mail or email, and also held public meetings explaining its contents to enable feedback from those who could not read it. Despite this attempt at inclusion, many South Africans did not participate in the deliberative process because they understood too little about the meaning of the constitution, or were too preoccupied with survival.[33] But inclusion is a first step toward deliberation, and the less the forum excludes relevant information, the better.[34]

Nevertheless, merely dumping information into a public forum is not enough for deliberation. Deliberative inclusivity has an additional meaning. Information in the forum should be weighed on its merits – the most relevant, valid, true, weighty, or coherent inputs to be sifted and separated from the rest. Democracy was traditionally often thought simply to aggregate and weigh citizens' subjective preferences, tallying them up to determine which preferences enjoy the greatest backing within the polity. By contrast, a deliberative forum ideally assigns weight to information or decisional options largely independently of their origins, and not chiefly as a function of their bald, numeric popularity. (An aggregative vote is held only at the conclusion of deliberations.) In reality, as John Dryzek points out, certain types of people might be 'better than others at arguing in rational terms'.[35] Yet, better deliberation, throughout the forum generally, can be expected to promote more robust inclusion on equal terms.

Information in the deliberative forum is partly *disembodied*, in that an ideal forum is open to the ideas of all comers mostly irrespective of who they are.[36] According to James Bohman, deliberation is said to involve some degree of impartial 'abstraction from one's own point of view'.[37] More generally, ideal deliberation is relatively free of the coercive effects of the statuses of deliberators. In Jürgen Habermas's famous articulation, the focus of the forum is on the 'unforced force of the better argument'.[38] The value of inputs into the forum depends not on physical force, nor the authority or influence of official state power and law, nor of high social position, wealth, popularity, or any other identity largely irrelevant to the merits of the input.[39] The focus on cogent information and reasons allows all positions to be considered, criticised, defended, and revised based on their merits, rather than on participants' preconceptions linked to the statuses of speakers.[40]

In the now-classic example of Citizens' Assemblies, 100+ randomly selected, but demographically representative, citizens each enjoy time to speak and deliberate on a circumscribed matter such as a constitutional reform.[41] A Citizens'

126   The Law of Deliberative Democracy

Assembly is small enough, and its deliberations lengthy enough (up to nearly a year of weekly meetings), that in time most of the participants' points of view are brought forward in discussions.[42] How *often* each position is voiced matters less than the position's cogence. A range of perspectives, including many overlooked in the more polarised debates of standard legislative decision-making, enter the crucible of deliberation. Arguments raised by the Assembly's diverse members can have equal potential weight and influence.

All this is contrary to the common critique that deliberative outcomes 'are more likely to reflect the initial views of the most advantaged deliberators'.[43] To this critique, Amy Gutmann and Dennis Thompson reply that:

> deliberation offers a better chance of overcoming the influence of status in the political process. Compared to bargaining, deliberation, properly structured, can diminish the discriminatory influence of class, race, and gender inequalities.[44]

In support of this claim, in their seminal work in 1996 Gutmann and Thompson relied on studies of trial juries to yield clues that deliberators who carefully sift evidence ('instead of simply voting') remain open-minded and 'pay more attention to the merits of arguments than to the status of fellow jurors'.[45] This observation has since been repeatedly affirmed in studies of public policy decision-making involving micropublics.[46] Of course, macro-level deliberation inevitably lies somewhat further from the egalitarian ideal.

None of this is meant to imply that the identities of deliberators are irrelevant. The ideal of inclusivity does not dismiss identity, but incorporates inputs from varying identities in order to ensure that no group dominates unless it has put forward the most meritorious ideas. Indeed, people representing assorted identities should stay involved throughout deliberations to help present their points of view – to illustrate, in detail, the relevance and contours of these views.[47] And, as we explore in chapter 6, knowledge of a deliberator's identity frequently conveys information about her unique perspective or expertise. Hence, the disembodiment of information in a deliberative forum is far from absolute.

In practice, the design of deliberative democracy raises difficult choices about which groups the forum should include. Should those united by common ideology or identity, or who aggregate simply in order to pool political power, have standing in the forum? One problem is that some groups employ extensive internal decision-making procedures that may be at odds with deliberative democracy. It is best if the 'internal processes of groups' allow deliberation in which 'members develop and modify their own interests and their views of the interest of the group'.[48] This in turn requires engaging with those outside the group 'by listening to what they have to say and by trying to take it into account or by rationally arguing against what they have to say'.[49] Some groups, however, hold rigid positions from start to finish of a public decision-making process, and employ internal procedures largely cut off from the larger deliberative forum. For instance, Ireland's

Social Partnership participatory initiative included a 'community and voluntary pillar' comprising various civic groups meant to deliberate on social policy issues, with the results fed into public policy-making.[50] The constituent groups generally favoured factional over collective interests, with one member stating 'every one of the fifteen of us is out for our own agenda and we really couldn't give a hoot about the others'.[51]

The paradigm inflexible group arguably is the political party. On the one hand, in chapter 3 we saw that parties can pool and clarify the ideas and perspectives of their members, and even therefore potentially aid public deliberation. This optimistic assessment draws on Jane Mansbridge et al and their expanded understanding of deliberation. That concept understands some self-interested reasoning as useful if it helps to draw out both the salient differences and common ground of deliberators.[52] As we also saw, some deliberativists have addressed political parties more directly.[53] For instance, some suggest that parties can serve an 'ideational coordination function' for voters.[54] Furthermore, Archon Fung argues that partisan deliberators might improve the quality and sustainability of a deliberative forum because 'participants who have much at stake make for better deliberation. More participants will be drawn into [such] deliberations and they will be more sustainable over time'.[55] Parties are not all bad, then, for deliberation.

On the other hand, to the extent that political parties coalesce ideas, interests, and ideologies into a relatively fixed product, parties may be far from ideal participants in the broader arena of deliberation. Often – for instance, during elections – political parties do not seek to engage with their counterparts in a communicative process of preference change.[56] As forces of factionalism and the entrenchment of agonistic positions, parties are often classically strategic. Parties generally strive to reach the end of a democratic decision-making process with their own preferences intact. Indeed, empirical research conducted by David Pelletier et al confirms that party partisans are less likely to modify their initial beliefs as a result of deliberation.[57] By contrast, as Carolyn Hendriks et al argue, '[n]on-partisan forums have participants with greater autonomy to change preferences, so their deliberative capacity can be judged superior to that of partisan forums'.[58] In part this is because, '[f]rom the perspective of *deliberation*, partisans make poor deliberators because they have committed agendas'.[59]

This is perhaps inevitable as, for instance, Kathleen Bawn et al find that parties 'develop common agendas and screen candidates for party nominations based on loyalty to their agendas'.[60] It has also been suggested that inflexibility in the stances of political parties can be explained by the responsibility that group representatives owe to their constituencies. Once elected, and now acting in their capacity as representatives, members of a political party may lack the autonomy to change their preferences. John Parkinson suggests that the delegate model of representation (according to which elected representatives mostly serve to implement their constituents' choices) is incompatible with the deliberative ideal of openness to preference shifts.[61] Parties, then, do not merely adduce information to be sifted

128   The Law of Deliberative Democracy

in a deliberative forum, but often substitute their own decisional procedures and fixed decisions for those of the wider forum.

These observations help to explain why we are critical of the thin view of political equality in law. The rise to prominence of equality reasoning in the law of politics is unproblematic in itself. Yet the thin view may serve as a judicial crutch. In the following case studies, we see that it often induces judges to rest their decisions on relatively observable, yet simplistic, comparisons of the electoral fortunes of political parties. The potential to realise either political equality or political deliberation is generally not greatly enhanced by such judicial tweaking of the balance of power between parties. Based on our critique of the case studies, we conclude that decision-making should instead be calibrated towards deliberative democracy's distinctive, and far more comprehensive, vision of equality.

Campaign speech

Cases on the regulation of election-period speech often exemplify the themes above. Legislative schemes can seek to improve deliberation in the campaign speech of political candidates and parties. Many such schemes raise liberty and integrity considerations. But our focus here is on equality. We begin by looking at an Australian case that invoked a thin doctrine of equality and rejected a comprehensive deliberative intervention into electoral campaign speech. Similarly sweeping legislative schemes to enhance deliberation would almost certainly be unviable under current US law. And yet, as we will see when exploring instances in the UK and elsewhere where such schemes have been permitted to run, a thicker equality model can be feasible in practice.

a. Thin equality: Australian Capital Television (ACTV)

The Australian High Court's signature early free expression case, *ACTV*, concerned a law mandating publicly funded broadcast airtime for political parties.[62] An amendment to the Broadcasting Act[63] had granted free television airtime to electoral candidates to deliver extended policy addresses in a prescribed format: static, featureless, and bland – a 'talking head' presentation unencumbered by visual gimmickry or dramatic distraction.[64] The scheme also disallowed alternative forms of paid broadcast advertising of a political nature during election campaigns. This became one of several political equality cases, dating from the 1990s to the mid-2010s, in which the Australian court established a more muscular pattern of review of parliamentary choices about the regulation of democracy.

The Court struck down the scheme. We considered the liberty aspect of this case in chapter 4. Now we focus on its equality reasoning. One rationale for the Court's decision was that 90 per cent of the free broadcast time was reserved for parties currently represented in Parliament; the remainder went to micro or upstart parties lacking any elected members.[65]

Discussing the law's objectives, judges in both the majority and minority alluded

Equality v Deliberation 129

to unmistakable deliberative goals, including that of remedying the typical brevity and triviality of campaign speech.[66] The judgment of Justice Brennan, in dissent, was clearest on this point. He explained that '[t]elevision advertising is brief; its brevity tends to trivialize the subject; it cannot deal in any depth with the complex issues of government. Its appeal is therefore directed more to the emotions than to the intellect'.[67] Brennan J also cited expert evidence on 'the debased nature of most political advertising' and 'its universal failure to convey information about policies to the voters'.[68]

Judges in both the majority and dissent also noted how the law might mitigate some of the political inequality caused by wealthy speakers' outsized ability to buy broadcast time.[69] This 'level playing field' argument potentially implicates deliberative democracy theory's goal of inclusion of a plurality of voices. Some judges also referenced safeguarding integrity as a legislative goal. To pay for campaign publicity and other costs, candidates are increasingly fixated on fundraising. A distinct risk of corruption emerges as they try to secure commitments from donors.[70]

But the legislative scheme's unequal allotment of airtime as between the political parties particularly moved the majority.[71] Chief Justice Mason and others suggested that the most salient equality issue lay in the conflict between established and developing parties. The free airtime:

discriminates against new and independent candidates ... [and] denies them meaningful access on a non-discriminatory basis. ... I do not accept that, because absolute equality in the sharing of free time is unattainable, the inequalities inherent in the regime introduced by [the amendment] are justified or legitimate.[72]

As it had seldom done before,[73] the Court therefore overruled parliamentary choices about trade-offs in democratic system design.

By viewing the dispute in the fairly simple terms of a conflict between mainline parties and more minor upstarts, the decision poorly served both deliberation and minority interests. A difficulty arises when the main persons and interests with de jure or de facto standing in a dispute are those associated with political parties. To promote deliberation, laws should prioritise not only the views of established major and minor parties, but also views commonly represented by no party at all. Legislative schemes to generate more robustly deliberative campaign speech have at least the potential to transcend the narrow categories of reasoning generated by the usual party-focused democracy. The scheme in the present case strove to do this, not by denying the centrality of parties, but by promoting a more open discussion of policy choices from within the existing party system.

As discussed above, and in chapter 2, modern election campaigns feature a host of deliberative pathologies. For instance, at campaign time, policy proposals are generally inflexible, and habitually presented as *faits accomplis*. (Changes mid-campaign even tend to be inhibited by charges of inconstancy, or 'flip-flopping'.)

The legislative scheme considered in *ACTV* provided a considered response to such instances of poor electoral deliberation. Offering extensive, free, and substantively focused airtime, an aim of the law was to free the established parties and their candidates from their usual oppositional and narrowly reactive campaigning patterns. The law encouraged the parties to focus on wider-ranging policy options.

Our preferred outcome would have been for the Court to leave the scheme untouched, or perhaps to tweak the broadcast allocations to mitigate concerns about inter-party equality. The *ACTV* majority's largely party-focused model of equality undersold the law's wider deliberative benefits. A thicker notion of equality would conceptualise equality not in terms of strategic balance between parties, but as widely inclusive of myriad interests and participants. Justice Brennan's dissent came the closest to voicing this position. He considered that the law 'would go far to ensuring ... openness of political discussion and the equality of the participants in the democratic process'.[74]

Intriguingly, members of the *ACTV* majority also touched on this view. Chief Justice Mason derided the legislation's lack of help for the speech of '[e]mployers' organizations, trade unions, manufacturers' and farmers' organizations, social welfare groups and societies generally'.[75] Indeed, free airtime for these and other groups might usefully inform election campaign debates. But the judge's reference to such non-party voices recalls the adage that the best is the enemy of the good. His all-or-nothing scenario contemplated that either a large (even perhaps unwieldy) assortment of civic associations should receive state help, or none should. Yet striking down the law only left the primacy of the parties, and their narrow and often rigid perspectives, unchallenged.

It is usually in vain to conceive of a democratic politics in which parties are relatively sidelined, as Chief Justice Mason seemed to. To be sure, parties play only minimal roles within deliberative micropublics such as Citizens' Assemblies, and parties are sometimes unimportant in local politics and in certain small and relatively homogenous polities (eg, Nebraska, where a unicameral legislature ostensibly abandoned parties in the 1930s).[76] Yet, for the most part, wishing parties away is unrealistic. Election campaign narratives largely converge around voters' choices between and among parties. Whether an electoral system relies on party-lists (as with proportional representation) or another model, the election of non-party independents is still the exception.

High-minded references to the desirability of diminishing the mainline parties' dominance thus distract from more plausible avenues for the reform of democracy. These would take the present assortment of parties as largely a given, while improving the parties' deliberative habits. (We also depart here from the positions of both Chad Flanders and Richard Pildes, who would prefer to disrupt the hegemony of the main parties.[77]) Legislative schemes can try to change the parties' internal decision-making procedures, for example by mandating more inclusive and informed intra-party policy-making. Alternatively, they can seek to modify how parties engage deliberatively with the wider polity – as the amendments to the Broadcasting Act sought to do. Either option can potentially make parties at least marginally better deliberative participants in a democracy.

Apart from the Court's brief utopian reverie, the main thrust of its equality analysis focused on rebalancing the two classes of political parties noted. Indeed, from the perspective of deliberative inclusion, giving upstart parties comparatively little broadcasting assistance might stymie the rise of new parties and the fresh perspectives they stand for. But the impugned legislation's prioritisation of mainstream parties over upstart parties apparently rested on the assessment – arguably reasonable, at least up to a point – that including upstart parties more robustly would generate a cacophonous, incoherent, or superficial campaign discourse. (Parties in Australia now include, eg, groups devoted to hunting, fishing, motoring, stopping immigration, sex, high-speed rail, voluntary euthanasia, marijuana legalisation, and smokers' rights.[78]) Nevertheless, the Court held that gross disparities between political parties, if induced by government action, were to be avoided. Its decision could have pursued this principle with greater discretion, as we noted, by adjusting the airtime allotment to make it more equitable.[79] Instead, the Court overruled the legislative amendments in their entirety.[80] Clearly there was no guarantee that the amendments would succeed at their aim of encouraging better policy discussion from within the party system. Yet in our view the Court should have let the experiment run.

Why might a thin, party-comparative model of equality win out in the law of politics? One reason is doubtless the very human habit of fixating on differences between groups, even when such distinctions are trivial.[81] This tyranny of differences stands out in several decades of social and psychological experimentation.[82] In essence, focusing on *relative* wealth, status, etc – the need for one person or group to best another – is often more affectively relevant than the attribute's absolute value.[83] Political parties are teams of individuals organised classically according to a competitive, group-forming impulse. Their contests with each other often steal the spotlight of electoral campaign politics. It should thus be no surprise that party competition is central to the law of politics as well.

Another reason is more complex. Recall from chapter 3 that balancing uses relative rather than absolute judgment to aid in the common law's often troubled pursuit of objective judgment. Balancing is a creature of common law practicality. Judges must do their best to look beyond the fact that objective judgment may be impossible, and to issue final decisions anyway. Balancing can reduce complex, cross-cutting, and vague arguments about justice or injustice to numeric or otherwise simple comparisons (eg, a 'balance of probabilities'). The law imposes balancing on human affairs in order to construct simpler and more easily regulable patterns of conduct.

Regulating *democratic* conduct, however, is a uniquely freighted task. Given how extensively the normative systems of democracy and of law differ, the former frequently resists simple ordering by the latter. One important distinction between them is that normativity in democratic campaigns is 'overdetermined', as we said in chapter 2. There we noted how citizens assess voting options at elections against a surfeit of evaluative standards: candidate trustworthiness, appeal, familiarity, competence, etc. Elections raise numberless varieties of policy preferences from which voters must choose. As a very general rule, electoral democracy's normative guidelines are more numerous, varied, and vague, and hence more ambiguous, than those of law. Statute and case law are relatively formalised: they enunciate principles of general scope and application, and are often comparatively unambiguous and firmly set. Individual laws are arranged in a relatively clear relation to each other. And they are enforced or elaborated by judges and lawyers in another defined hierarchy. Most of the time, then, law is a more perspicuous guide to conduct than are the mostly unspoken and cross-cutting normative principles in the discourse of electioneering.

Political equality might then focus selectively on political parties because the law seeks clear targets to regulate. Political parties present points where – unusually – the two normative systems of law and electoral democracy best recognise each other. Here they use a partly common language and share certain structural features. Political parties are relatively hierarchical, stable, and tangible. Parties play similar roles in politics and in law – aggregating people and points of view, and forming these into more or less coherent unities. Contemporary law now therefore displays an enthusiasm for regulating political parties (even if historically this was not the case[84]). Where political parties are involved, judges often shed their usual reticence about settling questions of democratic design.

The difficulty for deliberative democracy is that the affinity between politics and law at these points of mutual recognition can drag politics toward a model of practice inconsistent with deliberative democracy. Seizing on similarities between political parties and parties to litigation, law does not always leave democratic politics untouched. Legal decision-making sometimes forces electoral politics to make points of contact, prioritising and reinforcing relatively familiar features like political parties. In this way law can undermine a more deliberative vision of equality premised on inclusion beyond political parties.

b. Thick equality: UK examples

As noted earlier, in the US, a non-voluntary deliberative scheme as comprehensive as the law challenged in *ACTV* would be a legal non-starter, given the First Amendment's strict associational and speech rights (see chapter 4). In the UK, however, comprehensive regulation is not only legally viable, but culturally entrenched. UK laws have long mandated free airtime for political parties and their candidates. Indeed the UK inspired the common law world's initiatives in this regard. UK political actors have never been free to purchase airtime for political advertisements.[85] Not only is electoral broadcast advertising prohibited, but so are all paid political broadcasts at any time. The ban dates to the 1924 general election and the dawn of radio broadcasting itself.

This prohibition was originally motivated in part by fears of the potency and even demagogic potential of such powerful new media as radio and television.

A second, more positive aspiration at the time flowed from the incipient public service model of broadcasting. In this model, a publicly owned broadcaster is given a special charter to report current affairs and news with breadth, intelligence, and independence. As part of this public service mandate, the founder of the BBC, Sir John Reith, believed that broadcasters should offer free airtime to parties to enable them to inform the public of their platforms.[86] This model remains to this day, with the predominance of the BBC assured through a funding system tied to a fee on each owner of a television, and restrictions on the issue of licences to rival networks. In short, the UK scheme was born in a belief that powerful new media were to be neither limitlessly open to political contestants, nor completely off-limits. Rather, they were to be tamed and moderated.

These originary justifications embody clear deliberative concerns. The contemporary rationale for the prohibition on the purchase of broadcast time for political advertising, as explained by the UK Electoral Commission, involves a mix of deliberative and egalitarian values:

> allowing political advertising in the broadcast media would give an advantage to the best financed candidates or parties and could reduce an election campaign to soundbites and slogans. Political advertising in the broadcast media is therefore prohibited in the UK. [Party broadcasts] are designed to offset the differential ability of parties to attract campaign funds. This free airtime is provided prior to elections and other significant events (such as the budget) and allows qualifying parties an opportunity to deliver their messages directly to the electorate through the broadcast media.[87]

So, in place of paid broadcast advertising, registered parties in the UK are allocated time for 'party political' and 'party electoral' broadcasts (the latter being the focus in election years). These broadcasts were designed to avoid not just the trivialising effects of 15–30-second advertisements, but also the worst aspects of negative or attack campaigns. Indeed, in their early days, broadcasts essentially aired the totality of a party's policies, with party speeches and manifestos read over the airwaves. Initially, party broadcasts were 20-minute speeches; later, and for a considerable time, they remained 10-minute-long presentations.[88] But revised rules now permit parties to choose television broadcasts of between 160 seconds and 280 seconds and radio broadcasts of up to 150 seconds.[89] This truncation has been a concession to both the parties' desires to reach more citizens with higher frequency messages and the broadcasters' programming preferences. From a deliberative perspective it reflects an unfortunate assumption that modern audiences have limited attention spans.

The original UK model has much going for it as a way of integrating deliberative and equality considerations. Certainly the system of rationing airtime has functioned reasonably well – giving lie to the concerns that ostensibly haunted the Australian High Court, in relation to the narrower scheme in the *ACTV* case. While all mechanisms of administering airtime have flaws, as discussed in the previous

134 The Law of Deliberative Democracy

section the Australian court let the perfect be the enemy of the good. Meanwhile, the UK Government has resisted claims, based in European rights jurisprudence, that its political broadcasting regime is unjustified.[90] In a case brought by Animal Defenders International, a lobby group for animal rights, the European Court of Human Rights upheld the UK prohibition on political broadcast advertising.[91] The UK defended the rule as the manifestation of a 'desire to protect pluralist debate and the democratic process from distortion by powerful financial groups' while still preserving the general liberty to campaign on social and political issues through less expensive media.[92] The rationale of protecting pluralist debate with an eye to cost and disproportionate wealth is an example of a legislative concern for both deliberative and equality concerns at once.

It is worth noting that New Zealand also manages a system where paid electoral broadcast advertising is not permitted during the electoral campaign period.[93] Instead, parties share a fund permitting them to obtain broadcast airtime. As in the UK, the design accommodates deliberative and equality concerns. New Zealand rules require, for instance, that such 'election programmes' may not incorporate material that denigrates a political opponent (a deliberative concern with the preponderance of attack advertising in contemporary electoral discourse).[94] Critics of the system claim that its restriction on a pure liberty-to-advertise is unwarranted, at least since New Zealand also caps electoral expenditure.[95] But this falls into the trap, identified in chapter 4, of ignoring deliberative considerations and invoking liberty as a value that outweighs all others. The New Zealand model, not unlike the aborted Australian model, is not in place at all times. And, unlike in the UK, it allows non-party actors to promote issues through broadcast advertising campaigns. They can even do this at election time, provided the broadcast raises issues for discussion, rather than being advocacy for or against any particular candidate or party. This model therefore seeks to accommodate liberty values throughout the political cycle, with equality and deliberative concerns brought to the fore at election time.[96]

Perhaps unsurprisingly, in a society with inevitably competing ideas about what is best for democracy, UK laws also occasionally depart from thick equality. Just as the Australian High Court used its focus on strategic balancing to undervalue deliberative notions of equality, UK lawmakers have also occasionally done the same. In the UK, third parties not only are forbidden at any time from promoting political causes through broadcast advertising, but they are also subject to stringent limits on what they can spend on electioneering. The problem with the UK restrictions on third party electioneering, however, is that they attempt to seal off election campaigns from third party campaigning in the name of party equality. The term 'third parties' is revealing in itself, since it lumps a myriad of civil society groups into a lesser category defined by reference to what they are not, namely political parties.[97]

Until 1998, UK law prohibited third parties spending more than £5, in the six weeks prior to election day, on material that might promote the election of any *candidate*. After litigation by an anti-abortion campaigner who overspent that limit to produce tens of thousands of electoral pamphlets, the European Court of Human Rights invalidated the limit as unreasonably low.[98] However, the Court accepted the principle that legislatures could cap third party expenditure at low levels. The UK simply re-enacted the cap at just £500, spread over a longer period.[99] Third parties are able to mount *national campaigns* on issues at election time, but only to the value of about £450,000, barely one-fortieth of the expenditures permitted to each national political party (which also benefit from free broadcast time).[100]

Such highly restrictive limits on actors other than candidates and political parties are rationalised as measures to support the system of equalising party electioneering expenses. The effect, however, is to focus campaigning almost entirely on the voices and platforms of the parties. The goal of limiting expenses is reasonable when in pursuit of both deliberative and equality aims. But the deliberative interest in hearing from third party actors is sacrificed in the UK to a strategic concern to achieve an equal playing field among parties. The repression of third party electoral speech seeks to avoid an imbalance of partisan voices or interests. For instance, the £500 limit on third party campaigning focused on candidates is explicitly tied to a rule about non-coordination with candidates.[101] Unreasonably low limits fail to accommodate deliberative conceptions of elections as times of inclusive debate about the merits of party platforms and future leaders. The resulting notion of equality and deliberation is thin because it reinforces election times as periods of partisan oppositionalism, rather than conceiving them as more deliberatively rich occasions.

In sum, we have seen two ways in which a thin equality concern – focused on strategic balancing between political parties – can conflict with a regulatory aim of promoting deliberation in electoral speech. First, in *ACTV*, the Australian High Court struck down a law that could have helped nudge the speech of parties and candidates toward a more deliberative tenor. In part, the Court objected to what it saw as a gross inequality between major and minor parties under the scheme. We argued that this aspect of the law was indeed regrettable, and should be mitigated. But in our view the law's efforts to institutionalise deliberation otherwise had promise. Secondly, UK legislation has sought to diminish the roles of third parties in order to maintain greater equality among the parties regulated under a public funding scheme. On the one hand, we saw that maintaining inter-party balance is the pre-eminent concern here, more than promoting deliberation. On the other hand, we also saw that other parts of the UK law, much like a comparable New Zealand law, demonstrate how a comprehensive regulatory scheme for electoral speech can enhance deliberation while remaining consistent with equality – provided that the form of equality is itself deliberatively thick.

Voter equality and malapportionment

Our next examples largely concern voters, not parties. Over time, perfectionist judicial reasoning about voter equality has become more common in the law of politics. Yet such reasoning can generate an impoverished, and impoverishing, strictly *numeric* and *aggregative* legal methodology. Equality perfectionism in the law of politics tends to focus on the equal influence of the final electoral choices of individual voters (ie, their candidate preferences, as gauged at the ballot box). Deliberative democracy also frequently seeks to promote the equality of individuals; however, as noted, it prioritises the equality of perspectives – of interests, ideas, arguments, identities, reasons, etc. In deliberative theory's model of citizen inclusion, it is the plural perspectives of citizens, and not merely their final choices, that 'must be given equal consideration'.[102] Whether presented by the individual or by a group to which she belongs, these perspectives ought to enjoy equal access in a deliberative forum.

It is understandable that courts and lawmakers should seek to phase out these flexible approaches to equality. Numeric voter disparities can look manifestly unfair. For example, where different electoral districts have different quantities of voters, on some level this is self-evidently unjust. Yet a numeric equality test can be counter-productive for deliberation. It can generate relatively superficial insights into what political equality requires. Deliberative democracy's equal inclusion condition is not always straightforwardly expressible as a quantity. The flexibility to achieve unequal numbers can, in some cases, be a necessary tool to yield thicker, less abstract, more *deliberative* and inclusive equality.

Let us continue with the example of electoral districts. Any polity in which legislators represent districts (eg, in the lower legislative houses of each country of our study) must redraw those districts from time to time. But the process can be open to abuse. 'Malapportionment' usually thus denotes undue departures from the principle of 'one person, one vote' (as it is known in the US) or, more accurately, 'one vote, one value'. The basic intuition here is that each citizen should enjoy the same level of voting influence at elections. Electoral districts should therefore contain equal numbers of citizens or of eligible voters. (This model has some obvious fictive elements. For example, more realistically, the power of a vote is a function of where one votes – whether in an electorally 'competitive' district or state, where the electoral outcome is not a forgone conclusion.[103])

The numeric equality principle manifests most uncompromisingly, even obsessively, in relation to the US House of Representatives. There the approach to voter apportionment is about as perfectionist as electoral mapmaking can be. Narrow tolerances allow districts to depart no more than $+/-1$ per cent from the average of about 710,000 citizens.[104] (Some states' small populations necessitate departures from this rule, because districts do not cross state lines.[105]) By contrast, in Canada the principle is not so perfectionist. Districts, or 'ridings', in Canada can vary substantially. Table 5.1 shows the lowest- and highest-population ridings in Canada's federal system in 2006.[106]

The greatest ratios were 6.5:1 by population and 8:1 for eligible voters (electors).[107] Other ridings fell along a fairly linear continuum between these extremes. Meanwhile, in Australia and the UK, district equality is tightening.

Table 5.1 Populations of selected federal Canadian ridings

Riding	Province/ Territory	Riding Population	Electors in Riding
Nunavut	Nunavut	29,474	17,089
Labrador	Newfoundland and Labrador	26,364	20,175
Oak Ridges – Markham	Ontario	169,642	136,755
Brampton West	Ontario	170,422	109,151

For example, until the enactment of the Parliamentary Voting System and Constituencies Act 2011 (UK) ensuring representation of identifiable communities was the core principle of the British redistribution system. The Act now mandates that 'arithmetic equality' be the predominant criterion used by the independent commissions.[108]

But standards in the UK and Australia are still more flexible than those in relation to the US House. Congress originally legislated nationwide standards for redistricting in the Apportionment Act of 1842, which set out requirements such as geographic contiguity for each district.[109] Later developments, in 1872, imposed standards including one person, one vote.[110] The Reapportionment Act of 1929 replaced all earlier standards and took the federal government out of readjustment for the next three decades, leaving the task wholly to the states.[111] But in 1962 in *Baker v Carr*, abandoning earlier deference to legislatures, the US Supreme Court stepped into the role of regulating redistricting, invoking the Fourteenth Amendment's equal protection clause.[112] Soon after, *Reynolds v Sims* judicially re-established the principle of one person, one vote. This case, and others later on (along with legislation), elaborated more restrictive equality tests.[113] The *Reynolds* case itself arose in response to state-level districts in Alabama, including, at the extreme, a voter disparity of 81:1.[114]

Leading Canadian and Australian court decisions have thus far avoided equality perfectionism, expressing doubts about one vote, one value as boundary-drawing's single or overarching concern. The *Carter* case in Canada stands for a qualified principle of review, especially in the face of the need to represent large and remote areas of the vast country with ridings of manageable size.[115] In Australia, highly malapportioned electorates (alternatively 'zones' or 'areas' in which multiple electorates are bound together) were still the norm in some states of Australia in the 1970s, and some large disparities even lingered through to the 1990s.[116] In cases such as *McKinlay*[117] and *McGinty*,[118] the Australian High Court refused to overturn departures from one vote, one value.[119] In *McGinty*, as earlier noted, the High Court let stand an apportionment in Western Australia in which districts ranged up to 4:1 by population. A proposed amendment to the federal

Constitution, which would have created a nationwide one vote, one value standard in law, also failed in a 1988 reform referendum.

It is arguable that by neglecting to impose judicial review on the basis of strict equality at these junctures, Australia and Canada avoided the thickets of US judicial involvement in redistricting. In chapter 6 we describe some of the seemingly intractable difficulties that US judicial involvement in the field has spawned, including (perversely) catalysing extreme partisan gerrymandering. The federal governments of Australia and Canada, as well as both countries' state and provincial governments, are generally recognised as having developed smooth-running, impartial electoral mapmaking processes over time. It is notable that they did so without close judicial involvement. The standard of judicial review in both countries essentially remains one of qualified deference – qualified in the noted sense, that judges in future may still serve as backstops to block more egregious inequalities. Across Australia there are also tolerant cut-offs for state parliaments, usually in the order of 10 per cent. In certain vast rural electorates, two states (Queensland and Western Australia) expressly allow more dramatic departures from the mean.[120] In some cases in Canada, too, such as the federal guidelines of +/– 25 per cent variation (and even greater disparities in practice), the one vote, one value rule is so flexible that it is in no way meaningfully perfectionist.

The Canadian and Australian courts worried that a rule of rigid voter parity could have sacrificed certain other democratic objectives. One is the practical 'ombudsman' role of representatives, which the *Carter* court pointed out requires legislators to serve as roving problem-solvers, often in close contact with their constituents.[121] The realities of Canadian and Australian (and sometimes US) geography can make this a trying task. For instance, before its demise, the thinly populated and remote federal Australian electorate of Kalgoorlie was approximately ten times larger than the whole of the UK.[122] Equality perfectionism would insist that such a vast district should be even vaster – that it should be held to a strict rule of voter parity among districts.

Equality perfectionism also potentially conflicts with deliberative ideals. For instance, remote-area voters often have distinct interests. These may centre, for example, around agricultural activity, or indigenous community and culture. Returning to Table 5.1 above, note that the most overpopulated ridings, in Ontario, are located in fast-growing satellite communities around the city of Toronto, while the thinly populated Labrador and Nunavut ridings, in the far north and north-east of Canada, are largely indigenous in their populations. But indigenous people constitute only 2.5, 4.3 and 2 per cent of citizens in Australia, Canada, and the US, respectively. Spread thinly across each country, they can be systemically excluded under standard voting systems.

Deliberative notions of equal inclusion, as we have seen, put stress on the expression of distinctive perspectives. Groups with small numbers as a proportion of national population, but with discrete interests, may be unable to be heard via some forms of democratic representation. This concern is somewhat less urgent for relatively large or geographically concentrated minority groups (eg, members of sizeable immigrant enclaves in cities). Yet, for others, the rules of electoral mapmaking play roles in ensuring deliberative inclusion. The mapmaking process in all four countries of our study has long centred on what we can now recognise as a deliberative concept, that of *communities of interest*: redistricting must focus on keeping groups of like citizens together within voting districts. The communities of interest principle stems from a key rationale for district-linked democratic representation. Local identity groups are more coherently represented in their own district than they would be if bisected and scattered among several districts. Pooled thus into voting units with interests in common, distinct communities in theory can better highlight – to both electoral candidates and, later, legislators – any interests that their members share in common.[123] (This does not necessarily mean that members will vote for the same candidates.) Pooling perspectives in this way also prevents the community from being wholly swamped by others in the region or the country. The communities of interest principle can be read as deliberative, then, to the extent that it aims to secure the reliable inclusion of discrete voter interests and voices.

The *Raîche* case in Canada helps to make this clear. A New Brunswick boundary-drawing commission applied a relatively perfectionist one vote, one value test, in effect prioritising this over the communities of interest principle.[124] A court reversed the commission's self-imposed rule of $+/-$ 10 per cent tolerance, which had been different from the far greater leeway of $+/-$ 25 per cent set by legislation. The stricter rule in effect ousted Acadians, a distinct community of French-speakers, from dominance in their riding. The commission had split the community and distributed its pieces into majority-Anglophone electorates. In a country where French is constitutionally enshrined,[125] it is difficult to deny that Acadians – settled from France in 1604, exiled in the mid-1700s, and resettled again – constitute a coherent and historically distinctive group. Yet the example also illustrates how, in any number of cases, communities of interest might not neatly fit within electorate boundaries set by a strict test of quantitative equality.

It might be argued that it should not matter how often marginal views are voiced: whether very often, or just once. Persuasiveness in deliberative democracy is not primarily a function of how many people hold a certain view, or how often they express it, but of the view's inclusion in the forum and of its cogence. Thus perhaps even the most marginal views should be able to transcend their modest numbers if their views are inherently persuasive. Yet, in practice, overlooked perspectives will remain so unless expressed consistently and loudly enough for others to be at least made aware of them. The communities of interest principle can sometimes help make district-based democracy more inclusive and deliberative. In large part for this reason, we contend that electoral boundary systems should resist the encroachments of equality perfectionism.

Despite our view, the communities of interest principle has lost some currency, and a perfectionist and numeric principle of equality is ascendant. This is broadly evident in legislative and judicial trends. In Australia, each federal electorate

140 The Law of Deliberative Democracy

must have, 'as far as practicable', a number of voters within 3.5 per cent of the average.[126] In addition, the Australian High Court's increasingly common political-equality-based decisions (eg, in voting franchise cases[127]) may have primed the Court to shed its remaining reserve about reviewing voter apportionment. In Canada, too, while lower courts are bound to follow *Carter's* flexible approach, they have appeared to do so grudgingly.[128] Canada's judges appear ready to begin disciplining readjustment under more perfectionist equality formulae, should the issue return to the Supreme Court.

Note, however, that numeric equality perfectionism is not limited to cases involving voters as individuals. It has sometimes been combined with the party-focused approach mentioned earlier in the chapter. For instance, since a 1991 amendment, the Constitution of the state of South Australia has instructed electoral boundary commissioners to try to predict party seat tallies. The unusual 'electoral fairness and other criteria' provision provides that:

> [i]n making an electoral redistribution the Commission must ensure, as far as practicable, that the electoral redistribution is fair to prospective candidates and groups of candidates so that, if candidates of a particular group attract more than 50 per cent of the popular vote ... they will be elected in sufficient numbers to enable a government to be formed.[129]

Equality is thus cast in terms not of voters, but of candidates and 'groups' (that is, parties – especially the two major parties). Interestingly, a later subsection reaffirms the role of traditional redistricting factors such as geography, topography, and communities of interest; yet these are relegated to 'other criteria'. The law's drafters promoted the 50 per cent rule as a tool to curb the infamous distortions of single-member district voting, which periodically keep parties out of government even when they secure majorities of the popular vote.[130]

An extreme measure based almost solely on strategic balancing, the 50 per cent rule rewrites the results of boundary redistributions – and potentially of elections – with the parties' interests foremost in mind. Also extraordinarily, it gives the main parties rough equality not of opportunities, but of *outcomes*. In effect, it seeks to settle the results of elections based on presumed bottom-line party support.

This model excludes broader equality and deliberative factors. Major parties are broad tents. For example, centre-left parties (eg, Australian and UK Labor/Labour, Canada's Liberals, and the Democrats of the US) tend to attract support from postgraduate-educated, urban, immigrant, non-white, religious-minority, and many working-class voters. Even if they habitually vote for the same party, these groups often disagree on substantive matters of policy. But the perfectionist and party-based construction of political parties in the South Australian model is largely insensible to the varying preferences within the party. By foregrounding the equality of parties, the model groups together communities with little more in common than presumed voting intention. This places the cart before the horse. It gives parties priority over discrete groups of voters in the community – the voters whose representation the communities of interest principle had sought to secure.

Conclusion

Deliberative reform schemes aim to increase the degree of deliberative practice in a democracy, even if only marginally. In our view, such schemes occasionally hold promise. Yet they can have limited impact on their own, so long as the forms of the law of politics do not align with them. In light of perennial concerns about the woeful quality of electoral campaigning in modern democracies, deliberative reform schemes deserve a more nuanced and sympathetic judicial response.

We have argued that the law of politics often advances, at best, a simplistic view of political equality. Too often, it lets the political parties set the terms and boundaries of democratic expression, rather than the other way around. And it singles out evocative but simple quantitative comparisons, using these to trump wider notions of political equality understood as deliberative inclusion. A legal system that aims to rebalance only that which is most visibly out of balance may do damage to deeper and more comprehensive ideals of equality.

Notes

1 *Democracy and Disagreement* (Harvard University Press, 1996) 133.
2 Cited in Jeffrey Toobin, 'The Absolutist', *The New Yorker*, 30 June 2014, 41.
3 'Factions' here denote groups (including, but not limited to, sub-groups within political parties) organised according to common interest, but not themselves formalised political parties. For simplicity, we use 'party' to refer to both formal and informal political groups.
4 Amy Gutmann and Dennis F Thompson, *Why Deliberative Democracy?* (Princeton University Press, 2004) 256, 210.
5 Ibid 43.
6 James Bohman, 'Deliberative Democracy and the Epistemic Benefits of Diversity' (2006) 3 *Episteme* 175; Joshua Cohen, 'Deliberative and Democratic Legitimacy' in A Hamlin and P Pettit (eds), *The Good Polity* (Oxford University Press, 1989) 17, 18; John Parkinson, 'Democratizing Deliberative Systems' in Jane Mansbridge and John Parkinson (eds), *Deliberative Systems* (Cambridge University Press, 2012) 155.
7 See, eg, Julie Novkov, 'The Miscegenation/Same-Sex Marriage Analogy: What Can We Learn from Legal History?' (2008) 33 *Law & Social Inquiry* 345. Similarly, movements for gender and racial equality have borrowed normative and legal propositions from each other: Reva B Siegel, 'She the People: The Nineteenth Amendment, Sex Equality, Federalism and the Family' (2002) 115 *Harvard Law Review* 947.
8 See, eg, Transcript of Proceedings, *Obergefell v Hodges* (US Supreme Court, 14-556-Question-1, Ginsburg J, 28 April 2015) 70 ('[U]nder the common law tradition ... [m]arriage was a relationship of a dominant male to a subordinate female'. No state is 'allowed to have such a ... marriage anymore'); *Baskin v Bogan*, 766 F 3d 648, 661–3; 666–8 (7th Cir, 2014) ('Tradition per se ... cannot be a lawful ground for discrimination – regardless of the age of the tradition' (at 666, Posner J)).
9 For more on equality and deliberation in the same-sex marriage controversy, see Hoi Kong and Ron Levy, 'Deliberative Constitutionalism' in André Bächtiger, John

Dryzek, Jane Mansbridge and Mark Warren (eds), *Oxford Handbook of Deliberative Democracy* (Oxford University Press, forthcoming).

10 Dennis F Thompson, *Just Elections* (University of Chicago Press, 2002) 20.

11 See, eg, David Dyzenhaus, 'Law as Justification: Etienne Mureinik's Conception of Legal Culture' (1998) 14 *South African Journal on Human Rights* 11, 34. See also Albie Sachs, *The Strange Alchemy of Life and Law* (Oxford University Press, 2009) 33.

12 David Dyzenhaus, 'Dignity in Administrative Law: Judicial Deference in a Culture of Justification' (2012) 17 *Review of Constitutional Studies* 87, 92–3. More controversially, Peter Westen famously observed that equality claims derive 'entirely from rights': '[equality] is a "form" for stating moral and legal propositions whose substance' is based elsewhere: Peter Westen, 'The Empty Idea of Equality' (1982) 95 *Harvard Law Review* 537, 542, 556–68, 577–8, 592. Cf Steven J Burton, 'Comment On "Empty Ideas": Logical Positivist Analyses of Equality and Rules' (1981–1982) 91 *Yale Law Journal* 1136, noting how viewing disputes in comparative rather than absolute terms gives judgments a distinctive perspective.

13 *Reynolds v Sims*, 377 US 533 (1964).

14 *Attorney-General (Cth); ex rel McKinlay v Commonwealth* (1975) 135 CLR 1, 21 (Barwick CJ) ('*McKinlay*'). See also Michael Coper, *Encounters with the Constitution* (CCH Books, 1987) 335.

15 *Roach v Electoral Commissioner* (2007) 233 CLR 162 ('*Roach*').

16 Ibid 174 (Gleeson CJ), 188 (Gummow, Kirby and Crennan JJ). For discussion see, eg, Graeme Orr and George Williams, 'The People's Choice: The Prisoner Franchise and the Constitutional Protection of Voting Rights in Australia' (2009) 8 *Election Law Journal* 123; Nicholas Aroney, 'Towards the "Best Explanation" of the Constitution: Text, Structure, History and Principle in *Roach v Electoral Commissioner*' (2011) 30 *University of Queensland Law Journal* 145.

17 Women gained the right to vote federally in the Commonwealth Franchise Act 1902 (Australia), s 3. Note, however, that they were already voting in some pre-federation colonies: Helen Irving, 'The People and Their Conventions' in Michael Coper and George Williams (eds), *Power, Parliament and the People* (Federation Press, 1997) 113, 122.

18 *Sauvé v Canada (Chief Electoral Officer)* [2002] 3 SCR 519.

19 The European Court of Human Rights in *Hirst v United Kingdom (No 2)* (2006) 42 EHRR 849, [82] held that a complete ban on prisoner voting (in the Representation of the People Act 1983 (UK), s 3(1)) was a 'general, automatic and indiscriminate restriction on a vitally important Convention right'. The UK legislature has resisted liberalising the law.

20 *McGinty v Western Australia* (1996) 186 CLR 140, 183 (Dawson J) ('*McGinty*'). In the seminal American case on malapportionment, the Supreme Court chose to intervene but acknowledged that the separation of powers (along with other rationales) imposes limits on political questions' justiciability: *Baker v Carr*, 369 US 186 (1962), 210, 217 ('*Baker*').

21 Kenneth J Arrow, 'A Difficulty in the Concept of Social Welfare' (1950) 58 *Journal of Political Economy* 328, 328–33.

22 *Richardson v Ramirez*, 418 US 24, 55 (1973). For discussion see, eg, Abigail M Hinchcliff, 'The "Other" Side of *Richardson v Ramirez*: A Textual Challenge to Felon Disenfranchisement' (2011) 121 *Yale Law Journal* 194.

23 *McGinty*, above n 20, 166. For discussion see, eg, David Ball, 'The Lion That Squeaked: Representative Government and the High Court: *McGinty & Ors v the State of Western Australia*' (1996) 18 *Sydney Law Review* 372; Greg Carne 'Representing Democracy or Reinforcing Inequality? Electoral Distribution and *McGinty v Western Australia*' (1997) 25 *Federal Law Review* 351; Jeremy Kirk, 'Constitutional Limitations (II): Doctrines of Equality and Democracy' (2001) 25 *Melbourne University Law Review* 24.

24 A minority of the Court, Toohey and Gaudron JJ, held that the Western Australian malapportionment was 'so great as to be distinctly at odds with democratic standards' and amounted to an 'arbitrary and inflexible' distribution (*McGinty*, above, n 20, 215, 223). Also relevant to the majority's reasoning was the fact that the Court was asked to apply the federal Constitution to a state law in this case. Not until later cases (eg *Coleman v Power* (2004) 220 CLR 1; *Unions New South Wales v New South Wales* (2013) 304 ALR 266) did the Court clearly signal that the federal Constitution could apply to the states in this way.

25 *McGinty*, above n 20, 189 (Dawson J), 215 (Toohey J), 222–3 (Gaudron J), 286–7 (Gummow J), citing obiter comments by Mason J in *McKinlay* , above n 14, 61.

26 See, eg, *Crawford v Marion County Election Board*, 553 US 181 (2008) (upholding a voter ID law which opponents argued disadvantaged old and poor voters).

27 Orr and Williams, above n 16, 124.

28 Thomas Christiano, *The Rule of the Many* (Westview Press, 1996) 53–6; Jack Knight and James Johnson, 'What Sort of Equality Does Deliberative Democracy Require?' in James Bohman and William Rehg (eds), *Deliberative Democracy: Essays on Reason and Politics* (MIT Press, 1997) 279, 280.

29 Zsuzsanna Chappell, *Deliberative Democracy: A Critical Introduction* (Palgrave Macmillan, 2012) 75.

30 Ibid; Gutmann and Thompson, above n 1, 28.

31 Chappell, above n 29, 74.

32 Ibid 80 (inclusion of arguments); Iris Marion Young, *Inclusion and Democracy* (Oxford University Press, 2000) (social perspectives); John Dryzek, 'Democratization as Deliberative Capacity Building' (2009) 42 *Comparative Political Studies* 1379 (interests and voices); John Dryzek, 'Discursive Representation' (2008) 102 *American Political Science Review* 481, 481 (discourses).

33 Iris Marion Young, 'Activist Challenges to Deliberative Democracy' (2001) 29 *Political Theory* 670, 679–80.

34 James Bohman, *Democracy across Borders: from Demos to Demoi* (MIT Press, 2007) 92; Dryzek, 'Democratization as Deliberative Capacity Building', above n 32, 1385.

35 John Dryzek, *Deliberative Democracy and Beyond: Liberals, Critics, Contestations* (Oxford University Press, 2000) 59. For instance, some individuals or groups are predisposed to rely more on emotive than rational forms of communication: Niamh Gaynor, 'Associations, Deliberation and Democracy: The Case of Ireland's Social Partnership' (2011) 39 *Politics and Society* 497, 502.

36 John Rawls, *Political Liberalism* (Columbia, Expanded Edition, 2005) 137.

37 James Bohman, *Public Deliberation: Pluralism, Complexity, and Democracy* (MIT Press, 1996) 81 (describing and critiquing this notion).

38 Jürgen Habermas, *Between Facts and Norms: Contributions to a Discourse Theory of Law and Democracy* (MIT Press, 1996) ch 7, 306.

39 Harry Brighouse, 'Egalitarianism and Equal Availability of Political Influence' (1996) 4 *The Journal of Political Philosophy* 118. In chapter 6, we return to the notion of coercion and provide additional description and analysis.

40 Nicole Curato, 'A Sequential Analysis of Democratic Deliberation' (2012) 2 *Acta Politica* 423, 435; Ian O'Flynn, 'Deliberative Democracy for a Great Society' (2015) 13 *Political Studies Review* 207, 210–11.

41 Note the objection that the Assembly's stratified random sample, which has members roughly representative of demographic groups in the broader society, is proportionate rather than equal: John Parkinson, *Deliberating in the Real World: Problems of Legitimacy in Deliberative Democracy* (Oxford University Press, 2006) 33–4.

42 See, eg, contributions to Mark E Warren and Hilary Pearse (eds), *Designing Deliberative Democracy: The British Columbia Citizens' Assembly* (Cambridge University Press, 2008).

43 Gutmann and Thompson, above n 1, 133.
44 Ibid.
45 Ibid.
46 See Warren and Pearse, above n 42.
47 On the tensions in deliberative democracy's universalism and its accommodation of minority cultural groups see, eg, Seyla Benhabib, *The Claims of Culture: Equality and Diversity in the Global Era* (Princeton University Press, 2002).
48 Gutmann and Thompson, above n 1, 33.
49 Thomas Christiano, *The Constitution of Equality: Democratic Authority and its Limits* (Oxford University Press, 2008) 199.
50 Gaynor, above n 35, 508.
51 Ibid 511.
52 Jane Mansbridge et al, 'The Place of Self-Interest and the Role of Power in Deliberative Democracy' (2010) 18 *Journal of Political Philosophy* 64. See also Nancy Rosenblum, *On the Side of Angels: An Appreciation of Parties and Partisanship* (Princeton University Press, 2008) 306; Gerald C Wright and Brian F Schaffner, 'The Influence of Party: Evidence from the State Legislatures' (2002) 96 *American Political Science Review* 367 (arguing, though not from a deliberative perspective, that parties provide clear lines of electoral accountability).
53 Bernard Manin, 'On Legitimacy and Democratic Deliberation' (1987) 15 *Political Theory* 338, 357; Cohen, above n 6, 31–2; James Johnson, 'Political Parties and Deliberative Democracy?' in Richard S Katz and William Crotty (eds), *Handbook of Party Politics* (Sage, 2006) 47.
54 Robert E Goodin, *Innovating Democracy: Democratic Theory and Practice after the Deliberative Turn* (Oxford University Press, 2008) 258.
55 Archon Fung, 'Survey Article: Recipes for Public Spheres: Eight Institutional Design Choices and Their Consequences' (2003) 11 *Journal of Political Philosophy* 338, 345.
56 Russell Muirhead, 'Can Deliberative Democracy be Partisan?' (2010) 22 *Critical Review* 129, 134–5.
57 David Pelletier et al, 'The Shaping of Collective Values through Deliberative Democracy: An Empirical Study from New York's North Country' (1999) 32 *Policy Sciences* 103.
58 Carolyn M Hendriks, John S Dryzek and Christian Hunold, 'Turning up the Heat: Partisanship in Deliberative Innovation' (2007) 55 *Political Studies* 362, 362.
59 Ibid, 371.
60 Kathleen Bawn et al, 'A Theory of Political Parties: Groups, Policy Demands and Nominations in American Politics' (2012) 10 *Perspectives on Politics* 571, 579.
61 John Parkinson, 'Legitimacy Problems in Deliberative Democracy' (2003) 51 *Political Studies* 180, 187–8.
62 *Australian Capital Television Pty Ltd v Commonwealth* (1992) 177 CLR 106 ('*ACTV*'). See further Arthur Glass, 'Freedom of Speech and the Constitution: *Australian Capital Television* and the Application of Constitutional Rights' (1995) 17 *Sydney Law Review* 29; Donald Speagle, '*Australian Capital Television Pty Ltd v Commonwealth*' (1992) 18 *Melbourne Law Review* 938; George Williams, 'Freedom of Political Discussion and Australian Electoral Laws' (1998) 5 *Canberra Law Review* 151.
63 Broadcasting Act 1942 (Australia) Pt IIID, amended by the Political Broadcasts and Political Disclosures Act 1991 (Australia).
64 *ACTV*, above n 62, 128 (Mason CJ).
65 Ibid 127 (Mason CJ), 237 (McHugh J).
66 Ibid 131, 144–5 (Mason CJ).
67 Ibid 160 (Brennan J, dissenting).
68 Ibid 161.

69 Ibid 130, 144 (Mason CJ), 155–6 (Brennan J, dissenting); 188–9 (Dawson J); 238 (McHugh J).

70 Ibid 129, 144 (Mason CJ), 155, 159 (Brennan J, dissenting).

71 Ibid 172, 174 (Deane and Toohey JJ), 237–8, 245 (McHugh J); for a contrary view, see 190–1 (Dawson J)

72 Ibid 146; see also 129 (Mason CJ), 172 (Deane and Toohey JJ).

73 A rare early exception is *Australian Communist Party v Commonwealth* (1951) 83 CLR 1, which, however, involved an egregiously poorly drafted and overreaching law.

74 *ACTV*, n 62 above, 161 (Brennan J).

75 Ibid 132. See similarly at 237 (McHugh J).

76 Wright and Schaffner, above n 52.

77 Chad Flanders, 'Deliberative Dilemmas: A Critique of Deliberation Day from the Perspective of Election Law' (2007) 23 *Journal of Law and Politics* 147, 155–6; Richard H Pildes, 'Democracy and Disorder' in Cass R Sunstein and Richard A Epstein (eds), *The Vote: Bush, Gore, and the Supreme Court* (University of Chicago Press, 2001) 140.

78 Australian Electoral Commission, *Current Register of Political Parties* (16 February 2016) <www.aec.gov.au/parties_and_representatives/party_registration/Registered_parties/> accessed 22 February 2016.

79 To be sure, judges often choose blanket invalidation over a more surgical re-writing of statutes, perhaps (ironically) because the latter feels more like a usurpation of the legislature's role.

80 *ACTV*, above n 62, 146 (Mason CJ).

81 Test subjects, organised into groups essentially at random, quickly develop antipathy to each other: Henri Tajfel, 'Intergroup Behavior, Social Comparison and Social Change' (Katz-Newcomb Lectures, University of Michigan, Ann Arbor, mimeo, 1974). See also Michael Billig and Henri Tajfel, 'Social Categorization and Similarity in Intergroup Behaviour' (1973) 3 *European Journal of Social Psychology* 27.

82 Even an infant's sense of injustice, which develops as early as the first two years of life, centres on comparison: J Kiley Hamlin et al, 'Not Like Me = Bad: Infants Prefer Those Who Harm Dissimilar Others' (2013) 24 *Psychological Science* 589; Stephanie Sloane, Renée Baillargeon and David Premack, 'Do Infants Have a Sense of Fairness?' (2012) 23 *Psychological Science* 196.

83 See, eg, Donald L Horowitz, *Ethnic Groups in Conflict* (University of California Press, 2001) 143–7; Leon Festinger, 'A Theory of Social Comparison Processes' (1954) 7 *Human Relations* 117; Joanne V Wood, 'Theory and Research Concerning Social Comparisons of Personal Attributes' (1989) 106 *Psychological Bulletin* 231. See also studies of income levels and employee satisfaction correlated with levels of relative income: Andrew E Clark and Andrew J Oswald, 'Satisfaction and Comparison Income' (1996) 61 *Journal of Public Economics* 359.

84 Graeme Orr, 'Private Association and Public Brand: the Dualistic Conception of Political Parties in the Common Law World' (2014) 17 *Critical Review of International Social and Political Philosophy* 332, 338–9.

85 Jacob Rowbottom, 'Access to the Airwaves and Equality: The Case against Political Advertising on the Broadcast Media' in Keith D Ewing and Samuel Issacharoff (eds), *Party Funding and Campaign Financing in International Perspective* (Hart, 2006) 77. See Communications Act 2003 (UK), s 321.

86 The Electoral Commission (UK), *Party Political Broadcasting Review, 2001–02* (December 2001) 7.

87 The Electoral Commission (UK), 'Factsheet: Party Election Broadcasts and Referendum Campaign Broadcasts' (November 2010), quoted in Isobel White and Oonagh Gay, 'Party Political Broadcasts' (House of Commons Library Note, 17 March 2015, SN/PC 00354).

146 The Law of Deliberative Democracy

88 Jacob Rowbottom, 'Deliberation and Mass Media Communication' (2013) 12 *Election Law Journal* 435, 452.

89 Ofcom, 'Ofcom Rules on Party Political and Referendum Broadcasts' (21 March 2013) <http://stakeholders.ofcom.org.uk/broadcasting/guidance/programme-guidance/ppbrules/> accessed 22 February 2016, [22].

90 Rowbottom, above n 85, 78–9. See also The Committee on Standards in Public Life (Parliament of the UK), *Standards in Public Life: The Funding of Political Parties in the United Kingdom* (Fifth Report, Vol 1, October 1998) 174–6.

91 *Animal Defenders International v The United Kingdom* [2013] ECHR 362 ('*Animal Defenders*'); see also Jacob Rowbottom, 'Animal Defenders International: Speech, Spending and a Change of Direction in Strasbourg' (2013) 5 *Journal of Media Law* 1.

92 *Animal Defenders*, above n 91, [112], [117].

93 For details see Andrew Geddis, *Electoral Law in New Zealand: Practice and Policy* (LexisNexis, 2nd ed, 2014) ch 10.

94 Ibid 203.

95 Ibid 204–205.

96 It is also an example of electoral exceptionalism – the concept that special regulation is desirable at election time but might be unwarranted at other periods of the political cycle. Frederick Schauer and Richard H Pildes, 'Electoral Exceptionalism and the First Amendment' (1999) 77 *Texas Law Review* 1803.

97 Compare Anika Gauja and Graeme Orr, 'Regulating "Third Parties" as Electoral Actors: Comparative Insights and Questions for Democracy' (2015) 4 *Interest Groups and Advocacy* 249.

98 *Bowman v United Kingdom* [1998] ECHR 4 (invoking the freedom of expression in the European Convention of Human Rights).

99 Representation of the People Act 1983 (UK), s 75.

100 See Gauja and Orr, above n 97

101 Representation of the People Act 1983 (UK), s 75(1ZZB)–(1ZA).

102 Bohman, above n 37, 321.

103 David Lublin and Michael McDonald, 'Is It Time to Draw the Line? The Impact of Redistricting on Competition in State House Elections' (2006) 5 *Election Law Journal* 144.

104 *Karcher v Daggett*, 462 US 725 (1983) (elaborating on an implied rule of equality in art I, § 2 of the US Constitution). *Karcher* actually stands for the proposition that population differences among districts are permissible on the basis of legitimate state objectives: at 734. *Karcher* was in that respect a softening of the earlier *Wesberry* standard, which had established the requirement that 'as nearly as is practicable one man's vote in a congressional election is to be worth as much as another's': *Wesberry v Sanders*, 376 US 1, 7–8 (1964). However, the amount of flexibility is still limited. A recent Supreme Court decision applied the *Karcher* standard and found that West Virginia was justified in choosing a redistricting plan which had a 0.79 per cent population variance as opposed to one which had a population difference of only a single individual: *Tennant v Jefferson County Commission*, 567 US __ (2012) (*per curiam*).

105 For example the ratio between the Montana at-large District and the Rhode Island 1st District has been approximately 1.6:1. Congressional districts do not cross state lines.

106 Note that voter numbers in the Nunavut riding are constrained by the Nunavut territory's small population; as in other federations like the US and Australia, constituencies do not transcend provincial/territorial lines.

107 The disparities climbed higher shortly after, before they were scaled back somewhat by the Fair Representation Act, SC 2011 (Can), c 26.

108 Ron Johnston and Charles Pattie, 'From the Organic to the Arithmetic: New Redistricting Rules for the United Kingdom' (2012) 11(1) *Election Law Journal* 70,

70. There is a single national electoral quota for the UK and, with four exceptions, no electorate is to have more than 5 per cent above or below the quota: s 11 of the Parliamentary Voting System and Constituencies Act 2011, amending Sch 2 to the Parliamentary Constituencies Act 1986 (UK) c 56. At the federal level in Australia, the Electoral Commissioner sets the quota for each state and territory, and the aim is to ensure that the number of electors is no less than 3.5 per cent from the average in that state or territory: Commonwealth Electoral Act 1918 (Australia), ss 65 and 66.

109 Apportionment Act of 1842, 5 Stat 491.

110 Apportionment Act of 1872, 17 Stat 28.

111 Reapportionment Act of 1929, Pub L No 71–13, 46 Stat 21.

112 *Baker*, 369 US 186 (1962).

113 Eg, *Voter Information Project, Inc v City of Baton Rouge*, 612 F 2d 208 (5th Cir 1980) (schemes that serve to dilute the voting power of certain voters may violate the Fourteenth and Fifteenth Amendments even if the one person, one vote rule does not apply to non-legislative elections); *Tennant*, above n 104. Cf *Brown v Thomson*, 462 US 835 (1983) (deviations are acceptable for legitimate goals 'free from any taint of arbitrariness or discrimination', eg, to fit district borders to county borders).

114 *Reynolds v Sims*, 377 US 533, 568 (1964) ('an individual's right to vote for state legislators is unconstitutionally impaired when its weight is in a substantial fashion diluted when compared with votes of citizens living in other parts of the State') (elaborating on *Gray v Sanders*, 372 US 368, 379 (1963)).

115 *Reference re Electoral Boundaries Commission Act (Saskatchewan)* [1991] 2 SCR 158 ('*Carter*'). See generally Ronald E Fritz, 'Challenging Electoral Boundaries under the Charter: Judicial Deference and Burden of Proof' (1999) 5 *Review of Constitutional Studies* 1; Duff Spafford, '"Effective Representation": *Reference Re Provincial Election Boundaries*' (1992) 56 *Saskatchewan Law Review* 197. For a comparison between *Carter* and the comparable US law's equality perfectionism, see Robert W Behrman, 'Equal or Effective Representation: Redistricting Jurisprudence in Canada and the United States' (2011) 51 *American Journal of Legal History* 277. For an argument that the Supreme Court in *Carter* should have placed more emphasis on population size in determining electoral boundaries, see David Johnson, 'Canadian Electoral Boundaries and the Courts: Practices, Principles and Problems' (1994) 39 *McGill Law Journal* 224.

116 Graeme Orr and Ron Levy, 'Electoral Malapportionment: Partisanship, Rhetoric and Reform in the Shadow of the Agrarian Strongman' (2009) 18 *Griffith Law Review* 638; George Williams, 'Sounding the Core of Representative Democracy: Implied Freedoms and Electoral Reform' (1995) 20 *Melbourne University Law Review* 848, 856; Michael Stokes, 'A Tangled Web: Redistributing Electoral Boundaries for Tasmania's Legislative Council' (1996) 15 *University of Tasmania Law Review* 143.

117 *McKinlay*, above n 14.

118 *McGinty*, above n 20.

119 For a defence of the flexible approach, see Peter Creighton, 'Apportioning Electoral Districts in a Representative Democracy' (1994) 24 *University of West Australia Law Review* 78.

120 Orr and Levy, above n 116.

121 *Carter*, above n 115, 183–4 (McLachlin J).

122 Australian Electoral Commission, *2001 Profile of the Division of Kalgoorlie* (9 February 2011) <www.aec.gov.au/Elections/federal_elections/2001/Profiles/kalgoorlie.htm> accessed 22 February 2016.

123 See *contra* Nicholas O Stephanopoulos, 'Political Powerlessness' (2015) 90 *New York University Law Review* 1527.

124 *Raîche v Canada (Attorney General)* [2004] FC 679. *Raîche* arguably goes further than *Carter*, prioritising effective representation over equality perfectionism: Kim

Poffenroth, '*Raîche v Canada*: A New Direction in Drawing Electoral Boundaries?' (2005) 31 *Commonwealth Law Bulletin* 53.
125 Canada Act 1982 (UK), Sch B, ss 16–23.
126 Commonwealth Electoral Act 1902 (Australia), s 66(3)(a), as amended by the Electoral and Referendum Amendment Act 1998 (Australia).
127 See, eg, *Roach v Electoral Commissioner* (2007) 233 CLR 162; *Rowe v Electoral Commissioner* (2010) 243 CLR 1.
128 *Charlottetown (City) v Prince Edward Island* (1998) 168 DLR (4th) 79; *East York (Borough) v Ontario* (1997) 36 OR (3d) 733; *Friends of Democracy* [1999] NWTJ No 28; *Reference re Electoral Boundaries Commission Act [Alberta]* [1992] 1 WWR 481.
129 Constitution Act 1934 (South Australia), s 83.
130 For a favourable account of Constitution Act 1934 (South Australia), s 83 as a fairness guarantee, see Jenni Newton-Farrelly, 'From Gerry-Built to Purpose-Built: Drawing Electoral Boundaries for Unbiased Election Outcomes' (2009) 45 *Representation* 471.

Chapter 6

Integrity v Deliberation (The Partisanship and Coercion Problems)

Now the country suffered from its laws, as it had hitherto suffered from its vices.
Tacitus[1]

From time to time most democratic polities struggle to keep partisans from gaining control over the ground rules of politics. Nowhere is this clearer than in the drawing and redrawing of electoral district boundaries. Most jurisdictions now impose a legal rule of 'one vote, one value' (also known as 'one person, one vote'), which insists on the roughly equal apportionment of voters among districts. Yet this still leaves room to gerrymander. Gerrymanderers draw associations between, for example, working-class or postgraduate-educated citizens on the one hand, and Democratic Party voters on the other. The locations of demographic groups, and therefore of particular voters, can be gleaned from census data. Specialised computer software ramped up the opportunities for sophisticated electoral boundary manipulations starting in the 1980s. At a mouse click, incumbents (if they control electoral mapmaking) can spread opponents out in sub-majority numbers across many districts ('cracking') or concentrate them in outsized majorities in very few ('packing').[2] The results have often represented democracy's most outlandish manifestations of partisan decision making, producing exotic figures on electoral maps. Long and slender fingers follow country back roads to unite disparate enclaves of voters.[3] And boundaries wend round demographic blocs, serving as Rorschach shapes for scholars of democracy who see parson's noses,[4] nipples,[5] and of course salamanders.

Partisan maps surface repeatedly throughout the democratic histories of the countries of our study. In the United Kingdom, prior to the Great Reform Act of 1832,[6] many MPs were elected from tiny 'rotten' or 'pocket boroughs', each having just a handful of electors.[7] One of the most notorious, Old Sarum, had no voters at all for decades until its abolition.[8] Some of these odd disparities arose out of simple neglect. But often gerrymandering has been a more active affair. Canada's pugnacious first Prime Minister, Sir John A Macdonald, is remembered in part for the Gerrymander of 1882, '[p]erhaps the most ruthless of Macdonald's operations for party advantage'.[9] Macdonald 'follow[ed] the behests of the more exigent and greedy of his supporters, carving up Ontario in the most ruthless fashion for party advantage, and what is worse, taunting the Opposition at nearly every stage of the process'.[10] The parliamentary record documents the furious exchange among legislators over the 1882 boundary readjustment, which one opposition Liberal Member called an 'Act to bull-doze the Liberal Party of Canada'. On the other side Macdonald admitted: 'We meant to make you [Liberals] howl'.[11]

More recent episodes have been just as frank. As reported (and censored) in litigation over the case, election official and Democratic Party affiliate Wayne Bridgewater declared to his opponents that: 'We are going to shove ... [this map] up your f------ ass and you are going to like it, and I'll f--- any Republican I can'.[12] And in Australia, severely unequal voter apportionments were common at state level until approximately the 1990s.[13]

In chapter 5 we uncovered the problem of the law of politics' narrowly strategic treatment of inequality. *Strategic balancing* referred to processes whereby decision-makers tweak laws to correct outsized inequalities between the main political parties' chances of influencing voters and gaining power. Such balancing therefore conceives of political equality as mainly a matter of placing the competing parties on a more equal electoral footing. We noted how this narrow variety of equality can become a judicial crutch. Easy to operate, strategic balancing is nevertheless inattentive to wider normative values, not least deliberation. We suggested that a better way to resolve political equality cases would be to adopt a more deliberative notion of equality ranging beyond the equality of political parties.

Yet these fine arguments do not fit all situations. They can apply comfortably to cases where there is limited evidence that partisanship has motivated a legal change (eg, the amendments to Australia's Broadcasting Act considered in chapter 5).[14] But they are less convincing amid an established political culture of extreme partisanship. In such cases, exhorting judges to look past the partisan contest of parties can be unrealistic.

Recall from past chapters that, to deliberativists, 'strategic' groups or individuals compete with each other for dominance. Strategic contenders generally aim to see their own fixed allegiance groups, interests, and preferences prevail in the contest. In the law of politics – with its second-order focus on the ground rules of democracy – partisan conduct can be determinedly strategic. It may even challenge the integrity of the political order itself. Partisan capture of political rules poses the distinct risk to democracy of parties *entrenching* themselves in power contrary to the 'preferences of their constituents'.[15] This amounts to a risk of corruption in the broadest sense: not just the abuse of official power for private gain, political corruption also includes using existing power to *gain an undeserved hold on public office*.[16] Conversely, we may say that *integrity* (as we read it here) avoids such political corruption.

These definitions are hardly crystal clear. Conduct that may look corrupt to some is, to others, just the zealous push-and-pull between groups in a democracy, especially groups with different views about the common good. Yet the definitions identify pre-eminent concerns in scholarship and practice in the law of politics. 'Corruption', in Mark Warren's words, 'breaks the link between collective decision making and people's powers to influence collective decisions through speaking and voting, the very link that defines democracy'.[17] Deliberative democrats and others sometimes expand the definition of corruption beyond the narrow and traditional concept, which focuses on special access and favours ('governmental corruption'), to embrace a greater assortment of distortive influences on democracy ('electoral corruption').[18] For instance, wealthy benefactors' unequal donations to political parties are a worry when they influence electoral discourse based on factors 'irrelevant' to the campaign – a very deliberative concern.[19]

Partisan entrenchment is a particularly potent kind of electoral corruption.[20] If they control redistricting, partisans can both make and benefit from significant changes to districts. (The same is true of other decisions in the law of politics: eg, campaign financing regulation, constitutional amendment, judicial selections.) Gerrymanders can exert a multiplier effect: a party locked into power by gerrymandering can further manipulate boundaries.[21] And gerrymandering can be politically consequential: it affects general election outcomes and thus the broad policy directions of the state; and it is long-lasting, given the multi-year duration of a standard redistricting cycle.[22]

Hence, a court that values political integrity may need to deal with partisan rule manipulations – and the threat of strategic *im*balance of parties – as a first priority. Unlike the cases in chapter 5, then, sometimes strategic readings identify a controlling political problem. A court's prime concern should be to put out immediate fires by mitigating extreme partisanship.

Even so, strategic balancing is still not the law's best remedial option. A key obstacle is that partisanship and deficits of integrity are chiefly features of human conduct and attitudes, rather than of law. The values of previous chapters – liberty (chapter 4) and equality (chapter 5) – were either qualities of law (eg, law can mandate formally equal treatment and freedoms) or qualities to some extent directly regulable by law (eg, law can enhance substantive equality by redistributing social resources). Integrity is different. Laws cannot, at a stroke, mandate attitudes, motivations, worldviews, or 'moral dispositions'[23] – any of the internal states of mind that constitute a decision-maker's commitment to integrity. When law attempts to influence individual choices and predilections, there are few guarantees that such attempts will succeed. Individual human behaviour is a wild-card.

Yet, despite these difficulties, in this chapter we find that certain carefully tailored laws and institutions may engender integrity, even in the face of ingrained practices of extreme partisanship. We begin by outlining two alternative definitions/ legal models of integrity:

- *Thin integrity*: A relatively barebones approach, 'thin' regulation for integrity uses law as a tool of *negative* regulation: it defines and prohibits only that which does not count as integrity in decision-making. Often this means that decision-making is not substantially dominated by one political party or cartel of parties. Negative regulatory models often follow the strategic balancing approach: they call for maintaining tensions among counterbalanced

152   The Law of Deliberative Democracy

parties, each of whom acts to oppose and 'restrain'[24] the others in a system of 'institutionaliz[ed] conflict'.[25]

- *Thick integrity*: Thick integrity relies instead on a particular kind of *positive* regulation to stipulate what integrity affirmatively entails – a much harder task requiring a definition beyond the mere absence of extreme partisanship. On the thick definition we detail below, integrity requires decision-making to be broad-ranging in its sources and substantially rational in its methods. It should canvass relevant and probative arguments, points of view, and items of information. And it should sift and weigh these before reaching a decision. Significantly, this thick understanding of integrity echoes deliberative notions of judgment. (From this point we will often use 'deliberation' and 'thick integrity' interchangeably.)

Positive laws mandating thick integrity, then, take the relatively hard tack of stipulating substantive guidelines for thick integrity. It is no wonder that this is a comparatively unpopular regulatory method: it deals in substantially vague definitions. However, we find that positive regulation can effectively promote integrity far more than can negative regulation. Careful legal and institutional tailoring can promote integrity even in its thicker and more complex, deliberative form. Yet apart from Warren, and more indirectly John Uhr and Dennis Thompson,[26] until recently few deliberative democrats had mined the connections between deliberation and integrity.[27]

To begin the chapter we focus on a raft of problems stemming from excessive thin/negative regulation. Most legal commentators spend relatively little time conceiving of means of regulating political integrity other than under this thin model. Yet the model falls short both in terms of deliberation and on its own terms – as a tool for preventing partisan entrenchment. Such regulation assumes that power-holders inevitably and powerfully incline toward strategic self-dealing. The jurisdictions of our study are thus forever finding new ways to discipline partisan excesses in the laws of politics under more precisely codified rules of political conduct, in order to limit the discretion of power-holders. To concretise the discussion, the chapter focuses on the example of gerrymandering and its mitigation.

We initially outline the *partisanship problem*, or how elaborating legal rules to curb partisanship fails to address the attitudinal problem at the source of partisanship. We also explore the more complex *coercion problem*. Thin regulations fail in a deliberative sense when they coerce democratic outcomes. Non-coercion is a hallmark of deliberation, as we established in chapter 2. With regulation's negative form dominant in the law of politics, there may be comparatively little space for genuine democratic deliberation to run its course.

Hence, as in previous chapters, we first highlight how deliberation appears to conflict with other political values. But, making our usual move, we finish by challenging that perception. We develop a thick integrity model that incorporates deliberative values. Using case studies, we then show how this model has been effective despite the formidable challenges that partisanship and coercion present for the law of politics.

Thin integrity

Partisan redistricting in the United States has seen periods of quiescence and resurgence,[28] but in recent decades the rise of extreme partisanship has been undeniable.[29] At the same time, non-partisan redistricting has become the norm in Australia, the UK, and Canada. Australia was the first to assign the task to an independent bureaucracy. There, redistricting is in practice an essentially 'quasi-judicial, or even bureaucratic, task' performed largely without partisan referents.[30] There has been, comparatively, limited juridification of Australian electoral law, and a long history of judicial deference to the 'professional, relatively well-funded and centralized electoral authorities'.[31] Borrowing from Australia, in 1944 the UK created four permanent and independent boundary commissions, one for each of its constituent parts; the bodies' 'bona fides have only rarely been queried' since.[32] A little later, in Canada, a similar model of decision-making over electoral boundaries developed with the advent of federal commissions.[33] Since the early 1960s, one federal electoral boundaries commission (FEBC) for each province has governed redistricting.[34] Federal redistricting in Canada now attracts few charges of partisan self-dealing.

What has sent some other jurisdictions, notably the US, in strikingly divergent directions in recent decades? Some might attribute it to a question of manners, for instance seeing a relative 'civility and moderation' of politics in countries like Canada.[35] But this characterisation is unconvincing today,[36] as indeed it was in the past. Vigorous Canadian attempts to gerrymander were common for a full century before the advent of the FEBCs.[37] And certain boundary commissions set up by the Canadian provinces have been less impressive than their federal counterparts.[38] Factors more complex than the bare presence of commissions or the presumptively mild Canadian (or Australian or UK) political culture are at work. A main reason for the divergence, we suggest, is the overreliance on thin integrity regulation in the law of politics in the US.

Thin integrity regulation, as noted, is negative in form. In the law of politics, its main varieties are *strategic balancing* and *constraint*.[39] Strategic balancing aims to thwart official overreach by granting to the parties themselves the power to block partisan rule-making. Strategic balancing counterpoises partisan decision-makers, for instance, by installing partisans of different stripes on decision-making bodies such as electoral commissions, legislative committees, and even courts. It offers established parties a kind of self-help remedy. Part of the intent – and certainly the effect – of balancing opposed decision-makers is to have them hold each other in mutual check. Each is watchful for overreach by the others, seeking to block and counter the others' attempts to gain the upper hand.[40]

Constraint is negative in a more direct way. It attempts to bring the complex political world to order by formalising and clarifying reviewable limits on political

154 The Law of Deliberative Democracy

power. But, like balancing, constraint is often framed as a check on a political party's power *relative to all the others*. (This conflates integrity with equality: even constraint relies not on absolute but comparative judgments about when power-holders are too far out of sync.)

Strategic balancing and constraint frequently surface in the long catalogue of legal efforts to mitigate gerrymandering. For now, let us focus on the US, where (to generalise) thin regulatory models dominate in redistricting at both the state and federal levels. The majority of state legislatures draw state and federal boundaries by normal acts of legislation. Some states grant commissions control over redistricting. But the extent to which these commissions are independent from direct legislative control varies significantly across the states.[41] And, despite some movement in recent years to minimise legislative interference,[42] commissions are often politicised: membership is usually split between commissioners affiliated with the two main political parties.[43] (Several apparently non-partisan state commissions offer intriguing exceptions.[44]) In addition, under the US Voting Rights Act of 1965, individuals and the federal government may bring court actions against voting rules with deleterious impacts on the voting of historically disadvantaged ethno-racial groups.[45]

In the main, US redistricting is a product of finely tuned tensions between, for example, the two pre-eminent political parties, or between presumptively contending social factions (eg, white versus black or Latino). Integrity in decision-making in the US law of politics is thus often conceived of as the product of managed competition between opposing citizen or voter groups. In this area the law's modest objective is bipartisanship, rather than more robust non-partisanship. Samuel Issacharoff notes that the US Supreme Court's interventions into redistricting, while notionally based on constitutional individual rights and antidiscrimination norms, are actually driven by the Court's sense of the unfairness of partisan entrenchment by one side of politics.[46]

The notion that the law can and should step in to prevent partisan overreach dominates US commentary. Proposals commonly call for more 'process-based regulation',[47] including the implementation of independent commissions,[48] but also suggest far-reaching constraints on these commissions – for example, stricter administrative or judicial procedures to reconsider and review redistricting decisions;[49] transparency in the appointment of commissioners;[50] and, more generally, rationalisation, coordination, and simplification of decision-making. Rick Hasen thus proposes rules gradually perfected to remove 'the opportunity for partisan election officials to make discretionary decisions', in part by implementing 'periodic election law audits' to progressively eliminate 'potential ambiguities' from the law.[51] To Hasen, ambiguities are failures of vigilance, presenting decision-makers with irresistible opportunities for exploitation.

Most of all, balanced representation – for example splitting agencies between or among political parties – is a common approach to integrity in the US.[52] The assumption is that integrity emerges from institutions designed to 'enhance ... political contestation',[53] with powers counterposed to prompt mutual constraint, a struggle for dominance, and a hawkish distrust between decision-makers.[54] This is why representation on US state electoral bodies is generally split between the two major parties equally, or in proportion to legislative representation, such that commissioners each typically promote the interests of one party.[55] This strategic balancing model has long prevailed in the US law of politics. The commission created by Congress to adjudicate on the 1876 Hayes-Tilden election is a classic example of a commission split along party lines, and reproducing the partisan conflict it was established to resolve.[56] Even today, the six commissioners of the Federal Elections Commission (in charge of implementing federal campaign finance rules in particular) divide into three Republicans and three Democrats, and are noted for their occasional inability to reach any decision at all.[57] Many US commentators nevertheless remain committed to strategic balancing.[58]

Even for Westminster-model governments (the UK and, more approximately, Canada and Australia), where constitutional checks and balances were historically less prominent than in the US,[59] there have been continued calls for greater negative regulation. In the UK, statutory changes to the criteria used by the commissions have removed some discretionary powers.[60] This has rigidified the previously 'organic' statutory criteria used by the commissions to determine constituencies.[61] In Canada, as well, there is a stream of advocacy for greater constraint. Mark Carter believes that there is a 'need for a *Charter* jurisprudence' to elaborate rules to 'more clearly restrict' the management of redistricting.[62] His notion of a 'more consistent vision' that 'promises to structure and place limits upon the scope of interpretive discretion'[63] is another call for rationalisation and elaborate rule-making to curtail ambiguity.[64] Official reports also default to suggestions for tightening controls on boundary-drawing, for example by setting more rigid definitions of standards like 'communities of interest' (the main, rather vague criterion for drawing lower house districts).[65] The need for clarity, and the current 'lack of discipline' imposed on redistricting by the law, trouble many observers.[66]

Rooted in certain varieties of liberal tradition, negative regulation informs the design of essential political institutions in the US, and to a lesser extent in the UK, Australia, and Canada.[67] However, in at least two key ways thin/negative regulation taken to the extreme is problematic for the law of politics. Let us examine each in turn.

The partisanship problem

Political integrity and corruption defy precise definition. What amounts to a corrupt public act for private gain (eg, bribery) is not always clear.[68] But it is even more difficult to define the conduct that a negative rule against extreme political partisanship should disallow. Partisanship can elude judicial scrutiny, not because judges do not know partisanship when they see it, but because judges are bound by the rigidities of legal reasoning.

A straightforward legal prohibition against partisan districting might succeed in easy cases: judges can surely spot certain egregious gerrymanders, such as that of the Texas 25th Congressional District, which was redrawn to run for nearly 500 km from Austin to the Gulf of Mexico along a jagged line incorporating Hispanic (Democratic-voting) communities.[69] But most cases are harder. Deciding whether boundaries are drawn for partisan reasons would require judges to balance complex considerations like geography; social and economic similarities and differences; historical ties among local groups; and a range of other factors they cannot possibly master.[70] There are also evidentiary difficulties: litigants are unable conclusively to demonstrate harm caused by gerrymandering, as 'proving the exact reason why one candidate lost and another won may be impossible'.[71] Furthermore, if preventing 'excessive' partisanship is the goal, courts must somehow pinpoint when partisanship reaches this threshold.[72] In 1986 the US Supreme Court affirmed that partisan gerrymandering was a judiciable issue,[73] but after almost two decades of at best chequered success in the lower courts' attempts to enunciate 'judicially discernible and manageable standards', the Court retreated from that decision.[74]

Still, ambiguity in law is not in itself unusual. It is only when such definitional problems combine with abjectly partisan patterns of decision-making that more intractable problems seem to arise. Recall that integrity is at root not a property of law, but a description of human habits and attitudes. Laying down new negative rules rarely closes off every loophole and ambiguity.[75] Laws would do better to try to manage the partisans themselves – those who are motivated to push the envelope of propriety and to litigate aggressively to free themselves of the law of politics' constraints.

Yet how shall laws do this? Negative legal interventions are regularly ineffective in part as they can simply aggravate behavioural responses such as loophole-seeking and informal non-compliance. Numerous authors have explored the difficulty of influencing political behaviour through law.[76] Among the most relevant, Gerald Rosenberg collects a number of studies on judicial control of US redistricting during the Warren Court (1953–69), when it became a justiciable issue and judges stepped forcefully into the field. He concludes that there was at best a 'spotty' record of real-world reform.[77] For example, only some states saw their assemblies dislodge entrenched legislators from power any more often than before.[78]

More particularly, Issacharoff notes how 'constricting' regulations are frequently futile.[79] And Issacharoff and Pamela Karlan together introduce the metaphor of the 'hydraulics' of regulation, meaning the tendency of political behaviours (eg, campaign financing) to dodge legal constraints imposed upon them:

> political money, like water, has to go somewhere. It never really disappears into thin air ... [The 1976 *Buckley v Valeo* case on spending and donation regulations] produced a system in which candidates face an unlimited demand for campaign funds (because expenditures generally cannot be capped) but a constricted supply (because there is often a ceiling on the amount each contributor can give). ... In campaigns, the result is an unceasing preoccupation with fundraising.[80]

In our view such critiques bear principally on *negative* regulation. As a tool for regulating democratic practice, negative rules can be conceptually simple. Yet they can misfire precisely due to this simplicity. Instituting formalised rules via the tools of constraint and strategic balance risks doing more to catalyse than to suppress partisan rule manipulation. Political partisanship, like political money, can be hard to contain within formal legal channels.[81]

Formalised rules sometimes merely give partisans clearer targets for contestation. Many laws of politics shift political contests to the courts, where the laws can aggravate and concentrate competitions for power around narrow doctrinal disputes. This may only reinforce a political system's own tendencies toward agonism. A now classic illustration occurred in 2004–2005 as President George W Bush revealed his intentions to appoint apparent ideological partisans to US federal appellate courts. Partisan conflict began with the possibility of a vote on the Senate floor, then moved quickly to the issue of minority filibuster by Senate Democrats. In response, Republican senators, then in the majority, threatened changes to filibuster rules – the so-called 'nuclear option', which would depart from the old rule that only a supermajority vote could end debate in the Senate.[82] A bipartisan 'Gang of Fourteen' centrist senators then agreed to vote against the changes except in 'extraordinary circumstances' – thereby laying down a rule governing rules governing filibusters governing judicial appointments. Later the contest over appointments edged toward a fifth layer of rule-making, when debate centred around the boundaries of 'extraordinary circumstances'.[83]

In debate among politicians, and in broader public discourse, the appointments controversy focused attention on a discrete set of procedural problems.[84] At each step, the cascade of negative rules did not stop, but only relocated, the partisan contest. The parties fought each other under the last rule laid down. While elaborating ever more precise rules restricted the leeway for such battles, the process also narrowed and focused the resulting conflict, introducing greater clarity to the process and facilitating further conflict.

The benefit of elaborating new constraint rules is often at best temporary: there is a chaos period, or a lag phase, while parties adapt to shifting and still uncertain rules. There may be partisan peace during this brief calm. However, periods of lag and calm can decline as partisan efforts systematise and professionalise, with escalating rates of turnover.[85] As the political drama over judicial appointments played out in public and behind the closed doors of Senate offices, its main players seemed to hold out hope that each new rule would break the cycle. In reality, new rules frequently faltered just like their predecessors. The parties seemed blind to the possibility of counter-attacks, determinedly following the same negative pattern through cycle after cycle.[86]

Note the strong performative element in the problem of partisanship and its regulation. In Warren's words, when '[p]eople come to expect duplicity in public speech, the expectation tarnishes all public officials, whether or not they are corrupt'.[87] Yet not only behaviours, but laws too, can provoke this expectation. Negative regulations can cause their own cynical assumptions about political behaviour to self-fulfil when the regulations express the inevitability of partisanship. John Braithwaite observes:

> There are grave dangers in following the advice of Thomas Hobbes and David Hume and designing institutions that are fit for knaves, and based on distrust. The trouble with institutions that assume that people ... will not be virtuous is that they destroy virtue.[88]

Negative solutions tend to presuppose decision-makers who are wholly partisan. In a system dominated by negative balance and constraint strongly symbolising partisanship's inevitability, there may be little room left for a robust culture of integrity.

To be sure, some negative regulation will always be necessary. Recall from chapter 5 the 'backstop' function in the case of *Carter*, where Canada's Supreme Court extended merely qualified deference to boundary commissions. Yet, even if some governmental overreach is inevitable, the relevant question is how prevalent it is, and what therefore should be the degree of response. When we fashion negative regulations that are insensitive to the real levels of risk of partisan entrenchment in a given context, these remedies can be worse than the risks themselves. The law of politics' predominantly negative model of regulation of integrity, then, is often deficient on its own terms. It frequently fails to stanch efforts at entrenchment, which is the very aim of such regulation.

As we see next, some have argued that entrenchment might be merely transient, mitigated by the inevitable reverse swing of the political pendulum; in time, another set of partisans then becomes entrenched instead. This rejoinder embraces a long-term form of strategic balancing. Yet, even if this picture of negative regulation is empirically plausible (and this is far from clear), what are its deliberative consequences? We argue that it is generally anti-deliberative. The laws of politics' predominantly thin and negative model for integrity coercively determines the course – and even the outcome – of democratic decision-making.

The coercion problem

As chapter 1 noted, rapid juridification since the 1960s has laid down, atop existing democratic practice, a dense stratum of laws. This accretion of laws might have been unproblematic but for recurring patterns of practice in the law of politics – including strategic balancing and constraint – that truncate or reshape public deliberation. As they stand, laws of politics extensively influence the substance of debates and results in elections. A central hallmark of deliberative theory is that nothing except rational persuasion should compel decision-makers to reach a particular decision.[89] Yet the aim of law is often precisely to coerce: to use the force of the state to pressure a law's subjects to conform to mandates and restrictions. Can deliberative democracy be compatible with the law of politics when the two are apparently so contradictory in their methods?

Integrity v Deliberation   159

A preliminary answer, drawing on Jürgen Habermas, is that laws might coerce up to a point.[90] Hence, after mandating the creation of certain decision-making bodies, procedures, and criteria in broad terms, laws can step back to permit a democratic polity's actors to deliberate freely.[91] This is an important and partly convincing response to the coercion problem. But this preliminary answer may fall short. The potential for anti-deliberative coercion has increased with the laws of politics' proliferation throughout the sites of democratic choice. Laws now influence deliberation not merely by creating broad foundations for political deliberation, but also by establishing a fine matrix of rules.[92]

The principle of non-coercion is entailed from core assumptions in deliberative democratic theory. One is that the essence of decision-making should be rational persuasion – often described in Habermas's formulation of 'the unforced force of the better argument'.[93] This conception is far from unique to our era. Ancient and modern observers alike remark on the basic tension between governing by rational persuasion or by other forces, for example *strength*, the *identity and status* of speakers, and even *majority preferences*.[94]

Governing by brute strength raises the clearest (and fortunately now the rarest) cases of anti-deliberative coercion. Blasphemy laws aimed to exclude, on pain of penal sanctions, certain – or all – dissenting perspectives or arguments from theological discourse in the public sphere.[95]

The identity and status of a speaker raise cases both more complex and more prevalent. Identity and status can be socially persuasive despite only a tenuous logical link between the speaker's influential role (eg, divine or hereditary right, celebrity, wealth) and her argumentative claim.[96] Hence, as Habermas puts it, 'social power' and the 'strength of privileged interests' can give rise to 'illegitimate interventions' in deliberation.[97] To be sure, identitarian reasoning can sometimes enhance deliberation. As Jane Mansbridge et al point out, expressions about group identity can highlight distinctive and relevant perspectives, especially when the group's preferences and interests have previously been overlooked.[98] Also, deferring to a speaker with special knowledge and expertise may amount to choosing to be 'rationally ignorant', because everyone has only finite time and capacity to become well-briefed on public policy issues.[99] These are important exceptions to the anti-deliberative nature of social influence. But, more generally, by inserting heuristics or other decisional shortcuts, identities and statuses can cut deliberation short and precommit it to a relatively limited range of substantive outcomes.[100] (On this, see chapter 3.)

Finally, majority preference can also bypass deliberation. Crude forms of majoritarian democracy simply aggregate majority (or plurality) preferences to determine which set of citizens should hold sway in the making of policy and law. But when decision-making slavishly incorporates majority popular views it risks being unduly coercive. Deliberativists, like others, are acutely aware that bald majoritarian rule in decision-making is inattentive to a range of non-mainstream citizen interests. Conversely, when democracy is *structured to be deliberative*, it can be both more deliberative and more democratic.[101] (See chapter 2.) Deliberative

160   The Law of Deliberative Democracy

democracy caters to more than just the electorally dominant citizen bloc of the moment. However, it does not simply aim to unseat majorities from dominant positions. Rather, its objective is to loosen a majority's attachment to its existing preferences in order, at least to some degree, to reconcile and give expression to both majority and minority preferences.

To do this, there may need to be coercive power in the 'facilitating structures' of society; this limited coercion may 'be necessary to maintain basic rights, equal opportunity, and the other conditions that help participants approach the deliberative ideal'.[102] Admittedly, some (eg, some participatory democrats) would object to the idea that laws should mandate certain norms over others.[103] Such critics would want to see bottom-up participation that is uninfluenced by elite-defined norms. We recognise this objection. Yet deliberative democracy may well require laws to ensure that the structure of decision-making meets deliberation's required standards.

However, the notion of structuring democracy to be deliberative only gets us back to the larger problem stated at the outset: that laws should go no further than to create deliberative institutions and procedures. After this, the laws should step back and allow deliberation to carry on largely uncoerced by law. But are modes of decision-making in the law of politics indeed limited to structuring the procedures and initial conditions of deliberation? We argue that the law of politics is often not so limited, at least in its standard forms. This problem has both *external* and *cognitive* aspects.

a. External perspective on coercion

First, consider the *external* perspective – the perspective of outward appearances. How do the interventions of the law of politics affect relatively objective markers of uncoerced democratic deliberation? To the extent that laws bypass a more elaborate deliberative course of political decision-making (whether among elites or in the public sphere), laws may predetermine outcomes. The external signs of such legal shortcutting can be easy or hard to observe. Easier cases include laws that aim directly to curtail political deliberation, such as prohibitions on flag burning or other dissentient acts and words. Every now and then legal decision-makers even determine the outcomes of whole elections. *Bush v Gore* is deservedly notorious for this.[104] We also saw in the last chapter how some equalitarian interventions (eg, South Australia's electoral fairness provision) are perfectionist to such a degree that they predetermine elections, albeit with more benign motives. Such interventions enable wholesale transfers of political controversies into the courts or other independent bodies. There, if the decision-makers' partisan preferences do not resolve the issue, then legal tests (eg, of formal voter or party equality) may instead.

Most external indications of legal shortcutting are subtler, however. The coercive consequences of strategic balancing may not be immediately obvious. For instance, gerrymandering may reduce the number of competitive seats in a legislature,[105] and thus foreordain election results in some districts. Due in part to gerrymandering, only a few dozen of the US House of Representatives' 435 districts in a given election year tend to swing.[106] From a deliberative perspective, this effect is worryingly coercive. Since attempts at persuasion can do little to influence electoral outcomes in a non-competitive district, the local candidate has little cause to campaign, either deliberatively (setting out a coherent and popularly accessible policy platform) or otherwise. James Gardner therefore notes that when the law of politics assumes 'that the purpose of campaigns is primarily to tabulate exogenous voter preferences', rather than to stimulate deliberation, the effect is that 'political actors cannot reasonably expect, and therefore need not by law enjoy, meaningful opportunities during the campaign period to persuade voters to their points of view'.[107]

As we mentioned earlier, some observers defend entrenchment as part of an ongoing process of dominance-trading – a back-and-forth between roughly equal and opposite partisan groups.[108] Partisan electoral redistricting is therefore perhaps self-limiting in light of the political pendulum's inevitable swings: in time another side will take control of the electoral map. This notion is reflected in US Justice O'Connor's observation in *Davis v Bandemer* that '[t]here is no proof before us that political gerrymandering is an evil that cannot be checked or cured by the people or by the parties themselves'.[109] Hence, the opposing party, or voters, might in time even the score. This may or may not be a persuasive reading of the dynamics of partisan capture; it is, at best, significantly oversimplified.[110] Yet what is reasonably certain is the effect of this long-term strategic balance upon deliberation. Even if partisan entrenchment evens out over time, in the interim it is decidedly anti-deliberative. At a given time one group (a leading party, or a cartel of parties) has co-opted legal processes to control or strongly bias election outcomes.

Gerrymandered electoral maps are anti-deliberative when they pose in this way a very high bar for opposition parties to gain office.[111] Substantial public disaffection must first build toward an incumbent party that has overstayed its welcome.[112] This may coincide with a voting public's collective feeling that an overstaying government is no longer trustworthy and responsive. From time to time, voters prefer fresh governments, largely irrespective of the policy implications of the change.[113] In addition, partisan capture of the instruments of government can generate, for good reason, electoral revolts against the abuse of procedures of power.[114] But reversing entrenched partisan control is only weakly deliberative if – as is often the case – doing so is not chiefly an expression of public sentiment about a government's accumulated policy choices, but a reaction to a government in power for too long. There is minimal deliberation in the return-swing of a pendulum.

b. Cognitive perspective on coercion

Integrity is unique, as we have mentioned, in part for being based in states of mind. Integrity is essentially *cognitive*. It denotes a good-faith commitment to particular kinds of decision-making. This makes integrity an especially nebulous value. But the cognitive aspect of integrity is, in our view, a central incident of the Habermasian aspiration for restrained legal coercion. We saw above that, according to Habermas and others, the laws of politics should structure the procedures and initial conditions of deliberation, but should go no further. The cognitive view considers what this aspiration requires of the decision-makers who, by adjudicating, executing, and modifying rules, give life to these laws. What internal attitudes must such decision-makers adopt?

Our answer is that they should seek a cognitive separation between two categories of factors potentially bearing on their decisions: (1) *institutionally appropriate substantive principles* and (2) *downstream partisan consequences*. What is institutionally appropriate of course depends on the institution. For instance, the substantive guidelines for redistricting often include geographic contiguity, district compactness, and communities of interest. These are rational factors in light of the particular democratic objectives of the national lower houses in our study: legislators in these chambers each represent people in geographically defined districts. The redistricting guidelines assist that representation by combining, within a given district, coherent and identifiable communities of citizens (eg, historic communities; discrete immigrant groups; labourers; inhabitants of a rural township).[115] By contrast, decision-makers might instead, or in addition, be swayed by their awareness of how rule changes affect the parties' political fortunes – their likelihood of taking or holding office. In the redistricting context these latter considerations are institutionally inappropriate. Heeding them upends the goal of giving coherent voice to a society's many pre-political citizen groupings.

In cognitive terms, deciding with integrity in essence means that a decision-maker proceeds through the stages of the process by applying appropriate substantive criteria without fixating on the wider process. For instance, she should not consider how manipulating electoral boundary maps could allow her to influence election outcomes. Highly partisan decision-makers would tend to be fixated precisely on such concerns downstream of the decisional task at hand.[116] We saw another, recurring example above: the cycles of process manipulation in the US Senate on the matter of judicial selections. In the 2004–2005 controversy, in wave after wave of ad hoc rule-making, the substance of decision-making was secondary in importance. To partisans in this contest, focused foremost on winning the contest, there was relatively little genuine substantive deliberation, for example, about what qualities are required of a good judge. Most rhetorical and intellectual energy of the parties involved went instead toward manipulating procedural rules to angle for a win.

We have seen throughout this book that partisans often cement the substantive preferences and interests for which they stand well before the political contest even begins. The fixation on process manipulation can be such that no substantive choice is even required. Partisan struggle can sustain itself in a substanceless exercise of procedural competition. The fact that competition can thrive even absent differences of substance is long established in social psychology.[117] In the law of politics, the negative legal model often instigates this mode of exclusive cognitive fixation upon process and partisan electoral consequences. For example, Karlan notes that the partisan groups who engage in endless US litigation over gerrymandering invoke ostensible substantive reasons for changes to laws. But these changes merely give cover to partisan efforts: 'the political parties [have] learned to use one person, one vote, the *Voting Rights Act*, and the *Shaw* principle' – setting out a requirement of strict scrutiny for redistricting in order to watch for impacts on minority representation – 'as "stalking horses" for pursuing partisan ends'.[118] This has had the 'incongruous result of producing plaintiffs whose motivation for litigation is almost entirely divorced from the doctrinal basis for their suit'.[119]

Viewing integrity as a cognitive practice permits us to see how difficult deciding with integrity in the law of politics can be. In a situation where the partisan stakes of a decision are high, can a decision-maker commit to *following* a process without *manipulating* it for partisan ends? One problem is that substantive factors do not readily lend themselves to clear definition.[120] It may be easy to slide between the two categories of cognitive factors in decision-making. For instance, a map might in one sense be gerrymandered if it favours Republicans by packing Democratic-leaning African-American voters into relatively few districts. But, seen from a different angle, this same map might aid black political representation by helping to elect black candidates in select districts.[121] Hence, it can be easy to hide partisan manipulations under the cover of ostensibly appropriate rationales. And even those people who are consciously committed to integrity in decision-making may have difficulty keeping institutionally appropriate criteria separate from partisan considerations. It can take Herculean efforts of self-control to ignore information (eg, that about 90 per cent of African-Americans vote for Democratic candidates[122]) in favour of appropriate criteria – in effect casting downstream political consequences out of one's mind.

The upshot is that such regulation can collapse the Habermasian separation between starting conditions, on the one hand, and subsequent uncoerced substantive deliberation, on the other. The rise of negative regulation can erase the cognitive division between partisan and institutionally appropriate reasoning. Negative regulation therefore presents a catch-22: by creating new procedural rules to constrain partisanship directly, such regulation prompts more focus upon process, thus recreating the very problem it aims to solve.

As juridification on the negative model of regulation has expanded across the sites of democratic politics, it has brought with it a more coercive pattern of regulation. Why such regulation remains so common, both in practice and in the works of reform-minded commentators, is clear: it is simpler than the alternatives. Negative regulation requires of laws only that they define and limit extreme partisanship. This is not easy, but it is not so hard as defining what integrity affirmatively would entail in the absence of partisanship. Nevertheless, the simpler, negative approach often self-defeats. There is therefore a need for alternatives. In the remainder of this chapter we explore one promising positive legal model that appears able to engender thick integrity and mitigate both the partisanship and coercion problems.

Thick integrity

From the burgeoning empirical record on institutional aspects of deliberative democracy, there is now a fairly strong sense of how – and to what degree – institutional design can promote deliberation. Can we adapt this body of knowledge to resolve the two problems in our sights? In the remainder of this chapter we address this question.

Our major focus remains, as always, on the *law* of deliberative democracy. A principal question is how the law of politics engenders thick integrity, when it does. We observe that some positive mandates impel certain political behaviours associated with thick/deliberative integrity more powerfully than do negative constraints. Also important is the loose and open-ended nature of such mandates. Using the Canadian FEBCs to illustrate, we describe what we call the *guidance model* of regulation in the law of politics. This model helps to account for how, beginning in the early 1960s, the FEBCs rapidly supplanted a century's worth of partisan gerrymandering. The model also appears able to avoid at least some of the habitual (and otherwise intensifying) coercion of democratic politics under law.

Few forms of regulation are surer to produce unintended consequences than those functioning at the interface of law and human motive and attitude.[123] Such attempts go against the grain of prevailing assumptions, especially in the historical and contemporary American traditions.[124] Nevertheless, our look at Canada's FEBCs and their enabling laws shows how some innovative bodies, charged with pivotal decision-making in the law of politics, can deliberate even in otherwise politically polarised settings. We base this conclusion in part on empirical work by one of us on these bodies, a selection of which is reproduced below. The FEBCs developed processes characterised by thick integrity soon after their creation. These bodies are now deliberative in key respects: communicatively rational, flexible, and open-minded; open to mutual learning among participants; engaged in extensive and holistic weighing of decisional factors; sensitive to representations about public preferences and interests; and apparently able to separate institutionally appropriate representations from those of interested partisans.[125]

Like any historical narrative, the full account of the rise of thick integrity federally in Canadian redistricting includes many causes.[126] However, the FEBCs' particular model of regulation by guidance seems at least to have played an influential role. We understand this model as having four key attributes:

- *Thick/deliberative.* The FEBCs' principal, if unstated, goal is to engender integrity in its thick/deliberative form. As we see below, a number of the bodies' institutional features reflect this implicit goal. The FEBCs are roughly akin to archetypal small deliberative democratic bodies, such as Citizens' Juries and Assemblies.
- *Independent.* As with other micro-deliberative bodies, FEBC decision-making is insulated from the partisan political fray.[127] Generally this requires a process to be situated within a commission, court, or even Citizens' Jury/Assembly

separate from other government processes. Further steps may be needed to ensure that a body remains independent and is not itself subject to partisan capture.

The FEBC model is also legally distinctive:

- *Qualified deference.* The model contemplates only a loose standard of judicial (or other) legal review of commission decisions. In chapter 5, we saw that under the 'backstop' approach, legal decision-makers may step in to reverse only the most egregious partisan rule manipulations. On this approach, negative regulation is not absent, but neither is it dominant.
- *Ambiguous positive guidance.* Finally, in place of negative regulation, the commissions' enabling rules affirmatively stipulate what thick integrity in decision-making entails. These are the positive legal standards we have mentioned. Crucially, to avoid the exacting and coercive scrutiny typical of negative regulation, positive norms are formulated ambiguously. They employ open-ended terms that loosely direct (or 'guide') decision-makers.

To give an example of the latter feature, federal Canadian legislation makes few attempts to clarify exactly what 'communities of interest' denote in electoral mapmaking. The contours of the principle are intentionally left obscure, leaving the principle's precise effects unpredictable. This may help laws to *begin* a process – to stipulate broad and basic substantive and procedural guidelines – without going as far as to foreordain a given decision-making result.

One benefit of ambiguous regulatory models is already widely recognised: flexibility. Several authors have noted the rise of new models of governance in public administration that depart from the traditional regulatory approach of rigid constraint, for example in the European Union[128] and the US.[129] Orly Lobel thus describes models providing 'a range of interpretation, deviance, and trial and error without the constraints of rigid orders and fear of formal sanctions'.[130] Such newer approaches to governance also tend to be characterised by 'softness' rather than coercion,[131] revisability rather than rigidity,[132] and informality rather than formality.[133] As evidence of the rise of such regulation in administrative law, Todd Rakoff observes that the number of US Food and Drug Administration (FDA) regulations adopted each year dropped, while the number of annual FDA-issued documents that more loosely guide conduct increased 400 per cent in the 1990s from the 1980s.[134] The rise of the new governance model is usually attributed to dissatisfaction with the inflexibility of the traditional regulatory model. Rakoff reasons that in a fast-changing world, rigid and formal laws are often incapable of anticipating and accommodating new loopholes and challenges, leaving room for abuse:

Open-ended, general grants of authority are needed in a fast-changing world where not all evils can be foreseen. If administrators must wait to enact through public processes new, precisely-tailored rules, before they can act, much harm can be done, which can only be undone later at much greater cost. Regulated parties who wish to disregard the public welfare will have an incentive to look for gaps in the rules and exploit them during the delay required to put new laws on the books.[135]

In our view the guidance model's benefits also go further. We offer here a distinctive take on integrity in the law of politics by relying not only on work in regulatory theory, the law of politics, and other public law, but additionally on deliberative democracy. Our interest is in ways of introducing – through both legal and general institutional design – deliberative democracy-based thick integrity into politically contentious settings. The FEBCs' example of the rise of integrity offers an intriguing study, but it is worth stressing that our aim is not to isolate the best or only option for regulation. Our goal is more modest: to outline just one approach capable of improving on the status quo. However, we do incidentally draw the wider conclusion that, especially outside the courts, the toolbox of legal design includes far more than merely the well-worn tools of negative regulation.

The guidance model requires regulators and lawmakers to become comfortable with indeterminacy and ambiguity in legal norms, despite the contrary global trend toward more exacting legal scrutiny. Yet, though harder to articulate, and open to objections raised below, this model of promoting integrity may be worth the effort and risk. Indeed, we are optimistic, if cautiously, about the guidance model's duplicability elsewhere. We consider next how the guidance model potentially responds to both the partisanship and coercion problems.

Thick integrity and the partisanship problem

In Canada's FEBCs, the guidance model appears to have contributed to the dampening of partisanship and the promotion of thick integrity in its place, via two complementary regulatory routes. The first is an instance of the growing use of so-called *veil of ignorance rules*. The second – more unique – is the deliberative effect of *disembodied representation*.

a. Veil of ignorance rules

A number of authors, both within and outside the law of politics, have proposed veil of ignorance rules.[136] These build upon John Rawls's hypothetical in which a group of constitutional founders, oblivious to their own identities, elaborate their community's keystone principles.[137] Veil of ignorance rules elevate this notion from thought experiment to concrete regulatory strategy, where rules function 'not by clarifying, but by blurring'.[138]

For our purposes, a key observation is that ambiguous guidance laws might help to avoid the regulatory traps of negative regulation. Lobel notes that a 'soft law approach reduces the often perverse incentives imposed by liability and sanctions'.[139] We previously discussed the law of politics' challenge of keeping decision-makers from fixating on decisional process instead of substance. Negative regulatory solutions often aggravate this problem by presenting a clear focus for partisan contention and loophole-seeking, and therefore catalysing cycles of partisan manipulation of process. By contrast, guidance norms are obscure, their directives ambiguous or even contradictory. These features can quell at least some of the usual partisan conflict over competing interpretations of the laws of politics.

A number of interesting examples of veil of ignorance rules directly concern partisanship. An international legal advisory group, helping to rewrite Malawi's post-conflict founding document, called for a 'Rawlsian moment': the first election was to be held only after passage of a new Constitution detailing incumbent government powers.[140] Others have highlighted the beneficial effects of ambiguity in a federal division of powers[141] and in other national administrative regimes such as the post-Revolutionary French system of départements. The latter model's designer, the Abbé Sieyès, 'adopted this ambiguous strategy of decentralizing the administrative system in order to regenerate the state'.[142] The new structure deliberately cut across geographic lines and historic communities, dividing the country into several hundred units in order to blur social divisions and durably construct French national unity.

In the area of our focus in this chapter, partisan redistricting, Adam Cox has written in praise of the long periods ('temporal floors'), such as ten years, between typical rounds of electoral mapmaking.[143] The long wait can 'curb the effects of partisan gerrymandering' by 'promot[ing] beneficial uncertainty in the redistricting process'. Cox explains: 'While redistricting authorities can make some predictions about voting behavior ... the accuracy of those predictions decreases as one moves further in time from the point of prediction'.[144] Indeed, most electoral districts undergo sizeable demographic shifts over normal redistricting cycles of five to ten years.[145]

One ironic measure of the usefulness of veil of ignorance rules in the law of politics is how often political partisans have sought to undermine them. In Texas, an extreme gerrymander occurred only two years after the last district change, well outside the usual ten-year cycle.[146] And, in a rare departure from federal Canadian practice, in the early-1990s Canada's Parliament *extended* – apparently for partisan benefit – the usual decennial timeline.[147] In the Malawian example, too, elections went ahead before completion of the Constitution, to the consternation of both the advisors and some locals. As predicted, the party then elected wrote wide governing powers into the new document. Such examples suggest that ambiguous rules might be useful only when entrenched and immune from casual modification or repeal. In the Texas controversy, however, the US Supreme Court held that the Constitution's decennial redistricting rule is not a legal minimum but a maximum.[148] Such a 'temporal ceiling' may do little to reduce partisan gerrymandering.

Turning to the FEBCs, which as we have seen are widely understood to be non-partisan, the system's elaborate ambiguous features generate unpredictable outcomes likely to befuddle partisan boundary plans. As one Canadian commissioner put it, 'most of the time, we don't even know the effect' – that is, how redistricting impacts on election outcomes.[149] There is little of the clarity and focus that elsewhere prompt partisans to compete to win self-favourable changes to the laws and regulations of politics. The FEBCs ambiguate first via *procedural ambiguity*. The stages of the process are numerous and their total duration extensive, typically lasting two years or more.[150] Decision-making runs an obstacle course of diverse and redundant stages. The commissions feature a mixture of advisory and direct influences: parliamentarians and members of the public make recommendations, and commissioners finally decide. There are alternately open- and closed-door sessions (the latter encouraging frank discussion).

Also relevant is the FEBCs' *role ambiguity*: the diverse assortment of professional cultures and participants in these Commissions. Thirty members of the FEBCs do the work of readjustment across the country. The chief justice of a province appoints a judge to chair each three-person commission (one for each province), while the federal parliamentary speaker appoints the other two members. Esteemed judges and political scientists, who still predominate, tend to share membership with other respected professionals, such as social workers and police officers.[151] Notices invite public and parliamentarian input in open hearings after the publication of the proposals.

Lastly, the FEBCs feature exceptional levels of *substantive ambiguity*. Laws must sketch out what count as institutionally appropriate criteria – the reasons why a decision is called in the first place. For example, as noted earlier, redistricting criteria such as communities of interest are geared to the district-based electoral model. Most redistricting systems have positive and negative elements in varying proportions. Even in US states where redistricting focuses overwhelmingly on negative regulation, laws are not wholly rudderless in substantive terms, but still also stipulate positive criteria.[152]

But the FEBCs' enabling laws,[153] constitutional provisions,[154] court decisions,[155] and assorted customary rules,[156] which together govern redistricting, contain a particularly copious set of open-ended and sometimes incommensurable substantive rules. A number of commentators and courts have noted this. The guiding representational principles look 'willfully "muddled"'.[157] The 'commissions are required to balance conflicting policies'.[158] On the one hand, the practical problems of representing a large rural electorate can be a concern; on the other hand, so might be 'human dignity' and 'social justice'.[159] Many principles overlap or conflict with others in the abstract: geography, community history, community interests, practical problems of representation, numeric parity among districts, and effective representation. Others overlap in their application, as where multiple communities with distinct histories occupy the same region. Rules are pitched at varying levels of specificity and breadth, as well as of clarity and vagueness. The rules for numeric apportionment of voters among ridings alone are elaborately complex.[160] There is in general a marked indeterminacy in the correct application of redistricting criteria.[161] The substantive guidelines applied are capable of resolving in a great many alternative ways, and have an 'elusive and imprecise quality about them'.[162] In contrast '[n]o equivalent rabbit-warren of representational rules exists in the United States'.[163]

FEBC rules and process provide no overriding theory or central substantive decision-making authority. There is little country-wide unification of redistricting efforts. Apart from rare exceptions, no single faction exercises top-down control. Courts review federal Canadian readjustment infrequently and seldom reverse commission decisions. The leading Canadian case is still the decades-old *Carter* decision, enunciating a qualified standard of review in imprecise terms.[164] Additionally, the ten commissions work 'highly independently of one another'.[165] 'We were not', reports one commissioner, 'aware of the specifics of [other FEBCs'] proposals nor the approaches they were taking in their decision-making'.[166] Input by parliamentarians provides a potentially unifying national perspective; however, most input and objections filed are province- or district-specific.[167] Moreover, the regulatory body in charge, Elections Canada, is a 'passive procedural overseer' of readjustment with neither a dispute-settlement function nor any other substantive decision-making responsibility.[168] The process is decentralised by design. Debates in Parliament around the time of the bodies' inception show a government aware of the confusion that ten disparate commissions would, and should, bring to redistricting.[169] In early days a single national representation commissioner authored first drafts country-wide, but the office wound up in 1979 after critics warned against 'central control over all the maps'.[170]

The situation is markedly different in the US, where state legislative majorities usually control redistricting – including redistricting by commissions – leaving little mystery as to which political party will come out on top in the process. Gerrymandering is also a frequent subject of nationwide interest. In the Texas gerrymandering battle, the US Senate Majority leader openly masterminded the plan, and the President expressed support.[171] Frequent litigation in federal courts under the Voting Rights Act of 1965 and the Fourteenth Amendment also generates central coordination. Litigation over election disputes has burgeoned dramatically,[172] a trend that Karlan believes will continue as the 'proliferation of constraints on the reapportionment process' moves political contests into the courts.[173] On the one hand, the redistricting case law is complex and even incoherent;[174] some substantive rules are markedly ambiguous, relying on concepts such as 'bizarrely shaped districts'.[175] Yet the readiness of a central umpire, especially a court, to settle redistricting disputes can both focus and clarify – particularly in light of the well-defined partisan divisions within many US courts. (Canadian courts differ markedly in this regard.[176]) As we have also seen, the substantive grounds for judicial review of US redistricting remain conceptually narrow, focusing on minority disenfranchisement rather than on broader notions of integrity.

There is a strong likelihood that federal Canadian boundary drawing has suppressed its once endemic partisanship in part by deploying the suite of ambiguous regulatory devices seen here. But note that nothing we have yet described is patently

170 The Law of Deliberative Democracy

deliberative in character. In addition, in our description so far, veil of ignorance rules ultimately follow a negative strategy of *precluding the effects* of partisanship. This relatively modest model has attracted attention particularly among scholars in the US, where efforts to secure more fundamental change in decision-makers' approaches to governance often prompt scepticism. A host of current authors share James Madison's view that 'the CAUSES of faction cannot be removed' and that 'relief is only to be sought in the means of controlling its EFFECTS'.[177] Such statements tend to picture official decision-making as irredeemably partisan at its core. Though we have challenged this assumption throughout this book, we can never entirely discount it. Nevertheless, as we argue next, the usefulness of the guidance model may go beyond suppressing partisan effects.

b. Disembodied political representation

The guidance model of regulation also may change decision-makers' attitudes and approaches toward decision-making. The mechanisms we now consider are specifically deliberative. They affect not just consequences but also methods of decision-making. At the broadest level our argument is that, absent partisanship, decision-makers can instead be prompted toward thick integrity. This broad argument has at least four (overlapping) aspects or subcomponents.

First, deliberative decision-making is partly *disembodied*. As previous chapters described, disembodiment, with its Rawlsian echoes, refers to deliberators who reason not exclusively from their own fixed preconceptions, statuses, or identities, but also via communicatively rational process. Here, one's preferences and interests are not always fixed, but remain contingent and open to reconsideration – especially in the course of searching for common ground with other deliberators.[178] Communicative rationality does not radically upend every commitment a person once held. But it entails participants who are open to at least some changes of preference, and of their views of what is in their own best interests.

Some of the hallmarks of deliberation first outlined in chapter 2 reflect aspects of this ideal: deliberators should be *other-regarding, inclusive*, and *cooperative* with others in a deliberative forum, and thus *open-minded* about preference change. Deliberators are also ideally *reflective* about choices, and *holistic* in their views of benefits and drawbacks of those choices. All of these hallmarks involve – to some degree – impartial 'abstraction from one's own point of view'.[179] By contrast, partisan decision-making is dominated by its narrowness, occasional superficiality, and fixity of view.

Disembodiment in effect describes the partial separation of final decisions from their authors. The disembodiment ideal is particularly useful to the law of politics as a potential response to the partisanship risk. Disembodiment may lend the appearance, or the reality, of decision-making that is 'above politics'. (Below we consider the value of appearances per se.) In ideal deliberation, facts and arguments persuade based on their inherent informational or rational value, and not chiefly as a function of speaker status or power. Deliberators take the time to hear

Integrity v Deliberation **171**

and consider all or most inputs into the deliberative forum. As a result, deliberation is open to the representations of all comers, mostly irrespective of who they are.[180]

Secondly, in previous chapters we discussed the deliberative criterion of public *reason-giving*. We quoted from John Elster on 'the civilizing force of hypocrisy',[181] similar to Bob Goodin's observation that 'you cannot expect others to buy an argument from you that you would not buy from them'.[182] In practice not all talk adheres to this high ideal. Yet, when it does, disembodiment is implicit: decision-making must not remain mired in self-interested arguments of individuals and discrete social subgroups, but should be generalisable to propositions that others 'may reasonably be expected to endorse'.[183] Hence, Emmanuel Ani argues that, since private deliberation is possible but not reliable, 'reason and evaluation' of arguments should occur publicly in order to 'probe the corrupt behaviour' of officials.[184] Ani advocates combating corrupt practices not merely through transparency, but by joining transparency to public deliberation, where 'reason is compelled to function at its best'.[185]

Making a similar point about publicity's role in testing policy and averting scandal, Amy Gutmann and Dennis Thompson comment on President Reagan's infamous covert plan to channel weapons to Iran in return for the release of US hostages: 'The Iran-Contra affair is replete with decisions and policies which, if they had become public, would have been opposed and probably overturned'.[186] They describe Reagan's belief in the rightness of the policy as sincerely held, but misguided and uncontested as long as it remained secret; publicity could have exposed the 'the fundamental moral flaw in the policy'.[187] Publicity and debate do not merely expose, then, but also help to test, understand, and interpret what counts as political misconduct.

Thirdly, while disembodiment can be equated with 'non-partisanship', the former also has a deeper connotation. Deliberative decisions transcend both the partisan and the quotidian. They derive not from power-based negotiations between the self-interested positions of actors in ordinary politics, but from a polity's more *foundational* and broadly shared normative commitments. For instance, Gutmann and Thompson describe some deliberation as seeking to clarify – and thereafter if possible to minimise – basic moral differences among disagreeing deliberators.[188] Rawls's notion of 'overlapping consensus' similarly seeks out partial agreement only after acknowledging various citizens' basic differences of view.[189] While some commentators point out that *avoiding* deep reasoning can help achieve agreement,[190] deliberation must often engage with conceptual and moral fundamentals. In this way deliberation may appear to be 'above politics' – or at least above the many petty incidents of partisan polarisation (eg, the horse-race of the electoral campaign; mutual carping and insult; and accusations of scandal, real and imagined).

Fourthly and finally, however, deliberation is not actually separate from politics, but entails a different form of politics. Deliberation can result in *disembodied political representation*, which strips away some of the usual strategic-political focus of decision-making in the law of politics, leaving a comparatively non-partisan model of representation. Recasting politics in this mould, deliberation is also – as we saw in chapter 2 – often more democratically robust to the extent that it accommodates a more diverse array of citizen views.

This is an important point, and a possible rejoinder to any claims that legislatures are a more democratically legitimate means for deciding basic democratic ground rules.[191] Indeed, the FEBCs are not elected but appointed bodies, and their ambiguous procedures sometimes block internal decision-making from public view. As we have noted, however, the ambiguous FEBC system places assorted deliberators – from MPs to lay citizens – on roughly equal footing. Within the FEBCs, democracy is potentially more direct, egalitarian, and focused – providing citizens with a defined opportunity to voice ideas about boundary design, unfiltered by the representatives who stand to gain or lose from boundary changes. Whether apolitical, or merely political in a novel sense, disembodied representation partly answers the law of politics' endemic partisanship problem. It replaces some partisanship with deliberation that is untied to rigid categories of conceptual, factional, or identitarian reasoning.

At least this is the ideal. The next question is whether and how deliberative bodies in general, and the FEBCs in particular, achieve the ideal. Federal redistricting in Canada is a longstanding but under-examined case of small-scale, independent bodies transcending partisan decision-making and replacing it with a more flexible and deliberatively rigorous methodology.[192]

Let us consider some methods by which deliberative institutions trade partisanship for thick integrity. Again, as a function of human motive and attitude, thick integrity is not readily regulable in law. Negative laws often fail to constrain partisanship or stanch loophole-seeking. Even positive mandates usually cannot directly mandate non-partisanship or integrity, for instance by baldly instructing decision-makers to 'deliberate', or using cognate terms.[193] Nevertheless, institutions and laws can sometimes engender integrity indirectly. Deliberative democrats appreciate that careful institutional design can place people in circumstances where they are more likely to deliberate. Well-examined instances include Deliberative Polls and Citizens' Assemblies. These bodies' randomly selected, but demographically diverse, citizen-members are ushered through several stages of learning and collective deliberation.[194] It is worth rehearsing the Citizens' Assemblies' technique, which includes:

- relying on ordinary citizens, most of whom lack strong party or ideological affiliations, in order to select for relative open-mindedness among members;
- including members from many walks of life, to ensure breadth of perspective;
- elevating political neophytes to decision-making roles, to avoid much of the elitism of two-track deliberation mediated by long-term governmental insiders;
- stipulating principles of mutual respect and cooperation in advance, to promote cooperative deliberation in lieu of agonistic negotiation; and

- subjecting members to months-long processes of facilitated and broadly based learning, to ensure that participants are apprised of the substantive issues under debate.[195]

A lesson from these experiments is that carefully tailored institutions, laws, and other rules may yield decision-making that is characteristic of thick/deliberative integrity. To regulate in favour of so nebulous a value it is best to target the value's subcomponents; individually these may be easier to control. By manipulating the structure of a process and its starting conditions, the least ephemeral elements of a deliberative system may be orchestrated even though the ultimate goal – deliberation – remains ephemeral.

Deliberative bodies subject their members to the 'full blast of ... sundry opinions', to borrow Frank Michelman's phrase from another context.[196] No function is more central to deliberative democracy. Deliberative institutions use prolonged mutual exposure and learning to make participants more sensitive to perspectives they would not otherwise encounter. In the crucible of deliberation, the final decisions that emerge may not be attributable to a single contributor or faction. Without the usual degree of dominance of discrete identities, choices might instead be considered, criticised, defended, and revised more freely.

The ambiguous normative background of the Canadian FEBCs, seen in the last section, may help to scramble the lines of authorship of representations made in the course of decision-making. Decisions that emerge after a complex course of deliberation might not be attributable to a single author. This approach contradicts standard anti-corruption prescriptions, most of which stress the needs for greater transparency and clear lines of accountability.[197] But ambiguous guidance gambles that if the guidance model can disrupt clear lines of responsibility and authorship, helping to uncouple decisions from their decision-makers, members of the FEBCs may be hard-pressed to sustain sharp polarities, conceptual simplifications, and counterbalanced fixed interests.

The FEBCs engage in what may be termed political deliberation yet, by nearly all accounts, they do this without the polarising influence of political parties and candidates.[198] Like other deliberative bodies, the FEBCs are largely insulated from direct political party or candidate involvement; they may listen to, but need not heed, the representations of politicians. Thus they are largely left to deliberate over other kinds of inputs into the process.[199] A commissioner reported that 'by and large we welcomed the submissions more so from the public than the politicians'. 'The politicians' submissions were more political and were received as such'. Parliamentarians' submissions are influential primarily when 'echoed by community input'. Some 'had useful observations, but many just wanted to make the Commission the target of attacks, and that was not helpful'.[200]

The FEBCs carry out the classic elite deliberative function of receiving and translating democratic input (see chapters 2 and 3), by letting in a range of bona fide representations of citizens' preferences and interests.[201] This is no accident: the commissions solicit public views through many formal opportunities for participation, including prolonged periods for in-person and written submissions. The developing electoral maps are evidently flexible and open to change in the course of deliberation. Commissioners typically modify their proposals in response to public hearings and other deliberative stages, before submitting their final report to the Chief Electoral Officer of Canada. In comments that John Courtney (the FEBCs' leading academic observer) broadly affirms,[202] commissioners reported being strongly influenced by citizen submissions about facts on the ground in any given community.[203] Said one commissioner: 'We took very seriously the objections and proposals presented to us and tried to accommodate community sentiment as we understood it from the hearings'.[204] 'We extensively redrew our initial map in response to public submissions', reported another commissioner.[205] A third commissioner recalled that submissions were '[a]bsolutely crucial' and led to 'huge changes. … Public submissions are key inputs into the whole thing'.[206] Public participation seems to incline the commissions toward practical reasoning based less on party-political and other abstract pre-commitments than on fine-grained geographic, historical, and demographic facts.

The comments of the commissioners also suggest a reflective, open-minded, and cooperative approach. For instance, many commissioners reported not perceiving each other as competitors, but rather deciding via collective deliberation and even consensus: 'Decision-making was highly cooperative. We listened to one another's suggestions and ideas and made decisions based on what seemed to work best. It was consensus reasoning'.[207] The same appears to have been true in several FEBCs.[208] Moreover, the lay and neophyte status of some commissioners seems to aid reflective and open-minded process, in part as these members can push deliberations toward first-principle reasoning. Hence, the key democratic values at stake in redistricting decisions (eg, communities of interest, equality), in addition to more technical arcana, can play complementary roles.

Some reasonable doubt about all of the above is justified. We have already seen sceptical critiques of ideals of disembodiment (chapter 5 and this chapter), and deliberation more broadly (chapter 2). Recall that *wholly* excluding identity is neither possible in practice, nor is it in the best interests of deliberation.[209] Yet, even when it is more illusory than real, disembodiment can still affect the tenor of decision-making in the law of politics. The mere semblance of the phenomenon may influence decision-makers. The FEBC system both is and *appears to be* unconnected to any partisan camp, authored by no one in particular, and apart from or above the political fray. It may seem beyond the pale to manipulate a rule in the law of politics originally issued from a deliberative democratic process. Ordinary citizens generally ascribe special legitimacy to the judgments of deliberative democratic institutions.[210]

Even an imperfect deliberative process, then, which yields only slightly better deliberation, may help to counter the escalation of partisanship.[211] The appearance that rules are apolitical can self-fulfil to some degree, potentially arresting, slowing, or even reversing cycles of increasingly partisan rule-making. Warren and others describe the obverse situation: 'When people lose confidence that public decisions are taken for reasons that are publicly available and justifiable, they often become cynical about public speech and deliberation'.[212] This is one reason why appearances matter. In the words of one Canadian boundary commissioner, 'so long as people believe in the myth [of impartial judgment], and govern themselves accordingly, then the myth becomes a reality'.[213] Indeed, the 'mythology [of] the neutral fair system' may itself be a potent guarantee of integrity.[214]

Note, finally, that after the advent of the FEBCs in the 1960s, a prior decision-making culture of thoroughgoing partisanship quickly faded. Isolating the reasons for cultural change always calls for speculation, indeed more than we wish to engage in here. But the perspectives of Habermas,[215] Lawrence Lessig,[216] and others are worth noting. These authors suggest how laws create or shape cultures, including cultures of deliberation.[217] According to Habermas, mandated behaviours over time inculcate attitudes and generate lasting informal norms related to those behaviours.[218] While an activity may initially be forced, the habit or the perceived moral necessity of carrying out the activity can become second nature. Repeated actions thus help to internalise predispositions, assumptions, social meanings, expectations, and the like, which develop from or rationalise those actions.

If accurate, this description of cultural change can be particularly relevant and useful to the law of politics. Informal norms suggest origins in the 'underlying natural order'.[219] They may not appear 'contingent or contested', but rather 'natural', 'internalized' or 'taken for granted'.[220] Informal norms favouring more deliberative decision-making can perhaps help to reinforce the 'myth' of integrity, which political actors may hesitate to challenge. Such norms may help to determine the kinds of speech or conduct that find favour: polemic versus civil, extreme versus moderate, agonistic versus deliberative, selfish versus public-spirited. (An example is the definition of bribery in public office. In marginal cases, the meaning of corrupt bribery derives from prevailing assumptions shared, if only in approximate terms, among lawmakers, judges, prosecutors, and the broader public as to what kinds of donations are corrupt.[221]) Additionally, it is plausible – though again speculative – that the FEBCs developed a culture of integrity in part by relying on their diverse and ambiguous norms of guidance.[222] A number of authors observe that regulatory complexity can help seed informal normative development by mimicking informal norms' ambiguous complexes of networks, agreements, social meanings, practices, etc.[223]

To sum up, we have seen that law can seldom mandate deliberation directly, any more than it can control other states of mind and attitudes. However, laws can mandate the creation of institutions known to be associated with deliberation. The best strategy may thus be indirect and passive. This approach is apprised of, and thus deploys, the best institutional supports for *deliberation*. And, in concert with these institutional techniques, ambiguous positive guidance in law can improve on traditional strategies of regulation. Loose and open-ended mandates may prompt decision-makers to learn from each other at length, abandon some of their own pre-commitments, and refine their preferences in a large number of reciprocal speech acts.

Thick integrity and the coercion problem

The same ambiguous positive guidance that seems to supress partisanship and scramble authorship and allegiances on a multimember body may also safeguard against coercion in the law of politics. In this section we develop the claim that guidance is more consistent with a non-coercive course of regulation. We also raise – but largely dispel – a suite of objections from the rule of law.

The norms that inform the guidance model are *binding* rather than merely optional or aspirational. This distinguishes the model from other 'soft' or indirect normative systems (more on this below). Yet, significantly, the model remains agnostic as to what precise outcome decision-making should achieve, and how its complex starting conditions play out. Guidance only rarely involves courts or other legal reviewers in determining a range of final decisions. Rather than scrutinise and prohibit conduct or outcomes post hoc, it promotes robust deliberation in the course of decision-making.

Since it seldom predetermines outcomes, this model is relatively non-coercive in the *external* sense outlined above. Based on the ambiguous set of rules regulating the commissions, multiple and equally legitimate electoral maps are possible. We saw above how profoundly complex are the substantive norms involved. Applying them is, again, 'an enormous task', which requires 'a delicate balancing act that must take into account human interests as well as geographic characteristics'.[224] Weighing the redistricting criteria is 'not an exact science'.[225] For instance, especially within major urban centres, ethnic, linguistic, socio-economic, or other groups can overlap, and each may have a legitimate claim to being a community of interest. Other factors are still less deterministic, and less amenable to numeric analysis (eg, local history and considerations of social justice).[226] Decision-making in the FEBCs is thus chaotic in a literal but non-pejorative sense: there is a causal link between starting conditions and end result, and yet the result remains unpredictable.

As we saw, the FEBCs also feature significant procedural ambiguity. Their guiding laws use positive, open-ended mandates to place people in circumstances where they are more likely to deliberate. For instance, the FEBCs bring diverse participants, including members of the wider public, into sustained contact. The laws do little more than stipulate, at the outset, rules to ensure that deliberation occurs. The fact that this kind of deliberative intervention might change decisional outcomes is not itself a sign of significant coercion: the intervention neither directs outcomes nor shortcuts the course of deliberation.

The model of guidance we describe here does not eliminate rules, then, but makes these more numerous, complex, and conflictual. The rules are written but open-ended. Even this is coercive to some extent. But a basic level of coercive regulation is unavoidable in political system design. Recall that Habermas favours creating institutions by coercion, but otherwise letting decision-makers follow a largely autonomous course. In our view this is a pragmatic and tenable approach. And there is only relatively modest coercion when regulations stipulate criteria and procedures at the outset, without clarifying how the rules should interact – nor certainly how they should resolve.[227] Says one commissioner: 'while we were aware we were to consider community of interest or identity and history pattern, how we would do that was left up to us'.[228]

In the *cognitive* sense, too, ambiguous positive guidance may be relatively non-coercive. An ambiguous course of decision-making potentially complicates or severs the cognitive connections between a decision-maker's immediate substantive choices and the political consequences of those choices. To be sure, in contrast with procedurally ambiguous guidance, it may be harder to stipulate substantive starting conditions without going on to regulate outcomes coercively. Since the substance here defies clear characterisation in law, it may be difficult to describe or verify when decision-makers fulfil substantive criteria, and therefore to draw a distinction between starting conditions and end results.

However, we think the best view is that, in the haze of substantive principles directing the FEBCs, commissioners are freer to focus upon the immediate task of implementing criteria and managing conflicting public or parliamentarian submissions. The downstream electoral outcomes that may follow after the long course of decision-making may attract correspondingly less attention. Ambiguous substantive guidance may provide some cognitive insulation between initial conditions and downstream effects. As noted, commissioners reported that 'decisions did not appear to be … geared to manipulating electoral outcomes', in part because (as noted above) 'most of the time, [commissioners] don't even know the effect' – that is, how redistricting impacts on election outcomes.[229] This report is particularly plausible if ambiguous regulation forces participants to deliberate, most of all, on the immediate task at hand – deciding how best to fulfil the host of open-ended substantive mandates noted. It may be difficult to maintain a self-serving position when engaged in such a process. Admittedly, here we enter into more speculative territory, and we thus offer this conclusion cautiously. Still more study is needed on the cognitive states of decision-makers like the FEBC commissioners who, despite working in otherwise highly charged partisan environments, develop reputations for robust integrity in their decisions.

Objections from the rule of law

There are, in addition, a more normative set of possible objections to our view here. The guidance model's multi-layered, redundant, and contradictory mandates are at least superficially difficult to square with certain aspects of the rule of law. Not merely an arid theoretical concern, lawyers and judges often find any departures from the rule of law (as it is conventionally understood), including substantial legal indeterminacy, distinctly discomfiting. At least three rule of law principles are particularly engaged by the model we have outlined.

First, according to Joseph Raz, an essential principle of the rule of law is 'that the law should be such that people will be able to be guided by it'.[230] And Lon Fuller adds that the law must avoid contradiction.[231] A law must disclose a clear course of action to those it binds, giving clear forewarning of the kinds of acts targeted.[232] This principle of *predictability* classically sought to avoid arbitrary sanction, such as criminal liability based on unclear or retrospective grounds.[233] The FEBCs have no such power to impose liability. However, the principle of predictability may cast the FEBCs' governing laws as problematic if they guide too vaguely, especially given that they regulate governmental authority.[234]

In our view, however, the ambiguous positive guidance model is mostly unproblematic for the rule of law. While as a whole they are unpredictable, the norms individually each have a rational function. Every rule of guidance must follow what we call an *equivalence condition*: its addition to the body of rules must not prevent decision-makers from deciding approximately as rationally as they would under a more predictable system. A 'rational' rule is institutionally appropriate, in the sense in which we used this term above.

Hence, not just anything goes; some new rules would inject irrelevancies into redistricting. In practice, however, the FEBCs' governing rules seem rationally to guide redistricting. Each rule mandates a relatively circumscribed course of action with an identifiable purpose. Some rules are straightforward (eg, avoiding bisecting demographic enclaves), and others vague (eg, accounting for community history). In either case, commissioners can readily act upon each such rule without substantial difficulty. Only the sum of all the redistricting norms – how they combine to yield the final boundary map – is profoundly indeterminate. It can be difficult to predict how the final map will look based merely on the substantive criteria established at the outset. But though the process may be unpredictable as a whole, it lacks neither cause nor sense.

Another important rejoinder to concerns about predictability is that criteria for good democratic design are themselves, as a whole, irreducibly indeterminate. Kenneth Arrow's seminal work showed that normative expectations for democracy inevitably conflict, such that no single democratic model fulfils all such expectations.[235] Arrow's insight is important for our purposes. It suggests why legal scholars and practitioners should make peace with legal ambiguity and indeterminate outcomes, at least when the target of legal regulation is democracy. Indeterminacy is neither inappropriate nor unusual in the field of democracy. Here, legal ambiguity merely matches the contradictory and vague foundations of democratic politics.

More clearly articulating what would make a decision-maker act with greater integrity in the democratic context often is not therefore feasible.[236] One commissioner believes that the redistricting 'criteria inevitably cannot be clearer'.[237] Courtney similarly thinks that 'clarification' in 'statutes and guidelines' may not be possible.[238] Hence, the mandates to define discrete communities and fit them within electoral boundaries conflict with a host of other criteria, depend on judgments about the value of assorted communities, and yield no obvious single boundary line. This should be no surprise: ambiguous and contested criteria and procedures predominate in most law of politics contexts, including judicial appointments,[239] and electoral campaign rules.[240] Given the '[c]uriosities, anomalies and contradictions' of democracy,[241] rule of law principles of prospectivity must be more loosely applied in the law of politics. Ambiguous positive guidance aims far less than standard negative regulations to use artificially determinate criteria to simplify and short-cut decision-making.

Modern deliberativists also recognise the inevitability of substantive disagreement. Rather than bank on the possibility of consensus, they seek procedural outlets for deciding normatively ambiguous matters. For instance, two of the original Citizens' Assemblies – one in British Columbia in 2004 and the other in Ontario in 2007 – were assigned the same task: to design a new provincial electoral system. The two, however, reached different electoral reform recommendations. This may reflect differences in membership and the distinctive cultures of the two provinces. Yet, most of all, it seems to reinforce the notion that no single best decision exists for democratic design.

The second objection concerns the rule of law principle of *stability*. Some writers assume that extensive ambiguity and unpredictability produce laws that do not last long as functional and coherent norms[242] – a potential problem for stability. For example, Elizabeth Magill analogises the confusing American case law on the separation of legislative, executive, and judicial powers to the chaos of the 'three-body problem' known to physics.[243] On the other hand, turning Magill's metaphor around, even chaotic systems (eg, weather systems) have stable features (eg, the distinctive spiral of a hurricane). Unlike the redistricting and judicial appointments cases we saw from the US, Canadian federal redistricting rules are in the main not subject to rapid and continuous change, despite relying on thoroughly ambiguous norms. These norms persist, or change only slowly and modestly, from start to finish of each redistricting process and even across multiple cycles of redistricting.

Thirdly and finally, the guidance model may conflict with the rule of law principle that everyone is bound *equally* by law.[244] Even governments or their arms and delegates should be predictably bound, and they should enjoy no prerogative to decide when to be so bound. However, note that the guidance model's ambiguity does not extend to questions of compliance with/binding under law. In practice in the FEBCs, the binding force of guidance norms remains clear. This differs from more thoroughly ambiguous normative systems: for example, certain norms of international law, and alternative models of 'soft law',[245] which remain hazy as to whether people targeted by the norms need comply in the first place.[246]

We have seen that FEBC commissioners, bound only by qualified judicial oversight, are seldom subject to any punitive or corrective legal sanction. It may thus seem that guidance norms do not sufficiently bind, nor therefore meet rule of law standards. Raz, for one, assumes that courts must be easily accessed and available to review laws for compliance with rule of law principles.[247] Though often a reasonable expectation, this assumption becomes problematic when applied to the regulation of democracy. It may reinforce the common assumption that only precisely formulated (usually negative) and readily invoked legal norms can effectively inhibit partisanship or constrain excess governmental power. Indeed, it

180 The Law of Deliberative Democracy

is thought that ambiguous norms may leave partisans 'room in which to hide'.[248] Yet, in this chapter generally, we have argued that ambiguous positive guidance can be more effective at influencing whether partisanship or its alternatives dominate political practice. The FEBCs demonstrate strong compliance, even though their laws are ambiguous in both substance and process. In Canada (and, we might add, in Australia[249]), guidance has helped to reduce political coercion while keeping boundary commissions rationally bound by rules.

Interestingly, at least one author has suggested an alternative solution that addresses the first element of this problem (non-coercion), but not the second (rationality). Issacharoff advocates a laissez-faire strategy – withdrawing key constraints under the Voting Rights Act of 1965, in order to prevent the habitual manipulation of formal rules. This, he thinks, might free political actors to develop informal cultures of integrity.[250] Elsewhere he even calls for randomising redistricting.[251] The computer-generated maps he contemplates would bear little relation to the locations of cohesive communities and other traditional factors. But he predicts that both strategies could stem the endemic partisan manipulation of US redistricting – a higher concern.

We think that decision-making over electoral maps should remain rationally and formally rule-bound. A commission should not select boundaries arbitrarily and without stipulated governing criteria. Their record over several decades demonstrates that, despite the overall indeterminacy of the task, the FEBCs diligently follow their own governing rules. Issacharoff's laissez-faire and randomisation approaches would sacrifice rational redistricting to the cause of integrity. By contrast, though unpredictable, under an ambiguous positive guidance scheme decisional outcomes can remain both rational and characterised by substantial integrity. Of course, this model's applicability in the US context remains an open question.

Conclusion

Ultimately, the hardest challenge for the guidance model may be rhetorical – convincing law of politics practitioners, commentators, judges, and drafters to overcome anxieties about non-determinism in the law of politics. Guidance in law embraces complexity, ambiguity, indeterminacy, and even contradiction. Understandably, judges and lawmakers are often tempted to retreat to simpler, negative forms of regulation with more easily articulated content. In this chapter we saw courts and other bodies coping with the issue of partisan contestation over the law of politics by taking this, the easier of two regulatory routes.

This kind of legal intervention – blunt, coercive, agonistic, and inflexible – substantially renders public debate in its own image. Of the two countries at the focus of this chapter, Canada has kept clear of the particular tangle of laws into which US civil life and politics have long been enmeshed, and which are the sites of so much contemporary social struggle. But politics in Canada is not lawless; its law of politics, in the redistricting context, is just more consistent with relatively non-coercive, relatively disembodied, deliberative democracy. This again illustrates one of the recurring observations of this book: that the spread of law through the many corners of political practice is not problematic in itself. Deliberation can be woven into the fabric of law. Each of the values we have seen across the book – liberty, equality, integrity – can have either thin presence in the law of politics, or a thicker manifestation more consonant with deliberation. Thick integrity is complex and indeterminate, and harder to implement than its alternatives. Yet courts and legislatures should, we have argued, become as comfortable with indeterminacy as deliberative democracy already is.

Notes

1 Cornelius Tacitus, *The Complete Works of Tacitus* (Alfred John Church and William Jackson Brodribb trans, Random House, 1942) [3.25].
2 David Lublin and Michael P McDonald, 'Is It Time to Draw the Line? The Impact of Redistricting on Competition in State House Elections' (2006) 5 *Election Law Journal* 144, 154; Samuel Issacharoff, 'Gerrymandering and Political Cartels' (2002) 116 *Harvard Law Review* 593, 624.
3 Timothy P Brennan, 'Cleaning Out the Augean Stables: Pennsylvania's Most Recent Redistricting and a Call to Clean up This Messy Process' (2003) 13 *Widener Law Journal* 235, 279–80.
4 Peter Coaldrake, *Working the System: Government in Queensland* (University of Queensland Press, 1989) 40–51.
5 Ibid.
6 Officially titled the Representation of the People Act of 1832 (UK), 2 & 3 Will IV, c 45
7 Thomas Ertman, 'The Great Reform Act of 1832 and British Democratization' (2010) 43 *Comparative Political Studies* 1000, 1005.
8 DR Fisher (ed), *A History of Parliament: The House of Commons, 1820–1832* (Cambridge University Press, 2010) vol VI.
9 Peter B Waite, 'Chartered Libertine? A Case against Sir John A Macdonald and Some Answers' (1975–76) 3 *Manitoba Historical Society Transactions* 3.
10 Ibid. For later history see Terence H Qualter, *The Election Process in Canada* (McGraw-Hill, 1970).
11 House of Commons (Canada), *House of Commons Debates*, 4th Parl, 4th Sess, vol XII (9 May 1882) 1392, 1409.
12 *Hulme v Madison County*, 188 F Supp 2d 1041, 1051 (SD Ill, 2001).
13 Graeme Orr and Ron Levy, 'Electoral Malapportionment: Partisanship, Rhetoric and Reform in the Shadow of the Agrarian Strong-man' (2009) 18 *Griffith Law Review* 638.
14 Broadcasting Act 1942 (Cth) Pt IIID, amended by the Political Broadcasts and Political Disclosures Act 1991 (Cth).
15 Michael Klarman, 'Majoritarian Judicial Review: The Entrenchment Problem' (1997) 85 *Georgetown Law Review* 491, 498.
16 Mark E Warren, 'What Does Corruption Mean in a Democracy?' (2004) 48 *American Journal of Political Science* 328, 329 (expanding corruption's definition to include 'corruption of democratic institutions and practices').
17 Ibid 328.
18 Dennis F Thompson, 'Two Concepts of Corruption: Making Campaigns Safe for Democracy' (2005) 73 *George Washington Law Review* 1036, 1037, 1046–9. See also

Dennis F Thompson, *Just Elections: Creating a Fair Electoral Process in the United States* (University of Chicago Press, 2002) 112–13.

19 Thompson, 'Two Concepts of Corruption', above n 18, 1047–8.

20 Thompson expressly rejects partisanship as 'electoral corruption': ibid 1047. His focus is on private power. We differ with Thompson here because, irrespective of who the actor is, the act of manipulating electoral rules raises a profound risk of campaign distortion.

21 Michael E Lewyn, 'How to Limit Gerrymandering' (1993) 45 *Florida Law Review* 403, 407.

22 United States Constitution, art I § 2, cl 3 (ten-year maximum); *League of Latin American Citizens v Perry*, 548 US 399, 415 (2006) ('*Perry*') (mid-decennial redistricting allowed); Electoral Boundaries Readjustment Act (Canada) RSC 1985, c E-3, s 3(2) (ten years) ('EBRA'); Commonwealth Electoral Act 1918 (Australia), s 59(2)(c) (seven years); Parliamentary Voting System and Constituencies Act 2011 (UK) c 1, s 10(3) (five years).

23 Emmanuel Ani, 'Combatting Corruption with Public Deliberation' (2015) 34 *South African Journal of Philosophy* 13, 17.

24 James Madison, 'The Federalist No 48' in Isaac Kramnick (ed), *The Federalist Papers* (Penguin, 1987) 311.

25 Steven G Calabresi and Kevin H Rhodes, 'The Structural Constitution: Unitary Executive, Plural Judiciary' (1992) 105 *Harvard Law Review* 1153.

26 John Uhr, 'Institutions of Integrity: Balancing Values and Verification in Democratic Governance' (1999) 1 *Public Integrity* 94; Thompson, 'Two Concepts of Corruption', above n 18.

27 Recent works include Curtis Ventriss, 'Democratic Citizenship and Public Ethics' (2012) 14 *Public Integrity* 283; Guy Adams and Danny Balfour, 'Towards Restoring Integrity in "Praetorian Times"' (2012) 14 *Public Integrity* 325; Ani, above n 23. Cf Doron Navot, 'The Concept of Political Corruption' (2014) 16 *Public Integrity* 357, 367.

28 Adam Cox, 'Partisan Fairness and Redistricting Politics' (2004) 79 *New York University Law Review* 751, 772–3; Daniel Galvin and Colleen Shogan, 'Presidential Politicization and Centralization across the Modern-Traditional Divide' (2004) 36 *Polity* 477.

29 Lublin and McDonald, above n 2, 154; Mark Monmonier, *Bushmanders and Bullwinkles: How Politicians Manipulate Electronic Maps and Census Data to Win Elections* (University of Chicago Press, 2001); Gary C Jacobson, 'Partisan Polarization in Presidential Support: The Electoral Connection' (2003) 30 *Congress and the Presidency* 1.

30 Richard L Engstrom, *Revising Constituency Boundaries in the United States and Australia: It Couldn't be More Different* (2005) Democratic Audit of Australia <democraticaudit.org.au> accessed 22 February 2016; Norm Kelly, *Directions in Australian Electoral Reform: Professionalism and Partisanship in Electoral Management* (ANU E-Press, 2012) chs 2–3.

31 Graeme Orr, Bryan Mercurio and George Williams, 'Australian Electoral Law: A Stocktake' (2003) 2 *Election Law Journal* 383, 384.

32 Colin Rallings, Ron Johnston and Michael Thrasher, 'Changing the Boundaries but Keeping the Disproportionality: The Electoral Impact of the Fifth Periodical Reviews by the Parliamentary Boundary Commissions for England and Wales' (2008) 79 *Political Quarterly* 80, 83.

33 WE Lyons, 'Legislative Redistricting by Independent Commissions: Operationalizing the One Man-One Vote Doctrine in Canada' (1969) 1 *Polity* 428, 458–9.

34 EBRA, above n 22, ss 4–6. In Canada the process is usually called 'readjustment'.

35 Peter Hogg, 'Appointment of Justice Marshall Rothstein to the Supreme Court of Canada' (2006) 44 *Osgoode Hall Law Journal* 527, 537 (Appendix).

36 David Smith, 'A Question of Trust: Parliamentary Democracy and Canadian Society' (2004) 27 *Canadian Parliamentary Review* 24, 24–7 (on more polemical Canadian electoral politics).

37 Lyons, above n 33, 429.

38 John Courtney, *Commissioned Ridings: Designing Canada's Electoral Districts* (McGill-Queen's, 2001).

39 Use of the term 'constraint' in similar ways appears across the law of politics and, more broadly, the regulation of public power: see, eg, Bruce Ackerman, 'The New Separation of Powers' (2000) 113 *Harvard Law Review* 633, 640; Denis J Galligan, *Discretionary Powers: A Legal Study of Official Discretion* (Clarendon Press, 1986) 20.

40 Calabresi and Rhodes, above n 25, 1156; Madison, above n 24, 311.

41 Bruce E Cain, 'Redistricting Commissions: A Better Political Buffer' (2012) 121 *Yale Law Journal* 1808.

42 Ibid 1820.

43 Michael P McDonald, 'A Comparative Analysis of Redistricting Institutions in the United States, 2001–2002' (2004) 4 *State Politics and Policy Quarterly* 371.

44 Notably, the US Supreme Court affirmed the validity, under the Elections Clause of the US Constitution, of a commission created by a ballot initiative of Arizona voters: *Arizona State Legislature v Arizona Independent Redistricting Commission*, 576 US __ (2015).

45 42 USC § 1973c (2000); *League of Woman Voters of North Carolina v North Carolina*, 769 F 3d 224, 239 (4th Cir, 2014) (s 2 of the Voting Rights Act forbids any 'standard, practice, or procedure' that 'results in a denial or abridgement of the right of any citizen of the United States to vote on account of race or color') (citing 52 USC § 10301(a)). The Voting Rights Act of 1965 also provided for federal Justice Department 'preclearance' of any such changes in certain jurisdictions until the Supreme Court struck parts of it down in *Shelby County v Holder*, 570 US ___ (2013).

46 Issacharoff, above n 2, 600.

47 Michael P McDonald, 'Regulating Redistricting' (2007) 40 *Political Science & Politics* 675, 676.

48 Cain, above n 41. This is a common suggestion, not in itself problematic.

49 Common Cause, 'Common Cause Redistricting Guidelines' (February 2005) s 5.

50 *Reference Re Provincial Electoral Boundaries (Saskatchewan)* [1991] 2 SCR 158 ('*Carter*'); House of Commons Standing Committee on Procedure and House Affairs, Parliament of Canada, *Procedure and House Affairs Report* (1995) ('*Milliken Report*'); Common Cause, above n 49, s 3.

51 Richard L Hasen, 'Beyond the Margin of Litigation: Reforming US Election Administration to Avoid Electoral Meltdown' (2005) 62 *Washington and Lee Law Review* 937, 983–5.

52 See, eg, John Fund, *Stealing Elections. How Voter Fraud Threatens Our Democracy* (Encounter Books, 2004) 147. *Contra* Ronald J Krotoszynski, Johnjerica Hodge and Wesley W Wintermyer, 'Partisan Balance Requirements in the Age of New Formalism' (2015) 90 *Notre Dame Law Review* 941.

53 Hasen, above n 51, 944.

54 See, eg, Denise Scheberle, *Federalism and Environmental Policy: Trust and the Politics of Implementation* (Georgetown, 2nd ed, 2004); Robert D Putnam, Robert Leonardi and Rafaella Y Nanetti, *Making Democracy Work: Civic Traditions in Modern Italy* (Princeton University Press, 2002) 167.

55 See McDonald, above n 43, 380–4.

56 Thompson, *Just Elections*, above n 18, 170.

57 Douglas Oosterhouse, 'Campaign Finance Reform and Disclosure: Stepping Up IRS Enforcement as a Remedial Measure to Partisan Deadlock in Congress and the FEC' (2012) 65 *Rutgers Law Review* 261, 282–3.

58 See, eg, Cain, above n 41, 1827–41; Z Landau, O Reid and I Yershov, 'A Fair Division Solution to the Problem of Redistricting' (2009) 32 *Social Choice and Welfare* 479.

59 For example, in the Australian context, the constitutional drafters were mostly silent on the separation of powers: Fiona Wheeler, 'Original Intent and the Doctrine of Separation of Powers in Australia' (1996) 7 *Public Law Review* 96, 100.

60 Parliamentary Voting System and Constituencies Act 2011 (UK) c 1.

61 Ron Johnston and Charles Pattie, 'From the Organic to the Arithmetic: New Redistricting/Redistribution Rules for the United Kingdom' (2012) 11 *Election Law Journal* 70, 71.

62 Mark Carter, 'Reconsidering the *Charter* and Electoral Boundaries' (1999) 22 *Dalhousie Law Journal* 53, 71.

63 Ibid.

64 See also Courtney, above n 38, 259 (lamenting that little more can be done to clarify 'elusive and imprecise' standards).

65 *Milliken Report*, above n 50; Canadian Government, Royal Commission on Electoral Reform and Party Financing, *Reforming Electoral Democracy: Final Report* (1991) I, 150, 157–8 ('*Lortie Commission Report*').

66 Common Cause, above n 49. See also Michael Pal and Sujit Choudhry, 'Is Every Ballot Equal? Visible-Minority Vote Dilution in Canada' (2007) 13 *IRPP Choices* (January 2007) (Institute for Research on Public Policy) 14–16.

67 See, eg, Madison, above n 24, 303. Federalists were animated by a dark vision of the 'nature of man': James Madison, 'The Federalist No 10' in Isaac Kramnick (ed), *The Federalist Papers* (Penguin, 1987) 124; Thomas Hobbes, *De Cive* (Sterling P Lamprecht (ed), Appleton-Century-Crofts, 1949); David Hume, *Of the Independency of Parliament: Essays, Moral, Political and Literary*, vol 1 (Oxford University Press, 1963).

68 Graeme Orr, 'Dealing in Votes: Regulating Electoral Bribery?' in Graeme Orr, Bryan Mercurio and George Williams (eds), *Realising Democracy: Electoral Law in Australia* (Federation Press, 2003) 130, 141.

69 Texas Legislative Council (Texas Redistricting), *Redistricting Plan 01374C* (10 September 2003).

70 Guy-Uriel E Charles, 'Democracy and Distortion' (2007) 92 *Cornell Law Review* 601, 656.

71 Joshua Butera, 'Partisan Gerrymandering and the Qualifications Clause' (2015) 95 *Boston University Law Review* 303, 305.

72 Mitchell N Berman, 'Managing Gerrymandering' (2005) 83 *Texas Law Review* 781, 812.

73 *Davis v Bandemer*, 478 US 109 (1985).

74 *Vieth v Jubelirer*, 541 US 267, 281 (2004) (Scalia J for plurality). The absence of a majority decision in this case meant that *Bandemer* was not in fact overruled. Kennedy J (concurring) 'would not foreclose all possibility of judicial relief if some limited and precise rationale were found … in some redistricting cases': 306. See also *Perry*, 547 US 1017 (2006). For discussion see Michael S Kang, 'When Courts Won't Make Law: Partisan Gerrymandering and a Structural Approach to the Law of Democracy' (2007) 68 *Ohio State Law Journal* 1097; Richard L Hasen, 'Looking for Standards (in All the Wrong Places): Partisan Gerrymandering Claims after *Vieth*' (2004) 3 *Election Law Journal* 626.

75 Russell Muirhead, 'Can Deliberative Democracy be Partisan?' (2010) 22 *Critical Review* 129, 142.

76 See, eg, Cass R Sunstein, 'Social Norms and Social Roles' (1996) 96 *Columbia Law Review* 903; Richard H Pildes, 'The Destruction of Social Capital through Law' (1996) 144 *University of Pennsylvania Law Review* 2055.

77 Gerald Rosenberg, *The Hollow Hope: Can Courts Bring About Social Change?* (University of Chicago Press, 1993) 296–303. See similarly Richard G Niemi and Laura R Winsky, 'The Persistence of Partisan Redistricting Effects in Congressional Elections in the

1970s and 1980s' (1992) 54 *Journal of Politics* 565, 571; Samuel Issacharoff, 'Is Section 5 of the Voting Rights Act a Victim of Its Own Success?' (2004) 104 *Columbia Law Review* 1710, 1714.

78 Rosenberg, above n 77.

79 Issacharoff, above n 2, 612.

80 Samuel Issacharoff and Pamela Karlan, 'The Hydraulics of Campaign Finance Reform' (1999) 77 *Texas Law Review* 1705, 1713, 1715 (citing *Buckley v Valeo*, 424 US 1 (1976)). See also David Butler and Bruce Cain, *Congressional Redistricting: Comparative and Theoretical Perspectives* (Macmillan, 1992) 149–50.

81 See also Pamela Karlan, 'The Rights to Vote: Some Pessimism about Formalism' (1993) 71 *Texas Law Review* 1705, 1726–37.

82 Sarah A Binder, Anthony J Madonna and Steven S Smith, 'Going Nuclear, Senate Style' (2007) 5 *Perspectives on Politics* 729, 729.

83 Carl Hulse, 'Compromise in the Senate: The Nominees; Many Republicans Are Already Eager To Challenge Agreement on Filibusters', *The New York Times*, 25 May 2015, A18. This cycle ended with the takeover of the Senate by Democrats in 2006. In 2013, Senate Democrats changed the rules so that a simple majority became sufficient to allow a vote on a presidential nominee, as opposed to the 60 votes once required.

84 Charles Babington and Susan Schmidt, 'Filibuster Deal Puts Democrats in a Bind', *Washington Post*, 4 July 2005, A1.

85 Karlan, above n 81, 1726–37; Hasen, above n 51, 949.

86 Binder et al, above n 82.

87 Warren, above n 16, 328.

88 John Braithwaite, 'Institutionalizing Distrust, Enculturating Trust' in Valerie Braithwaite and Margaret Levi (eds), *Trust and Governance* (Russell Sage Foundation, 1998) 343, 351. See similarly Pildes, above n 76, 2058; Philip Pettit, 'The Cunning of Trust' (1995) 24 *Philosophy and Public Affairs* 202, 221–2.

89 Jürgen Habermas, *The Theory of Communicative Action: Reason and the Rationalization of Society* (Thomas McCarthy trans, Beacon Press, 1984, first published 1981) vol 1, 25.

90 Jürgen Habermas, *Between Facts and Norms: Contributions to a Discourse Theory of Law and Democracy* (Polity Press, 1996) 37–8.

91 See also Jane Mansbridge et al, 'The Place of Self-Interest and the Role of Power in Deliberative Democracy' (2010) 18 *The Journal of Political Philosophy* 64, 69–70, 80–3.

92 For an alternative critique of Habermas's limited coercion ideal, see Amy Allen, 'The Unforced Force of the Better Argument: Reason and Power in Habermas' Political Theory' (2012) 19 *Constellations* 353.

93 Habermas, above n 90, 306.

94 See, eg, Plato, *Republic* (Christopher Emlyn-Jones and William Preddy, eds and trans, Harvard University Press, 2013) vol I, book 1.

95 For discussion see Russell Sandberg and Norman Doe, 'The Strange Death of Blasphemy' (2008) 71 *Modern Law Review* 971.

96 James Bohman, 'Deliberative Democracy and Effective Social Freedom: Capabilities, Resources, and Opportunities' in James Bohman and William Rehg (eds), *Deliberative Democracy: Essays on Reason and Politics* (MIT Press, 1997) 321, 332 (effects of wealth disparity on deliberation).

97 Habermas, above n 90, 150.

98 Mansbridge et al, above n 91.

99 Ilya Somin, 'Deliberative Democracy and Political Ignorance' (2010) 22 *Critical Review* 253, 257–62. Similar ideas drive Burke's deliberative justification for representative democracy: Edmund Burke, 'Speech to the Electors in Bristol (1774)', *Works* (Bohn's Standard Library, 1902).

186   The Law of Deliberative Democracy

100 Shelly Chaiken and Yaacov Trope (eds), *Dual-Process Theories in Social Psychology* (Guildford Press, 1999); cf Dan M Kahan, 'Ideology, Motivated Reasoning, and Cognitive Reflection' (2013) 8 *Judgment and Decision Making* 407.

101 Ian O'Flynn, 'Deliberative Democracy for a Great Society' (2015) 13 *Political Studies Review* 207, 210–11.

102 Mansbridge et al, above n 91, 82.

103 See, eg, Robert Post, 'Managing Deliberation: The Quandary of Democratic Dialogue' (1993) 103 *Ethics* 654, 661.

104 *Bush v Gore*, 531 US 98 (2000).

105 Stephen Ansolabehere and James M Snyder Jr, 'The Effects of Redistricting on Incumbents' (2012) 11 *Election Law Journal* 490; Lublin and McDonald, above n 2.

106 Nathan S Catanese, 'Gerrymandered Gridlock: Addressing the Hazardous Impact of Partisan Redistricting' (2014) 28 *Notre Dame Journal of Law, Ethics and Public Policy* 323, 330.

107 James A Gardner, 'Deliberation or Tabulation? The Self-Undermining Constitutional Architecture of Election Campaigns' (2006) 2006–013 *Buffalo Legal Studies Research Paper* 1. Gardner also explores this theme throughout *What Are Campaigns For? The Role of Persuasion in Electoral Law and Politics* (Oxford University Press, 2009).

108 Daniel Lowenstein and Jonathan Steinberg, 'The Quest for Legislative Districting in the Public Interest: Elusive or Illusory?' (1985) 33 *UCLA Law Review* 1, 4; Nathaniel Persily, 'Reply: In Defense of Foxes Guarding Henhouses: The Case for Judicial Acquiescence to Incumbent-Protecting Gerrymanders' (2002) 116 *Harvard Law Review* 649, 679–91; Franita Tolson, 'Benign Partisanship' (2012) 88 *Notre Dame Law Review* 395, 398.

109 *Davis v Bandemer*, 478 US 109, 152 (1986) (O'Connor J) (concurring).

110 See, eg, Mark Tushnet, 'Constitutional Hardball' (2004) 37 *John Marshall Law Review* 523, 533–4; Patricia M Wald, 'A Response to Tiller and Cross' (1999) 99 *Columbia Law Review* 235, 256–7.

111 Thompson, *Just Elections*, above n 18, 41.

112 Orr and Levy, above n 13.

113 Hélène Landemore, 'Democratic Reason: The Mechanisms of Collective Intelligence in Politics' in Hélène Landemore and Jon Elster (eds), *Collective Wisdom: Principles and Mechanisms* (Cambridge University Press, 2012) 251.

114 Richard E Matland and Donley T Studlar, 'Determinants of Legislative Turnover: A Cross-National Analysis' (2004) 34 *British Journal of Political Science* 87.

115 This arguably presents to legislators a more coherent picture of those they serve, and allows voters of distinct communities to enhance their electoral power. For critical discussion see Michael P Crozier and Adrian Little, 'Democratic Voice: Popular Sovereignty in Conditions of Pluralisation' (2012) 47 *Australian Journal of Political Science* 333; Nicholas Stephanopoulos, 'Political Powerlessness' (2015) 90 *NYU Law Review* 1527.

116 Issacharoff, above n 2, 595.

117 See, eg, Henri Tajfel et al, 'Social Categorization and Intergroup Behaviour' (1971) 1 *European Journal of Social Psychology* 149.

118 Pamela S Karlan, 'The Fire Next Time: Reapportionment After the 2000 Census' (1998) 50 *Stanford Law Review* 731, 762.

119 Ibid 736.

120 See, eg, Courtney, above n 38, 259; *Lortie Commission Report*, above n 65, 150, 157–8; cf Hasen, above n 51, 983.

121 Kenneth W Shotts, 'Does Racial Redistricting Cause Conservative Policy Outcomes? Policy Preferences of Southern Representatives in the 1980s and 1990s' (2003) 65 *Journal of Politics* 216.

122 David Bositis, *Blacks and the 2012 Elections: A Preliminary Analysis* (Joint Centre For Political and Economic Studies, 4 September 2012) 7.

123 Lessig notes that '[g]overnments, as other institutions, are inept; changes are very often not as intended': Lawrence Lessig, 'The Regulation of Social Meaning' (1995) 62 *University of Chicago Law Review* 943, 957. See also Rosenberg, above n 77; Cass R Sunstein, *Radicals in Robes* (Basic Books, 2005) 100–101.

124 Madison, 'The Federalist No 10', above n 67, 125.

125 There is evidence of the bodies' designers taking a great deal of effort to design effective non-partisan bodies, though of course this was well before the modern rise of deliberative democracy scholarship. This is no anachronism. Deliberative scholarship has long been interested in existing cases of deliberative democracy, and is not merely a literature focused on institutional prescription. As we have noted throughout, deliberation as a concept in theory, and as a driving motivation in practical design of governance, has been evident in every era of democracy, antiquity included.

126 One cause may be the 1950s'–1960s' shift toward a politics regarding the interests of the country as a whole: Courtney, above n 38, 44–52, 55. In addition, differences between Canada and the US may be due to acknowledged differences in structure between parliamentary and presidential democracies, and Canada's multiparty system, which might encourage polarisation less than does the American two-party system. (But neither distinction explains why Canada diverged from the US in the 1960s.) Finally, the US has experienced a more dramatic series of political scandals in recent decades: David Farrell, *Comparing Electoral Systems* (Prentice Hall, 1997); PR Abramson, *Political Attitudes in America* (Freeman, 1983). Scandals perhaps undercut public trust and inspire more punitive, negative regulation of political actors.

127 In Canada, Australia, and the UK, there is at most glancing involvement by the political branches, and a wall of separation divides the process of redistricting from political actors who stand to gain or lose from the result. See Commonwealth Electoral Act 1918 (Australia), ss 6(4), 60, 70 (government chooses from a list of three candidates nominated by the Chief Justice of the Federal Court); Graeme Orr, *The Law of Politics: Elections, Parties and Money in Australia* (Federation Press, 2010) ch 2.

128 Joanna Scott and David M Trubek, 'Mind the Gap: Law and New Approaches to Governance in the European Union' (2002) 8 *European Law Journal* 1.

129 Orly Lobel, 'The Renew Deal: The Fall of Regulation and the Rise of Governance in Contemporary Legal Thought' (2004) 89 *Minnesota Law Review* 262; Todd D Rakoff, 'The Choice between Formal and Informal Modes of Administrative Regulation' (2000) 52 *Administrative Law Review* 159.

130 Lobel, above n 129, 314.

131 Ibid 314.

132 Scott and Trubek, above n 128, 6.

133 Rakoff, above n 129, 202.

134 Ibid 168.

135 Ibid 171–2.

136 Chad Flanders, 'Election Law Behind a Veil of Ignorance' (2012) 64 *Florida Law Review* 1369 (election law); Justin Levitt, 'You're Gonna Need a Thicker Veil' (2013) 65 *Florida Law Review Forum* 1 (election law); Adrian Vermeule, 'Veil of Ignorance Rules in Constitutional Law' (2001) 111 *Yale Law Journal* 399; Christopher Tarver Robertson, 'Blind Expertise' (2010) 85 *New York University Law Review* 174 (civil litigation); Russell Korobkin, 'Determining Health Care Rights From Behind a Veil of Ignorance' (1998) 3 *University of Illinois Law Review* 801 (health law).

137 John Rawls, *A Theory of Justice* (Belknap Press, 1971) 136–42.

138 Lessig, above n 123, 1010 (Lessig is an early implicit adopter of the notion of veil of ignorance rules.)

139 Lobel, above n 129, 314.
140 For this account we are indebted to Malawi advisory group member John Barker, University of Cambridge.
141 Jason Mazzone, 'The Social Capital Argument for Federalism' (2001) 11 *Southern California Interdisciplinary Law Journal* 27, 58.
142 Ted Margadant, 'Review' (1991) 63 *Journal of Modern History* 396, 397, reviewing Marie-Vic Ozouf-Marignier, *La Formation des Départements: La Représentation du Territoire Français à la fin du 18e Siècle* (École des Hautes Études en Sciences Sociales, 1989).
143 Cox, above n 28.
144 Ibid 769–70.
145 See above n 22.
146 See above n 69.
147 Ron Levy, 'Regulating Impartiality: Electoral Boundary Politics in the Administrative Arena' (2008) 53 *McGill Law Journal* 1, 20 n 118, 44.
148 *Perry*, 548 US 399 (2006).
149 Interview with anonymous federal electoral commissioner, cited in Levy, above n 147, 45.
150 Elections Canada, *Representation in the House of Commons* (Elections Canada, 2002) 14.
151 Elections Canada, *2012 Redistribution* <www.redecoupage-federal-redistribution.ca/content.asp?document=home&lang=e> accessed 23 February 2016.
152 Justin Levitt, 'Communities of Interest' (The Brennan Center for Justice at NYU School of Law, 26 November 2010).
153 EBRA, above n 22.
154 Constitution Act 1867 (Canada), ss 8, 40, 51, 51A, 52.
155 See ch 4.
156 Louis Massicotte, André Blais and Antoine Yoshinaka, *Establishing the Rules of the Game: Election Laws in Democracies* (University of Toronto Press, 2004) 97–8.
157 Russell Williams, 'Canada's System of Representation in Crisis: the "279 Formula" and Federal Electoral Redistributions' (2005) 35 *The American Review of Canadian Studies* 99, 101.
158 *Raîche v Canada (AG)* 2004 FC 679 [32].
159 *Carter* [1991] 2 SCR 158 [62].
160 Courtney, above n 38, 29–31.
161 Levy, above n 149, 37.
162 Courtney, above n 38, 259.
163 Ibid.
164 *Carter*, above n 159.
165 Interview with anonymous federal electoral commissioner, cited in Levy, above n 147, 54. See similarly interview with Commissioner Ritu Khullar (ibid 8 (n 29)).
166 Ibid 54.
167 Elections Canada, above n 151.
168 Levy, Interview with anonymous federal electoral commissioner, cited in Levy, above n 147, 54.
169 Parliament of Canada, *Parliamentary Debates*, House of Commons, 16 April 1964, 2261–4, 2266–7.
170 Norman Ward, 'A Century of Constituencies' (1967) 10 *Canadian Public Administration* 105, 113; Harvey Pasis, 'Achieving Population Equality among the Constituencies of the Canadian House, 1903–1976' (1983) 8 *Legislative Studies Quarterly* 111, 115.
171 Charles Lane, 'White House Defends Texas's GOP Remapping Plan to Justices', *Washington Post* (Washington DC), 2 February 2006, A3.
172 Hasen, above n 51, 958.

173 Karlan, above n 118, 735.

174 Ibid 733–5, 741 (n 7).

175 *Shaw v Reno*, 509 US 630, 685 n 7 (1993).

176 See, eg, Peter McCormick, 'Birds of a Feather: Alliances and Influences on the Lamer Court, 1990–1997' (1998) 36 *Osgoode Law Journal* 339.

177 Madison, above n 67, 125 (original capitalisation).

178 Habermas, above n 90, ch 7. See also Harry Brighouse, 'Egalitarianism and Equal Availability of Political Influence' (1996) 4 *The Journal of Political Philosophy* 118; Nicole Curato, 'A Sequential Analysis of Democratic Deliberation' (2012) 2 *Acta Politica* 423, 435.

179 James Bohman, *Public Deliberation: Pluralism, Complexity, and Democracy* (MIT Press, 1996) 81 (describing and critiquing this notion).

180 Jon Elster, 'The Market and the Forum: Three Varieties of Political Theory' in James Bohman and William Rehg (eds), *Deliberative Democracy: Essays on Reason and Politics* (MIT Press, 1997) 12

181 Jon Elster, 'Deliberation and Constitution-Making' in Jon Elster (ed), *Deliberative Democracy* (Cambridge University Press, 1998) 97–122.

182 Robert Goodin, *Motivating Political Morality* (Blackwell, 1992) 132–3.

183 John Rawls, *Political Liberalism* (Columbia, Expanded Edition, 2005) 137; Amy Gutmann and Dennis F Thompson, *Why Deliberative Democracy?* (Princeton University Press, 2004) 153–4; John Parkinson, *Deliberating in the Real World: Problems of Legitimacy in Deliberative Democracy* (Oxford University Press, 2006) 99.

184 Ani, above n 23, 24.

185 Ibid.

186 Amy Gutmann and Dennis F Thompson, *Democracy and Disagreement* (Harvard University Press, 1995) 102–103.

187 Ibid.

188 Gutmann and Thompson, above n 183, 4.

189 John Rawls, 'The Idea of an Overlapping Consensus' (1987) 7 *Oxford Journal of Legal Studies* 1.

190 Cass R Sunstein, 'Incompletely Theorized Agreements' (1995) 62 *Harvard Law Review* 1733.

191 Robert Post, 'Democracy, Popular Sovereignty, and Judicial Review' (1998) 86 *California Law Review* 429.

192 Lyons, above n 33, 432–9.

193 *Contra* Levy, above n 147, citing interview with Jean Pierre Kingsley, former Chief Electoral Officer of Canada (5 July 2007).

194 See James Fishkin, *When the People Speak: Deliberative Democracy and Public Consultation* (Oxford University Press, 2009).

195 Mark Warren and Hilary Pearse, *Designing Deliberative Democracy: The British Columbian Citizens' Assembly* (Cambridge University Press, 2008).

196 Frank Michelman, *Brennan and Democracy* (Princeton University Press, 1999) 423.

197 See, eg, Gabriella R Montinola, and Robert W Jackman, 'Sources of Corruption: A Cross-Country Study' (2002) 32 *British Journal of Political Science* 147; Christopher Hood and David Heald, *Transparency: The Key to Better Governance?* (Oxford University Press, 2006); Daniel Berliner, 'The Political Origins of Transparency' (2014) 76 *The Journal of Politics* 479.

198 Courtney, above n 38, 8, but cf infrequent exceptions at 144–9; Christopher S Elmendorf, 'Representation Reinforcement through Advisory Commissions: The Case of the Law of Politics' (2005) 80 *New York University Law Review* 1366, 1393; Jean-Pierre Kingsley, 'The Administration of Canada's Independent, Non-Partisan Approach' (2004) 3 *Election Law Journal* 406, 406–407; Hasen, above n 51, 985.

199 Keith Hamilton, 'Drawing Electoral Boundaries in British Columbia' (2008) 2 *Journal of Parliamentary and Political Law* 27, 30–31 (commissioners rigorously educate themselves for the task).

200 Levy, Interview with anonymous federal electoral commissioner, cited in Levy, above n 147, n 247; see also Kingsley, above n 193.

201 Hamilton, above n 199 (500 oral submissions were heard over 12 weeks by just one commission).

202 Courtney, above n 38, 136.

203 Cf an instance where four unusually knowledgeable constituents had been coached by members of an affected political party: Levy, Interview with anonymous federal electoral commissioner, cited in Levy, above n 147, n 245.

204 Ibid n 246 ('we did consider suggestions that would better incorporate local residents' sense of local community ... taking out or putting in boundaries in ways that left communities more intact').

205 Ibid 41 (this was echoed by a second commissioner); Kingsley, above n 193 (public submissions 'significantly impact' the process).

206 Ibid 42.

207 Ibid 43.

208 Commissioner Ritu Khullar, cited in ibid n 255 ('the three of us worked well together, and I guess also shared some fundamental values of how to approach the task'). See also Kingsley, above n 193.

209 Heather Gerken suggests that 'introducing a little bit of politics into a reform commission's decision making process may inoculate its decisions against the political fray': Heather Gerken, 'Inoculating Electoral Reform against Everyday Politics' (2007) 6 *Election Law Journal* 184, 201.

210 Ron Levy, 'Breaking the Constitutional Deadlock: Lessons from Deliberative Experiments in Constitutional Change' (2010) 34 *Melbourne University Law Review* 805, 836.

211 For a different take on the value of appearances see Mark E Warren, 'Democracy and Deceit: Regulating Appearances of Corruption' (2006) 50 *American Journal of Political Science* 160.

212 Warren, above n 16, 328. *McConnell v FEC*, 540 US 93, 143 (2003) similarly holds that appearances per se are relevant.

213 Commissioner Ritu Khullar, cited in Levy, above n 147, n 118.

214 Ibid 45.

215 Habermas, above n 90, 67–9.

216 Lessig, above n 123, 958.

217 Political 'culture' serves here as a catch-all, denoting, for instance, the influential 'meanings', 'trust', 'social capital', 'values' and 'symbols' ascribed socially – rather than in common or codified law – to particular political acts. With some simplification, 'informal norms' captures these many forms.

218 Habermas, above n 90, 67–9.

219 Roberto Mangabeira Unger, *Social Theory: Its Situation and Its Task* (Cambridge University Press, 1987) 1.

220 Lessig, above n 123, 958. See also Harold Koh, 'Contemporary Conceptions of Customary International Law' (1998) 92 *American Society of International Law Proceedings* 37, 38.

221 Orr, above n 68, 141.

222 For a fuller account see Levy, above n 147.

223 See, eg, JB Ruhl, 'The Fitness of Law: Using Complexity Theory to Describe the Evolution of Law and Society and Its Practical Meaning for Democracy' (1996) 49 *Vanderbilt Law Review* 1407, 1467; Julian Webb, 'Law, Ethics and Complexity:

Complexity Theory and the Normative Reconstruction of Law' (2005) 52 *Cleveland State Law Review* 227.

224 Elections Canada, above n 151, 13.

225 *Raîche* 2004 FC 679 [32].

226 Interview with Kingsley, above n 193.

227 On the distinction between 'guiding' and 'constraining' rules see, eg, Joseph Raz, 'The Rule of Law and Its Virtue' (1977) 93 *Law Quarterly Review* 195, 198; TRS Allan, 'The Rule of Law as the Rule of Reason: Consent and Constitutionalism' (1999) 115 *Law Quarterly Review* 221, 225–7.

228 Levy, above n 147, 40.

229 Ibid 45, n 271.

230 Joseph Raz, *The Authority of Law: Essays on Law and Morality* (Clarendon Press, 1979) 213–19.

231 Lon Fuller, *The Morality of Law* (Yale University Press, 1969) 39.

232 Ibid; Raz, above n 230, 198–201.

233 Brian Z Tamanaha, *On the Rule of Law: History, Politics, Theory* (Cambridge University Press, 2004) 97. On retrospectivity see Raz, above n 230, 214–15; but cf Charles Sampford, *Retrospectivity and the Rule of Law* (Oxford University Press, 2006) 58–9.

234 Raz, above n 230, 216.

235 Kenneth Arrow, 'A Difficulty in the Concept of Social Welfare' (1950) 58(4) *Journal of Political Economy* 328.

236 *Lortie Commission Report*, above n 65, 157–8.

237 Levy, above n 147, 39.

238 Courtney, above n 38, 259.

239 Lorraine Weinrib, 'Appointing Judges to the Supreme Court of Canada in the Charter Era: A Study in Institutional Function and Design' in Ontario Law Reform Commission, *Appointing Judges: Philosophy, Politics and Practice* (1991) 109, 110.

240 Issacharoff and Karlan, above n 80.

241 Lord Longford, *A History of the House of Lords* (Sutton Publishing, 1999) 10l. See also Sunstein, above n 123, 102–106.

242 Fuller, above n 231, 33–94; Raz, above n 230, 198–201.

243 M Elizabeth Magill, 'The Real Separation in Separation of Powers Law' (2000) 86 *Virginia Law Review* 1127, 1128–9. In another context see Daniel Fitzpatrick, 'Evolution and Chaos in Property Rights Systems: The Third World Tragedy of Contested Access' (2006) 115 *Yale Law Journal* 996, 1001, 1003 (chaotic norms generate failure in property rights regimes).

244 Fuller, above n 231, 39; Raz, above n 230, 198–201.

245 Lobel, above n 129, 315; Raz, above n 230, 167–8. According to Raz, laws can have indirect effects including the enhancement, or diminishment, of the respect paid to particular moral values: ibid 168, 176–7.

246 Note that even weakly binding law might play an important deliberative role by inserting into decision-making otherwise overlooked perspectives, eg, about human rights and reciprocal multilateral obligations: see Hoi Kong and Ron Levy, 'Deliberative Constitutionalism' in André Bächtiger, John Dryzek, Jane Mansbridge and Mark Warren (eds), *Oxford Handbook of Deliberative Democracy* (Oxford University Press, forthcoming).

247 Raz, above n 230, 216–7.

248 Carter, above n 62, 58.

249 Orr, above n 127.

250 Issacharoff, above n 77, 1714.

251 Samuel Issacharoff, 'Judging Politics: The Elusive Quest for Judicial Review of Political Fairness' (1993) 71 *Texas Law Review* 1643, 1647, 1693–5.

Part IV

Conclusion

Chapter 7

Deliberative Democracy as an Holistic Value

The Constitution was intended less to resolve arguments than to make argument itself the solution.

Joseph J Ellis[1]

Deliberation is a *sine qua non* of good decision-making in general. Deliberative forms of democracy, in turn, are requisites for good decision-making in politics and government. These claims animated this book. They are not asserted as axiomatic; instead, earlier chapters have sought to justify them. (We would apologise to readers who reject them, but they are unlikely to have persisted this far.) Drawing on these claims, the purpose of the book has been to apply insights, assembled by others over recent decades of deliberative democratic theory, to the field of the law of politics. In doing so, we have directed special attention to the regulation of elections and to judicial reasoning about democratic process.

Law and deliberation exist in a reflexive relationship, which can be captured in a pair of interconnected questions. We have dubbed these the law-deliberation question, and the deliberation-law question. The former concerns how law shapes, enables, or constrains deliberation. The latter concerns how deliberation shapes law, whether by generating new regulatory models or understandings, or reinforcing existing rules and their interpretation.

In doing this, we have been acutely conscious of the limitations of deliberative democratic theory, both normative and pragmatic. Our outlook would best be described as guarded optimism. Our account has, we hope, been balanced, rather than naïvely idealistic. So, we have sought throughout, and in some detail in the opening chapters,[2] to paint a rounded tableau of deliberative democratic ideals. After all, the law is a pragmatic endeavour – an attempt to channel human interactions in socially productive ways without unduly constraining human potential. It is not, ultimately, a realm for dreamers. This is especially the case when it comes to the law of politics, which exists at the intersection of constitutional and administrative law, political theory, and the rough and tumble of parliamentary and electoral activity.

Relatedly, our focus has not been on law as an abstraction, but on law as a varied set of norms. Our aim has been to use, and further develop, a set of conceptual tools primarily in order to inform further analysis and juristic development in the law of politics: an exercise in what William Twining dubs middle-level theorising.[3] In particular, we have sought to inject the insights and values of deliberative democracy into both the critique and potentially the reform of the law of politics. According to David Schultz, elements of this law have been relatively rudderless, guided reactively by legal concerns and concepts but insufficiently informed by democratic theory.[4] Schultz's view bears some truth, although it is overstated. The problem is not so much a lack of democratic theory, but its fragmented nature and limited vision.

As we have identified, a triad of normative and instrumental values – liberty, equality, and integrity – *do* surface time and again in consideration of the structures and rules that shape electoral politics. Our lament, as we have been at pains to demonstrate, is that those values have been defined and applied in ways that may best be described as 'thin'. The values tend to be played off each other in pairwise comparisons and balancing exercises. Worse, they have been focused upon in ways that tend to occlude consideration of deliberative democratic values.

This occlusion – a failure of both the legal imagination to embrace deliberative considerations and of political theorists to attend to the woof and warp of legal regulation – might superficially be passed off as a product of the complex and nuanced demands of deliberative theory. After all, at first glance values like political liberty, equality, and integrity may seem compellingly simple and focused, especially in specific application. For example the slogan 'free and fair elections' embodies the ideal that everyone should have a freedom to exercise an equally weighted vote that is guaranteed to be counted. Yet we need only scratch the surface to appreciate that there are numerous variations of the ideals of equality and freedom. Similarly, stray just a short distance from the technocratic question of how to safeguard ballots and their scrutiny, and terms like 'integrity' are problematised. What these values mean in the context of campaign finance, or party regulation, is hotly contested.[5] Complexity is thus a feature of each democratic value we have looked at.

A main thrust of this book has been the argument that deliberative democracy, properly understood and applied, offers an holistic approach that can in some instances rise above apparent competitions between values. Democratic values are not locked in ineluctable conflict. Deliberative democratic understandings can assist us to accommodate the disparate normative commitments of the law of politics. This accommodation does not magically erode all tension within political values. But it does offer a more enriched understanding of politics and governance as something more than a jungle of individuated rights, a numerical notion of equality, or an elite game (understandings associated with naïve, siloed approaches to liberty, equality, and integrity).

Concretising the concepts

In keeping with the genre of this book as an exercise in middle-level theory, chapters 4 to 6 were exercises in specialised legal analysis. As such, they sought to mediate between higher level questions in political and, to a lesser extent, legal theory;[6] and critical analysis of a specialist field, namely the law of politics. The book's *raison d'être* is to introduce the law of deliberative democracy as a discrete field of inquiry, rather than to attempt a comprehensive survey of regulatory issues in the law of politics. We concentrated on offering detailed case studies of two key clusters of issues of ongoing interest to political activists, electoral officials, regulators, and concerned citizens alike. One of these clusters involved electoral speech and campaign activity, particularly the regulation of campaign air-time, opinion polling, and 'truth' in political advertising.[7] The other cluster involved electoral redistricting and vote weighting.[8]

Examined from the vantage point of deliberative democratic ideas, the law of politics is a field richly strewn with second-order questions – that is, questions about the design of the institutions and practice of democratic decision-making. As a result, we have sought to escape the relative pragmatism of some past studies of the relationship of democratic deliberation and legal regulation, which have addressed first-order concerns. 'First-order' here means the generation of substantive responses to thorny but genre-specific public problems, such as responses to climate change and other environmental challenges; social inclusion of racial, sexual, and ethnic minorities; or decisions about land or resource allocation. But this is not to say that the law-deliberation and deliberation-law questions, which we identified at the outset, are not important to such first-order conundrums. For instance, in dealing with land planning, the law may provide for representative deliberation (say in local government debates over projects) or more juridical and hence elite, but less easily capturable forms of deliberation (such as hearings in planning tribunals offering broad standing to citizen interests).

Instead, second-order questions are meta-questions, especially in our case about the design of deliberation in electoral democracy. In relation to the law of politics there is an acute recursion. The laws governing elections, campaigns, parties, voting, and referendums (all elements of democratic deliberation) are themselves products of deliberation, at parliamentary, judicial, and community levels. Juristic argumentation and decision-making – itself a particular species of elite deliberation – in turn offers a particularly legal, as opposed to say party-political, form of deliberation about the law of politics. The guts of the book have been spent exploring the by-ways of this deliberation about deliberation.

Electoral bribery as an evolving (and deliberative) regulatory issue

In the interests of concretising the interplay of the four values we have identified, it may be worth evaluating a particular picturesque, yet nevertheless revealing, issue in election law. That is electoral bribery, and the evolving relevance and purposes of its legal understanding. The term 'electoral bribery', a distinct pejorative, is intriguing in how it has waxed and waned in its scope, while implicating all of the core values of political liberty, equality, integrity, and deliberation.

Bribery – the use of largesse to sway or reward decision-makers, whether citizens or officials – has ancient roots.[9] In elections up until the late Victorian era (and longer in parts of the United States), currying electors' favour around election time persisted through various means, including dispensing alcohol and money. Yet although notionally criminal since at least 1695 in British elections,[10] much of what looks like outright vote-buying to modern eyes was part of a social norm of reciprocity in pre-democratic times. It formed a 'complicated dance of patronage and deference',[11] an element of social reciprocity. Indeed, to the extent that those who lacked the franchise still took part in the great libations at election time, it was more inclusive, and hence 'democratic', than the limited franchise itself.

The values that infused pre-modern elections were not, of course, those that came to be desired in modern and more democratic times. Liberty and equality, for instance, were privileges attaching to freemen, rather than 'rights for all'.[12] Electoral integrity has a distinct history, first captured in the legislative plea of 1275 that 'There shall be no Disturbance of Free Elections'.[13] But it was an integrity primarily concerned with limiting violence and intimidation, or fraud in polling, rather than a more intricate ideal. And pre-modern elections were barely conceived of as deliberative exercises at all.

Nonetheless, as we described in chapter 2, the emergence of recognisably modern elections in the later Victorian era involved a confluence of Whiggish and radical principles, with legal and technological adaptations. These reforms instituted a bold and hopeful experiment with electoral democracy – through what we can now recognise as an attempt to blend deliberative principles holistically with emerging values of equality, individual liberty, and a more robust notion of integrity.

The deliberative shift within, and democratic hope for, modern elections rested on various social and regulatory developments in the Victorian era, of which the move against electoral bribery was part of a larger whole. Above all there was the expansion of the franchise, an ideal reflecting equality and liberty. The expansion of the franchise, as we noted in chapter 5, in itself advanced the deliberative goal of broad inclusivity. Broader voting rights were themselves linked to the spread of literacy and the rise of print as a mass medium for the spread of political ideas and information,[14] developments that increased the potential of elections as moments of mass deliberative choice.

In the same Victorian period, eliminating vote-buying came to be seen as a crusade, which went hand in glove with the push for the secret ballot.[15] The secret ballot itself was argued as a benefit for equality, liberty, and integrity. Liberty was to be enhanced by guaranteeing the freedom of electoral conscience. Equality was to be improved by protecting newly enfranchised but often economically dependent voters from having their choice suborned by intimidatory employers or husbands. And integrity was to be reinforced by rendering promises to sell votes unreliable, thereby de-commodifying the ballot. In Westminster systems too, candidates were made subject to expenditure limits for the first time, along with restrictions on the gaudily flamboyant style of campaigning.[16] The explicit point of such limits was not to leech colour from electioneering,[17] but to rein in costs (an equality goal, albeit with potential impacts on freedom of expression), as well as to limit disguised vote-buying in a practical way.

It would be a stretch of historical revisionism to argue that deliberative democracy was the unifying theme in these fundamental reforms. But it is a thread that helps explain the accommodation between potentially sparring normative aims of the law of politics. The ultimate point of de-commodifying the ballot, reining in the cost of elections, and nudging campaigns towards a more discursive focus was not simply a fairer or cleaner contest, but one that was potentially more deliberatively democratic. None of this is to say that the accommodation was perfect: on the contrary. Every reform has unintended, sometimes unavoidable consequences. For instance, few today would want to wind back the secret ballot, although, as Bruce Ackerman and Jim Fishkin observe, secrecy generates a certain 'civic privatism': some citizens and electors are shy about discussing politics.[18] Modern elections are clearly more democratic and deliberative than their forbears. But they are also flawed exercises. In part these flaws relate to agonistic partisanship. In part it is also because deliberative ideals have not had much conscious sway in shaping the law of politics for many decades.

What then of electoral bribery today? The contemporary conceit is that the battle against vote-buying was won long ago, in developed democracies at least, so that the law is 'largely obsolete'.[19] Outside of pockets of the desperately poor, who is going to sell their vote for a few notes or a bottle of whisky?[20] But the law of electoral bribery remains important. It is not a mere vestige of a discrete battle to harmonise political equality, liberty, and integrity. It remains relevant in tracing the boundaries of what is acceptable in campaign discourse, and thus has a continuing significance from a deliberative democratic perspective. Indeed, it was in a similar context that we presented (in chapter 6) one of our most contestable findings: that potentially coercive regulation meant to secure electoral integrity can work best when it possesses some indeterminacy. In the case of electoral bribery, such ambiguity similarly has a salutary effect for political deliberation. It can be a tool in deliberative discourse, generating reflection and debate about the ethics of campaigning. For instance, when members of the media label a policy to lower taxation an electoral 'bribe' by a candidate, they invoke the legal term 'bribery' in a metaphorical sense.[21] The point is not to censor open debate about taxation rates. Rather it is to open up a discussion about whether the policy is sufficiently reasoned, other-regarding, and inclusive, or whether it is targeted cynically at a class of swinging voters. These are all concerns for good democratic deliberation.

Onwards, in conclusion

The key concepts developed in this work – such as accommodative versus conceptual balancing, and the problems arising from arithmetical approaches to political equality, exclusionary concerns with partisanship, and narrowly coercive regulation – have, we believe, broad explanatory power and possible impact. Indeed, the problem in legal deliberation of naïve balancing tests is unlikely to infect the judicial development of electoral law alone. It may not even be confined to the law of politics and courts, but may also hobble parliamentary committees and other bodies seeking to negotiate apparently competing values.

In a book that aims to sketch out a new field, there is not space to catalogue, let alone explore, all the potential applications of deliberative democratic theory to the law of politics. The terrain is fertile though. To take but one emerging example, convenience voting – voting early or online – is expanding at dramatic rates in western democracies. Its proponents defend its roll-out as either an equality measure (especially in the US), or a liberty or even lifestyle entitlement. Its detractors fret about integrity.[22] In the middle of this discussion, the upsides and downsides from a deliberative perspective have been largely lost. Mass early voting requires a re-thinking of the very notion of the election campaign as a staged and focused period, and of how parties and other advocates frame campaigns and how undecided voters interact with campaign material and debates. On the other hand, as more and more voters engage with balloting through the post and the internet, there is potential to explore a shared, minimum level of interaction (physical and online) and information prior to the act of casting the ballot.

Such analysis remains for another day. Our overarching theme, that deliberative democracy offers a relatively holistic and integrative vision, rests on the promise of deliberation to reinforce democracy and democracy to reinforce deliberation. For that to occur, it cannot be wished into being. The law of politics plays a central role in mediating democratic activity; ideally, to adapt Ellis above, it exists less to resolve arguments than to open space for deliberative and democratic arguments to proffer solutions.

Notes

1 Joseph J Ellis, *Quartet: Orchestrating the Second American Revolution 1783–1789* (Random House, 2015).
2 Especially chs 1 and 2.
3 William Twining, 'Introduction' in William Twining (ed), *Legal Theory and Common Law* (Basil Blackwell, 1986) 4–5.
4 David Schultz, *Election Law and Democratic Theory* (Ashgate, 2015) ch 1.
5 Is public funding of elections a measure to advance integrity and equality (by limiting corrupting private donations and balancing the ability of rival parties to campaign) or is it a measure that challenges integrity and equality (by corrupting the relationship of parties and the state and entrenching incumbents)? Compare Ingrid van Biezen, 'State Intervention in Party Politics: the Public Funding and Regulation of Political Parties' (2008) 16 *European Review* 337 and related work by the same author. On contested

norms internationally in regulating party affairs generally, see Anika Gauja, 'The Legal Regulation of Political Parties: Is there a Global Normative Standard?' (2016) 15 *Election Law Journal* 4.

6 The higher-order legal questions we invoked centred on juridical theory in constitutional law, especially the role of superior courts in reviewing legislation.

7 Chapters 4–5.

8 Chapters 5–6.

9 As has discussion of whether it was corrupting, or bred a useful kind of loyalty: see John T Noonan, *Bribes: the Intellectual History of a Moral Idea* (Diane Publishing Company, 1984) 39–41; compare Augustine, *On Free Choice of the Will* (Thomas Williams trans, Hackett Publishing Company, 1993) 10–11 (who saw it as a form of depravity, of the triumph of private interest over the public good).

10 See 7&8 William III, c 4.

11 Hannah Barker and David Vincent, *Lange, Print and Electoral Politics 1790–1832* (Boydell Press, 2001) xiv. See, for more, Frank O'Gorman, *Voters, Patrons and Parties: the Unreformed Electoral System of Hanoverian England 1734–1832* (Clarendon Press, 1982); and Frank O'Gorman, 'Campaign Rituals and Ceremonies: the Social Meaning of Elections in England 1780–1860' (1992) 134 *Past and Present* 79.

12 The etymology of the 'franchise' (from 'frank', freedom, or privilege) reflects that.

13 3 Edward I, c 5.

14 James Vernon, *Politics and the People: A Study in English Political Culture c.1815–1867* (Cambridge University Press, 1993).

15 Graeme Orr, 'Suppressing Vote-Buying: the "War" on Electoral Bribery from 1868' (2006) 27 *Journal of Legal History* 289.

16 Corrupt and Illegal Practices Prevention Act 1883 (UK). Excess expenditure was an illegal practice that could void an election. An example of the reining-in of flamboyant style was the criminalisation of payments for 'bands of music, torches, flags, banners, cockades, ribbons or other marks of distinction' at election time (see s 16 of the Act).

17 Though this was a by-product welcomed by many. See generally Graeme Orr, *Ritual and Rhythm in Electoral Systems: a Comparative Legal Account* (Ashgate, 2015) ch 8 (focusing on strictures against 'treating', a form of electoral bribery).

18 Bruce Ackerman and James Fishkin, 'Deliberation Day' (2002) 10 *Journal of Political Philosophy* 129, 129-30.

19 Colin A Hughes, 'Electoral Bribery' (1998) 7 *Griffith Law Review* 209, 209.

20 For exceptions proving the rule, in the US, see Pamela Karlan, 'Not by Money but by Virtue Won? Vote Trafficking and the Voting Rights System' (1994) 80 *Virginia Law Review* 1455, 1460, 1470.

21 Graeme Orr, 'Dealing in Votes: Regulating Electoral Bribery' in Graeme Orr, Bryan Mercurio and George Williams (eds), *Realising Democracy: Electoral Law in Australia* (Federation Press, 2003) 127, 134–5. Karlan, above n 20, employs a distinction between 'retail' (unlawful) and 'wholesale' vote-buying.

22 Postal and online voting cannot guarantee secrecy and both are susceptible to fraud through interception or hacking.

Bibliography

A Articles/Books/Reports

Abramowitz, Alan I and Kyle L Saunders, 'Is Polarisation a Myth?' (2008) 70 *Journal of Politics* 542

Abramson, PR, *Political Attitudes in America* (Freeman, 1983)

Ackerman, Bruce, 'The New Separation of Powers' (2000) 113 *Harvard Law Review* 633

Ackerman, Bruce and James Fishkin, 'Deliberation Day' (2002) 10 *Journal of Political Philosophy* 129

Ackerman, Bruce and James Fishkin, *Deliberation Day* (Yale University Press, 2004)

Adams, Guy and Danny Balfour, 'Towards Restoring Integrity in "Praetorian Times"' (2012) 14 *Public Integrity* 325

Alarie, Benjamin RD and Andrew J Green, 'Interventions at the Supreme Court of Canada: Accuracy, Affiliation and Acceptance' (2010) 48 *Osgoode Hall Law Journal* 381

Aleinikoff, T Alexander, 'Constitutional Law in the Age of Balancing' (1987) 96 *Yale Law Journal* 943

Alexy, Robert, 'Balancing, Constitutional Review, and Representation' (2005) 3 *International Journal of Constitutional Law* 578

Allan, TRS, 'The Rule of Law as the Rule of Reason: Consent and Constitutionalism' (1999) 115 *Law Quarterly Review* 221

Allan, TRS, 'Democracy, Legality and Proportionality' in Grant Huscroft, Bradley W Miller and Gregoire Webber (eds), *Proportionality and the Rule of Law* (Cambridge University Press, 2014)

Allen, Amy, 'The Unforced Force of the Better Argument: Reason and Power in Habermas' Political Theory' (2012) 19 *Constellations* 353

Altman, D and B Mollyann, 'Opinion on Public Opinion Polling' (2003) *Health Affairs* W276

Amazeen, Michelle A, Emily Thorson, Ashley Muddiman and Lucas Graves, 'A Comparison of Correction Formats: The Effectiveness and Effects of Rating Scale versus Contextual Corrections on Misinformation' (American Press Institute, February 2015) <www.americanpressinstitute.org/wp-content/uploads/2015/04/The-Effectiveness-of-Rating-Scales.pdf> accessed 19 February 2016

Anderson, Elizabeth S and Richard H Pildes, 'Expressive Theories of Law: A General Restatement' (2000) 148 *University of Pennsylvania Law Review* 1503

204 Bibliography

Anderson, Robert, 'Reporting Public Opinion Polls: The Media and the 1997 Canadian Election' (2000) 12 *International Journal of Public Opinion Research* 285

Ani, Emmanuel, 'Combatting Corruption with Public Deliberation' (2015) 34 *South African Journal of Philosophy* 13

Ansolabehere, Stephen and James M Snyder Jr, 'The Effects of Redistricting on Incumbents' (2012) 11 *Election Law Journal* 490

Aristotle, *Complete Works* (Jonathan Barnes (ed), Princeton University Press, 1984)

Aroney, Nicholas, 'Towards the "Best Explanation" of the Constitution: Text, Structure, History and Principle in *Roach v Electoral Commissioner*' (2011) 30(1) *University of Queensland Law Journal* 145

Arrow, Kenneth J, 'A Difficulty in the Concept of Social Welfare' (1950) 58 *Journal of Political Economy* 328

Arthur, W Brian, 'Inductive Reasoning and Bounded Rationality' (1994) 84 *American Economic Review* 406

Asimov, Isaac, 'The Franchise' in Isaac Asimov and Martin H Greenberg (eds), *Election Day 2084* (Prometheus Books, 1984)

Atkin, Charles K and James Gaudino, 'The Impact of Polling and the Mass Media' (1984) 472 *Annals of the American Academy of Political and Social Science* 119

Augustine, *On Free Choice of the Will* (Thomas Williams trans, Hackett Publishing Company, 1993)

Avraham, Ronen and Liu Zhiyong, 'Incomplete Contracts with Asymmetric Information: Exclusive Versus Optional Remedies' (2006) 8 *American Law and Economics Review* 523

Bächtiger, André, Simon Niemeyer, Michael Neblo, Marco R. Steenbergen and Jürg Steiner, 'Disentangling Diversity in Deliberative Democracy: Competing Theories, Their Blind Spots and Complementarities' (2010) 18 *Journal of Political Philosophy* 32

Baker, Edwin C, *Human Liberty and Freedom of Speech* (Oxford University Press, 1989)

Bale, Tim, 'Restricting the Broadcast and Publication of Pre-Election and Exit Polls: Some Selected Examples' (2002) 39 *Representation* 15

Ball, David, 'The Lion That Squeaked: Representative Government and the High Court: *McGinty & Ors v the State of Western Australia*' (1996) 18(3) *Sydney Law Review* 372

Barker, Hannah and David Vincent, *Lange, Print and Electoral Politics 1790–1832* (Boydell Press, 2001)

Baunach, Dawn Michelle, 'Changing Same-Sex Marriage Attitudes in America From 1988 Through 2010' (2012) 76 *Public Opinion Quarterly* 364

Bawn, Kathleen, Martin Cohen, David Karol, Seth Masket, Hans Noel and John Zaller, 'A Theory of Political Parties: Groups, Policy Demands and Nominations in American Politics' (2012) 10(3) *Perspectives on Politics* 571

Behrman, Robert W, 'Equal or Effective Representation: Redistricting Jurisprudence in Canada and the United States' (2011) 51 *American Journal of Legal History* 277

Benhabib, Seyla, 'Deliberative Rationality and Models of Democratic Legitimacy' (1994) 1 *Constellations* 26

Benhabib, Seyla, 'Toward a Deliberative Model of Democratic Legitimacy' in Seyla Benhabib (ed), *Democracy and Difference: Contesting the Boundaries of the Political* (Princeton University Press, 1996)

Benhabib, Seyla, *The Claims of Culture: Equality and Diversity in the Global Era* (Princeton University Press, 2002)

Bibliography 205

Bennett, WL, 'News Polls: Constructing an Engaged Public' in George C Edwards III, Lawrence R Jacobs and Robert Y Shapiro (eds), *The Oxford Handbook of American Public Opinion and Media* (Oxford University Press, 2011)

Berinsky, Amy J, 'American Public Opinion in the 1930s and 1940s: The Analysis of Quota-Controlled Sample Survey Data' (2006) 40 *Public Opinion Quarterly* 499

Berliner, Daniel, 'The Political Origins of Transparency' (2014) 76 *The Journal of Politics* 479

Berman, Mitchell N, 'Managing Gerrymandering' (2005) 83 *Texas Law Review* 781

Bhattacharya, Mita and Russell Smyth, 'The Determinants of Judicial Prestige and Influence: Some Empirical Evidence from the High Court of Australia' (2001) 30 *Journal of Legal Studies* 223

Bhattacharya, Mita and Russell Smyth, 'What Determines Judicial Prestige? An Empirical Analysis for Judges of the Federal Court of Australia' (2003) 5 *American Law and Economics Review* 233

Billig, Michael and Henri Tajfel, 'Social Categorization and Similarity in Intergroup Behavior' (1973) 3 *European Journal of Social Psychology* 27

Binder, Sarah A, Anthony J Madonna and Steven S Smith, 'Going Nuclear, Senate Style' (2007) 5 *Perspectives on Politics* 729

Birch, AH, *Representation* (Macmillan, 1972)

Bohman, James, *Public Deliberation: Pluralism, Complexity, and Democracy* (MIT Press, 1996)

Bohman, James, 'Deliberative Democracy and Effective Social Freedom: Capabilities, Resources, and Opportunities' in James Bohman and William Rehg (eds), *Deliberative Democracy: Essays on Reason and Politics* (MIT Press, 1997)

Bohman, James, 'Deliberative Democracy and the Epistemic Benefits of Diversity' (2006) 3 *Episteme* 175

Bohman, James, *Democracy across Borders: From Demos to Demoi* (MIT Press, 2007)

Bohman, James, 'Representation in the Deliberative System' in J Mansbridge and J Parkinson (eds), *Deliberative Systems* (Cambridge University Press, 2012)

Bohman, James and William Rehg (eds), *Deliberative Democracy: Essays on Reasons and Politics* (MIT Press, 1997)

Bositis, David, *Blacks and the 2012 Elections: A Preliminary Analysis* (Joint Centre For Political and Economic Studies, 4 September 2012)

Boughey, Janina, 'The Reasonableness of Proportionality in the Australian Administrative Law Context' (2015) 43 *Federal Law Review* 59

Bracton, *Bracton on the Laws and Customs of England* (Samuel E Thorne trans, Belknap Press, 1968)

Braithwaite, John, 'Institutionalizing Distrust, Enculturating Trust' in Valerie Braithwaite and Margaret Levi (eds), *Trust and Governance* (Russell Sage Foundation, 1998)

Brennan, Timothy P, 'Cleaning Out the Augean Stables: Pennsylvania's Most Recent Redistricting and a Call to Clean up This Messy Process' (2003) 13 *Widener Law Journal* 235

Brighouse, Harry, 'Egalitarianism and Equal Availability of Political Influence' (1996) 4 *The Journal of Political Philosophy* 118

Brink, David O, 'Legal Theory, Legal Interpretation, and Judicial Review' (1988) 17 *Philosophy & Public Affairs* 105

Burke, Edmund, 'Speech to the Electors in Bristol (1774)' in *Works* (Bohn's Standard Library, 1902)

206 Bibliography

Burke, Edmund, *Select Works of Edmund Burke* (A New Imprint of the Payne Edition, Liberty Fund, 1999) vol IV

Burton, Steven J, 'Comment On "Empty Ideas": Logical Positivist Analyses of Equality and Rules' (1981–1982) 91 *Yale Law Journal* 1136

Butera, Joshua, 'Partisan Gerrymandering and the Qualifications Clause' (2015) 95 *Boston University Law Review* 303

Butler, David and Bruce Cain, *Congressional Redistricting: Comparative and Theoretical Perspectives* (Macmillan, 1992)

Cain, Bruce E, 'Redistricting Commissions: A Better Political Buffer' (2012) 121 *Yale Law Journal* 1808

Calabresi, Steven G and Kevin H Rhodes, 'The Structural Constitution: Unitary Executive, Plural Judiciary' (1992) 105 *Harvard Law Review* 1153

Campbell, Angus, 'Polling, Open Interviewing, and The Problem of Interpretation' (1946) 2 *Journal of Social Issues* 67

Campbell, Enid, *Parliamentary Privilege* (Federation Press, 2003)

Canadian Government, Royal Commission on Electoral Reform and Party Financing, *Reforming Electoral Democracy: Final Report* (1991) ('*Lortie Commission Report*')

Carne, Greg, 'Representing Democracy or Reinforcing Inequality? Electoral Distribution and *McGinty v Western Australia*' (1997) 25 *Federal Law Review* 351

Carney, Gerard, *Members of Parliament: Law and Ethics* (Prospect Media, 2000)

Carter, Mark, 'Reconsidering the *Charter* and Electoral Boundaries' (1999) 22 *Dalhousie Law Journal* 53

Casillas, CJ, PK Enns and PC Wohlfarth, 'How Public Opinion Constrains the US Supreme Court' (2011) 55 *American Journal of Political Science* 74

Catanese, Nathan S, 'Gerrymandered Gridlock: Addressing the Hazardous Impact of Partisan Redistricting' (2014) 28 *Notre Dame Journal of Law, Ethics & Public Policy* 323

Chaiken, Shelly and Yaacov Trope (eds), *Dual-Process Theories in Social Psychology* (Guildford Press, 1999)

Chambers, Simone, 'Deliberative Democracy Theory' (2003) 6 *Annual Review of Political Science* 307

Chambers, Simone, 'Rhetoric and the Public Sphere: Has Deliberative Democracy Abandoned Mass Democracy?' (2009) 37 *Political Theory* 323

Chappell, Zsuzsanna, *Deliberative Democracy: A Critical Introduction* (Palgrave Macmillan, 2012)

Charles, Guy-Uriel E, 'Democracy and Distortion' (2007) 92 *Cornell Law Review* 601

Christiano, Thomas, *The Rule of the Many* (Westview Press, 1996)

Christiano, Thomas, *The Constitution of Equality: Democratic Authority and its Limits* (Oxford University Press, 2008)

Chung, Robert, 'The Freedom to Publish Opinion Poll Results: A Worldwide Update of 2012' (The University of Hong Kong, December 2012) <http://hkupop.hku.hk/english/report/freedom/FTP_2012.pdf> accessed 19 February 2016

Clark, Andrew E and Andrew J Oswald, 'Satisfaction and Comparison Income' (1996) 61 *Journal of Public Economics* 359

Coaldrake, Peter, *Working the System: Government in Queensland* (University of Queensland Press, 1989)

Cohen, Henry, *Election Projections: First Amendment Issues* (CRS Report for Congress, 23 January 2001)

Cohen, Joshua, 'Deliberation and Democratic Legitimacy' in Alan P Hamlin and Philip Pettit (eds), *The Good Polity: Normative Analysis of the State* (Blackwell, 1989)

Cohen, Joshua, 'Deliberation and Democratic Legitimacy' in James Bohman and William Rheg (eds), *Deliberative Democracy: Essays on Reason and Politics* (MIT Press, 1997)

Coleman, Jules and Brian Leiter, 'Determinacy, Objectivity, and Authority' (1993) 142 *University of Pennsylvania Law Review* 549

Coper, Michael, *Encounters with the Constitution* (CCH Books, 1987)

Courtney, John, *Commissioned Ridings: Designing Canada's Electoral Districts* (McGill-Queen's, 2001)

Cox, Adam, 'Partisan Fairness and Redistricting Politics' (2004) 79 *New York University Law Review* 751

Cranston, Ross, *Consumers and the Law* (Weidenfeld and Nicholson, 1978)

Creighton, Peter, 'Apportioning Electoral Districts in a Representative Democracy' (1994) 24 *UWA Law Review* 78

Crespi, Leo P, 'The Cheater Problem in Polling' (1945) 9 *Public Opinion Quarterly* 431

Crozier, Michael P and Adrian Little, 'Democratic Voice: Popular Sovereignty in Conditions of Pluralisation' (2012) 47 *Australian Journal of Political Science* 333

Curato, Nicole, 'A Sequential Analysis of Democratic Deliberation' (2012) 2 *Acta Politica* 423

Cutler, Fred and Richard Johnston, with R Ken Carty, André Blais, and Patrick Fournier, 'Deliberation, Information, and Trust: The British Columbia Citizens' Assembly as Agenda Setter' in Mark E Warren and Hilary Pearse (eds), *Designing Deliberative Democracy: The British Columbia Citizens' Assembly* (Cambridge University Press, 2008)

Dalton, Russell J, *Citizen Politics: Public Opinion and Political Parties in Advanced Industrial Democracies* (Congressional Quarterly Press, 5th ed, 2008)

de Vreese, CH and HA Semetko, 'Public Perception of Polls and Support for Restrictions on the Publication of Polls: Denmark's 2000 Euro Referendum' (2002) 14 *International Journal of Public Opinion Research* 410

Devlin, Nicholas, 'Opinion Polls and the Protection of Political Speech – A Comment on *Thomson Newspapers Co v Canada*' (1997) 28 *Ottawa Law Review* 411

Donsbach, Wolfgang, *Who's Afraid of Opinion Polls? Normative and Empirical Arguments for the Freedom of Pre-Election Surveys* (European Society for Opinion and Marketing Research, 2001) <http://wapor.org/pdf/who-is-afraid-of-opinion-polls.pdf> accessed 19 February 2016

Donsbach, Wolfgang and Uwe Hartung, 'The Legal Status of Public Opinion Research in the World' in Wolfgang Donsbach and Michael Traugott (eds), *The SAGE Handbook of Public Opinion Research in the World* (SAGE, 2008)

Dovi, Suzanne, 'Political Representation' (17 October 2011) *Stanford Encyclopedia of Philosophy* <http://plato.stanford.edu/entries/political-representation/> accessed 1 March 2016

Dryzek, John, *Discursive Democracy* (Cambridge University Press, 1990)

Dryzek, John, *Deliberative Democracy and Beyond: Liberals, Critics, Contestations* (Oxford University Press, 2000)

Dryzek, John, 'Discursive Representation' (2008) 102(4) *American Political Science Review* 481

Dryzek, John, 'Democratization as Deliberative Capacity Building' (2009) 42 *Comparative Political Studies* 1379

Dryzek, John S and Christian List, 'Social Choice Theory and Deliberative Democracy: A Reconciliation' (2003) 33 *British Journal of Political Science* 1

208   Bibliography

Dryzek, John S and Simon J Niemeyer, 'Reconciling Pluralism and Consensus as Political Ideals' (2006) 50 *American Journal of Political Science* 634

Dworkin, Ronald, *A Matter of Principle* (Harvard University Press, 1985)

Dworkin, Ronald, *Law's Empire* (Harvard University Press, 1986)

Dworkin, Ronald, *Freedom's Law* (Harvard University Press, 1997)

Dyzenhaus, David, 'Law as Justification: Etienne Mureinik's Conception of Legal Culture' (1998) 14 *South African Journal on Human Rights* 11

Dyzenhaus, David, 'Dignity in Administrative Law: Judicial Deference in a Culture of Justification' (2012) 17 *Review of Constitutional Studies* 87

Dyzenhaus, David, 'Proportionality and Deference in a Culture of Justification' in Grant Huscroft, Bradley W Miller and Gregoire Webber (eds), *Proportionality and the Rule of Law* (Cambridge University Press, 2014)

Elections Canada, *Representation in the House of Commons* (Elections Canada, 2002) <www.redecoupage-federal-redistribution.ca/content.asp?document=home&lang=e> accessed 1 March 2016

Ellis, Joseph J, *Quartet: Orchestrating the Second American Revolution 1783–1789* (Random House, 2015)

Elmendorf, Christopher S, 'Representation Reinforcement Through Advisory Commissions: The Case of the Law of Politics' (2005) 80 *New York University Law Review* 1366

Elster, Jon, 'The Market and the Forum: Three Varieties of Political Theory' in James Bohman and William Rehg (eds), *Deliberative Democracy: Essays on Reason and Politics* (MIT Press, 1997)

Elster, Jon, 'Deliberation and Constitution-Making' in Jon Elster (ed), *Deliberative Democracy* (Cambridge University Press, 1998)

Elster, Jon, 'Introduction' in John Elster (ed), *Deliberative Democracy* (Cambridge University Press, 1998)

Emerson, Thomas, *The System of Freedom of Expression* (Harvard University Press, 1970)

Engstrom, Richard L, *Revising Constituency Boundaries in the United States and Australia: It Couldn't be More Different* (Democratic Audit of Australia, 2005) <democraticaudit.org. au> accessed 22 February 2016

Ertman, Thomas, 'The Great Reform Act of 1832 and British Democratization' (2010) 43 *Comparative Political Studies* 1000

Estlund, David, *Democratic Authority: A Philosophical Framework* (Princeton University Press, 2008)

Ewing, Keith D, 'A Theory of Democratic Adjudication: Towards a Representative, Accountable and Independent Judiciary' (2000) 38 *Alberta Law Review* 312

Farrell, David, *Comparing Electoral Systems* (Prentice Hall, 1997)

Feasby, Colin, 'Public Opinion Poll Restrictions, Elections and the *Charter*' (1997) 55 *University of Toronto Faculty of Law Review* 241

Ferejohn, John, 'Judicializing Politics, Politicizing Law' (2002) 61 *Law and Contemporary Problems* 41

Festinger, Leon, 'A Theory of Social Comparison Processes' (1954) 7 *Human Relations* 117

Finkelstein, Ray, *Report of the Independent Inquiry into the Media and Media Regulation* (Australian Government, 28 February 2012)

Fisher, DR (ed), *A History of Parliament: The House of Commons, 1820–1832* (Cambridge University Press, 2010)

Fishkin, James, *Democracy and Deliberation: New Directions for Democratic Reform* (Yale University Press, 1991)

Fishkin, James S, 'Virtual Democratic Possibilities: Prospects for Internet Democracy' (Paper presented at Conference on Internet, Democracy and Public Goods, Belo Horizonte, Brazil, 6–10 November 2000)

Fishkin, James S, 'Consulting the Public Through Deliberative Polling' (2002) 22 *Journal of Policy Analysis and Management* 128

Fishkin, James, *When the People Speak: Deliberative Democracy and Public Consultation* (Oxford University Press, 2009)

Fiss, Owen, 'Free Speech and Social Structure' (1985) 71 *Iowa Law Review* 1405

Fiss, Owen, 'Why the State?' (1987) 100 *Harvard Law Review* 781

Fitzgerald, Thomas, 'Public Opinion Sampling' (2002) 39 *Society* 53

Fitzpatrick, Daniel, 'Evolution and Chaos in Property Rights Systems: The Third World Tragedy of Contested Access' (2006) 115 *Yale Law Journal* 996

Flanders, Chad, 'Deliberative Dilemmas: A Critique of Deliberation Day from the Perspective of Election Law' (2007) 23 *Journal of Law and Politics* 147

Flanders, Chad, 'What Do We Want in a Presidential Primary? An Election Law Perspective' (2011) 44 *University of Michigan Journal of Law Reform* 901.

Flanders, Chad, 'Election Law Behind a Veil of Ignorance' (2012) 64 *Florida Law Review* 1369

Fletcher, George P and Jens David Ohlin, *Defending Humanity: When Force Is Justified and Why* (Oxford University Press, 2008)

Fried, A, *A Crisis in Public Opinion Polling* (Routledge, 2011)

Fritz, Ronald E, 'Challenging Electoral Boundaries Under the Charter: Judicial Deference and Burden of Proof' (1999) 5 *Review of Constitutional Studies* 1

Fuller, Lon, 'Adjudication and the Rule of Law' (1960) 54 *American Society for International Law and Process* 1

Fuller, Lon, *The Morality of Law* (Yale University Press, 1969)

Fund, John, *Stealing Elections: How Voter Fraud Threatens Our Democracy* (Encounter Books, 2004)

Fung, Archon, 'Survey Article: Recipes for Public Spheres: Eight Institutional Design Choices and Their Consequences' (2003) 11 *Journal of Political Philosophy* 338

Gageler, Stephen, 'Why Write Judgments?' (2014) 36 *Sydney Law Review* 189

Galligan, Denis J, *Discretionary Powers: A Legal Study of Official Discretion* (Clarendon Press, 1986)

Galvin, Daniel and Colleen Shogan, 'Presidential Politicization and Centralization across the Modern-Traditional Divide' (2004) 36 *Polity* 477

Gardner, James A, 'Deliberation or Tabulation? The Self-Undermining Constitutional Architecture of Election Campaigns' (2006) 2006–013 *Buffalo Legal Studies Research Paper* 1

Gardner, James, *What Are Campaigns For? The Role of Persuasion in Electoral Law and Politics* (Oxford University Press, 2009)

Gastil, John, *By Popular Demand: Revitalizing Representative Democracy through Deliberative Elections* (University of California Press, 2000)

Gauja, Anika, *Political Parties and Elections: Legislating for Representative Democracy* (Ashgate, 2010)

Gauja, Anika, 'The Legal Regulation of Political Parties: Is There a Global Normative Standard?' (2016) 15 *Election Law Journal* 4)

210   Bibliography

Gauja, Anika and Graeme Orr, 'Regulating "Third Parties" as Electoral Actors: Comparative Insights and Questions for Democracy' (2015) 4 *Interest Groups and Advocacy* 249

Gaynor, Niamh, 'Associations, Deliberation and Democracy: The Case of Ireland's Social Partnership' (2011) 39 *Politics and Society* 497

Geddis, Andrew, 'Three Conceptions of the Electoral Moment' (2003) 28 *Australian Journal of Legal Philosophy* 53

Geddis, Andrew, *Electoral Law in New Zealand: Practice and Policy* (LexisNexis, 2nd ed, 2014)

Gelber, Katharine, 'Freedom of Political Speech, Hate Speech and the Argument from Democracy: The Transformative Contribution of Capabilities Theory' (2010) 9(3) *Contemporary Political Theory* 304

Gerken, Heather, 'Inoculating Electoral Reform Against Everyday Politics' (2007) 6 *Election Law Journal* 184

Ghosh, Eric, 'Deliberative Democracy and the Countermajoritarian Difficulty: Considering Constitutional Juries' (2010) 30 *Oxford Journal of Legal Studies* 327

Glass, Arthur, 'Freedom of Speech and the Constitution: *Australian Capital Television* and the Application of Constitutional Rights' (1995) 17 *Sydney Law Review* 29

Gleeson, Murray, *The Rule of Law and the Constitution* (ABC Books, 2000)

Glendon, Mary Ann, *Rights Talk: The Impoverishment of Political Discourse* (Free Press, 1993)

Goodin, Robert, *Motivating Political Morality* (Blackwell, 1992)

Goodin, Robert E, 'Talking Politics: Perils and Promise' (2006) 45 *European Journal of Political Research* 235

Goodin, Robert E, *Innovating Democracy: Democratic Theory and Practice after the Deliberative Turn* (Oxford University Press, 2008)

Goodin, Robert, 'Democratic Deliberation Within' (2009) 29 *Philosophy and Public Affairs* 81

Gray, Anthony, 'The Guaranteed Right to Vote in Australia' (2007) 7(2) *QUT Law Review* 178

Greenawalt, Kent, *Law and Objectivity* (Oxford University Press, 1992)

Gutmann, Amy and Dennis Thompson, *Democracy and Disagreement* (Harvard Belknap Press, 1996)

Gutmann, Amy and Dennis Thompson, *Why Deliberative Democracy?* (Princeton University Press, 2004)

Habermas, Jürgen, *The Theory of Communicative Action: Reason and the Rationalization of Society* (Thomas McCarthy trans, Beacon Press, 1984, first published 1981)

Habermas, Jürgen, 'Law as Medium and Law as Institution' in G Teubner (ed), *Dilemmas of Law in the Welfare State* (Walter de Gruyter, 1988)

Habermas, Jürgen, *Moral Consciousness and Communicative Action* (Christian Lenhardt and Shierry Weber Nicholsen trans, MIT Press, 1990)

Habermas, Jürgen, 'Reconciliation Through the Public Use of Reason: Remarks on John Rawls's Political Liberalism' (1995) 92 *Journal of Philosophy* 109

Habermas, Jurgen, *Between Facts and Norms: Contributions to a Discourse Theory of Law and Democracy* (William Rehg trans, MIT Press, 1996)

Habermas, Jürgen, 'Constitutional Democracy: A Paradoxical Union of Contradictory Principles?' (2001) 29(6) *Political Theory* 766

Haidt, Jonathan, *The Righteous Mind: Why Good People are Divided by Politics and Religion* (Pantheon, 2012)

Hamilton, Keith, 'Drawing Electoral Boundaries in British Columbia' (2008) 2 *Journal of Parliamentary and Political Law* 27

Hamlin, A and Philip Pettit, *The Good Polity* (Oxford University Press, 1989)

Hamlin, J Kiley, Neha Mahajan, Zoe Liberman and Karen Wynn, 'Not Like Me = Bad: Infants Prefer Those Who Harm Dissimilar Others' (2013) 24 *Psychological Science* 589

Hanretty, Chris, 'Political Preferment in English Judicial Appointments, 1880–2005' (2012) *APSA Annual Meeting Paper*

Hardmeier, Sibylle, 'The Effects of Published Polls on Citizens' in W Donsbach and M Traugott (eds), *The SAGE Handbook of Public Opinion Research in the World* (SAGE, 2008) 504

Harvey, Anna and Barry Friedman, 'Pulling Punches: Congressional Constraints on the Supreme Court's Constitutional Rulings 1987–2000' (2006) 31(4) *Legislative Studies Quarterly* 533

Hasen, Richard L, 'Looking for Standards (in All the Wrong Places): Partisan Gerrymandering Claims after *Vieth*' (2004) 3 *Election Law Journal* 626

Hasen, Richard L, 'Beyond the Margin of Litigation: Reforming US Election Administration to Avoid Electoral Meltdown' (2005) 62 *Washington and Lee Law Review* 937

Hasen, Richard L, 'A Constitutional Right to Lie in Campaigns and Elections' (2013) 74 *Montana Law Review* 53

Henderson, Rick, 'Polling Error' (1993) 25(1) *Reason* 11

Hendriks, Carolyn M, 'Integrated Deliberation: Reconciling Civil Society's Dual Role in Deliberative Democracy' (2006) 54 *Political Studies* 486

Hendriks, Carolyn M, John S Dryzek, and Christian Hunold, 'Turning up the Heat: Partisanship in Deliberative Innovation' (2007) 55 *Political Studies* 362

Henkin, Louis, *The Age of Rights* (Columbia University Press, 1990)

Henn, Matt, 'Opinion Polling in Central and Eastern Europe under Communism' (1998) 33 *Journal of Contemporary History* 229

Herbst, Susan, *Numbered Voices: How Opinion Polling has Shaped American Politics* (University of Chicago Press, 1993)

Hill, Lisa, 'Deliberative Democracy and Compulsory Voting' (2013) 12 *Election Law Journal* 454

Hinchcliff, Abigail M, 'The "Other" Side of *Richardson v Ramirez*: A Textual Challenge to Felon Disenfranchisement' (2011) 121 *Yale Law Journal* 194

Hirschl, Ran, 'The Judicialization of Politics' in Keith Whittington, R Daniel Keleman and Gregory A Caldeira (eds), *The Oxford Handbook of Law and Politics* (Oxford University Press, 2008)

Hobbes, Thomas, *De Cive* (Sterling P Lamprecht (ed), Appleton-Century-Crofts, 1949)

Hocking, Jenny, *Gough Whitlam: The Biography* (Melbourne University Publishing/MiegunyahPress, 2008)

Hogg, Peter, 'Appointment of Justice Marshall Rothstein to the Supreme Court of Canada' (2006) 44 *Osgoode Hall Law Journal* 527

Hogg, Peter W, *Constitutional Law of Canada* (Carswell, 2011)

Hood, Christopher and David Heald, *Transparency: The Key to Better Governance?* (Oxford University Press, 2006)

Horowitz, Donald L, *Ethnic Groups in Conflict* (University of California Press, 2001)

House of Commons Standing Committee on Procedure and House Affairs, Parliament of Canada, *Procedure and House Affairs Report* (1995) ('*Milliken Report*')

212 Bibliography

Howells, Geraint and Stephen Weatherill, *Consumer Protection Law* (Ashgate, 2nd ed, 2005)

Hughes, Colin A, 'The Rules of the Game' in Clive Bean, Ian McAllister and John Warhurst (eds), *The Greening of Australian Politics: The 1990 Federal Election* (Longman Cheshire, 1990)

Hughes, Colin A, 'Electoral Bribery' (1998) 7 *Griffith Law Review* 209

Human Rights Council, 'Report of the Special Rapporteur on the promotion and protection of the right to freedom of opinion and expression, Frank La Rue' (2014) UN Doc A/HRC/26/30 (30 May 2014)

Hume, David, *Of the Independency of Parliament: Essays, Moral, Political and Literary*, vol 1 (Oxford University Press, 1963)

Irving Helen, 'The People and Their Conventions' in Michael Coper and George Williams (eds), *Power, Parliament and the People* (Federation Press, 1997)

Issacharoff, Samuel, 'Judging Politics: The Elusive Quest for Judicial Review of Political Fairness' (1993) 71 *Texas Law Review* 1643

Issacharoff, Samuel, 'Gerrymandering and Political Cartels' (2002) 116 *Harvard Law Review* 593

Issacharoff, Samuel, 'Is Section 5 of the Voting Rights Act a Victim of Its Own Success?' (2004) 104 *Columbia Law Review* 1710

Issacharoff, Samuel and Pamela Karlan, 'The Hydraulics of Campaign Finance Reform' (1999) 77 *Texas Law Review* 1705

Jacobs, Laverne, 'From Rawls to Habermas: Towards A Theory of Grounded Impartiality in Canadian Administrative Law' (2014) 51 *Osgoode Hall Law Review* 543

Jacobson, Gary C, 'Partisan Polarization in Presidential Support: The Electoral Connection' (2003) 30 *Congress and the Presidency* 1

Johnson, David, 'Canadian Electoral Boundaries and the Courts: Practices, Principles and Problems' (1994) 39 *McGill Law Journal* 224

Johnson, James, 'Political Parties and Deliberative Democracy?' in Richard S Katz and William Crotty (eds), *Handbook of Party Politics* (SAGE, 2006)

Johnston, Ron and Charles Pattie, 'From the Organic to the Arithmetic: New Redistricting/Redistribution Rules for the United Kingdom' (2012) 11 *Election Law Journal* 70

Joint Standing Committee on Electoral Matters, Parliament of Australia, *Report on the Conduct of the 2007 Federal Election and Matters Relating Thereto* (2009)

Kahan, Dan M, 'Ideology, Motivated Reasoning, and Cognitive Reflection' (2013) 8 *Judgment and Decision Making* 407

Kahneman, Daniel, 'Maps of Bounded Rationality: Psychology for Behavioural Economics' (2003) 93 *The American Economic Review* 1449

Kang, Michael S, 'When Courts Won't Make Law: Partisan Gerrymandering and a Structural Approach to the Law of Democracy' (2007) 68 *Ohio State Law Journal* 1097

Karlan, Pamela, 'The Rights to Vote: Some Pessimism About Formalism' (1993) 71 *Texas Law Review* 1705

Karlan, Pamela, 'Not by Money but by Virtue Won? Vote Trafficking and the Voting Rights System' (1994) 80 *Virginia Law Review* 1455

Karlan, Pamela S, 'The Fire Next Time: Reapportionment After the 2000 Census' (1998) 50 *Stanford Law Review* 731

Karlan, Pamela, 'Politics by Other Means' (1999) 85 *Virginia Law Review* 1697

Katz, RS and W Crotty, *Handbook of Party Politics* (SAGE, 2006)

Kavanagh, A, *Constitutional Review under the UK Human Rights Act* (Cambridge University Press, 2009)

Kearney, D and Thomas W Merrill, 'Influence of Amicus Curiae Briefs on the Supreme Court' (1999) 148 *University of Pennsylvania Law Review* 743

Keating, Gregory C, 'Reasonableness and Rationality in Negligence Theory' (1996) 48 *Stanford Law Review* 311

Kelly, Norm, *Directions in Australian Electoral Reform: Professionalism and Partisanship in Electoral Management* (ANU E-Press, 2012)

Kildea, Paul, 'Worth Talking About? Modest Constitutional Amendment and Citizen Deliberation in Australia' (2013) 12 *Election Law Journal* 524

Kingsley, Jean-Pierre, 'The Administration of Canada's Independent, Non-Partisan Approach' (2004) 3 *Election Law Journal* 406

Kirk, Jeremy, 'Constitutional Limitations (II): Doctrines of Equality and Democracy' (2001) 25 *Melbourne University Law Review* 24

Kitto, Frank, 'Why Write Judgments?' (1992) 66 *Australian Law Journal* 787

Klarman, Michael, 'Majoritarian Judicial Review: The Entrenchment Problem' (1997) 85 *Georgetown Law Review* 491

Knight, Jack and James Johnson, 'What Sort of Equality Does Deliberative Democracy Require?' in J Bohman and W Rehg (eds), *Deliberative Democracy: Essays on Reason and Politics* (MIT Press, 1997)

Koch, Cornelia and Lisa Hill, 'The Ballot Behind Bars After *Roach*: Why Disenfranchise Prisoners?' (2008) 33 *Alternative Law Journal* 220

Koh, Harold, 'Contemporary Conceptions of Customary International Law' (1998) 92 *American Society of International Law Proceedings* 37

Kong, Hoi and Ron Levy, 'Deliberative Constitutionalism' in André Bächtiger, John Dryzek, Jane Mansbridge and Mark Warren (eds), *Oxford Handbook of Deliberative Democracy* (Oxford University Press, forthcoming)

Kornhauser, Lewis A and Lawrence G Sager, 'Unpacking the Court' (1986) 96 *Yale Law Journal* 82

Kornhauser, Lewis A and Lawrence G Sager, 'The One and the Many: Adjudication in Collegial Courts' (1993) 81 *California Law Review* 1

Korobkin, Russell, 'Determining Health Care Rights From Behind a Veil of Ignorance' (1998) 3 *University of Illinois Law Review* 801

Krotoszynski, Ronald J, Johnjerica Hodge and Wesley W Wintermyer, 'Partisan Balance Requirements in the Age of New Formalism' (2015) 90 *Notre Dame Law Review* 941

Kumm, Matthias, 'Constitutional Rights as Principles: On the Structure and Domain of Constitutional Justice' (2004) 2 *International Journal of Constitutional Law* 574

Kumm, Matthias, 'Institutionalising Socratic Contestation' (2007) 1 *European Journal of Legal Studies* 1

Kushner, H, 'Election Polls, Freedom of Speech and the Constitution' (1983) 15 *Ottawa Law Review* 515

Lachapelle, G, *Polls and the Media in Canadian Elections: Taking the Pulse* (Research Studies for the Royal Commission on Electoral Reform and Party Financing, vol 16 (Dundurn Press, 1991)

Landau, Z, O Reid and I Yershov, 'A Fair Division Solution to the Problem of Redistricting' (2009) 32 *Social Choice and Welfare* 479

214 Bibliography

Landemore, Hélène, 'Democratic Reason: The Mechanisms of Collective Intelligence in Politics' in Hélène Landemore and Jon Elster (eds), *Collective Wisdom: Principles and Mechanisms* (Cambridge University Press, 2012)

Landerkin, Hugh F, 'Custody Disputes in the Provincial Court of Alberta: A New Judicial Dispute Resolution Model' (1997) 35 *Alberta Law Review* 627

Lang, Kurt and Gladys E Lang, 'The Impact of Polls on Public Opinion' (1984) 472 *Annals of the American Academy of Political and Social Science* 129

Lawrence, Jon, *Electing our Masters: The Hustings in British Politics from Hogarth to Blair* (Oxford University Press, 2009)

Leiter, Brian (ed), *Objectivity in Law and Morals* (Cambridge University Press, 2001)

Lessig, Lawrence, 'The Regulation of Social Meaning' (1995) 62 *University of Chicago Law Review* 943

Leveson, Lord Justice Brian, *An Inquiry into the Culture, Practices and Ethics of the Press* (4 vols, The Stationery Office, November 2012)

Levitsky, Steven and Lucan A Way, 'Why Democracy Needs a Level Playing Field' (2010) 21 *Journal of Democracy* 57

Levitt, Justin, 'Communities of Interest' (The Brennan Center for Justice at NYU School of Law, 26 November 2010)

Levitt, Justin, 'You're Gonna Need a Thicker Veil' (2013) 65 *Florida Law Review Forum* 1

Levy, Ron, 'Regulating Impartiality: Electoral Boundary Politics in the Administrative Arena' (2008) 53 *McGill Law Journal* 1

Levy, Ron, 'Breaking the Constitutional Deadlock: Lessons from Deliberative Experiments in Constitutional Change' (2010) 34 *Melbourne University Law Review* 805

Levy, Ron, 'Drawing Boundaries: Election Law Fairness and Its Democratic Consequences' in Joo-Cheong Tham, Brian Costar and George Williams (eds), *Electoral Democracy: Australian Prospects* (Melbourne University Press, 2011)

Levy, Ron, 'Deliberative Constitutional Change in a Polarised Federation' in Paul Kildea, Andrew Lynch and George Williams (eds), *Tomorrow's Federation: Reforming Australian Government* (Federation Press, 2012)

Levy, Ron, 'Deliberative Voting: Realising Constitutional Referendum Democracy' (2013) *Public Law* 555

Levy, Ron and Graeme Orr (eds), 'Symposium: The Law of Deliberative Democracy' (2013) 12 *Election Law Journal* 355.

Lewis, David E, *The Politics of Presidential Appointments: Political Control and Bureaucratic Performance* (Princeton University Press, 2008)

Lewyn, Michael E, 'How to Limit Gerrymandering' (1993) 45 *Florida Law Review* 403

Lobel, Orly, 'The Renew Deal: The Fall of Regulation and the Rise of Governance in Contemporary Legal Thought' (2004) 89 *Minnesota Law Review* 262

Longford, Lord Frank Pakenham, *A History of the House of Lords* (Sutton Publishing, 1999)

Lovink, JAA, 'Is Canadian Politics Too Competitive?' (1973) 6 *Canadian Journal of Political Science* 341

Lowenstein, Daniel and Jonathan Steinberg, 'The Quest for Legislative Districting in the Public Interest: Elusive or Illusory?' (1985) 33 *UCLA Law Review* 1

Lublin, David and Michael P McDonald, 'Is It Time to Draw the Line? The Impact of Redistricting on Competition in State House Elections' (2006) 5 *Election Law Journal* 144

Lyons, WE, 'Legislative Redistricting by Independent Commissions: Operationalizing the One Man–One Vote Doctrine in Canada' (1969) 1 *Polity* 428

MacDonnell, Vanessa A, 'The Constitution as Framework for Governance' (2003) 63 *University of Toronto Law Journal* 624

Mackenzie, Michael K and Mark E Warren, 'Two Trust-Based Uses of Minipublics in Democratic Systems' in John Parkinson and Jane Mansbridge (eds), *Deliberative Systems* (Cambridge University Press, 2012)

Madison, James, 'The Federalist No 10' in Isaac Kramnick (ed), *The Federalist Papers* (Penguin, 1987)

Madison, James, 'The Federalist No 63' in Isaac Kramnick (ed), *The Federalist Papers* (Penguin, 1987).

Madison, James, 'The Federalist No 48' in Isaac Kramnick (ed), *The Federalist Papers* (Penguin, 1987)

Magill, M Elizabeth, 'The Real Separation in Separation of Powers Law' (2000) 86 *Virginia Law Review* 1127

Maguire, CB and Roy Radner (eds), *Decision and Organization* (North-Holland Publishing Company, 1972)

Manin, Bernard, 'On Legitimacy and Democratic Deliberation' (1987) 15 *Political Theory* 338

Manin, Bernard, *The Principles of Representative Government* (Cambridge University Press, 1997)

Manin, Bernard, 'Democratic Deliberation: Why We Should Promote Debate Rather than Discussion' (Paper to Program in Ethics and Public Affairs Seminar, Princeton University, 13 October 2005)

Mansbridge, Jane, James Bohman, Simone Chambers, David Estlund, Andreas Føllesdal, Archon Fung, Cristina Lafont, Bernard Manin and José luis Martí, 'The Place of Self-Interest and the Role of Power in Deliberative Democracy' (2010) 18 *The Journal of Political Philosophy* 64

Mansbridge, Jane, James Bohman, Simone Chambers, Thomas Christiano, Archon Fung, John Parkinson, Dennis F Thompson and Mark E Warren, 'A Systemic Approach to Deliberative Democracy' in John Parkinson and Jane Mansbridge (eds), *Deliberative Systems* (Cambridge University Press, 2012)

Margadant, Ted, 'Review' (1991) 63 *Journal of Modern History* 396

Marsh, David, David Richards and Martin Smith, 'Unequal Plurality: Towards an Asymmetric Power Model of British Politics' (2003) 38 *Government and Opposition* 306

Massaro, Toni M and Robin Stryker, 'Freedom of Speech, Liberal Democracy, and Emerging Evidence on Civility and Effective Democratic Engagement' (2012) 54 *Arizona Law Review* 375

Massicotte, Louis, André Blais and Antoine Yoshinaka, *Establishing the Rules of the Game: Election Laws in Democracies* (University of Toronto Press, 2004)

Mathews, Jud and Alec Stone Sweet, 'All Things in Proportion? American Rights Review and the Problem of Balancing' (2011) 60 *Emory Law Journal* 797

Matland, Richard E and Donley T Studlar, 'Determinants of Legislative Turnover: A Cross-National Analysis' (2004) 34 *British Journal of Political Science* 87

Matsusaka, John, 'Direct Democracy Works' (2005) 19 *Journal of Economic Perspectives* 185

Mattson, Kevin, 'Do Americans Really Want Deliberative Democracy?' (2002) 5 *Rhetoric & Public Affairs* 327

Mazzone, Jason, 'The Social Capital Argument for Federalism' (2001) 11 *Southern California Interdisciplinary Law Journal* 27

McAllister, Ian, *The Australian Voter: 50 Years of Change* (UNSW Press, 2011)

McCormick, Peter, 'Birds of a Feather: Alliances and Influences on the Lamer Court, 1990–1997' (1998) 36 *Osgoode Law Journal* 339

McDonald, Michael P, 'A Comparative Analysis of Redistricting Institutions in the United States, 2001–2002' (2004) 4 *State Politics and Policy Quarterly* 371

McDonald, Michael P, 'Regulating Redistricting' (2007) 40(4) *Political Science & Politics* 675

McGinnis, John O, 'Against the Scribes: Campaign Finance Reform Revisited' (2000–2001) 24 *Harvard Journal of Law & Public Policy* 25

McLeish, Stephen, 'Challenges to the Survival of the Common Law' (2014) 38(2) *Melbourne University Law Review* 818

Meguid, Bonnie M, *Party Competition Between Unequals: Strategies and Electoral Fortunes in Western Europe* (Cambridge University Press, 2008)

Meiklejohn, Alexander, *Political Freedom: The Constitutional Powers of the People* (Oxford University Press, 1965)

Mendes, Conrado Hübner, *Constitutional Courts and Deliberative Democracy* (Oxford University Press, 2013)

Michelman, Frank, 'Brennan and Democracy: The 1996–97 Brennan Center Symposium Lecture' (1998) 86 *California Law Review* 399

Michelman, Frank, *Brennan and Democracy* (Princeton University Press, 1999)

Mill, John Stuart, *Considerations on Representative Government* (Parker, Son, and Bourn, 1861)

Miller, David, 'Deliberative Democracy and Social Choice' (1992) 40 *Political Studies* 54

Milot, Micheline, 'Conceptions of the Good: Challenging the Premises of Deliberative Democracy' in David Kahane, Daniel Weinstock, Dominique Leydet and Melissa Williams (eds), *Deliberative Democracy in Practice* (UBC Press, 2010)

Möller, Kai, 'Proportionality and Rights Inflation' in Grant Huscroft, Bradley W Miller and Gregoire Webber (eds), *Proportionality and the Rule of Law* (Cambridge University Press, 2014)

Monmonier, Mark, *Bushmanders and Bullwinkles: How Politicians Manipulate Electronic Maps and Census Data to Win Elections* (University of Chicago Press, 2001)

Montinola, Gabriella R and Robert W Jackman, 'Sources of Corruption: A Cross-Country Study' (2002) 32(1) *British Journal of Political Science* 147

Moore, Michael, 'Moral Reality Revisited' (1992) 90 *Michigan Law Review* 2424

Morgan-Foster, Jason, 'Transnational Judicial Discourse and Felon Disenfranchisement: Re-Examining *Richardson v Ramirez*' (2006) 13 *Tulsa Journal of Comparative and International Law* 279

Mouffe, Chantal, 'Deliberative Democracy or Agonistic Pluralism?' (1999) 66 *Social Research* 745

Muirhead, Russell, 'Can Deliberative Democracy be Partisan?' (2010) 22 *Critical Review* 129

Mullan, David, *Administrative Law* (Irwin Law, 2001)

Navot, Doron, 'The Concept of Political Corruption' (2014) 16 *Public Integrity* 357

Newton-Farrelly, Jenni, 'From Gerry-Built to Purpose-Built: Drawing Electoral Boundaries for Unbiased Election Outcomes' (2009) 45 *Representation* 471

Nicol, Nancy and Miriam Smith, 'Legal Struggles and Political Resistance: Same-Sex Marriage in Canada and the USA' (2008) 11 *Sexualities* 667

Niemi, Richard G and Laura R Winsky, 'The Persistence of Partisan Redistricting Effects in Congressional Elections in the 1970s and 1980s' (1992) 54 *Journal of Politics* 565

Nino, Carlos, *The Constitution of Deliberative Democracy* (Yale University Press, 1996)

Noonan, John T, *Bribes: the Intellectual History of a Moral Idea* (Diane Publishing Company, 1984)

Novkov, Julie, 'The Miscegenation/Same-Sex Marriage Analogy: What Can We Learn from Legal History?' (2008) 33 *Law & Social Inquiry* 345

Nussbaum, Martha, 'Capabilities as Fundamental Entitlements: Sen and Social Justice' (2003) 9 *Feminist Economics* 33

Nyhan, Brendan and Jason Reifler, 'Estimating Fact-Checking's Effects: Evidence from a Long-Term Experiment during Campaign 2014' (American Press Institute, 28 April 2015) <www.americanpressinstitute.org/wp-content/uploads/2015/04/Estimating-Fact-Checkings-Effect.pdf> accessed 22 February 2016

O'Flynn, Ian, 'Deliberative Democracy for a Great Society' (2015) 13 *Political Studies Review* 207

O'Gorman, Frank, *Voters, Patrons and Parties: the Unreformed Electoral System of Hanoverian England 1734–1832* (Clarendon Press, 1982)

O'Gorman, Frank, 'Electoral Deference in Unreformed England, 1760–1832' (1984) *Journal of Modern History* 56

O'Gorman, Frank, *Voters, Patrons and Parties: the Unreformed Electorate of Hanoverian England, 1734–1832* (Clarendon Press, 1989)

O'Gorman, Frank, 'Campaign Rituals and Ceremonies: the Social Meaning of Elections in England 1780–1860' (1992) 134 *Past and Present* 79

Oosterhouse, Douglas, 'Campaign Finance Reform and Disclosure: Stepping Up IRS Enforcement as a Remedial Measure to Partisan Deadlock in Congress and the FEC' (2012) 65 *Rutgers Law Review* 261

Organization of American States, *Annual Report of the Inter-American Commission on Human Rights 2005: Report of the Special Rapporteur for Freedom of Expression* (Inter-American Commission on Human Rights OEA/Ser L/V/II.122, Washington DC, 27 February 2008)

Orr, Graeme (ed), 'Special Issue: Electoral Regulation and Representation' (1998) 7 *Griffith Law Review*

Orr, Graeme, 'The Conduct of Referenda and Plebiscites in Australia: A Legal Perspective' (2000) 11 *Public Law Review* 117

Orr, Graeme, 'The Law Comes to the Party: The Continuing Juridification of Australian Political Parties' (2002) 3 *Constitutional Law and Policy Rev* 41

Orr, Graeme, 'Dealing in Votes: Regulating Electoral Bribery?' in Graeme Orr, Bryan Mercurio and George Williams (eds), *Realising Democracy: Electoral Law in Australia* (Federation Press, 2003)

Orr, Graeme, 'Suppressing Vote-Buying: the "War" on Electoral Bribery from 1868' (2006) 27 *Journal of Legal History* 289

Orr, Graeme, *The Law of Politics: Elections, Parties and Money in Australia* (Federation Press, 2010)

Orr, Graeme, 'Legal Conceptions of Political Parties: Through the Lens of Anti-Discrimination Law' in Joo-Cheong Tham, Brian Costar and Graeme Orr (eds), *Electoral Democracy: Australian Prospects* (Melbourne University Press, 2011)

Orr, Graeme, 'Party Primaries for Candidate Selection? Right Question, Wrong Answer' (2011) 34 *University of New South Wales Law Journal* 964

Orr, Graeme, 'Deliberation and Electoral Law' (2013) 12 *Election Law Journal* 421

218   Bibliography

Orr, Graeme, 'Private Association and Public Brand: the Dualistic Conception of Political Parties in the Common Law World' (2014) 17 *Critical Review of International Social and Political Philosophy* 332

Orr, Graeme, *Ritual and Rhythm in Electoral Systems: a Comparative Legal Account* (Ashgate, 2015)

Orr, Graeme and George Williams, 'The People's Choice: The Prisoner Franchise and the Constitutional Protection of Voting Rights in Australia' (2009) 8 *Election Law Journal* 123

Orr, Graeme and Ron Levy, 'Electoral Malapportionment: Partisanship, Rhetoric and Reform in the Shadow of the Agrarian Strong-man' (2009) 18 *Griffith Law Review* 638

Orr, Graeme and Ron Levy, 'Regulating Opinion Polling: A Deliberative Democratic Perspective' (2016) 39 *UNSW Law Journal* 318

Orr, Graeme, Bryan Mercurio and George Williams, 'Australian Electoral Law: A Stocktake' (2003) 2 *Election Law Journal* 383

Orr, Graeme, Brian Mercurio and George Williams (eds), *Realising Democracy: Electoral Law in Australia* (The Federation Press, 2003)

Ozouf-Marignier, Marie-Vic, *La Formation des Départements: La Représentation du Territoire Français à la fin du 18e Siècle* (Recherches d'Histoire et de Sciences Sociales no 36, École des Hautes Études en Sciences Sociales, 1989)

Pal, Michael and Sujit Choudhry, 'Is Every Ballot Equal? Visible-Minority Vote Dilution in Canada' (2007) 13 *IRPP Choices* (Institute for Research on Public Policy, January 2007)

Pal, Michael, 'The Promise and Limits of Citizens' Assemblies: Deliberation, Institutions and the Law of Democracy' (2012) 38(1) *Queen's Law Journal* 259

Parker, Charles E, 'Polling Problems in State Primary Elections' (1948) 12 *Public Opinion Quarterly* 728

Parkinson, John, 'Legitimacy Problems in Deliberative Democracy' (2003) 51 *Political Studies* 180

Parkinson, John, *Deliberating in the Real World: Problems of Legitimacy in Deliberative Democracy* (Oxford University Press, 2006)

Parkinson, John, 'Democratizing Deliberative Systems' in J Mansbridge and J Parkinson (eds), *Deliberative Systems* (Cambridge University Press, 2012)

Parliament of Australia, House of Representatives Standing Committee on Legal and Constitutional Affairs, *A Time for Change: Yes/No? Inquiry into the Machinery of Referendums* (2009)

Pasis, Harvey, 'Achieving Population Equality among the Constituencies of the Canadian House, 1903–1976' (1983) 8 *Legislative Studies Quarterly* 111

Pelletier, David, Vivica Kraak, Christine McCullum, Ulla Uusitalo and Robert Rich, 'The Shaping of Collective Values through Deliberative Democracy: An Empirical Study from New York's North Country' (1999) 32 *Policy Sciences* 103

Persily, Nathaniel, 'Reply: In Defense of Foxes Guarding Henhouses: The Case for Judicial Acquiescence to Incumbent-Protecting Gerrymanders' (2002) 116 *Harvard Law Review* 649

Persily, Nathaniel, 'The Place of Competition in American Election Law in the Marketplace of Democracy: Electoral Competition and American Politics' in Michael P McDonald and John Samples, *The Marketplace of Democracy: Electoral Competition and American Politics* (Brookings Institution Press, 2007)

Petersen, Thomas, 'Regulation of Opinion Polls: A Comparative Perspective' in Christina Holtz-Bacha and Jesper Strömbäck (eds), *Opinion Polls and the Media: Reflecting and Shaping Public Opinion* (Palgrave-Macmillan, 2012)

Pettit, Philip, 'The Cunning of Trust' (1995) 24 *Philosophy and Public Affairs* 202

Pettit, Philip, 'Deliberative Democracy and the Discursive Dilemma' (2001) 11 *Philosophical Issues* 268

Pildes, Richard H, 'The Destruction of Social Capital Through Law' (1996) 144 *University of Pennsylvania Law Review* 2055

Pildes, Richard H, 'Democracy and Disorder' in Cass R Sunstein and Richard A Epstein (eds), *The Vote: Bush, Gore, and the Supreme Court* (University of Chicago Press, 2001)

Pildes, Richard, 'Competitive, Deliberative and Rights-Oriented Democracy' (2004) 3 *Election Law Journal* 685

Pildes, Richard, 'The Supreme Court, 2003 Term – Foreword: The Constitutionalization of Democratic Politics' (2004) 118 *Harvard Law Review* 29

Plato, *Republic* (Christopher Emlyn-Jones and William Preddy, eds and trans, Harvard University Press, 2013)

Poffenroth, Kim, '*Raîche v Canada*: A New Direction in Drawing Electoral Boundaries?' (2005) 31 *Commonwealth Law Bulletin* 53

Ponet, David and Ethan Leib, 'Fiduciary Law's Lessons for Deliberative Democracy' (2011) 91 *Boston University Law Review* 1249

Posner, Richard A, *Law, Pragmatism and Democracy* (Harvard University Press, 2003)

Post, Robert, 'Democracy, Popular Sovereignty, and Judicial Review' (1998) 86 *California Law Review* 429

Post, Robert, 'Managing Deliberation: The Quandary of Democratic Dialogue' (1993) 103 *Ethics* 654

Postema, Gerald R, 'Sweet Dissonance: Conflict, Consensus, and the Rule of Law' (2010) 17 *Harvard Review of Philosophy* 37

Putnam, Robert D, Robert Leonardi and Rafaella Y Nanetti, *Making Democracy Work: Civic Traditions in Modern Italy* (Princeton University Press, 2002)

Qualter, Terence H, *The Election Process in Canada* (McGraw-Hill, 1970)

Queensland Parliament, Legal, Constitutional and Administrative Review Committee, *Report on Truth in Political Advertising* (December 1996)

Rakoff, Todd D, 'The Choice between Formal and Informal Modes of Administrative Regulation' (2000) 52 *Administrative Law Review* 159

Rallings, Colin, Ron Johnston and Michael Thrasher, 'Changing the Boundaries but Keeping the Disproportionality: The Electoral Impact of the Fifth Periodical Reviews by the Parliamentary Boundary Commissions for England and Wales' (2008) 79 *Political Quarterly* 80

Rawlings, HF, *Law and the Electoral Process* (Sweet & Maxwell, 1988)

Rawls, John, *A Theory of Justice* (Belknap Press, 1971)

Rawls, John, 'The Idea of an Overlapping Consensus' (1987) 7 *Oxford Journal of Legal Studies* 1

Rawls, John, 'The Idea of Public Reason' in James Bohman and William Rehg (eds), *Deliberative Democracy: Essays on Reasons and Politics* (MIT Press, 1997)

Rawls, John, *Political Liberalism* (Columbia University Press, Expanded Edition, 2005)

Raz, Joseph, 'The Rule of Law and Its Virtue' (1977) 93 *Law Quarterly Review* 195

Raz, Joseph, *The Authority of Law: Essays on Law and Morality* (Clarendon Press, 1979)

Raz, Joseph, 'The Rule of Law and its Virtue' in Joseph Raz (ed), *The Authority of Law* (Oxford University Press, 1979)

220 Bibliography

Rehg, William, 'Translator's Introduction' in Jürgen Habermas, *Between Facts and Norms: Contributions to a Discourse Theory of Law and Democracy* (William Rehg trans, The MIT Press, 1996, first published 1992)

Rhodes, Glenn, *Votes for Australia: How Colonials Voted at the 1899–1900 Federation Referendums* (Centre for Australian Public Sector Management, Griffith University, 2002)

Robertson, Christopher Tarver, 'Blind Expertise' (2010) 85 *New York University Law Review* 174

Rosati, Connie S, 'Some Puzzles about the Objectivity of Law' (2004) 23(3) *Law and Philosophy* 273

Rosenberg, Gerald, *The Hollow Hope: Can Courts Bring About Social Change?* (University of Chicago Press, 1993)

Rosenblum, Nancy L, *On the Side of the Angels: An Appreciation of Parties and Partisanship* (Princeton University Press, 2010)

Rostbøll, Christian F, 'Freedom of Expression, Deliberation, Autonomy and Respect' (2011) 10 *European Journal of Political Theory* 5

Rostow, Eugene V, 'The Democratic Character of Judicial Review' (1952) 66 *Harvard Law Review* 208

Rowbottom, Jacob, 'Access to the Airwaves and Equality: The Case against Political Advertising on the Broadcast Media' in Keith D Ewing and Samuel Issacharoff (eds), *Party Funding and Campaign Financing in International Perspective* (Hart Publishing, 2006) 77

Rowbottom, Jacob, 'Animal Defenders International: Speech, Spending and a Change of Direction in Strasbourg' (2013) 5 *Journal of Media Law* 1

Royal Commission on Electoral Reform and Party Financing, *Reforming Electoral Democracy* (Canadian Government, June 1991)

Ruhl, JB, 'The Fitness of Law: Using Complexity Theory to Describe the Evolution of Law and Society and Its Practical Meaning for Democracy' (1996) 49 *Vanderbilt Law Review* 1407

Russell, A, 'The Truth about Youth? Media Portrayals of Young People and Politics in Britain' (2004) 4 *Journal of Public Affairs* 347

Sachs, Albie, *The Strange Alchemy of Life and Law* (Oxford University Press, 2009)

Sampford, Charles, *Retrospectivity and the Rule of Law* (Oxford University Press, 2006)

Sandberg, Russell and Norman Doe, 'The Strange Death of Blasphemy' (2008) 71 *Modern Law Review* 971

Sanders, Lynn M, 'Against Deliberation' (1997) 25 *Political Theory* 347

Santiago Nino, Carlos, *The Constitution of Deliberative Democracy* (Yale University Press, 1996)

Schaar, John, 'Legitimacy in the Modern State' in William Connolly (ed), *Legitimacy and the State* (Blackwell, 1984)

Schafer, Mark, *Groupthink Versus High-Quality Decision Making in International Relations* (Columbia University Press, 2010)

Schauer, Frederick, *Free Speech: A Philosophical Enquiry* (Cambridge University Press, 1982)

Schauer, Frederick, 'Slippery Slopes' (1985) 99 *Harvard Law Review* 361

Schauer, Frederick, 'Proportionality and the Question of Weight' in Grant Huscroft, Bradley W Miller and Gregoire Webber (eds), *Proportionality and the Rule of Law* (Cambridge University Press, 2014)

Schauer, Frederick and Richard Pildes, 'Electoral Exceptionalism and the First Amendment' (1999) 77 *Texas Law Review* 1803

Bibliography   221

Scheberle, Denise, *Federalism and Environmental Policy: Trust and the Politics of Implementation* (Georgetown University Press, 2nd ed, 2004)

Schultz, David, *Election Law and Democratic Theory* (Ashgate, 2015)

Schumpeter, Joseph, *Capitalism, Socialism and Democracy* (Harper Perennial Modern Classics, 3rd ed, 1950)

Scott, Joanna and David M Trubek, 'Mind the Gap: Law and New Approaches to Governance in the European Union' (2002) 8 *European Law Journal* 1

Sen, Maya, 'Courting Deliberation: An Essay on Deliberative Democracy in the American Judicial System' (2012) 27 *Notre Dame Journal of Law, Ethics & Public Policy* 303

Senate Joint Select Committee on Electoral Reform, Australian Parliament, *Second Report* (1984)

Sheff, Jeremy N, 'The Myth of the Level Playing Field: Knowledge, Affect and Repetition in Public Debate' (2010) 75 *Missouri Law Review* 143

Shotts, Kenneth W, 'Does Racial Redistricting Cause Conservative Policy Outcomes? Policy Preferences of Southern Representatives in the 1980s and 1990s' (2003) 65 *Journal of Politics* 216

Siegel, Reva B, 'She the People: The Nineteenth Amendment, Sex Equality, Federalism and the Family' (2002) 115 *Harvard Law Review* 947

Sikes, Earl R, *State and Federal Corrupt-Practices Legislation* (Duke University Press, 1928)

Silver, Brian L, *The Ascent of Science* (Oxford University Press, 1998)

Simon, Herbert A, 'Theories of Bounded Rationality' in CB Maguire and Roy Radner (eds), *Decision and Organization* (North-Holland Publishing Company, 1972)

Sloane, Stephanie, Renée Baillargeon and David Premack, 'Do Infants Have a Sense of Fairness?' (2012) 23 *Psychological Science* 196

Smith, David, 'A Question of Trust: Parliamentary Democracy and Canadian Society' (2004) 27 *Canadian Parliamentary Review* 24

Solum, Lawrence Byard, 'Freedom of Communicative Action: A Theory of the First Amendment Freedom of Speech' (1988) 83 *Northwestern University Law Review* 54

Somin, Ilya, 'Deliberative Democracy and Political Ignorance' (2010) 22 *Critical Review* 253

Sossin, Lorne, 'Speaking Truth to Power? The Search for Bureaucratic Independence in Canada' (2005) 55 *University of Toronto Law Review* 1

Spafford, Duff, '"Effective Representation": *Reference Re Provincial Election Boundaries*' (1992) 56 *Saskatchewan Law Review* 197

Spangenberg, F, *The Freedom to Publish Opinion Poll Results: Report on a Worldwide Update* (Foundation for Information, 2003)

Speagle, Donald, '*Australian Capital Television Pty Ltd v Commonwealth*' (1992) 18 *Melbourne Law Review* 938

Spector, Horatio, 'The Right to a Constitutional Jury' (2009) 3 *Legisprudence* 111

Stanyer, James, *Intimate Politics: Publicity, Privacy and the Personal Lives of Politicians in Media-Saturated Democracies* (Polity Books, 2012)

Stavropoulos, Nicos, *Objectivity in Law* (Clarendon Press, 1996)

Steiner, Jürg, *The Foundations of Deliberative Democracy: Empirical Research and Normative Implications* (Cambridge University Press, 2012)

Steiner, Jürg, Andre Bächtiger, Markus Spörndli and Marco R Steenbergen, *Deliberative Politics in Action: Analyzing Parliamentary Discourse* (Cambridge University Press, 2004)

Stephanopoulos, Nicholas O, 'Political Powerlessness' (2015) 90 *New York University Law Review* 1527

222 Bibliography

Stokes, Michael, 'A Tangled Web: Redistributing Electoral Boundaries for Tasmania's Legislative Council' (1996) 15 *University of Tasmania Law Review* 143

Stone, Adrienne, 'The Limits of Constitutional Text and Structure: Standards of Review and the Freedom of Political Communication' (1999) 23 *Melbourne University Law Review* 668

Stone, Harlan Fisk, 'The Common Law in the United States' (1936) 50 *Harvard Law Review* 4

Stone Sweet, Alec and Jud Mathews, 'Proportionality Balancing and Global Constitutionalism' (2008) 47 *Columbia Journal of Transnational Law* 72

Sunstein, Cass, 'Preferences and Politics' (1991) 20 *Philosophy and Public Affairs* 3

Sunstein, Cass, *Democracy and the Problem of Free Speech* (The Free Press, 1993)

Sunstein, Cass R, 'Incompletely Theorized Agreements' (1995) 62 *Harvard Law Review* 1733

Sunstein, Cass R, 'On the Expressive Function of Law' (1996) 144 *University of Pennsylvania Law Review* 2021

Sunstein, Cass R, 'Social Norms and Social Roles' (1996) 96 *Columbia Law Review* 903

Sunstein, Cass R, *Designing Democracy: What Constitutions Do* (Oxford University Press, 2001)

Sunstein, Cass R, 'The Law of Group Polarization' in James Fishkin and Peter Laslett (eds), *Debating Deliberative Democracy* (Blackwell, 2003)

Sunstein, Cass R, *Radicals in Robes* (Basic Books, 2005)

Sunstein, Cass R, *A Constitution of Many Minds: Why the Founding Document Doesn't Mean What It Meant Before* (Princeton University Press, 2009)

Tacitus, Cornelius, *The Complete Works of Tacitus* (Alfred John Church and William Jackson Brodribb trans, Random House, 1942)

Tajfel, Henri, 'Intergroup Behavior, Social Comparison and Social Change' (Katz-Newcomb Lectures, University of Michigan, Ann Arbor, mimeo, 1974)

Tajfel, Henri, MG Billig, RP Bundy and Claude Flament, 'Social Categorization and Intergroup Behaviour' (1971) 1 *European Journal of Social Psychology* 149

Tamanaha, Brian Z, *On the Rule of Law: History, Politics, Theory* (Cambridge University Press, 2004)

Taylor, Charles, 'Conditions of an Unforced Consensus on Human Rights' in Joanne R Bauer and Daniel A Bell, *The East Asian Challenge for Human Rights* (Cambridge University Press, 1999)

Teer, F and JD Spence, *Political Opinion Polls* (Hutchinson, 1973)

Tham, Joo-Cheong, *Money and Politics: The Democracy We Can't Afford* (UNSW Press, 2010)

Tham, Joo-Cheong, Brian Costar and Graeme Orr (eds), *Electoral Democracy: Australian Prospects* (Melbourne University Press, 2011)

Thompson, Dennis F, *John Stuart Mill and Representative Government* (Princeton University Press, 1976)

Thompson, Dennis F, *Just Elections: Creating a Fair Electoral Process in the United States* (University of Chicago Press, 2002)

Thompson, Dennis F, 'Two Concepts of Corruption: Making Campaigns Safe for Democracy' (2005) 73 *George Washington Law Review* 1036

Thompson, Dennis F, 'Deliberative Democratic Theory and Empirical Political Science' (2008) 11 *Annual Review of Political Science* 497

Thompson, Dennis F, 'Deliberate About, Not In, Elections' (2013) 12 *Election Law Journal* 372

Tierney, Stephen, *Constitutional Referendums: The Theory and Practice of Republican Deliberation* (Oxford University Press, 2012)

Tolson, Franita, 'Benign Partisanship' (2012) 88 *Notre Dame Law Review* 395

Tushnet, Mark, 'Constitutional Hardball' (2004) 37 *John Marshall Law Review* 523

Twining, William, 'Introduction' in William Twining (ed), *Legal Theory and Common Law* (Basil Blackwell, 1986)

Twomey, Anne, 'The Federal Constitutional Right to Vote in Australia' (2000) 28 *Federal Law Review* 125

Uhr, John, *Deliberative Democracy in Australia: The Changing Place of Parliament* (Cambridge University Press, 1998)

Uhr, John, 'Institutions of Integrity: Balancing Values and Verification in Democratic Governance' (1999) 1 *Public Integrity* 94

Unger, Roberto Mangabeira, *Social Theory: Its Situation and Its Task* (Cambridge University Press, 1987)

van Biezen, Ingrid, 'State Intervention in Party Politics: the Public Funding and Regulation of Political Parties' (2008) 16 *European Review* 337

Van de Walle, Steven, Steven Van Roosbroek and Geert Bouckaert, 'Trust in the Public Sector: Is There Any Evidence for a Long-Term Decline?' (2008) 74 *International Review of Administrative Sciences* 45

Ventriss, Curtis, 'Democratic Citizenship and Public Ethics' (2012) 14 *Public Integrity* 283

Vermeule, Adrian, 'Veil of Ignorance Rules in Constitutional Law' (2001) 111 *Yale Law Journal* 399

Vernon, James, *Politics and the People: A Study in English Political Culture c 1815–1867* (Cambridge University Press, 1993)

Waite, Peter B, 'Chartered Libertine? A Case Against Sir John A Macdonald and Some Answers' (1975–76) 3 *Manitoba Historical Society Transactions* 3

Wald, Patricia M, 'A Response to Tiller and Cross' (1999) 99 *Columbia Law Review* 235

Waldron, Jeremy, 'Judicial Review and the Conditions of Democracy' (1998) 4 *Journal of Political Philosophy* 6

Waldron, Jeremy, 'Judges as Moral Reasoners' (2009) 7 *International Journal of Constitutional Law* 2

Walsh, Elias, Sarah Dolfin and John DiNardo, 'Lies, Damn Lies, and Pre-Election Polling' (2009) 99 *American Economic Review* 316

Walzer, Michael, 'Deliberation, and What Else?' in Stephen Macedo (ed), *Deliberative Politics: Essays on Democracy and Disagreement* (Oxford University Press, 1999)

Ward, Norman, 'A Century of Constituencies' (1967) 10 *Canadian Public Administration* 105

Ward, SJA, *Ethics and the Media* (Cambridge University Press, 2011)

Warren, Mark E, 'What Does Corruption Mean in a Democracy?' (2004) 48 *American Journal of Political Science* 328

Warren, Mark E, 'Democracy and Deceit: Regulating Appearances of Corruption' (2006) 50 *American Journal of Political Science* 160

Warren, Mark E, 'Institutionalizing Deliberative Democracy' in Shawn W Rosenberg, *Deliberation, Participation and Democracy: Can the People Govern?* (Palgrave Macmillan, 2007)

Warren, Mark and Hilary Pearse (eds), *Designing Deliberative Democracy: The British Columbia Citizens' Assembly* (Cambridge University Press, 2008)

Warren, Mark and Hilary Pearse, 'Introduction' in Mark Warren and Hilary Pearse (eds), *Designing Deliberative Democracy: The British Columbia Citizens' Assembly* (Cambridge University Press, 2008)

224 Bibliography

Webb, Julian, 'Law, Ethics and Complexity: Complexity Theory and the Normative Reconstruction of Law' (2005) 52 *Cleveland State Law Review* 227

Webb, Paul, *The Modern British Party System* (SAGE, 2007)

Weiden, David, 'Judicial Politicization, Ideology and Activism at the High Courts of the United States, Canada, and Australia' (2011) 64 *Political Research Quarterly* 335

Weinrib, Lorraine, 'Appointing Judges to the Supreme Court of Canada in the Charter Era: A Study in Institutional Function and Design' in Ontario Law Reform Commission, *Appointing Judges: Philosophy, Politics and Practice* (1991)

Weissberg, R, 'The Problem with Polling' (2002) 148 *Public Interest* 37

Westen, Peter, 'The Empty Idea of Equality' (1982) 95 *Harvard Law Review* 537

Wheeler, Fiona, 'Original Intent and the Doctrine of Separation of Powers in Australia' (1996) 7 *Public Law Review* 96

Whittington, Keith, R Daniel Kelemen and Gregory A Caldeira (eds), *Oxford Handbook of Law and Politics* (Oxford University Press, 2008)

Williams, George, 'Sounding the Core of Representative Democracy: Implied Freedoms and Electoral Reform' (1995) 20 *Melbourne University Law Review* 848

Williams, George, *Truth in Political Advertising Legislation in Australia* (Australian Parliamentary Library, Research Paper No 13 of 1996–97)

Williams, George, 'Freedom of Political Discussion and Australian Electoral Laws' (1998) 5 *Canberra Law Review* 151

Williams, George and David Hume, *People Power: The History and Future of the Referendum in Australia* (UNSW Press, 2010)

Williams, George and Natalie Gray, 'A New Chapter in the Regulation of Truth in Political Advertising in Australia' (1997) 8 *Public Law Review* 110

Williams, Glanville L, 'The Law Reform (Contributory Negligence) Act, 1945' (1946) 9 *Modern Law Review* 105

Williams, Russell, 'Canada's System of Representation in Crisis: the "279 Formula" and Federal Electoral Redistributions' (2005) 35 *The American Review of Canadian Studies* 99

Wood, Diane P, 'When to Hold, When to Fold, and When to Reshuffle: The Art of Decisionmaking on a Multi-Member Court' (2012) 100 *California Law Review* 1445

Wood, Joanne V, 'Theory and Research Concerning Social Comparisons of Personal Attributes' (1989) 106 *Psychological Bulletin* 231

Wright, Gerald C and Brian F Schaffner, 'The Influence of Party: Evidence from the State Legislatures' (2002) 96 *American Political Science Review* 2

Young, Iris Marion, *Justice and the Politics of Difference* (Princeton University Press, 1990)

Young, Iris Marion, 'Justice, Inclusion and Deliberative Democracy' in Stephen Macedo (ed), *Deliberative Politics: Essays on Democracy and Disagreement* (Oxford University Press, 1999)

Young, Iris Marion, *Inclusion and Democracy* (Oxford University Press, 2000)

Young, Iris Marion, 'Activist Challenges to Deliberative Democracy' (2001) 29 *Political Theory* 670

Young, Sally, *Media Reporting on the Next Federal Election: What Can We Expect?* (Papers on Parliament No 58, Australian Senate, 2012)

Zurn, Christopher F, *Deliberative Democracy and the Institutions of Judicial Review* (Cambridge University Press, 2007)

B Cases

Argentina

Asociación de Teleradiodifusoras Argentina and Asociación de Radiodifusoras Privadas Argentina v Government of the City of Buenos Aires, A682.XXXVI (7 June 2005) (Supreme Court of Argentina)

Australia

Attorney-General (Cth); ex rel McKinlay v Commonwealth (1975) 135 CLR 1
Australian Capital Television Pty Ltd v Commonwealth (1992) 177 CLR 106
Australian Communist Party v Commonwealth (1951) 83 CLR 1
Cameron v Becker (1995) 64 SASR 238
Coleman v Power (2004) 220 CLR 1
Durant v Greiner (1990) 21 NSWLR 119
Featherston v Tully (2002) 83 SASR 302
Featherston v Tully (No 2) (2002) 83 SASR 347
Forge v ASIC (2006) 228 CLR 45
Global Sportsman Pty Ltd v Mirror Newspapers Ltd (1984) 55 ALR 25
King v Electoral Commissioner (1998) 78 SASR 172
McGinty v Western Australia (1996) 186 CLR 140
Monis v The Queen (2013) 249 CLR 92
Plimer v Roberts (1997) 150 ALR 235
Roach v Electoral Commissioner (2007) 233 CLR 162
Rowe v Electoral Commissioner (2010) 243 CLR 1
Smith v Oldham (1912) 15 CLR 355
Tajjour v New South Wales [2014] HCA 35
Taylor v McLean (Unreported, Court of Petty Sessions, Launceston, Schott CM, 9/6/2004)
Unions New South Wales v New South Wales (2013) 304 ALR 266
Woodward v Maltby [1959] VR 794 (UK)

Canada

British Columbia (Public Service Employee Relations Commission) v British Columbia Government and Service Employees' Union [1999] 3 SCR 3
Canadian Pacific Limited v Matsqui Indian Band [1995] 1 SCR 3
Charlottetown (City) v Prince Edward Island (1998) 168 DLR (4th) 79
East York (Borough) v Ontario (1997) 36 OR (3d) 733
Friends of Democracy [1999] NWTJ No 28
Irwin Toy Ltd v Quebec (Attorney General) [1989] 1 SCR 927
Libman v Quebec (Attorney General) [1997] 3 SCR 569
R v Bryan [2007] 1 SCR 527
R v Butler [1992] 1 SCR 452
R v Canadian Broadcasting Corporation et al [1993] 51 CPR (3d)
R v Oakes [1986] 1 SCR 103
Raîche v Canada (Attorney General) [2004] FC 679

Bibliography

Reference re Electoral Boundaries Commission Act (Alberta) [1992] 1 WWR 481
Reference re Electoral Boundaries Commission Act (Saskatchewan) [1991] 2 SCR 158
RJR-MacDonald Inc v Canada (Attorney General) [1995] 3 SCR 199
Sauvé v Canada (Chief Electoral Officer) [2002] 3 SCR 519
Thomson Newspapers Co Ltd v Canada (Attorney General) [1998] 1 SCR 877

Columbia

Constitutional Court of Colombia, Decision C-488/1993 (28 October 1993)
Constitutional Court of Colombia, Decision C-089/1994 (3 March 1994)

Europe

Animal Defenders International v United Kingdom [2013] ECHR 362
Bowman v United Kingdom [1998] ECHR 4
Hirst v United Kingdom (No 2) (2006) 42 EHRR 849

France

Cour de cassation [French Court of Cassation], 00-85329, 4 September 2001 reported in
(2001), Bull crim no 170, 562

International

Kim Jong-Cheol v Republic of Korea, Human Rights Committee, UN Doc CCPR/
C/84/D/968/2001 (23 August 2005)

Paraguay

Supreme Court of Justice of Paraguay, Constitutional Chamber, Decision 99 of 1998 (5
May 1998)

Philippines

Social Weather Stations v Commission on Elections, Philippines Supreme Court, GR No 147571
(5 May 2001)

South Africa

My Vote Counts NPC v Speaker of the National Assembly [2015] ZACC 31

United Kingdom

Edgington v Fitzmaurice (1885) 29 Ch D 459
Kruse v Johnson [1898] 2 QB 91
R (Daly) v Secretary of State for the Home Department [2001] 2 AC 532

United States

Abrams v United States, 250 US 616 (1919)
Arizona Free Enterprise Club v Bennett, 564 US __ (2011)
Arizona State Legislature v Arizona Independent Redistricting Commission, 576 US __ (2015)
Baker v Carr, 369 US 186 (1962)
Baskin v Bogan, 766 F 3d 648 (7th Cir 2014)
Bostic v Schaefer, 760 F 3d 352 (4th Cir 2014)
Brown v Hartlage, 456 US 45 (1982)
Brown v Thomson, 462 US 835 (1983)
Bush v Gore, 531 US 98 (2000)
Citizens United v Federal Election Commission, 558 US 310 (2010)
Crawford v Marion County Election Board, 553 US 181 (2008)
Daily Herald Co v Munro, 838 F 2d 380 (9th Cir Wash 1988)
Davis v Bandemer, 478 US 109 (1985)
FCC v League of Women Voters, 468 US 364 (1984)
Federal Election Commission v Wisconsin Right to Life Inc, 551 US 449 (2007)
Gray v Sanders, 372 US 368 (1963)
Grutter v Bolinger, (2003) 539 US 306
Hulme v Madison County, 188 F Supp 2d 1041 (SD Ill, 2001)
INS v Chadha, 462 US 919 (1983)
John Hagelin et al v Federal Election Commission, 411 F 3d 237 (DC Cir 2005)
Karcher v Daggett, 462 US 725 (1983)
Kitchen v Herbert, 755 F 3d 1193 (10th Cir 2014)
League of Latin American Citizens v Perry, 548 US 399 (2006)
League of Woman Voters of North Carolina v North Carolina, 769 F 3d 224 (4th Cir 2014)
Lochner v New York, 198 US 45 (1905)
Loving v Virginia, 388 US 1 (1967)
Marbury v Madison, 5 US 137 (1803)
McConnell v FEC, 540 US 93 (2003)
McCutcheon v Federal Election Commission, 572 US __ (2014)
Miami Herald Publishing Co v Tornillo, 418 US 241 (1974)
Mills v Alabama, 384 US 214 (1966)
New York Times Co v Sullivan, 376 US 254 (1964)
New York v United States, 505 US 144 (1992)
Olmstead v United States, 277 US 348 (1928)
Pestrak v Ohio Elections Commission, 926 F 2d 573 (6th Cir 1991)
Red Lion Broadcasting Co v FCC, 395 US 367 (1969)
Reynolds v Sims, 377 US 533 (1964)
Richardson v Ramirez, 418 US 24, 55 (1973)
Rickert v Washington Public Disclosure Commission 168 P 3d 826 (2007)
Sable Communications of California Inc v Federal Communications Commission, 492 US 115 (1989)
Shaw v Reno, 509 US 630 (1993)
Shelby County v Holder, 570 US ___ (2013)
Tennant v Jefferson County Commission, 567 US __ (2012)
Transcript of Proceedings, *Obergefell v Hodges* (US Supreme Court, 14-556-Question-1, Ginsburg J, 28 April 2015)

228 Bibliography

Turner Broadcasting System Inc v FCC, 512 US 622 (1994)
United States v Alvarez, 567 US__ (2012)
United States v Carolene Products Co, 304 US 144 (1938)
United States v Will, 449 US 200 (1980)
Vanasco v Schwartz, 401 F Supp 87, 100 (ED NY, 1975), affirmed by memorandum, *Schwartz v Vanasco* 423 US 1041 (1976)
Vanasco v Schwartz, 423 US 1041 (1976)
Vieth v Jubelirer, 541 US 267 (2004)
Voter Information Project Inc v City of Baton Rouge, 612 F 2d 208 (5th Cir 1980)
Wesberry v Sanders, 376 US 1 (1964)
Wisconsin v Yoder, 406 US 205 (1972)
Wyeth v Levine, 555 US 555 (2009)

C Legislation

Australia

Australia Constitution Broadcasting Act 1942 (Cth)
Commonwealth Electoral Act 1902 (Cth)
Commonwealth Electoral Act 1918 (Cth)
Commonwealth Electoral Legislation Amendment Act 1983 (Cth)
Commonwealth Franchise Act 1902 (Cth)
Constitution Act 1934 (SA)
Constitution of the Commonwealth of Australia
Criminal Code (Qld)
Electoral Act 1985 (SA)
Electoral Act 1992 (ACT)
Electoral Act 2004 (NT)
Electoral Act 2004 (Tas)
Electoral Amendment (Political Honesty) Bill 2003 (Parliament of Australia)
Electoral and Referendum Amendment Act 1998 (Cth)
Parliamentary Privileges Act 1987 (Cth)
Political Broadcasts and Political Disclosures Act 1991 (Cth)

Canada

Canada Elections Act, SC 2000
Constitution Act 1867 (Canada)
Electoral Boundaries Readjustment Act (Canada) RSC 1985
Fair Representation Act, SC 2011

Council of Europe

Council of Europe, Committee of Ministers, *Measures Concerning Media Coverage of Election Campaigns*, Recommendation No R 99 (15) (9 September 1999)

New Zealand

Electoral Act 1993 (NZ)

United Kingdom

Bill of Rights 1688 (UK) 1 Will & Mar 2, c 2
Canada Act 1982 (UK) c 11
Communications Act 2003 (UK) c 21
Corrupt and Illegal Practices Prevention Act 1883, 46 & 47 Vict, c 51 (UK)
Corrupt Practices Act 1695, 7&8 Will III, c 4 (UK)
Freedom of Election Act 1275, 3 Edward I, c 5 (UK)
Parliamentary Constituencies Act 1986 (UK) c 56
Parliamentary Voting System and Constituencies Act 2011 (UK) c 1
Representation of the People Act 1983 (UK) c 2
Representation of the People Act of 1832 (UK) 2 & 3 Will IV, c 45

United States

42 USC § 1973c (2000)
52 USC § 10301(a)
Communications Act of 1934, Pub L 98-549, 48 Stat 1064
Federal Rules of Civil Procedure; Law Reform (Contributory Negligence) Act 1945 (US)
United States Constitution

D Treaties

Convention for the Protection of Human Rights and Fundamental Freedoms, opened for signature 4 November 1950, 213 UNTS 221 (entered into force 3 September 1953), as amended by Protocol No 11 to the Convention for the Protection of Human Rights and Fundamental Freedoms, opened for signature 11 May 1994, ETS No 155 (entered into force 1 November 1998) and Protocol No 14 to the Convention for the Protection of Human Rights and Fundamental Freedoms, Amending the Control System of the Convention, opened for signature 13 May 2004, CETS No 194 (not yet in force)

E Other

'Moore in "Noodles for Votes" Row', *BBC News* (online), 7 October 2004 <http://news.bbc.co.uk/2/hi/entertainment/3719154.stm> accessed 23 February 2016

ACE Electoral Knowledge Network, *Blackout Period for Release of Opinion Poll Results* (26 November 2014) <https://aceproject.org/epic-fr/CDMap?question=ME062&questions=all&set_language=en> accessed 23 February 2016

Article 19 Global Campaign for Free Expression, *Comparative Study of Laws and Regulations Restricting the Publication of Election Opinion Polls* (Article 19, 2003) <www.article19.org/pdfs/publications/opinion-polls-paper.pdf> accessed 19 February 2016

230 Bibliography

Australian Electoral Commission, *2001 Profile of the Division of Kalgoorlie* (9 February 2011) <www.aec.gov.au/Elections/federal_elections/2001/Profiles/kalgoorlie.htm> accessed 23 February 2016

Australian Electoral Commission, *Current Register of Political Parties* (16 February 2016) <www.aec.gov.au/parties_and_representatives/party_registration/Registered_parties/> accessed 23 February 216

Australian Government, Finance and Public Administration Legislation Committee, Australian Senate, *Debate on the Citizen Initiated Referendum Bill 2013*, Melbourne, 29 April 2013, 16–17 (Scott Ryan)

Babington, Charles and Susan Schmidt, 'Filibuster Deal Puts Democrats In a Bind', *Washington Post*, 4 July 2005, A1

Blair, Tim, 'The Horror of a Year in Climate La La Land', *The Daily Telegraph*, 26 July 2010

Brock, David, 'Ontario Abdicates its Duty on Electoral Reform', *The Toronto Star*, 10 May 2007

Canadian Radio-television and Telecommunications Commission, 'Election-period broadcasting: Debates' (15 March 1995) Public Notice CRTC 1995-44

Common Cause, 'Common Cause Redistricting Guidelines' (February 2005)

Elections Canada, *2012 Redistribution* <www.redecoupage-federal-redistribution.ca/content.asp?document=home&lang=e> accessed 23 February 2016

Electoral Commission (UK), 'Factsheet: Party Election Broadcasts and Referendum Campaign Broadcasts' (November 2010)

Electoral Commission (UK), *Party Political Broadcasting Review, 2001–02* (December 2001)

Hartcher, Peter, 'Great Procrastinator Takes Reins of Inaction on Climate Change', *Sydney Morning Herald*, 24 July 2010

House of Commons (Canada), *House of Commons Debates*, 4th Parl, 4th Sess, vol XII (9 May 1882)

Hulse, Carl, 'Compromise in the Senate: The Nominees; Many Republicans Are Already Eager To Challenge Agreement on Filibusters', *The New York Times*, 25 May 2015, A18

Kelly, Paul, 'Labor Can't be Serious about Citizens' Plan,' *Weekend Australian*, 24 July 2010

Lane, Charles, 'White House Defends Texas's GOP Remapping Plan to Justices', *Washington Post* (Washington DC), 2 February 2006, A3

Ofcom, 'Ofcom Rules on Party Political and Referendum Broadcasts' (21 March 2013), <http://stakeholders.ofcom.org.uk/broadcasting/guidance/programme-guidance/ppbrules/> accessed 23 February 2016

Palmer, Vaughn, 'Liberals Sink into Quagmire of Electoral Reform', *Vancouver Sun*, 2 April 2003

Parliamentary Debates (Commons), 16 April 1964

Ronald Reagan, *Message to the Senate Returning Without Approval the Fairness in Broadcasting Bill* (19 June 1987) Ronald Reagan Presidential Library and Museum <www.reagan.utexas.edu/archives/speeches/1987/061987h.htm> accessed 23 February 2016

Texas Legislative Council (Texas Redistricting), *Redistricting Plan 01374C* (10 September 2003)

The Committee on Standards in Public Life (Parliament of the UK), *Standards in Public Life: The Funding of Political Parties in the United Kingdom* (Fifth Report of the Committee on Standards in Public Life, Vol 1, October 1998)

Toobin, Jeffrey, 'The Absolutist', *The New Yorker*, 30 June 2014

Urquhart, Ian, 'An Ill-Advised Leap in the Dark: Ontario Electoral Reform Panel will meet for Almost a Year and a Loopy Outcome is a Possibility', *The Hamilton Spectator*, 28 March, 2006

White, Isobel and Oonagh Gay, 'Party Political Broadcasts' (House of Commons Library Note, 17 March 2015, SN/PC 00354)

World Association for Public Opinion Research, *ESOMAR/WAPOR Guideline on Opinion Polls and Published Surveys* (ESOMAR/WAPOR, 2014) <http://wapor.org/esomar-wapor-guide-to-opinion-polls/> accessed 19 February 2016

Index

Abbé Sieyès 167
Abella, Rosalie 96–7
abstraction, deliberation and 125
accommodation: conceptual balancing contrasted 75; consensus and 25; decision making and 25; deliberative democracy as 49; institutional accommodation 76; preference accommodation 75; problem of 13, 48–50, 76, 108; proportionality and 60–1, 76–7, 85–6; second-order deliberation 75
Ackerman, Bruce 199
Aleinikoff, Alexander 53
ambiguous positive guidance *see* guidance model of regulation
analogy, reasoning by 44
Ani, Emmanuel 171
apportionment *see* voting
Aristotle 3
Arrow, Kenneth 178
Arthur, W Brian 55
Australia: accommodation problem 49–50; constitutional reform, popular preferences 62–3; consumer protection 101; electoral campaign speech 128–32, 133, 135; electoral district boundaries 153, 155, 160–1; electoral law, expansion of 5; equality 119, 122–4; journalism self-regulation 103; political advertising regulation 104–7; political expression 79–81, 83, 85; voter equality 136–40; voter understanding of political issues 31

balancing *see* proportionality
Bastarache, Michel 94–7
Bawn, Kathleen 127
Bohman, James 125
Braithwaite, John 158
bribery, electoral law regulation 197–9
Bridgewater, Wayne 150
Burke, Edmund 35, 89
Bush, George W 157

Canada: accommodation problem 49, 86; Citizens' Assemblies 4, 29, 32, 172–3, 179; electoral district boundaries 149–50, 153, 155, 158, 164–9, 172–80; equality 119, 122, 123, 124; federal electoral boundaries commissions (FEBCs) 153, 164–9, 172–80; first-order deliberation 9; judicial deference 96–7; narrow (bounded) framing 52; opinion poll regulation 86–7, 93–8; public judicial influence 63; veil of ignorance rules 167; voter equality 136–7, 138–40; voter persuasion 33
campaign *see* electoral campaign
Carter, Mark 155
Chambers, Simone 6, 89, 91
Citizens' Assemblies 4, 29, 32, 47, 124, 125–6, 172–3, 179
civility in deliberative discourse 23
Classic Deliberation 28, 57
coercion: absence of 23; cognitive perspective 161–3, 177; external perspective 160–1, 176–7; problem of 14, 48, 152, 158–63, 176–7

234 Index

cognition and integrity 161–3, 177
Cohen, Joshua 57, 82
collegiality 43
collegiate judgment 43
communicative action 28–30, 48, 53, 77–78, 81–82, 84–85, 127, 170
communicative rationality *see* communicative action
conceptual balancing: 13; equality and 120; liberty and 75; method 60; and political expression 79–80
consensus: accommodation and 25
constitutional law: deliberative legal theory 5; disembodied political representation 170–5; domain of 7; open-texturedness 30–1; veil of ignorance rules 166–70
constraint approach to regulation 153–4
consumer protection: opinion poll regulation compared 100–3
cooperative deliberation 22
corruption, integrity and 150–1
Council of Europe: opinion poll regulation 87
Courtney, John 174
courts: collegiality 43; collegiate judgment 43; deliberative role 8; elite direction and reception 46–7; evidentiary rules 43; first-order deliberation 9; impartiality 44; independence 44; individuals versus collectivities 81–3; judicial deference 96–7, 123; judicial review of deliberative measures 80; liberty versus deliberation 83–5; opinion poll regulation *see* opinion poll regulation; proportionality *see* proportionality; public judicial influence 63; public participation 44; reasoning *see* reasoning
Cox, Adam 167
Cruz, Ted 119
'culture of justification', law as 122

decision making: accommodation and 25; communicative rationality 25–6
deference: of courts 96–7, 123; qualified deference, guidance model of regulation 165

deliberation: abstraction 125; characteristics 22–4, 170; civility 23; Classic Deliberation 28, 57; coercion, absence of 23; cooperative 22; democracy and 26, 49–50; dialectic with law 8, 11–12, 195; equality and *see* equality; Expansion of the Classic Ideal of Deliberation 28, 57–8, 77–8; first-order *see* first-order deliberation; holistic 23, 195–200; and inclusion *see* inclusion; and information *see* information; informed 23; integrity and *see* integrity; liberty and *see* liberty; narrow (bounded) framing 55–7; open-minded 22; other-regarding 23; party framing 57–8; policy over personality 35; political expression and 75–108; proportionality and 51–5, 58–60; reason-giving 23; reflective 22; second-order *see* second-order deliberation; self-interested 27–8
Deliberation Day 24
'deliberative', meaning 21
deliberative democracy: ambiguities 27–9; communicative versus deliberative 28; conception of 78–9; content of book 11–15; critiques 27–9; deliberative electoral democracy *see* deliberative electoral democracy; democratic credentials 26; doctrinal focus on 11; elite-mediated varieties 24; empirical scepticism about 29; epistemic justification 25; future development 200; as holistic value 195–200; inclusiveness 26, 35; informed consent 26; institutional design 49; introduction to 12, 21–2; law and *see* law; law of politics; legitimacy 4; populist varieties 24; questions as to 64–5; rationales 25–7; reflection of public opinion 26; scepticism about 46–7; and social difference 27; tension within 4; 'two-track' model 24; tyranny, avoidance of 27; varieties 24–5
deliberative electoral democracy: inclusion and partnership 35–6; open-texturedness 30–1; personality politics 34–5; sites of mass persuasion 31–4

deliberative governance: and democratic governance 3–4; proportionality and 48; qualities of 3; tension within 3

deliberative measures: additive measures 82–3, 87, 108; disclosure of opinion polling methodology 87; embargo of opinion polls 87; judicial review of 80; subtractive measures 82, 87, 108

'deliberative referendums' *see* referendums

'deliberative voting' *see* voting

democracy *see also* deliberative democracy: deliberative electoral democracy; communicative versus deliberative 28; conception of 78–9; deliberation and 26, 49–50; discursive styles 28; virtual representation 35

democratic governance: and deliberative governance 3–4

difference, equality and 120

disclosure as deliberative measure 87

disembodied political representation 170–5

Dryzek, John 32, 34–5, 79, 125

Dyzenhaus, David 122

electoral campaign: competitiveness in elections 32; deliberation about versus deliberation during 32; Deliberation Day 24; electoral campaign speech 128–35; electoral district boundaries *see* electoral district boundaries; inclusiveness 35; mass persuasion 31–4; media reporting self-regulation 103–4; and open-texturedness 30–1; opinion polls *see* opinion poll regulation; personality politics 34–5; political advertising regulation 104–8; truth in political campaigning 99–100; voter understanding of political issues 31

election law: expansion of 4–5; scholarship 8; theme of 6–7

electoral district boundaries: balance and 151, 154-7, 161; coercion problem and 160–3; constraint and 153–8, 165, 169; gerrymandering 149, 151–4, 156, 160–1, 163–4, 167, 169; thick integrity and 164–5, 166–80; thin integrity and 153–5; partisanship problem 149, 155–158

elite-mediated deliberation 45–6

elites: conception of 3; as deliberative translators 45–6; empirical misrecognition 47; as governance gatekeepers 47; institutional misrecognition 46–7; receptiveness 46–7; scepticism about deliberative democracy 46–7

Ellis, Joseph 195, 200

Elster, John 78, 171

Embargo on reporting polling as deliberative measure 87

empirical misrecognition 47

equality: apportionment 135–41; authors' approach 13; as broad inclusivity 124; deliberative democracy as equality measure 200; difference and 120; electoral campaign speech case study 128–35; 'informational equality' 76; introduction to 13, 119–22; as political objective 48; problem of 13, 48, 119–41; rationales 124–8; rise of 122–4; sameness and 120; second-order deliberation 121–2; testing 120–1; thick forms 61, 121–2, 132–5; thin forms 122, 128–32; voter equality 135–41

European Union: ambiguous regulatory model 165

evidentiary rules 43

Expansion of the Classic Ideal 28, 57–8, 77–8

fact-checking *see* political journalism

federal electoral boundaries commissions (FEBCs) *see* Canada

first-order deliberation: courts' role in 9; law and 62–4, 197; scope of 9

Fish, Morris 95–7

Fishkin, James 23–4, 31, 48, 91, 199

Fiss, Owen 81, 84

Flanders, Chad 128

framing *see* reasoning

freedom of expression/speech *see* opinion poll regulation; political expression; voting

236 Index

Gardner, James 33, 161
Gelber, Katherine 82
gerrymandering *see* electoral district boundaries
Glendon, Mary Ann 55
Gonthier, Charles 98–9
Goodin, Robert 56, 78, 171
governance: conceptions of 3; deliberative *see* deliberative governance; democratic *see* democratic governance; lawyers as elite gatekeepers 47; and mass rule 3
greeting as deliberative 28
Greiner, Nick 101
guidance model of regulation: ambiguous positive guidance 165; deliberative integrity 164; disembodied political representation 170–5; independence 164–5; model 164; qualified deference 165; rule of law objections 177–80; thick integrity 164, 176; veil of ignorance rules 166–70
Gutmann, Amy 119, 126, 171

Habermas, Jürgen 6, 8, 21, 24–5, 44–8, 81, 125, 159, 162, 175–6
Hasen, Richard 102, 154
Hendriks, Carolyn 127
Herbst, Susan 90
Hobbes, Thomas 158
holistic deliberation 23, 195–200
human rights: judicial deference 96; legal norms 7; political advertising regulation 134–5
Hume, David 158

impartiality of courts 44
inclusion: alternative discourse styles 28; and deliberative electoral democracy 35–6; deliberative inclusivity 22, 26, 121, 125; equality as broad inclusivity 124; of information 32, 120, 124–5; and opinion poll regulation 88
independence: of courts 44; guidance model of regulation 164–5
information: consumer protection 100–1; disembodied 125; election results 95–6; inclusion of 120, 124–5; inclusiveness of

32; 'informational equality' 76; informed deliberation 23 *see* information; misleading 88–9; opinion polls 87–9, 90, 92, 93, 94, 95, 97; political misinformation 106; types of 124–5
institutional accommodation *see* accommodation
institutional design: guidance model *see* guidance model of regulation; synthesis of deliberation and democracy 49–50
institutional misrecognition 46–7
institutional reform, open-texturedness and 30–1
integrity: authors' approach 13–14; coercion problem 14, 152, 158–63, 176–7; cognitive aspect 161–3; concern over 200; corruption and 150–1; deliberation and 149–81; disembodied political representation 170–5; equality contrasted 151; guidance model of regulation *see* guidance model of regulation; introduction to 13–14, 149–53; liberty contrasted 151; partisanship problem 14, 152, 155–8, 166–75; as political objective 48; thick models 61, 152–3, 164–77, 181; thin models 151–2, 153–5; veil of ignorance rules 166–70
Ireland, Social Partnership participatory initiative 127
Issacharoff, Samuel 154, 156–7, 180

journalism *see* political journalism
judges *see* courts; elites

Kahan, Dan 56
Karlan, Pamela 156–7, 163, 169
Kavanagh, Aileen 58, 96
Kennedy, John F 26

Lang, Gladys 90
Lang, Kurt 90
law *see also* rule of law: accommodation problem 50; as 'culture of justification' 122; and deliberative democracy 4–6; of deliberative democracy 6–11; and deliberative democracy 42–6;

deliberative role 8; dialectic with deliberation 8, 11–12, 195; and first-order deliberation 62–4, 197; as locus of social deliberation 42

law of politics: authors' approach 12–13; constraint approach to regulation 153–4; introduction to 41–2; key values 48; proportionality types 61t; scholarship 5–6; second-order deliberation 10–11, 197; strategic balancing *see* proportionality

lawmaking: legitimacy and 7–8

lawyers *see* elites

legal elites *see* elites

legal reasoning *see* reasoning

legislatures *see* parliaments

legitimacy, lawmaking and 7–8

Lessig, Lawrence 175

liberty: accommodation problem 13; authors' approach 13; conceptual balancing 75; deliberation and 83–5, 108; deliberative democracy as liberty measure 200; integrity contrasted 151; introduction to 13, 75–7; political importance 75; as political objective 48

Lobel, Orly 165

Macdonald, John A 149–50

Magill, Elizabeth 179

Manin, Bernard 36, 57

Mansbridge, Jane 28, 78–9, 127, 159

mass rule, governance and 3

Mathews, Jud 53

Matsusaka, John 35

McLeish, Stephen 52

Meiklejohn, Alexander 81

Mendes, Conrado Hübner 43, 51, 55

Michelman, Frank 173

Mill, John Stuart 3

New Zealand: electoral campaign speech 134; opinion poll regulation 86–7

Nino, Carlos 57

O'Connor, Sandra Day 161

open-minded deliberation 22

openness and institutional reform 30–1

opinion *see* public opinion

opinion poll regulation: consumer protection analogy 100–3; feedback loops 89–90; flexible application by courts 87–8; inclusiveness 88; judicial deference to 96–7; judicial doctrinal amendment 98–9; judicial redefinition of deliberation 95–6; judicial responses to 92–5; misleading information 88–9; other-regarding deliberation 88; regulatory approaches 86–8; representation 89; strategic voting 90–1; substantive discourse 91–2; voters' true views, undermining of 90–1

other-regarding deliberation 23

Parkinson, John 24, 77, 127

parliaments, law of 7

partisanship: disembodied political representation 170–5; gerrymandering *see* electoral district boundaries; integrity 152; problem of 14, 48, 149, 152, 155–8, 166–75; veil of ignorance rules 166–70

Pelletier, David 127

personality politics 34–5

Pildes, Richard 32, 130

political campaigns *see* voting

political expression: deliberation and 75–108; individuals versus collectivities 81–3; journalism, fact-checking method of self-regulation 103–4; judicial review of deliberative measures 80; liberty versus deliberation 83–5

politics *see also* constitutional law: law of politics; voting; deliberatively thin conception 48; disembodied political representation 170–5; party framing 52–3, 57–8; political parties, deliberative inflexibility 127–8

Post, Robert 84, 85

Postema, Gerald 56, 63

precedent, reasoning from 44–6

preference accommodation *see* accommodation

238 Index

proportionality: accommodation and 76, 85–6; accommodative balancing 60–1, 77; authors' approach 12–13; binary method 53, 58–9; conceptual balancing *see* conceptual balancing; deliberation and 51–5, 58–60; and deliberative governance 48; framing model 53–5; law of politics 61t; method 48; multiple balancing 58–9; overreliance on 48; reasoning and 48; strategic balancing 61, 120, 150–1, 153; thick equality 61; thick integrity 61; thick models 55, 60–1; thin models 60–1

public opinion: communication to government 34; constitutional reform, popular preferences 62–3; judicial influence 63; opinion polls *see* opinion poll regulation; reflection by deliberative democracy 26

public participation in court process 44

Pufendorf, Samuel von 56

Rakoff, Todd 165–6

Rawls, John 8, 43–4, 54, 166, 171

Raz, Joseph 177, 179

Reagan, Ronald 83, 171

reasonable person test 43, 94

reasoning: by analogy 44, 121; communicative rationality 25–6; giving reasons 23, 43, 78; law as 'culture of justification' 122; narrow (bounded) framing 51–2, 55–7; party framing 52–3, 57–8; from precedent 44–6; proportionality and 48, 53–5; reciprocal reason-giving 26; value rationalisation 27

referendums 3, 5–6, 24, 30–1, 36, 45, 76, 92, 138, 197

reflective deliberation 22

Reith, John 133

rhetoric as deliberative 28

Rosenberg, Gerald 156

Rostbøll, Christian 81

rule of law: everyone equally bound by law 179–80; predictability principle 177–9; stability principle 179–80

sameness, equality and 120

scholarship *see* deliberativist theory

Schultz, David 196

Schumpeter, Joseph 33

second-order deliberation: accommodation and 75; equality and 121–2; law and 62–4; and law of politics 10–11, 197; scope of 9–10

self-interested deliberation 27–8

Sen, Maya 54

social difference, accommodation of 27

Solum, Lawrence 81, 84–5

South Africa: equality 125; political advertising regulation 106

Stone, Harlan Fisk 75

storytelling as deliberative 28

strategic balancing *see* proportionality

strategic individuals, concept of 25

Sunstein, Cass 81, 83, 85

Sweet, Alec Stone 53

theory *see* deliberativist theory

Thompson, Dennis 9, 32, 54, 62, 119, 126, 152, 171

translation: by elites 45–6; problems 48–50

Twining, William 196

United Kingdom: electoral bribery 198–9; electoral campaign speech 128, 132–5; electoral district boundaries 149, 153, 155; electoral law, expansion of 5; equality 119, 123–4; journalism self-regulation 103; judicial deference 96; political advertising regulation 104–5; proportionality 50, 58; voter equality 136–7, 140; voter persuasion 33

United States: ambiguous regulatory model 165; collegiality of courts 43; competitiveness in elections 32; electoral campaign speech 128; electoral district boundaries 153–6, 160, 162–3, 167–9, 180; elite-mediated deliberation 24; equality 119, 122, 123–4; first-order deliberation 9; journalism self-regulation 103; Kennedy's international diplomacy 26; open-texturedness 31; opinion poll regulation 91, 92–3; political advertising regulation 105, 107–8; political expression 81, 83–5, 102–3; proportionality 50, 53, 54–5; public judicial influence 63; translation problem 48; veil of ignorance rules 167; voter equality 136–8, 140; voter persuasion 33

veil of ignorance rules 166–70
virtual representation 35
voting: apportionment 135–41; bribery 197–9; corruption and 150–1;

'deliberative voting' 24; electoral district boundaries *see* electoral district boundaries; reporting of results 88; virtual representation 35; voter equality 122, 135–41;

Waldron, Jeremy 55
Warren, Mark 150–2, 157–8, 174–5

Young, Iris Marion 28, 56, 63, 125
Young, Sally 91

Zurn, Christopher 54–5